Stochastic Processes and Their Applications: In Honor of Prof. Sally McClean

Stochastic Processes and Their Applications: In Honor of Prof. Sally McClean

Guest Editors

Panagiotis-Christos Vassiliou
Andreas C. Georgiou

Basel • Beijing • Wuhan • Barcelona • Belgrade • Novi Sad • Cluj • Manchester

Guest Editors

Panagiotis-Christos Vassiliou
Department of Statistical
Science
University College London
London
UK

Andreas C. Georgiou
Quantitative Methods and
Decision Analytics Lab
Department of Business
Administration
University of Macedonia
Thessaloniki
Greece

Editorial Office
MDPI AG
Grosspeteranlage 5
4052 Basel, Switzerland

This is a reprint of the Special Issue, published open access by the journal *Mathematics* (ISSN 2227-7390), freely accessible at: https://www.mdpi.com/journal/mathematics/special_issues/Sally_McClean.

For citation purposes, cite each article independently as indicated on the article page online and as indicated below:

Lastname, A.A.; Lastname, B.B. Article Title. *Journal Name* **Year**, *Volume Number*, Page Range.

ISBN 978-3-7258-3223-1 (Hbk)
ISBN 978-3-7258-3224-8 (PDF)
https://doi.org/10.3390/books978-3-7258-3224-8

Contents

Editorial

Stochastic Processes and Their Applications: In Honor of Prof. Sally McClean

P.-C. G. Vassiliou [1,*] and Andreas C. Georgiou [2,*]

1   Department of Mathematics, Aristotle University of Thessaloniki, 54006 Thessaloniki, Greece
2   Quantitative Methods and Decision Analysis Lab, Department of Business Administration, University of Macedonia, 54636 Thessaloniki, Greece
*   Correspondence: vasiliou@math.auth.gr (P.-C.G.V.); acg@uom.edu.gr (A.C.G.)

1. Introductory Notes

Stochastic processes are foundational tools in many scientific disciplines, including biology, operational research, social sciences, and stochastic finance, among others. The important characteristics of systems in these areas evolve with time in a relatively random way, and since stochastic processes are mainly families of random variables, in which their index represents time, they are the natural tool to use. This origin aligns with its mathematical interpretation of randomness and probabilistic analysis.

The word "stochastic" comes from the Greek word "στοχαστικός", and in this context, it means "random". The same word, in its form as a verb, is used in Greek in a similar context, to express the process of thought when someone is searching for all the possible outcomes of a certain phenomenon that has an important influence on one's life.

The theory and applications of stochastic processes trace their roots to the development of one of the richest and most fundamental examples: Brownian motion. This was an unexpected starting point, as Brownian motion is a remarkable mathematical construct that simultaneously exhibits properties of a martingale, Gaussian process, diffusion, Lévy process, Markov process, and more—concepts that were formalized much later. The origins of Brownian motion can be traced back to the early 1900s.

On 29 March 1900, Louis Bachelier (11 March 1870–28 April 1946) successfully defended his celebrated thesis, *Theorie de la Speculation*, at the Sorbonne. In this groundbreaking work, he applied probability theory to stock markets, marking the first historical attempt to introduce stochastic thinking through mathematics. This thesis laid the foundation for what is now known as stochastic finance.

In 1933, Andrei Kolmogorov (1903–1987) published his seminal work *Foundations of the Theory of Probability*, which introduced the axiomatic foundations of probability theory. This groundbreaking book has withstood the test of time and remains the cornerstone upon which the entire field of probability and statistics has flourished. Following Kolmogorov's contributions during the 1930s and 1940s, the study of stochastic processes became one of the most mathematically rigorous disciplines, alongside certain areas of pure mathematics (see Cramer [1]).

The development of stochastic processes as a formal extension of probability theory owes much to the influential works of Joseph (Joe) Doob (1910–2004) and William Feller (1906–1970). Doob's *Stochastic Processes* [2] and Feller's two-volume *An Introduction to Probability Theory and Its Applications* [3,4] were instrumental in shaping the modern theory of stochastic processes. These foundational texts not only advanced the field, but also played a key role in establishing courses on probability and stochastic processes in mathematics departments worldwide.

Received: 6 January 2025
Revised: 7 January 2025
Accepted: 8 January 2025
Published: 16 January 2025

Citation: Vassiliou, P.-C.G.; Georgiou, A.C. Stochastic Processes and Their Applications: In Honor of Prof. Sally McClean. *Mathematics* 2025, 13, 276. https://doi.org/10.3390/math13020276

The term "probabilist", so commonly used today, owes much to the era in which Doob and Feller lived and collaborated. Their long and fruitful discussions helped define and solidify the identity of probabilists as a distinct group within mathematics, contributing to the global dissemination of probabilistic and stochastic ideas.

Doob's 1953 book, *Stochastic Processes*, became a classic in the John Wiley series and remains a "must read" for any probabilist. In this landmark work, Doob formally defined the concept of a martingale for the first time, which naturally led to the definitions of supermartingales and submartingales. He then developed the theory of martingales and Markov processes to a remarkable extent, laying the foundation for much of modern probability theory.

For an inspiring account of how this influential book came to be, one can refer to Doob's interview with Laurie Snell [5], where he shares fascinating insights into his writing process and the development of the field.

In a paper by Doob [6], we learn that Feller was tireless in revising his books, taking particular delight in discovering new approaches, applications, and examples to enhance them. His books are extraordinary for their almost bewildering diversity of perspectives and applications, both within and beyond pure mathematics. No other book remotely resembles Feller's work in its combination of the purest mathematics, dazzling technical virtuosity, and wide-ranging applications, all presented in a style that vividly conveys the author's enthusiasm.

2. In Honor of Prof. Sally McClean

A glance at the history of eminent mathematicians reveals a sobering truth: nature does not preserve its most exceptional minds indefinitely. Each had a finite lifespan and, eventually, they "left". For some, this span was tragically short, despite their profound contributions to the progress of mathematics. It is a common tradition, therefore, for colleagues to honor such individuals by publishing a volume of invited papers in their research area.

However, we believe this gesture of respect is far more meaningful when it occurs just before or at the time of their retirement, allowing them to witness and appreciate the recognition of their life's work.

The journal *Mathematics* (a Q1 journal in the Web of Science list) recognized the success of our first Special Issue by publishing a volume (book) containing all the papers we edited for that Issue [7]. Encouraged by this achievement, they invited us to edit another Special Issue. We proposed the theme, "Stochastic Processes and Their Applications: In Honor of Prof. Sally McClean", to mark her semi-retirement and to recognize her significant contributions to research. The Editorial Board was delighted to accept our proposal, expressing their enthusiasm for the project.

Prof. Sally Ida McClean, a distinguished Northern Irish statistician and operations researcher, has significantly advanced the fields of mathematical modeling and health care planning. Sally Ida McClean was born in Belfast and earned her first degree, an M.A. in Mathematics, from the University of Oxford in 1970. She went on to complete an M.Sc. in Mathematical Statistics and Operations Research at Cardiff University in 1972 and earned her Ph.D. from Ulster University at Coleraine in 1976.

Her research spans a wide range of topics, including workforce modeling, health administration, interactive architecture, and survey methodology. She has authored over 300 publications in areas such as mathematical modeling, applied probability, multivariate statistical analysis, and the application of mathematical and statistical methods to computer science.

Prof. McClean's contributions to mathematical modeling, particularly in health care planning, are immense. Her research has significantly impacted elderly care, with models that optimize health care planning and resource allocation.

Prof. McClean is a Fellow of both the Royal Statistical Society and the Operational Research Society, as well as an Associate Fellow of the Institute of Mathematics and its Applications. Her extensive research output is reflected in citation metrics from major databases. According to Google Scholar, she has over 600 research publications, cited 12,674 times, with an h-index of 54. In the Web of Science (WOS) database, she has 218 publications, cited 2710 times, with an h-index of 25.

Prof. McClean's outstanding contributions to research have been recognized through her receipt of Ulster University's Senior Distinguished Research Fellowship.

3. Stochastic Processes and Their Applications: In Honor of Prof. Sally McClean

The Guest Editors would like to express their sincere gratitude to the Chief Editors and the Editorial Board of *Mathematics* for extending the invitation to edit this special volume. We warmly thank the authors for their significant contributions to this publication, as well as for their diligence and enthusiasm in addressing all comments and suggestions during the review process.

Our heartfelt appreciation goes to the anonymous reviewers whose invaluable assistance and rigorous comments were crucial to the successful completion of this endeavor.

We are also deeply grateful to the Editorial Manager, Dr. Syna Mu, for his tireless efforts in facilitating the workflow for this Issue, his excellent collaboration with the Guest Editors, and for arranging partial funding for the publication of this volume.

Special thanks are extended to Professors Michael Voskoglou and Maria Mariani for serving as Academic Editors for our own contributed articles. Their names were known to the Guest Editors after the publication of their papers.

Finally, we wish to acknowledge the numerous Editorial Assistants who skillfully managed the considerable workload involved in handling the large number of submissions for this volume. Their commitment and effectiveness played a crucial role in successfully completing this project.

The following section provides an organized overview of the articles in this Special Issue, categorized into key thematic areas. Additionally, we provide the reader with some useful references to help introduce the mathematical background relevant to the papers. The sub-areas (sections) are arranged to generally reflect the title of the Special Issue, with the articles in each section sorted according to their publication dates.

(i) Markov Chains, Processes, and Markov Systems.

Markov processes are stochastic processes that exhibit the Markov property, while Markov chains are their discrete time and discrete state space counterpart. That is, the probabilistic dependence on the past is only through the present state, which contains all the necessary information for the evolution of the process. Useful introductory texts on probability theory and stochastic processes can be found in [8], and on homogeneous and non-homogeneous Markov chains and processes in [9–12] and [13] (Chapter 3). For Markov systems or Open Markov models, which are generalizations of the Markov chain, a research monograph on the subject is detailed in [14]. We now provide a brief description of the articles of the Special Issue that could be included in this category:

(i1) Strong Ergodicity in Non-homogeneous Markov Systems with Chronological Order, by P.-C.G. Vassiliou [15]. Consider a stochastic system with a population of members categorized into different states. Three types of movements are possible within this system. First, members can transition between states; second, members may exit the system from various states; and third, new members may enter the system to replace those who have left or to expand the population. When the dynamics of these movements are modeled by a non-homogeneous Markov chain, the system is referred to as a non-homogeneous Markov system (NHMS).

An NHMS generalizes the classical Markov chain by accounting for multiple particles moving among the states, with the possibility of leaving the system and being replaced by others, potentially with different characteristics. This is in contrast to the classical Markov chain, which typically models a single particle transitioning among states without exits or replacements.

In this context, the author studied the concept of strong ergodicity for NHMS, focusing on a novel relaxation of a critical assumption found in all prior studies, i.e., the study relaxes the standard assumption regarding the asymptotic behavior of NHMS. Specifically, the author did not assume that the underlying inhomogeneous Markov chain geometrically converges to a homogeneous Markov chain with a regular transition probability matrix as time approaches infinity. Instead, the author investigated and derived conditions under which the rate of convergence to strong ergodicity in an NHMS is geometrically fast, thereby broadening the understanding of NHMS dynamics.

(i2) Estimation–Calibration of Continuous-Time Non-Homogeneous Markov Chains with Finite State Space, by ML Esquível, NP Krasii, and GR Guerreiro [16]. The paper is divided into three parts. The first proposes a method to estimate the parameters of a set of transition intensities from ideal observed data. The second presents the result on regime-switching Markov chains that establishes the possibility of considering transition intensities made up of different sorts of functional forms, with each one of the functional forms depending on different sets of parameters. Finally, in the third part, the norm of the difference of two probability transition matrices is quantified in terms of the norm of the corresponding matrices of transition intensities, which justifies the choice of arbitrary functional forms for the transition intensities in ways that are more adequate for parameter estimation.

(i3) Educational Status as A Mediator of Intergenerational Social Mobility in Europe: A Positional Analysis Approach, by G. Stamatopoulou, E. Tsouparopoulou, and M. Symeonaki [17]. The study aimed to investigate both nominal (absolute) and relative (positional) patterns of intergenerational educational mobility in Europe by analyzing transitions across the educational levels of respondents and their parents in Europe using raw data drawn from the European Social Survey (ESS) from the year 2002 and onwards. It reveals all the necessary information concerning the proposed methodology and the ESS data that are utilized in order to estimate intergenerational educational mobility in absolute and relative terms. It presents the measurement results of intergenerational educational mobility, nominal and positional, and the validation tests performed.

(i4) The Arsenal of Perturbation Bounds for Finite Continuous-Time Markov Chains: A Perspective, by A.Y. Mitrophanov [18]. This perspective article describes what can be regarded as deterministic perturbations of the Kolmogorov equations. Thus, in effect, it considers deterministic perturbations of a stochastic process (i.e., the Markov chain under study). One could possibly imagine perturbation scenarios involving various deterministic or stochastic systems under deterministic or stochastic perturbations. Clearly, each scenario would require its own set of theoretical developments. Yet, the types of results discussed could be relevant in a broader context and may be applicable to other possible (and, possibly,

far more complex) perturbation scenarios. At the very least, they can provide a relevant standard for comparison or even help generate a viable working hypothesis.

(i5) A Throughput Analysis Using a Non-Saturated Markov Chain Model for LTE-LAA and WLAN Coexistence, by Mun-Suk Kim [19]. The paper proposes an analytical model to calculate the throughput for each system in a scenario where a single LTE-LAA system, dedicated to downlink transmission, shares an unlicensed channel with multiple WLAN systems. This study employs a Markov chain approach to model the random backoff operations of LTE-LAA eNodeB (eNB) and WLAN nodes under non-saturated traffic conditions. The Markov chain approach is limited by the need to define LTE-LAA eNB and WLAN node transmissions in discrete timeslots. Nevertheless, it enables a clear and detailed analysis of all sequential random backoff operations in the distributed coordination function of LTE-LAA and WLAN. In addition, this study analyzes the throughput of LTE-LAA and WLAN systems by integrating the impact of the clear channel assessment (CCA) threshold, which represents the sensitivity level required to detect ongoing transmissions, with Markov chain modeling of random backoff operations.

(ii) Semi-Markov Chains, Processes, and Semi-Markov Systems.

Semi-Markov chains are generalizations of Markov chains where the time of transition from each state to another is now a random variable. The same applies for semi-Markov processes, except that the time is now continuous. A very good text on semi-Markov chains and processes for the interested reader can be found in [20]. For semi-Markov systems or open semi-Markov models, which are, again, generalizations of Markov chains, the first paper that introduced them was [21], and this is a reliable publication to start from. We provide below a brief description of the articles that could be categorized in this section:

(ii1) Semi-Markov Models for Processes Mining in Smart Homes, by S. McClean and L. Yang [22]. This paper is concerned with developing and illustrating some specific mathematical expressions and results for models of human activity. It develops and uses Markov-type models to represent ADL processes and corresponding key performance indicators (KPIs) in smart homes, as well as in describing and evaluating strategies to determine anomalies in such transitions and durations. The approach is illustrated and evaluated using a publicly available smart home dataset comprising an event log of sensor activations, together with an annotated record of the actual activities, which is used for model development and validation.

(ii2) Attainability for Markov and Semi-Markov Chains, by B Verbeken and M.-A Guerry [23]. Firstly, the concept of attainability for Markov chains is reviewed and extended to systems with a growth factor $1 + \alpha$, where the parameter α signifies the rate of change in the size of the system over time. When α is negative, this indicates a contraction in the system size, i.e., a decline in the number of people in the system. Conversely, when α is positive, the system expands over time. Thereafter, it is introduced and the attainability is studied along with the state reunion attainability for semi-Markov chains starting from the concept of SR-maintainability for semi-Markov chains. It is shown that a general approach to state reunion attainability, where a structure is said to be state-reunion-attainable if there exists an arbitrary initial structure from which it can be attained, is not appropriate, and the concept of (n-step) state reunion attainability starting from a subset S of structures is introduced. A method to determine the associated region of attainable structures is also provided.

(ii3) Cost Evaluation for Capacity Planning based on Patient's Pathways via Semi-Markov Reward Modelling, by C. Chatzimichail, P. Kolias, and A. Papadopoulou [24]. In the study, a non-homogeneous semi-Markov reward model is considered, where rewards are random variables associated with state occupancies and transitions. The novelty of the paper lies in the inclusion of states' inflows and availability, which is critical for capacity-

planning based on service demands in an environment of fixed resources. The theory of the model is provided, followed by results related to the population's structure and states' inflows and the expressions related to the current availability of states. Also, expressions for the expected costs generated by the system and corresponding to patients' paths are developed.

(ii4) On a Mixed Transient–Asymptotic Result for the Sequential Interval Reliability for Semi-Markov Chains, by G. D'Amico and T. Gkelsinis [25]. The authors studied the sequential interval reliability, a measure recently introduced in the literature. This measure represents the probability of the system working during a sequence of non-overlapping time intervals. In their previous work, the authors proposed a recurrent-type formula for computing this indicator in the transient case and investigated the asymptotic behavior. The purpose of this work is to further explore the asymptotic behavior when only some of the time intervals are allowed to reach infinity while the remaining ones are not. In this way, a unique indicator that is able to describe the process evolution in transient and asymptotic cases is provided. It is important to note that this is not a straightforward result since, in order to achieve it, we need to develop several mathematical ingredients that generalize the classical renewal and Markov renewal frameworks.

(iii) Mathematical Optimization and Decision Analysis

This category addresses mathematical optimization and decision analysis with a specific focus on Data Envelopment Analysis (DEA) and stochastic programming. It addresses hierarchical efficiency evaluation and resource allocation, tailored for large organizations and enterprises, particularly within the banking sector. Key publications that can introduce the reader to this area of study are [26–28].

(iii1) A Bilevel DEA Model for Efficiency Evaluation and Target Setting with Stochastic Conditions, by A.C. Georgiou, K. Karapis, E.-M. Vretta, K. Bitsis, and G. Paltayian [29]. The paper presents a novel bilevel DEA model to evaluate organizational efficiency and set performance targets under stochastic conditions. It combines hierarchical decision-making with uncertainty modeling through discrete scenarios, which makes it particularly suitable for environments with volatile economic conditions. The model's integration of bilevel optimization and stochastic elements provides practical insights into resource allocation and output targeting while accommodating uncertainty. A major contribution of this work is its ability to address the complex interdependencies and hierarchical structures in large organizations, exemplified by a case study in the banking sector. This enhances its relevance to industries with similar operational complexities. The proposed approach offers dynamic strategies for decision-makers, allowing adjustments as scenarios unfold, thereby improving overall sustainability across economic, environmental, and social dimensions. The mathematical rigor and practical application make this paper a valuable addition to the literature on efficiency analysis, especially for sectors undergoing transformative changes such as banking.

(ix) General Stochastic Processes.

(ix1) A Class of Power Series q-Distributions, by Charalambos A. Charalambides † [30]. This is a seminal paper extending the work of the author devoted to q-distributions published on the research monograph Charalambides [31]. For example, the q-binomial distribution is the distribution of the number of successes in a sequence of n independent Bernoulli trials, with the odds of success at a trial varying geometrically with the number of trials. As a second example, the negative q-binomial distribution of the second kind is the distribution of the number of failures until the occurrence of the nth success in a sequence of independent Bernoulli trials, with the probability of success at a trial varying geometrically with the number of successes. A class of power series q-distributions, by considering a q-Taylor expansion of a parametric function, provides a unified approach to the study of

these distributions. Its q-factorial moments, for $0 < q < 1$ and $1 < q < \infty$, are obtained in terms of q-derivatives of its series function. Moreover, it is proven that a power series q-distribution is completely determined from its first two q-cumulants (or q-moments). Also, the convolution of power series q-distributions, using probability-generating functions, is shown to be a power series q-distribution. Furthermore, as part of demonstrating this approach, the q-factorial moments for $0 < q < 1$ and $1 < q < \infty$ of the q-Poisson (Heine and Euler) distributions, q-binomial distribution of the first kind, negative q-binomial distribution of the second kind, and q-logarithmic distribution are obtained as members of this class of distributions. In addition, interesting and useful structural information about these distributions is obtained through their probability-generating functions.

† Prof. Charalambos A. Charalambides has "left" us unexpectedly just after submitting the final form of his paper.

(ix2) Analyzing the Asymptotic Behavior of an Extended SEIR Model with Vaccination for COVID-19, by V.E. Papageorgiou, G. Vasiliadis, and G. Tsaklidis [32]. The paper provides valuable corrections concerning the theoretical results displayed in previous publications that pertain to the non-negativity and boundedness of a system of seven differential equations, which describe the transition of COVID-19 after the onset of the vaccination period. These modifications are crucial in validating the suitability of the epidemiological model for accurately describing the spread of COVID-19. More importantly, it provides novel properties regarding the global asymptotic stability of both the disease-free and endemic equilibria based on the values of the basic reproduction number. These theoretical aspects are more crucial than the local stability analysis, offering insights into long-term behavior when the system approaches the aforementioned equilibria. Finally, a novel addition to the literature is the computation of the convergence rate to the endemic equilibria, offering a more comprehensive understanding of the system's asymptotic behavior.

Conflicts of Interest: The author declares no conflicts of interest.

References

1. Cramer, H. Half a century with probability theory: Some personal recollections. *Ann. Probab.* **1976**, *4*, 509–546. [CrossRef]
2. Doob, J.L. *Stochastic Processes*; Wiley Classics Library, John Wiley: New York, NY, USA, 1990
3. Feller, W. *An Introduction to Probability and Its Applications*; John Wiley: New York, NY, USA, 1968; Volume 1.
4. Feller, W. *An Introduction to Probability and Its Applications*; John Wiley: New York, NY, USA, 1971; Volume 2.
5. Snell, J.L. A conversation with Joe Doob. *Stat. Sci.* **1997**, *12*, 301–311. [CrossRef]
6. Doob, J.L. William Feller and twentieth century probability. In Proceedings of the Sixth Berkeley Symposium, Berkeley, CA, USA, 21 June–18 July 1970; University of California Press: Berkeley, CA, USA, 1971; Volume 1, pp. XV–XX.
7. Vassiliou, P.-C.G.; Georgiou, A.C. Markov and Semi-Markov Chains, Processes, Systems, and Emerging Related Fields. *Mathematics* **2021**, *19*, 2490. [CrossRef]
8. Bremaud, P. *Probability Theory and Stochastic Processes*; Springer Nature: Cham, Switzerland, 2020.
9. Iosifescu, M. *Finite Markov Processes and Applications*; John Wiley: New York, NY, USA, 1980.
10. Isaacson, D.; Madsen, R. *Markov Chains Theory ana Applications*; John Wiley: New York, NY, USA, 1976
11. Seneta, E. *Non-Negative Matrices and Markov Chains*; Springer: Berlin/Heidelberg, Germany, 1981.
12. Bremaud, P. *Markov Chains*, 2nd ed.; Springer Nature: Cham, Switzerland, 2020.
13. Vassiliou, P.-C.G. *Discrete-Time Asset Pricing Models in Applied Stochastic Finance*; John Wiley: New York, NY, USA, 2010
14. Vassiliou, P.-C.G. *Non-Homogeneous Markov Chains and Systems, Theory and Applications*; Chapman and Hall: London, UK, 2023.
15. Vassiliou, P.-C.G. Strong Ergodicity in Nonhomogeneous Markov Systems with Chronological Order. *Mathematics* **2024**, *12*, 660. [CrossRef]
16. Esquivel, M.L.; Krasii, N.P.; Guerreiro, G.R. Estimation-Calibration of Continuous-Time Non-Homogeneous Markov Chain with Finite State Space. *Mathematics* **2024**, *12*, 668. [CrossRef]

17. Stamatopoulou, G.; Tsouparopoulou, E.; Symeonaki, M. Educational status as a mediator of intergenerational social mobility in Europe: A positional analysis approach. *Mathematics* **2024**, *12*, 996. [CrossRef]
18. Mitrophanov, A.Y. The arsenal of perturbation bounds for finite continuous-time Markov chains: A perspective. *Mathematics* **2024**, *12*, 1608. [CrossRef]
19. Kim, M.-S. A Throughput Analysis Using a Non-Saturated Markov Chain Model for LTE-LAA and WLAN Coexistence. *Mathematics* **2025**, *13*, 59. [CrossRef]
20. Howard, R. *Dynamic Probabilistic Systems: Semi-Markov and Decision Processes*; Dover Publications: New York, NY, USA, 2007.
21. Vassiliou, P.-C.G.; Papadopoulou, A.A. Non-homogeneous semi-Markov systems and maintainability of the state sizesl teams via second order Markov modelling. *J. Appl. Probab.* **1992**, *29*, 519–534. [CrossRef]
22. McClean, S.; Yang, L. Semi-Markov models for processes mining in smart homes. *Mathematics* **2024**, 11, 5001. [CrossRef]
23. Verbeken, B.; Guerry, M.-A. Attainability for Markov and Semi-Markov Chains. *Mathematics* **2024**, *12*, 1227. [CrossRef]
24. Chatzimichail, C.; Kolias, P.; Papadopoulou, A. Cost evaluation for capacity planning based on patient's pathways via semi-Markov reward modelling. *Mathematics* **2024**, *12*, 1430. [CrossRef]
25. D'Amico, G.; Gkelsinis, T. On a Mixed Transient—Asymptotic Result for the Sequential Interval Reliability for Semi-Markov Chains. *Mathematics* **1924**, *12*, 1842. [CrossRef]
26. Dempe, S. Bilevel optimization: Theory, algorithms, applications and a bibliography. In *Bilevel Optimization: Advances and Next Challenges*; Springer: Berlin, Germany, 2020; pp. 581–672.
27. Charnes, A.; Cooper, W.; Lewin, A.Y.; Seiford, L.M. Data envelopment analysis theory, methodology and applications. *J. The Operational Res. Soc.* **1997**, *48*, 332–333. [CrossRef]
28. Cooper, W.W.; Seiford, L.M.; Tone, K. *Introduction to Data Envelopment Analysis and Its Uses: With DEA-Solver Software and References*; Springer Science & Business Media: Berlin, Germany, 2006.
29. Georgiou, A.C.; Karapis, K.; Vretta, E.-M.; Bitsis, K.; Paltayian, G. A Bilevel DEA Model for Efficiency Evaluation and Target Setting with Stochastic Conditions. *Mathematics* **2024**, *12*, 529. [CrossRef]
30. Charalambides, C.A. A Class of Power Series q-Distributions. *Mathematics* **2024**, *12*, 712. [CrossRef]
31. Charalambides, C.A. *Discrete q-Distributions*; John Wiley & Sons: Hoboken, NJ, USA, 2016.
32. Papageorgiou, V.E.; Vasiliadis, G.; Tsaklidis, G. Analyzing the Asymptotic Behavior of an Extended SEIR Model with Vaccination for COVID-19. *Mathematics* **2024**, *12*, 55. [CrossRef]

Short Biography of Author

Panagiotis-C.G. Vassiliou is an Emeritous Professor at the Department of Mathematics, Aristotle University of Thessaloniki and was an Honorary Professor at the Department of Statistical Sciences, University College London for ten years. He has spend research and teaching time in cronological order at Ulster University, Ioannina University, Aristotle University of Thessaloniki, University College London. He has also spend research time at Imperial College London. He has also taught at the London Taught Course Center (LTCC), for 3rd and 4th year Ph.D. students of UCL, LSE, King's, Brunel and Kent. He has published more than 58 papers, indexed in the web of science mainly in the areas of non-homogeneous Markov systems, non-homogeneous semi Markov systems, and stochastic finance. His publications time span is 51 years and the two journals with the highest frequency were *Journal of Applied Probability* (11 papers, in 140 pages) and *Linear Algebra and its Applications* (8 papers in 224 pages). He has also written 4 books in English (J. Wiley, Chapman and Hall, UCL, MDPI) and 14 books in Greek. He has been the supervisor of 9 completed Ph.D thesis. Academic Services: Referee in more than 25 scientific journals, Guest Editor in 2 scientific journals and currently a member on the Editorial Board of *Mathematics*. Metrics: more than 915 citations in Web of Science, H-index = 19.

Andreas C. Georgiou is a Professor of Operational Research and the Director of the Quantitative Methods and Decision Analysis Lab in the Department of Business Administration at the University of Macedonia. He also serves as the Director of the MBA program and previously held the position of Director for the Master's Program in Business Analytics and Data Science. His research interests encompass a broad range of topics, including Mathematical Methods in Business Analytics, Stochastic Processes, Markov Chains, Mathematical Human Resource Planning, and Operations Research methodologies in Operations Management. He has also specialized expertise in discrete event simulation, multi-objective optimization, and efficiency and productivity evaluation using Data Envelopment Analysis (DEA). Prof. Georgiou has played a pivotal role in numerous research projects and doctoral dissertations, making significant contributions to the field. He has served on organizing and scientific committees for various conferences and holds positions on the editorial boards of several academic journals. His work has been published extensively in international conference proceedings and high-impact journals, earning over 1300 citations to date. In addition, Prof. Georgiou has provided peer reviews for more than 50 international journals and conferences, collaborating with leading publishing houses such as Elsevier, Springer, Sage, Emeral, Wiley, Taylor & Francis, and MDPI.

MDPI

Article

Semi-Markov Models for Process Mining in Smart Homes

Sally McClean [1,*,†] and Lingkai Yang [2,†]

[1] School of Computing, Ulster University, Belfast BT15 1AP, Northern Ireland, UK
[2] Research Institute of Mine Big Data, Chinese Institute of Coal Science, Beijing 100013, China;
      y1163376026@gmail.com
*   Correspondence: si.mcclean@ulster.ac.uk
†   These authors contributed equally to this work.

Abstract: Generally, these days people live longer but often with increased impairment and disabilities; therefore, they can benefit from assistive technologies. In this paper, we focus on the completion of activities of daily living (ADLs) by such patients, using so-called Smart Homes and Sensor Technology to collect data, and provide a suitable analysis to support the management of these conditions. The activities here are cast as states of a Markov-type process, while changes of state are indicated by sensor activations. This facilitates the extraction of key performance indicators (KPIs) in Smart Homes, e.g., the duration of an important activity, as well as the identification of anomalies in such transitions and durations. The use of semi-Markov models for such a scenario is described, where the state durations are represented by mixed gamma models. This approach is illustrated and evaluated using a publicly available Smart Home dataset comprising an event log of sensor activations, together with an annotated record of the actual activities. Results indicate that the methodology is well-suited to such scenarios.

Keywords: Markov-type model; process mining; Smart Homes; convolution of gamma mixture models

MSC: 60K15

Citation: McClean, S.; Yang, L. Semi-Markov Models for Process Mining in Smart Homes. *Mathematics* **2023**, *11*, 5001. https://doi.org/10.3390/math11245001

Academic Editors: Panagiotis-Christos Vassiliou and Andreas C. Georgiou

Received: 21 November 2023
Revised: 14 December 2023
Accepted: 15 December 2023
Published: 18 December 2023

1. Introduction

Worldwide, people are living longer, with increasing numbers of older people forming a larger proportion of the population [1]. It is predicted that, by 2050, the proportion of the world population over 60 years of age will have grown to over 20%. However, the downside of this prediction is that it comes with increased impairment and disability in older people, including cognitive decline, depressive illnesses, and dementia. At the same time, however, there have been major improvements in technology and, in particular, assistive technologies are increasingly being used to facilitate the functioning, independence, and well-being of older citizens.

Older people frequently experience physical and cognitive decline, typically preventing the completion of activities of daily living (ADLs) [2]. Such patients may need family or professional care at home or might require admission to a long-term nursing facility, with a resulting decrease in quality-of-life and an increase in costs. High-tech solutions can help improve such situations, using so-called Smart Homes, which utilise assistive technologies and employ sensors to collect appropriate data and provide suitable analysis to support the diagnosis, monitoring, and treatment of these conditions.

Typically, in Smart Homes, sensors are placed on household objects, such as doors, to monitor ADLs, or may instead utilise imaging techniques to infer (sub-)activities. The activation of sensors can be recorded as a time-stamped log of low-level events. Such data can be thought of as an event history, commonly used in process mining [3], where, in the Smart Home case, the events typically characterise the start or end of an activity, or sub-activity, of daily living. The activity can then be analysed to identify ADL behavioural

patterns or abnormalities. This may lead to a reminder to the patient, if required, or an alarm to alert carers or medical services that there may be an issue.

Markov models, and their extensions, offer a well-defined mathematical framework for the movements of individuals through processes, where the individual is known to enter and leave the system through a given state, at a given time. Such models have been widely explored and developed to allow for different application areas and settings, as well as for assessing the legitimacy of assumptions. More specifically, they have already been used for Smart Homes (e.g., [4]) and Process Mining (e.g., [5]). In this paper, we explore several possible directions that exploit the computational advantages of the Process Mining paradigm alongside the mathematical and operational benefits of Markov-type models. Several topics of interest are explored, namely: (i) first passage time distributions for classes of interest, such as specific activities or groups of activities; (ii) aggregation of states to identify levels of detail that are parsimonious and computationally efficient, while providing appropriate inference; (iii) detection of anomalies and concept drift for such activities of interest, which may be indicative of activities taking longer than previously or might signal a new emergent pattern.

This paper is concerned with developing and illustrating some specific mathematical expressions and results for models of human activity. If these are appropriate then computation should be efficient and can provide useful results, e.g., characterising and detecting outliers in performance indicators, such as the length of time taken to perform important (sub-)activities. Appropriate semi-Markov model assumptions can also be built into simulation or digital twin analysis, facilitating the study of different scenarios and their performance in various situations.

The novelty of this paper resides in the development and use of Markov-type models to represent ADL processes and corresponding key performance indicators (KPIs) in Smart Homes, as well as in describing and evaluating strategies to determine anomalies in such transitions and durations. The approach is illustrated and evaluated using a publicly available Smart Home dataset [6], comprising an event log of sensor activations, together with an annotated record of the actual activities, which we use for model development and validation.

2. Literature Review

Processes frequently occur in many different contexts, such as business, telecommunications, and healthcare. Previously, there have been substantial efforts to model and analyse such processes, with the aim of improving understanding and efficiency as well as predicting future outcomes. Also, with recent developments in IT, there exist more sophisticated computer systems to collect, store, process, and exchange data. This has led to the emergence of Process Mining, as a bridge between data mining and process modelling [3], which has already been applied to diverse areas, such as manufacturing (Lorenz et al. [7]), telecommunications (Mahendrawathi et al. [8]), and healthcare (Rojas et al. [9]).

In general, such processes are defined as consisting of a number of activities each with start and end times and corresponding durations. A process instance executes these activities in a sequence, following the logic and rules at work in real-world scenarios. Consequently, Process Mining may involve discovering the activities and trajectories that comprise the process, predicting trajectories, or identifying outliers. Such analysis may use standard data mining approaches such as classification, clustering, association rules, or deep learning. However, in addition, model-based approaches can provide possibilities for incorporating structural process knowledge into the analysis, thereby facilitating improved insight and enhanced forecasting.

A mathematical model can be used to provide a simplified version of a process, where analytic solutions or simulation models can imitate process behaviour without necessarily engaging with real-world scenarios [10]. Such models have frequently been used to address complex problems such as determining correctness, conformance, or performance. Performance analysis typically focuses on the dynamic behaviour of the

process, based on key performance indicators (KPIs) such as response time, uptime, or reliability. More specifically, the main KPIs for Markov-type models have been identified by [11] as (i) state occupancy probabilities, i.e., number of visits to a state during an arbitrary time interval; (ii) first passage time probabilities; and (iii) state occupancy duration probabilities [12]. Also, Markov models are widely used probabilistic process models where it is assumed that the Markov property holds, i.e., the current state only depends on the immediately previous state. This assumption facilitates both the prediction of individual transitions [13] and population forecasting [14]. Higher-order Markov models [15] may alternatively be employed if the Markov assumption is not appropriate [16,17]. Also, non-homogeneous Markov models can be used if the model parameters are changing with time [13].

Another type of Markov model is the hierarchical Markov model, where states may be ordered in levels belonging to a hierarchy, where a group of lower-level states may constitute a single state at a higher level ([4,18]). In addition, hierarchical Markov models may only be partially observable, with unobserved states at the lower levels; such situations can be considered as hierarchical hidden Markov models [19]. On the other hand, depending on the level of interest, the lower levels of the hierarchy may be aggregated to combine states, remove kth order effects, and reduce computational complexity [20]. Also, as well as the basic time-stamped events (change of state) data, we may have additional covariates (features) which can be incorporated into the Markov models. In the literature, this has been accomplished by using partitioning approaches [10], conditional Bayesian networks [21], or making the transition parameters functions of the covariates [22].

As a result of such breadth and diversity, Markov-type models are highly applicable to a variety of application areas. A few such examples are manpower planning, e.g., Papadopoulou and Vassiliou [23], Verbeken and Guerry [24], and McClean et al. [25]; hospital planning, e.g., Marshall and McClean [21], Shaw et al. [26]; business process modelling, e.g., Yang et al. [5], Chen et al. [27]. In addition, there have been a number of papers using Markov-like models for Smart Homes, which are our current focus, e.g., Youngblood and Cook [18], Wang et al. [4]. We have also co-authored an introductory paper on this topic which focuses on the use of semi-Markov models for state durations in Smart Homes (Yang et al. [28]). As we will discuss further, this application area is very well suited to a number of the approaches we have mentioned. As such, we believe that Process Mining and Markov-type models can make a very useful contribution to utilising data from Smart Homes, to great advantage.

3. First Passage Time from a Specified Class of States to the Complement of that Class

3.1. The General Case

In what follows, we will consider a notional Smart Home in which we represent human activities of daily living by way of a semi-Markov process, where the states represent changes of (sub-)activity and are typically detected by time-stamped sensor activations, although other mechanisms are possible, e.g., image-processing of a video feed.

We define Class C as a subset of the states of the semi-Markov system and C' its complement in S, the full set of states. Here, S is notionally a set of human activities of daily living carried out in the home and C is a subset of (sub-)activities that are performed to achieve a goal, e.g., making breakfast. Here, S might be the full set of activities of interest in the home, such as "make breakfast", "eat breakfast", "wash dishes", "make dinner", "take shower", and so on, while C is a subset of S, for example, we might have C = "Manage breakfast" = "cook breakfast", "eat breakfast", "wash dishes". On the other hand, $\tilde{C}$ is an aggregate of all activities in S that are not in C. Initially, we are interested in the distributions of durations in the states of C before the first transition to $\tilde{C}$.

Then, the sub-transition matrix for class C is $A = \{a_{ij}\}$, where k is the number of states and $i, j = 1, \cdots, k$. Here, we consider $\tilde{C}$ as an aggregate of all states in C' and b is the k-dimensional column vector of transition probabilities from states of C to the aggregated states of $\tilde{C}$. Then, $H(t) = \{h_i(t)\}$ is the $k \times k$ matrix with columns the probability density

function's (pdf's) of holding times in each state of C, respectively, and $f(t) = \{f_i(t)\}$ is the column vector of first passage times from each state of C to $\tilde{C}$, respectively. Then,

$$f^*(s) = (A \square H(s))f^*(s) + b\square h^*(s), \tag{1}$$

where $\square$ is the Hadamard product and $f^*(s)$ is the moment generating function of $f(t)$, while $h^*(s)$ is the moment generating function of $h(t)$. This is a special case of the result in [29]. Regrouping gives

$$f^*(s) = (I - A\square H^*(s))^{-1}b\square h^*(s). \tag{2}$$

We note that, in the relation in reference (2), the inverse of the matrix always exists (see [30], P710). We consider an example for $k = 2$, which has been explored previously. Here, states 1 and 2 form the class of interest and we assume that the holding times are exponentially distributed with parameters as in the diagram (Figure 1).

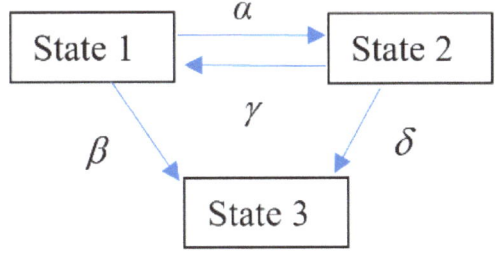

Figure 1. An example where $k = 2$.

In this case, $h(t) = (h_1(t), h_2(t))' = ((\alpha + \beta)e^{-(\alpha+\beta)t}, (\gamma + \delta)e^{-(\gamma+\delta)t})$.

$$A = \begin{pmatrix} 0 & \dfrac{\beta}{\alpha + \beta} \\ \dfrac{\gamma}{\gamma + \delta} & 0 \end{pmatrix}, \quad b = \begin{pmatrix} \dfrac{\alpha}{\alpha + \beta} \\ \dfrac{\delta}{\gamma + \delta} \end{pmatrix}, \tag{3}$$

$$H(t) = \begin{pmatrix} (\alpha + \beta)e^{-(\alpha+\beta)t} & (\alpha + \beta)e^{-(\alpha+\beta)t} \\ (\gamma + \delta)e^{-(\gamma+\delta)t} & (\gamma + \delta)e^{-(\gamma+\delta)t} \end{pmatrix}, \quad h(t) = \begin{pmatrix} (\alpha + \beta)e^{-(\alpha+\beta)t} \\ (\gamma + \delta)e^{-(\gamma+\delta)t} \end{pmatrix}, \tag{4}$$

and

$$H^*(s) = \begin{pmatrix} (\alpha + \beta)/(\alpha + \beta + s) & (\alpha + \beta)/(\alpha + \beta + s) \\ (\gamma + \delta)/(\gamma + \delta + s) & (\gamma + \delta)/(\gamma + \delta + s) \end{pmatrix}. \tag{5}$$

So,

$$\begin{aligned} f^*(s) &= \begin{pmatrix} 1 & -\beta/(\alpha + \beta + s) \\ -\gamma/(\gamma + \delta + s) & 1 \end{pmatrix}^{-1} \begin{pmatrix} \alpha/(\alpha + \beta + s) \\ \delta/(\gamma + \delta + s) \end{pmatrix} \\ &= \left(1 - \dfrac{\beta\gamma}{(\alpha + \beta + s)(\gamma + \delta + s)}\right)^{-1} \begin{pmatrix} 1 & \beta/(\alpha + \beta + s) \\ \gamma/(\gamma + \delta + s) & 1 \end{pmatrix} \begin{pmatrix} \alpha/(\alpha + \beta + s) \\ \delta/(\gamma + \delta + s) \end{pmatrix} \\ &= \left(1 - \dfrac{\beta\gamma}{(\alpha + \beta + s)(\gamma + \delta + s)}\right)^{-1} \begin{pmatrix} \dfrac{\alpha}{\alpha + \beta + s} + \dfrac{\beta\delta}{(\alpha + \beta + s)(\gamma + \delta + s)} \\ \dfrac{\delta}{\gamma + \delta + s} + \dfrac{\beta\gamma}{(\alpha + \beta + s)(\gamma + \delta + s)} \end{pmatrix}. \end{aligned} \tag{6}$$

Putting $\gamma = 0$ to give a Coxian phase type model with two phases, we get:

$$f^*(s) = \begin{pmatrix} \dfrac{\beta}{\alpha + \beta + s} + \dfrac{\beta\delta}{(\alpha + \beta + s)(\delta + s)} \\ \dfrac{\delta}{\delta + s} \end{pmatrix},$$

(7)

$$f(t) = \begin{pmatrix} \dfrac{\beta\delta}{\alpha + \beta - \delta} e^{-\delta t} + \dfrac{(\alpha + \beta)(\alpha - \delta)}{\alpha + \beta - \delta} e^{-(\alpha+\beta)t} \\ \delta e^{-\delta t} \end{pmatrix}.$$

(8)

We note that this equation was previously obtained in McClean [31].

3.2. The Coxian Model

For the general Smart Home case, we consider a Coxian transition matrix structure where transitions to transient states are sequential (Figure 2) and we envisage a phase-type model where there are a number of transient states and exit to a single, or possibly a group of, absorbing state(s). Exit to the absorbing state can occur from any transient case, otherwise, departure from a transient state is to the next transient state in the sequence. A classical phase-type distribution describes a non-negative random variable (usually the duration) generated by a Markov process having a number of transient states (or phases) and a single absorbing state. The duration in each state is therefore exponential. However, in the current case, we envisage a semi-Markov Coxian phase-type model, in particular, a model with mixed gamma durations in each state.

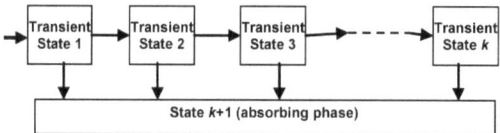

Figure 2. The Coxian phase-type model.

Here, the transient class of states could be all the activities in a visit to the kitchen. Entry to the class is flagged by a door sensor and the class comprises all possible states in the kitchen. For example, a state could be accessing the kettle, which may be accessed for making a cup of coffee (short duration) or for filling a cooking pot (long duration). We therefore assume that the inhabitant enters the kitchen, and then carries out one or more activities in the kitchen class, where an activity duration is described by a mixed gamma duration. In our notional example, these mixture components typically represent latent sub-states, e.g, the short and long kettle durations.

For this semi-Markov Coxian phase-type model, we let a_i be the transition probability from phase S_i to S_{i+1}, for $i = 1, \cdots, k-1$, and let b_i be the probability of transition from S_i to S_{k+1}, for $i = 1, \cdots, k$ where S_{k+1} is the absorbing state. Then, $f_i(t)$ is the pdf of duration in phase S_i, with corresponding generating function $f_i^*(s)$ for $i = 1, \cdots, k$.

In this case:

$$A = \begin{pmatrix} 0 & b_1 & 0 & \cdot & \cdot & 0 \\ 0 & 0 & b_2 & 0 & \cdot & 0 \\ \cdot & \cdot & & \cdot & \cdot & \cdot \\ \cdot & \cdot & & \cdot & \cdot & \cdot \cdot \\ \cdot & \cdot & & \cdot & \cdot & \cdot \\ 0 & 0 & 0 & \cdot & \cdot & b_{k-1} \\ 0 & 0 & 0 & \cdot & \cdot & 0 \end{pmatrix}, \quad b = \begin{pmatrix} a_1 \\ a_2 \\ \cdot \\ \cdot \\ \cdot \\ a_{k-1} \\ a_k \end{pmatrix},$$

(9)

$$
\boldsymbol{H}(t) = \begin{pmatrix}
h_1(t) & \cdot & \cdot & \cdot & \cdot & h_1(t) \\
h_2(t) & \cdot & & \cdot & \cdot & h_2(t) \\
& & \cdot & \cdot & \cdot & \\
& \cdot & \cdot & \cdot & \cdot & \cdot \\
& & \cdot & \cdot & \cdot & \cdot \\
h_{k-1}(t) & \cdot & & \cdot & \cdot & h_{k-1}(t) \\
h_k(t) & \cdot & & \cdot & \cdot & h_k(t)
\end{pmatrix}, \text{and } \boldsymbol{h}(t) = \begin{pmatrix}
h_1(t) \\
h_2(t) \\
\cdot \\
\cdot \\
\cdot \\
h_{k-1}(t) \\
h_k(t)
\end{pmatrix}. \tag{10}
$$

Then, we have:

$$
\boldsymbol{f}^*(s) = \begin{pmatrix}
1 & -b_1 h_1^*(s) & 0 & \cdot & \cdot & 0 \\
0 & 1 & -b_2 f_2^*(s) & 0 & \cdot & 0 \\
\cdot & \cdot & \cdot & \cdot & \cdot & \cdot \\
\cdot & \cdot & \cdot & \cdot & \cdot & \cdot \\
0 & 0 & 0 & \cdot & \cdot & -b_{k-1}f_{k-1}^*(s) \\
0 & 0 & 0 & \cdot & \cdot & 1
\end{pmatrix}^{-1} \begin{pmatrix}
a_1 h_1(t) \\
a_2 h_2(t) \\
\cdot \\
\cdot \\
\cdot \\
a_{k-1}h_{k-1}(t) \\
a_k h_k(t)
\end{pmatrix}
$$

$$
= \begin{pmatrix}
1 & b_1 h_1^*(s) & b_1 b_2 h_1^*(s)h_2^*(s) & \cdot & \cdot & b_1 b_2 \cdots b_{k-1} h_1^*(s) \cdots h_{k-1}^*(s) \\
0 & 1 & b_2 h_2^*(s) & 0 & \cdot & 0 \\
\cdot & \cdot & \cdot & \cdot & \cdot & \cdot \\
\cdot & \cdot & \cdot & \cdot & \cdot & \cdot \\
0 & 0 & 0 & \cdot & \cdot & b_{k-1}h_{k-1}^*(s) \\
0 & 0 & 0 & \cdot & \cdot & 1
\end{pmatrix} \begin{pmatrix}
a_1 h_1(t) \\
a_2 h_2(t) \\
\cdot \\
\cdot \\
\cdot \\
a_{k-1}h_{k-1}(t) \\
a_k h_k(t)
\end{pmatrix}. \tag{11}
$$

So,

$$
f_i^*(s) = \sum_{j=i}^{k} \alpha_j h_j * (s) \prod_{r=j}^{k-1} b_r h_r^*(s), i = 1, \cdots, k. \tag{12}
$$

For $k = 2$ and

$$
\boldsymbol{H}^*(s) = \begin{pmatrix}
(\alpha+\beta)/(\alpha+\beta+s) & (\alpha+\beta)/(\alpha+\beta+s) \\
(\gamma+\delta)/(\gamma+\delta+s) & (\gamma+\delta)/(\gamma+\delta+s)
\end{pmatrix}. \tag{13}
$$

We therefore obtain the previous result for a Coxian Markov phase-type model. If the initial state entered in C is unknown we use a probability vector $\pi = \{\pi_i\}$, where π_i is the probability of admission to state $S_i, i = 1, \cdots, k$. In this case, the transform of the unconditional pdf of duration in C is:

$$
g^*(s) = \pi f^*(s). \tag{14}
$$

For mixed gamma holding times and a semi-Markov Coxian phase-type model we have:

$$
h_i(t) = \sum_{r=1}^{R_i} \pi_{ir} \frac{1}{\Gamma(\alpha_{ir})\beta_{ir}^{\alpha_{ir}}} t^{\alpha_{ir}-1} e^{-\frac{t}{\beta_{ir}}}, t \geq 0, \tag{15}
$$

and

$$
h_i^*(s) = \sum_{r=1}^{R_i} \pi_{ir}(1+\beta_{ir}s)^{-\alpha_{ir}}, i = 1, \cdots, k. \tag{16}
$$

So, we need to compute $f_i^*(s)$, which is a mixture of terms with coefficients $\alpha_j \prod_{r=j}^{k-1} b_r$ of the convolution of exponentials. Thus, the time to exit from class C is

prob(exit from 1) × (mixed gamma 1) + prob(exit from 2) × (mixed gamma 1 ⊕ mixed gamma 2) + ⋯⋯. We can think of this as a mixture of terms relating to exits from successive states, where the corresponding duration is a convolution of times in all the states involved in this transition. We regard such terms as durations of time to exit from C, following entry to the hidden semi-Markov model, where the gamma mixture components are hidden states. Here, ⊕ denotes convolution (sum of two independent random variables). We write

$$f_i^*(s) = \sum_{j=i}^{k} a_j \left(\prod_{r=j}^{k-1} b_r h_j^*(s) h_r^*(s) \right), i = 1, \cdots, k. \tag{17}$$

For example, when $k = 2$:

$$f_1^*(s) = a_1 h_1^*(s) + a_2 b_1 h_1^*(s) h_2^*(s), \tag{18}$$

$$f_2^*(s) = a_2 h_2^*(s). \tag{19}$$

So, for entrance to state 1 and exit from state 1, we have a mixture of durations with an exit from state 1 directly, with probability a_1 and from state 1 to state 2, and then state 2 to exit, with probability $a_2 b_1$. Inverting the transforms, the corresponding durations have pdfs $h_1(t)$ and the convolution of $h_1(t)$ and $h_2(t)$, respectively. Here, $a_1 + b_1 = 1$ and $a_2 = 1$. For entrance to state 2, exit can only occur directly from state 2, and the duration has pdf $h_2(t)$.

In general, of course, different sequences may be formed from the same activities executed in different orders. Here, we have developed the theory for commonly occurring sequences and those potentially of particular interest, e.g., some sequences might indicate that the patient is not managing their activities successfully. In further work, we plan to further consider these aspects, particularly focusing on the aggregation of states, as an aid to understanding, and improved computational efficiency [20].

3.3. Gamma Convolutions

The sum of a number of independently and identically distributed random variables is called their convolution. The exact expressions for the convolutions of n gamma pdfs and cumulative distribution functions (cdfs) are complex and difficult to compute, but are of considerable practical interest [32]. In particular, some authors have proposed that a simple gamma distribution can give a good approximation, especially for convolutions with $n > 2$, (Stewart et al. [33], Covo and Elalouf [34]). On the other hand, approximations and high-performance algorithms have also been developed and are implemented in coga (r-project-org) [35]. In particular, exact solutions have been implemented for $n = 2$ [36] or $n > 2$ [37], while efficient approximate solutions have originated from Barnabani [38].

In our current context, some interesting work has been carried out by Guenther et al. [20] (and in other papers), who describe the modelling and computation of passage-time distributions between groups and aggregates of states.

4. Experiments on Artificially Generated Smart Home Data

In this Section, we generate mixed gamma data representing typical behaviours of each of two activities, in each case consisting of two possible sub-activities, where each sub-activity has two or three possible mixed gamma components. The chosen activities are Toileting and Breakfast, respectively. In each case, we simulate an activity instance by generating two mixed gamma sub-activity instance durations, where we assume these two sub-activities are followed sequentially. For each activity, we then simulate 10,000 representative activity instance durations as the sum of the corresponding mixed gamma sub-activity instance durations.

Using these simulated data, we carry out a series of experiments that, for each of the two activities, compare the empirical activity duration distribution with the convolution model, computed as the convolution of the two sub-activity durations, and the mixed

gamma model fitted to the actual (simulated) data for the activity duration. As discussed in the previous section, the latter has previously been shown to give a good approximation to such data [5].

4.1. Datasets

Toileting To generate data that simulates a scenario in which the inhabitant first performs 'use toilet' and then 'wash hands', we suppose the inhabitant has three patterns when using the toilet, requiring 1, 5, and 10 min on average and two duration patterns for washing hands, taking on average 20 and 40 s each. Such patterns are created by gamma distributions with parameters presented in Table 1. The sequential execution of the two activities is referred to as 'Toileting'.

Table 1. Toileting: real gamma distribution parameters and the parameters fitted by the model-based method.

		Real Parameters			Estimated Parameters			
	Activity	Shape	Scale	Mean	Mixing	Shape	Scale	Mean
		3	20	60	0.795	3.076	19.168	58.961
	Use toilet	50	6	300	0.165	43.040	6.946	298.963
Toileting		200	3	600	0.040	201.440	2.970	598.284
	Wash hands	20	1	20	0.701	21.257	0.939	19.951
		40	1	40	0.299	46.666	0.861	40.170

Breakfast To simulate a 'Breakfast' scenario including two consecutive activities, 'eat food' (three patterns taking 10, 20, and 40 min on average) and 'wash dishes' (two patterns, requiring 5 and 10 min), gamma distributions are employed with the parameters shown in Table 2.

Table 2. Breakfast: real gamma distribution parameters and the parameters fitted by the model-based method.

		Real Parameters			Mathematical Model			
	Activity	Shape	Scale	Mean	Mixing	Shape	Scale	Mean
		60.00	10.00	600.00	0.69	57.12	10.54	601.86
	Eat food	60.00	20.00	1200.00	0.24	66.77	18.07	1206.47
Breakfast		120.00	20.00	2400.00	0.07	121.83	19.69	2398.62
	Wash dishes	10.00	30.00	300.00	0.74	13.35	20.94	279.58
		30.00	20.00	600.00	0.26	29.78	19.08	568.22

4.2. Goodness of Fit of the Model-Based Method for 'Toileting'

Regarding 'Toileting', Table 1 displays real gamma parameters for generating the activities 'use toilet' and 'wash hands', alongside the model-based method estimated from gamma mixture models. Additionally, Table 3 shows the gamma mixture model parameters obtained from the data-driven-based method. Such mixture models are fitted by maximizing the likelihood using the Nelder–Mead simplex algorithm [5].

Table 3. Toileting: parameters fitted by the data-driven-based method.

	Mixing	Shape	Scale	Mean
	0.796	6.086	13.402	81.561
Toileting	0.164	51.745	6.529	337.822
	0.040	189.917	3.376	641.162

Figure 3 demonstrates the model-based method for estimating the duration distribution of the 'toileting' activity (red line). This is achieved by the convolution of estimated gamma mixture models for 'use toilet' (black line) and 'wash hands' (orange line) in Figure 4. The green line represents the distribution that is estimated by the data-driven method. In other words, instead of fitting 'toileting' data directly (the data-driven method), the model-based approach first separately fits the duration distributions of the two sub-activities and then combines them to estimate the 'toileting' duration distribution. The model-based method is therefore suitable for scenarios in which the distribution of sub-activities is known, without the need for additional computational resources.

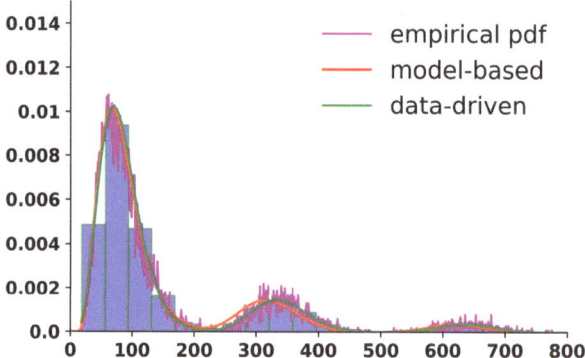

Figure 3. Toileting: pdf of the model- and data-driven-based methods.

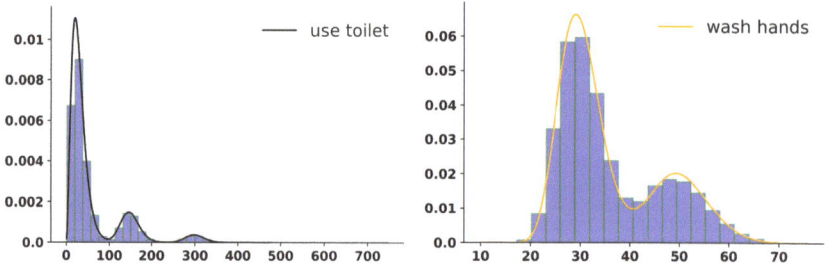

Figure 4. Toileting: pdf of activities 'use toilet' and 'wash hands'.

The KS test [39] is then employed to assess the goodness of fit of the model-based method, with the results presented in Table 4 and Figure 5. We note that the Anderson–Darling test could have been used here as a more powerful alternative to the Kolmogorov–Smirnov test. In summary, both the model-based and data-driven methods effectively represent the original data distribution, as indicated by p-values of 0.219 (model-based) and 0.181 (data-driven), which exceed the predetermined significance level of 0.05. Furthermore, the estimated duration distributions by the two methods is extremely similarly with a p-value of 0.610; the same result can be seen in Figure 5.

Table 4. Toileting: the goodness of data fitting by using the KS test.

Sample 1	Sample 2	Statistic	p-Value
Model-based	Real data	0.047	0.219
Data-driven-based	Real data	0.049	0.181
Model-based	Data-driven-based	0.034	0.610

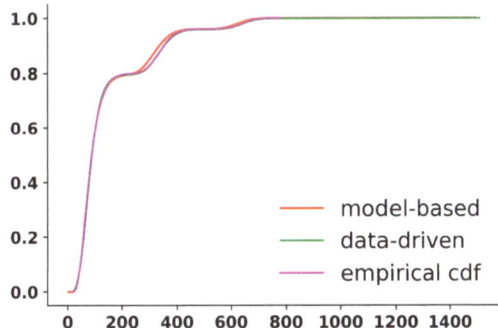

Figure 5. Toileting: cdf of the model- and data-driven-based methods.

4.3. Goodness of Fit of the Model-Based Method for 'Breakfast'

Similarly, parameters to generate the data of 'eating food' and 'washing dishes' and parameters fitted by the model-based method are presented in Table 2. Table 5 displays the data-driven method estimated gamma mixture model parameters. The fitted pdf curves are shown in Figure 6.

Table 5. Breakfast: parameters fitted by the data-driven-based method.

	Mixing	**Shape**	**Scale**	**Mean**
	0.698	51.105	17.714	905.274
Breakfast	0.233	59.564	27.811	1656.523
	0.069	145.588	20.580	2996.230

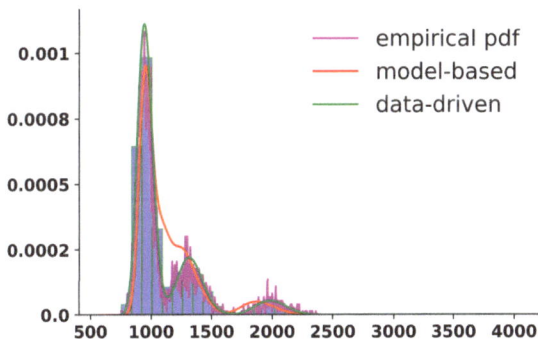

Figure 6. Breakfast: the pdf of model- and data-driven-based methods.

The pdf of activities 'eat food' and 'wash dishes' is given in Figure 7. The KS test results are given in Table 6 and Figure 8. The data-driven method fits the data the best with the highest p-value of 0.523 compared to 0.276 of the model-based method. We highlight that, although the performance of the data-driven method in data fitting outperforms the model-based method, they show less distribution difference with a p-value of 0.821.

Table 6. Breakfast: the goodness of data fitting by using the KS test.

Sample 1	Sample 2	Statistic	p-Value
Model-based	Real data	0.180	0.276
Data-driven-based	Real data	0.147	0.523
Model-based	Data-driven-based	0.114	0.821

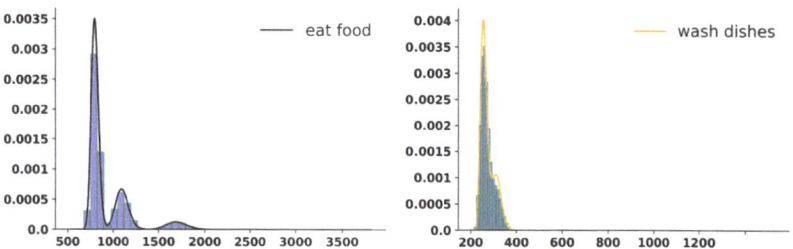

Figure 7. Toileting: pdf of activities 'eat food' and 'wash dishes'.

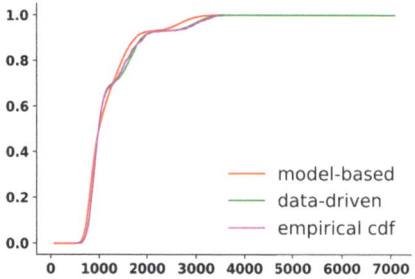

Figure 8. Breakfast: activites of the model- and data-driven-based methods.

5. Example Using Artificially Generated Data for Toileting to Assess Deterioration

Using the artificially generated data described in Section 4.2, we will illustrate the model described in Equations (17) to (19) and discussed in Section 3.3, for gamma convolution. We therefore consider a toileting model as described in the real data part of Table 1. However, we now use a mixed gamma with the given parameters for the two activities 'use toilet' and 'wash hands' but, unlike in Section 4, we assume that 'wash hands' is omitted with probability b. This might be of interest, for example, when assessing deteriorating cognitive or kidney function in an elderly patient.

In this case, the pdf for time spent on the toileting activity becomes a mixture of the pdf of time spent using the toilet, with probability b, and the convolution of time spent on 'use toilet' and 'wash hands', with probability $1 - b$. In Figure 9, we see the pdf of this distribution plotted as a function of b, which shows that, with the increase of b (higher probability to omit washing hands), the length of duration to complete activity 'toileting' is decreasing. Here, b may be regarded as a proxy for impairment, and we can therefore use a statistical test, such as likelihood ratio, to test for drift in b, signalling possible decline. Similarly, Figure 10 demonstrates the pdf that 'wash dishes' is omitted with probability b.

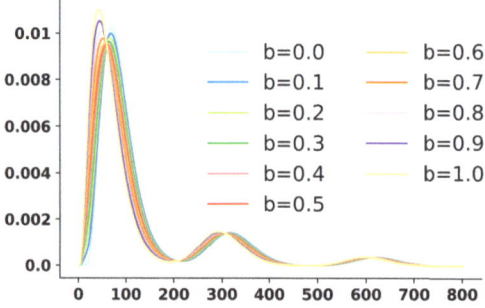

Figure 9. Toileting: pdf of the model-based method given that "wash hands" is omitted with probability b.

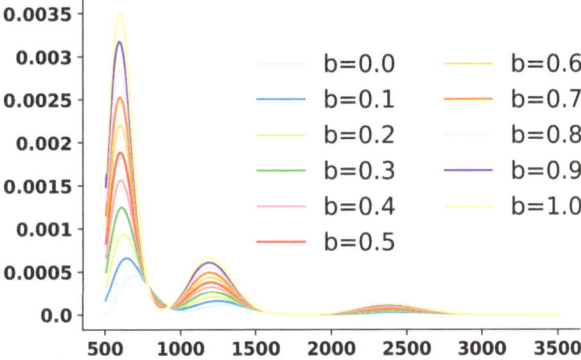

Figure 10. Breakfast: pdf of the model-based method given that "wash dishes" is omitted with probability *b*.

6. Experiments on Real-World Smart Home Data
Datasets

This section utilizes data pertaining to the daily activities of a 26-year-old individual living in a three-room apartment, as gathered by van Kasteren [6]. The data comprise 14 binary state-change sensors, representing the seven activities shown in Table 7 with the Markov transition probabilities shown in Table 8. These sensors were strategically positioned in various areas such as cupboards, refrigerators, and doors, and were left unattended for a duration of 28 days. Additional insights into the apartment's layout and sensor placement can be found in [6,40].

Table 7. Events in the activity, sensor, and location level [28].

Level	Events	#Events
Activity	'Get Drink', 'Go to Bed', 'Leave House', 'Prepare Breakfast', 'Prepare Dinner', 'Take Shower', 'Use Toilet'	7
Sensor	'Microwave', 'Hall Toilet Door', 'Hall Bathroom Door', 'Cups Cupboard', 'Fridge','Plates Cupboard', 'Front Door', 'Dish Washer', 'Toilet Flush', 'Freezer', 'Pans Cupboard', 'Washing Machine', 'Groceries Cupboard', 'Hall Bedroom Door'	14
Location	'Outdoor', 'Bedroom', 'Kitchen', 'Washroom'	4

Table 8. Transition probabilities between activities [28].

	GD	GTB	LH	PB	PD	TS	UT
Get Drink (GD)	0.15	0	0	0.05	0	0	0.8
Go to Bed (GTB)	0	0	0	0.042	0	0	0.958
Leave House (LH)	0.091	0.03	0.03	0	0.091	0.061	0.697
Prepare Breakfast (PB)	0.05	0	0	0	0	0.55	0.4
Prepare Dinner (PD)	0.6	0	0.1	0	0	0	0.3
Take Shower (TS)	0	0	0.913	0	0.043	0	0.043
Use Toilet (UT)	0.061	0.193	0.096	0.158	0.053	0.088	0.351

Since all seven activities have a high transition probability to activity 'use toilet', these transitions are of interest, with 16, 23, 23, 8, 3, 1, and 40 samples, respectively, starting from 'get drink', 'use toilet', 'go to bed', 'leave house', 'prepare breakfast', 'prepare dinner', 'take shower' and 'use toilet'. Due to the limited sample size and the lack of a representative, several transitions are ignored and, finally, data from 'go to bed' to 'use toilet' and 'use

toilet' to 'use toilet' are used as a case study. Their density distributions are shown in Figures 11 and 12. Figures 13 and 14 demonstrate their active curves with the KS test results in Tables 9 and 10.

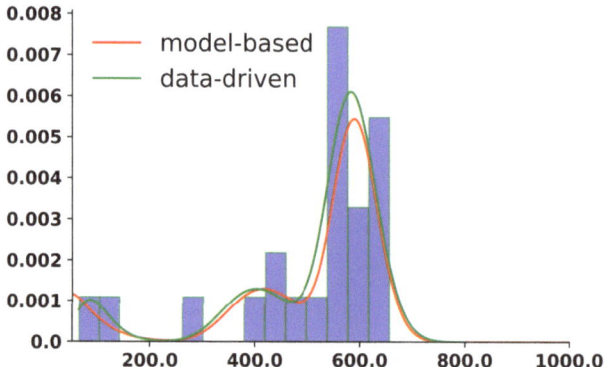

Figure 11. From 'go to bed' to 'use toilet': the pdf of model- and data-driven-based methods.

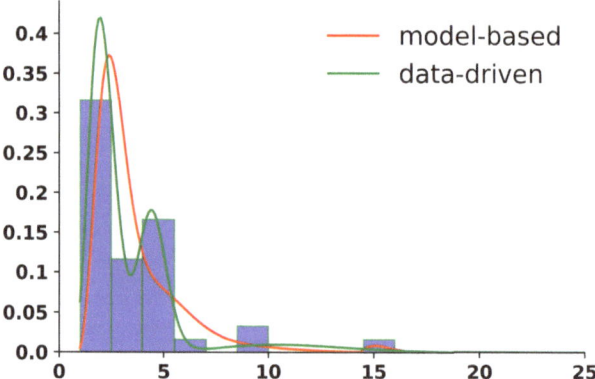

Figure 12. From 'use toilet' to 'use toilet': the pdf of model- and data-driven-based methods.

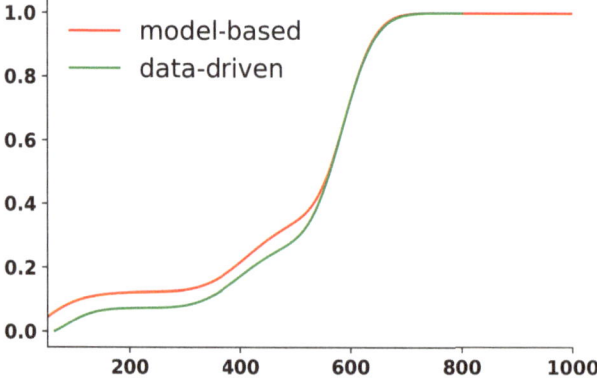

Figure 13. From 'go to bed' to 'use toilet': cdf of the model- and data-driven-based methods.

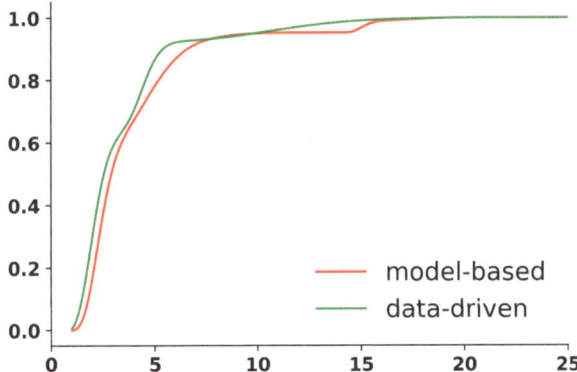

Figure 14. From 'use toilet' to 'use toilet': cdf of the model- and data-driven-based methods.

Table 9. From 'go to bed' to 'use toilet': the goodness of data fitting by using the KS test.

Sample 1	Sample 2	Statistic	*p*-Value
Model-based	Real data	0.215	0.685
Data-driven-based	Real data	0.205	0.705
Model-based	Data-driven-based	0.248	0.532

Table 10. From 'use toilet' to 'use toilet': the goodness of data fitting by using the KS test.

Sample 1	Sample 2	Statistic	*p*-Value
Model-based	Real data	0.582	0.217
Data-driven-based	Real data	0.481	0.384
Model-based	Data-driven-based	0.388	0.632

7. Conclusions and Further Work

Smart Homes and sensorized environments are becoming increasingly prevalent and can provide a useful source of support for disabled inhabitants. In this paper, we have developed suitable equations for semi-Markov models with mixed gamma duration distribution; these have been implemented and evaluated using simulated and real data and have been shown to produce promising results. Such durations can be interpreted as KPIs (Key Performance Indicators) and can be used to assess changes represented by anomalies/outliers or concept drift (changes in duration distribution).

In further work, we plan to extend the research to different Markov-type models, such as: (i) *n*th order models, where the Markov property no longer hold in all cases, and there may be situations when the next (sub-)activity depends on previous states; (ii) non-homogeneous Markov models [17], where the model parameters vary with time, e.g., day-time and night-time, or week-days and weekends, might have different activity patterns that are reflected in model parameters; and (iii) the aggregation of semi-Markov models with a view to providing key information at a suitable level of detail and to improve computational efficiency.

In general, such models can be used in healthcare situations in several important ways. Firstly, they can provide assistance for the patient, by reminding and prompting when a (sub-)activity has been ongoing for too long or omitted. By providing such services in the home, there are potentially huge financial benefits, in terms of reduced hospital and nursing home admissions, as well as improved quality-of-life for the patient and their carers. Secondly, by providing information to the medical professionals and identifying possible deterioration in the patient's condition, there can be improved monitoring, with the potential for more timely and effective treatment and reductions in hospital (re)admissions.

Finally, by having a suitable deployment of such Smart Home technologies, the care of relevant patients can be better managed, resourced, and planned. However, although there has been a considerable amount of research and some deployment of such solutions, there is still a lot of work that needs to be undertaken before the approach is fully fit-for-purpose and widely adopted ([41,42]).

Author Contributions: Conceptualization, S.M.; Methodology, S.M.; Software, L.Y.; Validation, L.Y.; Formal analysis, L.Y.; Investigation, L.Y.; Resources, S.M. and L.Y.; Data curation, L.Y.; Writing—original draft, S.M. and L.Y.; Writing—review & editing, S.M. and L.Y.; Supervision, S.M.; Project administration, S.M.; Funding acquisition, S.M. All authors have read and agreed to the published version of the manuscript.

Funding: This research received no external funding.

Data Availability Statement: The python script to generate the artificial data used in this paper is shared at https://github.com/LingkaiYang/SmatHomeArtificialData/tree/main. The real-world data is publicly available at https://ailab.wsu.edu/mavhome/research.html.

Conflicts of Interest: The authors declare no conflict of interest.

References

1. WHO. 2022. Available online: https://www.who.int/news-room/fact-sheets/detail/ageing-and-health (accessed on 13 November 2022).
2. Joe, E.; Ringman, J.M. Cognitive symptoms of Alzheimer's disease: Clinical management and prevention. *BMJ* **2019**, *367*, l6217. [CrossRef] [PubMed]
3. Van Der Aalst, W.; Adriansyah, A.; De Medeiros, A.K.A.; Arcieri, F.; Baier, T.; Blickle, T.; Bose, J.C.; Van Den Brand, P.; Brandtjen, R.; Buijs, J.; et al. Process mining manifesto. In Proceedings of the Business Process Management Workshops: BPM 2011 International Workshops, Clermont-Ferrand, France, 29 August 2011, Revised Selected Papers, Part I 9. Springer: Berlin/Heidelberg, Germany, 2012; pp. 169–194.
4. Wang, X.; Liu, J.; Moore, S.J.; Nugent, C.D.; Xu, Y. A behavioural hierarchical analysis framework in a smart home: Integrating HMM and probabilistic model checking. *Inf. Fusion* **2023**, *95*, 275–292. [CrossRef]
5. Yang, L.; McClean, S.; Donnelly, M.; Burke, K.; Khan, K. A multi-components approach to monitoring process structure and customer behaviour concept drift. *Expert Syst. Appl.* **2022**, *210*, 118533. [CrossRef]
6. Van Kasteren, T.; Noulas, A.; Englebienne, G.; Kröse, B. Accurate activity recognition in a home setting. In Proceedings of the 10th International Conference on Ubiquitous Computing, Seoul, Republic of Korea, 21–24 September 2008; pp. 1–9.
7. Lorenz, R.; Senoner, J.; Sihn, W.; Netland, T. Using process mining to improve productivity in make-to-stock manufacturing. *Int. J. Prod. Res.* **2021**, *59*, 4869–4880. [CrossRef]
8. Mahendrawathi, E.; Astuti, H.M.; Nastiti, A. Analysis of customer fulfilment with process mining: A case study in a telecommunication company. *Procedia Comput. Sci.* **2015**, *72*, 588–596. [CrossRef]
9. Rojas, E.; Munoz-Gama, J.; Sepúlveda, M.; Capurro, D. Process mining in healthcare: A literature review. *J. Biomed. Inform.* **2016**, *61*, 224–236. [CrossRef] [PubMed]
10. McClean, S.; Barton, M.; Garg, L.; Fullerton, K. A modeling framework that combines markov models and discrete-event simulation for stroke patient care. *ACM Trans. Model. Comput. Simul. (TOMACS)* **2011**, *21*, 1–26. [CrossRef]
11. Georgiou, A.C.; Papadopoulou, A.; Kolias, P.; Palikrousis, H.; Farmakioti, E. On state occupancies, first passage times and duration in non-homogeneous semi-Markov chains. *Mathematics* **2021**, *9*, 1745. [CrossRef]
12. Vassiliou, P.C.; Tsakiridou, H.L. Asymptotic behavior of first passage probabilities in the perturbed non-homogeneous semi-Markov systems. *Commun. Stat.-Theory Methods* **2004**, *33*, 651–679. [CrossRef]
13. Garg, L.; McClean, S.I.; Barton, M.; Meenan, B.J.; Fullerton, K. Intelligent patient management and resource planning for complex, heterogeneous, and stochastic healthcare systems. *IEEE Trans. Syst. Man Cybern. Part A Syst. Humans* **2012**, *42*, 1332–1345. [CrossRef]
14. Gillespie, J.; McClean, S.; Garg, L.; Barton, M.; Scotney, B.; Fullerton, K. A multi-phase DES modelling framework for patient-centred care. *J. Oper. Res. Soc.* **2016**, *67*, 1239–1249. [CrossRef]
15. Vassiliou, P.C.; Moysiadis, T. Inhomogeneous Markov Systems of High Order. *Methodol. Comput. Appl. Probab.* **2010**, *12*, 271–292. [CrossRef]
16. Moore, S.J.; Nugent, C.D.; Zhang, S.; Cleland, I.; Sani, S.; Healing, A. A markov model to detect sensor failure in IoT environments. In Proceedings of the 2020 IEEE World Congress on Services (SERVICES), Beijing, China, 18–23 October 2020; pp. 13–16.
17. Vassiliou, P.C. *Non-Homogeneous Markov Chains and Systems: Theory and Applications*; CRC Press: Boca Raton, FL, USA, 2022.
18. Youngblood, G.M.; Cook, D.J. Data mining for hierarchical model creation. *IEEE Trans. Syst. Man Cybern. Part C Appl. Rev.* **2007**, *37*, 561–572. [CrossRef]

19. Asghari, P.; Soleimani, E.; Nazerfard, E. Online human activity recognition employing hierarchical hidden Markov models. *J. Ambient. Intell. Humaniz. Comput.* **2020**, *11*, 1141–1152. [CrossRef]
20. Guenther, M.C.; Dingle, N.J.; Bradley, J.T.; Knottenbelt, W.J. Passage-time computation and aggregation strategies for large semi-Markov processes. *Perform. Eval.* **2011**, *68*, 221–236. [CrossRef]
21. Marshall, A.; McClean, S. Conditional phase-type distributions for modelling patient length of stay in hospital. *Int. Trans. Oper. Res.* **2003**, *10*, 565–576. [CrossRef]
22. Jones, B.; McClean, S.; Stanford, D. Modelling mortality and discharge of hospitalized stroke patients using a phase-type recovery model. *Health Care Manag. Sci.* **2019**, *22*, 570–588. [CrossRef]
23. Papadopoulou, A.; Vassiliou, P.C. On the variances and convariances of the duration state sizes of semi-Markov systems. *Commun. Stat. Theory Methods* **2014**, *43*, 1470–1483. [CrossRef]
24. Verbeken, B.; Guerry, M. Discrete Time Hybrid Semi-Markov Models in Manpower Planning. *Mathematics* **2021**, *9*, 1681. [CrossRef]
25. McClean, S.; Montgomery, E.; Ugwuowo, F. Non-homogeneous continuous-time Markov and semi-Markov manpower models. *Appl. Stoch. Model. Bus. Ind.* **1997**, *13*, 191–198. [CrossRef]
26. Shaw, B.; Marshall, A. Modelling the flow of congestive heart failure patients through a hospital system. *J. Oper. Res. Soc.* **2007**, *58*, 212–218. [CrossRef]
27. Chen, Z.; Zhang, S.; McClean, S.; Hart, F.; Milliken, M.; Allan, B.; Kegel, I. Process Mining IPTV Customer Eye Gaze Movement Using Discrete-Time Markov Chains. *Algorithms* **2023**, *16*, 82. [CrossRef]
28. Yang, L.; McClean, S.; Bashar, A.; Moore, S.; Tariq, Z. Using Semi-Markov Models to Identify Long Holding Times of Activities of Daily Living in Smart Homes. Available online: https://faculty.pmu.edu.sa/Admin/ckEditor_Uploads/133318033358462860_Camera_Ready_PROMISE_2023_draft.pdf (accessed on 20 November 2023).
29. Howard, R.A. *Dynamic Probabilistic Systems: Markov Models*; Courier Corporation: North Chelmsford, MA, USA, 2012; Volume 1.
30. Howard, R.A. *Dynamic Probabilistic Systems: Semi-Markov and Decision Processes*; Dover Publications: Mineola, NY, USA, 2007; Volume 2.
31. McClean, S. The two-stage model of personnel behaviour. *J. R. Stat. Soc. Ser. A Gen.* **1976**, *139*, 205–217. [CrossRef]
32. Khaledi, B.E.; Kochar, S. A review on convolutions of gamma random variables. In *Stochastic Orders in Reliability and Risk: In Honor of Professor Moshe Shaked*; Springer: New York, NY, USA, 2013; pp. 199–217.
33. Stewart, T.; Strijbosch, L.; Moors, H.; Batenburg, P.V. A Simple Approximation to the Convolution of Gamma Distributions. 2007. Available online: https://pure.uvt.nl/ws/portalfiles/portal/858139/dp2007-70.pdf (accessed on 20 November 2023).
34. Covo, S.; Elalouf, A. A novel single-gamma approximation to the sum of independent gamma variables, and a generalization to infinitely divisible distributions. *Electron. J. Stat.* **2014**, *8*, 894–926. [CrossRef]
35. Hu, C.; Pozdnyakov, V.; Yan, J. Density and distribution evaluation for convolution of independent gamma variables. *Comput. Stat.* **2020**, *35*, 327–342. [CrossRef]
36. Mathai, A.M. Storage capacity of a dam with gamma type inputs. *Ann. Inst. Stat. Math.* **1982**, *34*, 591–597. [CrossRef]
37. Moschopoulos, P.G. The distribution of the sum of independent gamma random variables. *Ann. Inst. Stat. Math.* **1985**, *37*, 541–544. [CrossRef]
38. Barnabani, M. An approximation to the convolution of gamma distributions. *Commun. Stat. Simul. Comput.* **2017**, *46*, 331–343. [CrossRef]
39. Yang, L.; McClean, S.; Donnelly, M.; Burke, K.; Khan, K. Process Duration Modelling and Concept Drift Detection for Business Process Mining. In Proceedings of the 2021 IEEE SmartWorld, Ubiquitous Intelligence & Computing, Advanced & Trusted Computing, Scalable Computing & Communications, Internet of People and Smart City Innovation (SmartWorld/SCALCOM/UIC/ATC/IOP/SCI), Atlanta, GA, USA, 18–21 October 2021; pp. 653–658.
40. Moore, S.; Nugent, C.D.; Cleland, I.; Zhang, S. Impact analysis of erroneous data on IoT reliability. In Proceedings of the 2019 IEEE SmartWorld/SCALCOM/UIC/ATC/CBDCom/IOP/SCI, Leicester, UK, 19–23 August 2019; pp. 1908–1915.
41. Chimamiwa, G.; Giaretta, A.; Alirezaie, M.; Pecora, F.; Loutfi, A. Are Smart Homes Adequate for Older Adults with Dementia? *Sensors* **2022**, *22*, 4254. [CrossRef]
42. Lee, L.N.; Kim, M.J. A critical review of smart residential environments for older adults with a focus on pleasurable experience. *Front. Psychol.* **2020**, *10*, 3080. [CrossRef]

mathematics

MDPI

Article

Analyzing the Asymptotic Behavior of an Extended SEIR Model with Vaccination for COVID-19

Vasileios E. Papageorgiou [1,*], Georgios Vasiliadis [2] and George Tsaklidis [1]

[1] Department of Mathematics, Aristotle University of Thessaloniki, 54124 Thessaloniki, Greece; tsaklidi@math.auth.gr
[2] Department of Mathematics, University of Western Macedonia, 52100 Kastoria, Greece; gvasiliadis@uowm.gr
* Correspondence: vpapageor@math.auth.gr

Abstract: Several research papers have attempted to describe the dynamics of COVID-19 based on systems of differential equations. These systems have taken into account quarantined or isolated cases, vaccinations, control measures, and demographic parameters, presenting propositions regarding theoretical results that often investigate the asymptotic behavior of the system. In this paper, we discuss issues that concern the theoretical results proposed in the paper "An Extended SEIR Model with Vaccination for Forecasting the COVID-19 Pandemic in Saudi Arabia Using an Ensemble Kalman Filter". We propose detailed explanations regarding the resolution of these issues. Additionally, this paper focuses on extending the local stability analysis of the disease-free equilibrium, as presented in the aforementioned paper, while emphasizing the derivation of theorems that validate the global stability of both epidemic equilibria. Emphasis is placed on the basic reproduction number R_0, which determines the asymptotic behavior of the system. This index represents the expected number of secondary infections that are generated from an already infected case in a population where almost all individuals are susceptible. The derived propositions can inform health authorities about the long-term behavior of the phenomenon, potentially leading to more precise and efficient public measures. Finally, it is worth noting that the examined paper still presents an interesting epidemiological scheme, and the utilization of the Kalman filtering approach remains one of the state-of-the-art methods for modeling epidemic phenomena.

Keywords: dynamical systems; stability analysis; asymptotic behavior; Kalman filters; epidemiological modelling; COVID-19

MSC: 65P40; 62P10; 37N35; 34D20

Citation: Papageorgiou, V.E.; Vasiliadis, G.; Tsaklidis, G. Analyzing the Asymptotic Behavior of an Extended SEIR Model with Vaccination for COVID-19. *Mathematics* **2024**, *12*, 55. https://doi.org/10.3390/math12010055

Academic Editors: Mihaela Neamțu, Eva Kaslik and Anca Rădulescu

Received: 30 October 2023
Revised: 20 December 2023
Accepted: 21 December 2023
Published: 23 December 2023

1. Introduction

The authors in [1] propose a compartmental model that contains a system of seven differential equations with the aim of describing the changing dynamics of the spread of COVID-19. The model divides the population into smaller parts, considering susceptible (S), exposed (E), infected (I), quarantine (Q), recovered (R), deceased (D), and vaccinated (V) cases. The first part of the aforementioned paper is dedicated to the proposal of theoretical results regarding the non-negativity of model's states, the boundedness of the total population, and the existence and local stability of the disease-free equilibrium (DFE), based on the basic reproduction number, R_0.

However, there are certain issues regarding the presented proofs and formulas. In the present analysis, we aim to introduce the existing errors, providing detailed comments that rectify them. Moreover, emphasis is placed on proposing theorems concerning the global stability analysis of epidemic equilibria, in accordance with the above-mentioned scheme. In this way, we extend the theoretical results displayed in [1], while providing valuable information regarding the asymptotic behavior of the epidemiological system.

This information can be employed for the establishment of more accurate measures that can facilitate the limiting of the virus's transmission.

Typically, the spread of infectious diseases is explained through compartmental models, among which the SIR model—representing susceptible-infected-recovered—is the most recognized [2]. Consequently, numerous studies delve into the dynamics of COVID-19 relying on the SIR model or its adaptations like SIRS [3], SEIR, or the SEIRD models [4]. Furthermore, Malkov [5] proposed a deterministic SEIRS model that incorporates time-varying transmission rates for the description of the transmission of COVID-19. Other compartmental extensions can be found in [6–11]. All the abovementioned endeavors are based on systems of differential equations that can be numerically solved.

Several techniques have been proposed in the literature to establish numerically stable methodologies for solving systems of differential equations. Many papers employ Runge–Kutta methodologies, with the 4th-order Runge–Kutta being the most widely known [12,13]. Several extensions have been proposed in the articles of Kalogiratou and Monovasilis, which refer to two-derivative Runge–Kutta methods with optimal phase properties [14], optimized dispersion and dissipation error [15], and constant and frequency dependent coefficients [16]. Moreover, additional advanced techniques for solving systems of partial differential equations have been proposed in [17–19].

In summary, the present paper provides valuable corrections concerning the theoretical results displayed in [1] that pertain to the non-negativity and boundedness of a system of seven differential equations, which describe the transition of COVID-19 after the onset of the vaccination period. These modifications are crucial in validating the suitability of the epidemiological model for accurately describing the spread of COVID-19. More importantly, we provide novel properties regarding the global asymptotic stability of both the disease-free and endemic equilibria based on the values of the basic reproduction number (R_0). These theoretical aspects are more crucial than the local stability analysis, offering insights into long-term behavior when the system approaches the aforementioned equilibria. Finally, a novel addition to the literature is the computation of the convergence rate to the endemic equilibria, offering a more comprehensive understanding of the system's asymptotic behavior. Using real values for the basic reproduction number derived from experimental data, we can evaluate the severity of the phenomenon and validate previous predictions about the future course of the pandemic in the literature.

The rest of the article is structured as follows: In Section 2, we present a series of issues regarding the non-negativity and boundedness theorems that are proposed in [1], while Sections 3 and 4 are dedicated to the rectification of issues concerning the local stability of the disease-free equilibrium and the existence and uniqueness of the endemic equilibrium, respectively. Finally, in Section 5, we present novel results regarding the global stability of the epidemic equilibria, while in Section 6, we conclude with the advantages of epidemiological modeling, emphasizing the main contribution of the present paper.

2. Non-Negativity of Model's States and Boundedness of the Total Population

To begin, the authors in [1] have proposed an ODE system of seven equations to describe the transmission of COVID-19 after the opening of the vaccination period. As a result, the examined population has been split into seven compartments (classes) based on the state of the population's members; Equation (1) displays the transitions between these classes, namely

$$
\begin{aligned}
\frac{dS(t)}{dt} &= \Lambda - \beta S(t)I(t) - aS(t) - \mu S(t), \\
\frac{dE(t)}{dt} &= \beta S(t)I(t) - \gamma E(t) + \sigma \beta V(t)I(t) - \mu E(t), \\
\frac{dI(t)}{dt} &= \gamma E(t) - \delta I(t) - \mu I(t), \\
\frac{dQ(t)}{dt} &= \delta I(t) - (1-\kappa)\lambda Q(t) - \kappa \rho Q(t) - \mu Q(t), \\
\frac{dR(t)}{dt} &= (1-\kappa)\lambda Q(t) - \mu R(t), \\
\frac{dD(t)}{dt} &= \kappa \rho Q(t), \\
\frac{dV(t)}{dt} &= aS(t) - \sigma \beta V(t)I(t) - \mu V(t),
\end{aligned}
\tag{1}
$$

with non-negative initial conditions. In Table 1, we present the definition of the system's states and parameters.

Table 1. Parameter and state definition of the proposed SEIHCRDV model.

Symbol	Definition of Parameter/State
S	Susceptible
E	Exposed
I	Infectious
Q	Quarantined
R	Recovered
D	Deceased
V	Vaccinated
Λ	New births and new residents
a	Vaccination rate
β	Transmission rate
γ	Incubation rate
δ	Infection rate
λ	Recovery rate
κ	Case fatality rate
μ	Natural death rate
ρ	Death rate
σ	Vaccine inefficacy

In the first theorem of [1], the authors aim to prove the non-negativity of the system's states based on the proposed system of differential equations. More specifically, an attempt to prove the non-negativity of the number of susceptible cases $S(t)$, $\forall t \geq 0$, when $S_0 > 0$ is displayed. This attempt leads to

$$S(t) \geq S_0 e^{-\mu t} \geq 0 . \tag{2}$$

However, this inequality does not seem to hold true when considering the first differential equation of the system. Equation

$$\frac{dS(t)}{dt} = \Lambda - \beta S(t) I(t) - a S(t) - \mu S(t) > -\mu S(t) , \tag{3}$$

holds true only when $\Lambda > \beta S(t) I(t) + a S(t)$. It is evident that there are several instances of parameter selections where the aforementioned expression is not satisfied. We note that all system's parameters are assumed to be positive constants, as they represent ingoing or outgoing transition rates of the system's states. Therefore, a modification of (2) is required to lead to the desired outcome. Specifically, we take

$$\begin{aligned}\frac{dS(t)}{dt} &= \Lambda - \beta S(t) I(t) - a S(t) - \mu S(t) > -\beta S(t) I(t) - a S(t) - \mu S(t) \\ &= -(\beta I(t) + a + \mu) S(t) \geq -\left(\beta \max_{t \in [0,\infty)} I(t) + a + \mu\right) S(t) .\end{aligned}$$

Using the infinity norm $\|I(t)\|_\infty = \max_{t \in [0,\infty)} I(t)$, we obtain

$$\frac{d \ln(S(t))}{dt} \geq -(\beta \|I(t)\|_\infty + a + \mu).$$

Consequently, by integrating the above expression with respect to t, and substituting $t = 0$, we result in

$$S(t) \geq S_0 e^{-(\beta \|I(t)\|_\infty + a + \mu)t} \geq 0 , \quad \forall t \geq 0 . \tag{4}$$

Notice that $\|I(t)\|_\infty < \infty$, as we refer to a finite population function, $N(t)$. We believe that this approach now rectifies the proof of Theorem 1. The utilization of the infinity norm

can be employed for proving the non-negativity of vaccinated cases, too, while the proof for the remaining states is omitted for the sake of brevity.

In the second theorem of [1], the authors aim to prove the boundedness of the total population function $N(t)$, $\forall t \geq 0$. They claim that since $N(t) = S(t) + E(t) + I(t) + Q(t) + R(t) + D(t) + V(t)$, for the derivative with respect to time, we have

$$\frac{dN(t)}{dt} = \frac{dS(t)}{dt} + \frac{dE(t)}{dt} + \frac{dI(t)}{dt} + \frac{dQ(t)}{dt} + \frac{dR(t)}{dt} + \frac{dD(t)}{dt} + \frac{dV(t)}{dt}, \tag{5}$$

which leads to

$$\frac{dN(t)}{dt} = \Lambda - \mu N(t), \quad \forall t \geq 0. \tag{6}$$

However, Equation (6) does not hold based on the proposed epidemiological system, which is presented in Equation (1). This derives from the inclusion of the deceased cases, $D(t)$, in the total population. The above expression should be rectified as

$$\frac{dN(t)}{dt} = \Lambda - \mu(S(t) + E(t) + I(t) + Q(t) + R(t) + V(t)) = \Lambda - \mu N(t) + \mu D(t), \tag{7}$$

after the summation of all equations of the ODE system, as $\frac{dN(t)}{dt} = \frac{dS(t)}{dt} + \frac{dE(t)}{dt} + \frac{dI(t)}{dt} + \frac{dQ(t)}{dt} + \frac{dR(t)}{dt} + \frac{dD(t)}{dt} + \frac{dV(t)}{dt}$. Thus, after moving $\mu N(t)$ to the left side, we lead to

$$\frac{dN(t)}{dt} + \mu N(t) = \Lambda + \mu D(t),$$

or

$$\frac{de^{\mu t} N(t)}{dt} = (\Lambda + \mu D(t))e^{\mu t}$$

and integrating with respect to t, we obtain

$$e^{\mu t} N(t) - N_0 = \frac{\Lambda}{\mu}(e^{\mu t} - 1) + \mu \int_0^t D(s)e^{\mu s}ds, \tag{8}$$

or

$$N(t) = \frac{\Lambda}{\mu} + \left(N_0 - \frac{\Lambda}{\mu}\right)e^{-\mu t} + \mu e^{-\mu t} \int_0^t D(s)e^{\mu s}ds. \tag{9}$$

As a result, $N(t)$ is bounded if and only if $\int_0^t D(s)e^{\mu s}ds$ is bounded for all $t > 0$.

Moreover, there is another major issue in the proof of Theorem 2 in [1]. The authors claim that $N(t) \leq \frac{\Lambda}{\mu}$ for all $t > 0$, regardless of the system's parameters. According to Expression (6), which as we mentioned earlier is not true, the authors lead to

$$N(t) = \frac{\Lambda}{\mu} + \left(N_0 - \frac{\Lambda}{\mu}\right)e^{-\mu t}, \quad \forall t > 0. \tag{10}$$

Apparently, $N(t) \leq \frac{\Lambda}{\mu}$ is not true for every parametric set. Based on Equation (10), this is valid for all $t > 0$, only when $N_0 < \frac{\Lambda}{\mu}$.

Finally based on (9) for $t \to \infty$, we lead to

$$\lim_{t \to \infty} N(t) = \frac{\Lambda}{\mu}, \tag{11}$$

in case $\lim_{t \to \infty} e^{-\mu t} \int_0^t D(s)e^{\mu s}ds = 0$.

As a result, it becomes evident that the authors' proof for Theorem 2 does not validate the theorem's statement.

3. Local Stability of the Disease-Free Equilibrium (DFE)

Moving on to Theorem 3, the authors claim that the disease-free equilibrium (DFE) is locally asymptotically stable if $R_0 < 1$ and unstable when $R_0 > 1$. First, we notice that during the computation of R_0, the vector $W(X)$ of Section 3.3 in [1] should be rectified to $W(X) = ((\mu + \delta)E, -\gamma E + (\mu + \delta)I)^T$, since the number of infected cases is missing from the second component of the vector. This modification does not alter the final formula for R_0, where

$$R_0 = \frac{\beta \gamma \Lambda (\mu + \alpha \sigma)}{\mu (\mu + \gamma)(\mu + \delta)(\mu + \alpha)} \ . \tag{12}$$

To prove the local asymptotic stability of the DFE X^0, the respective Jacobian matrix of the epidemiological system is employed. Equilibrium X^0 is locally asymptotically stable when all six eigenvalues of the Jacobian $J(X^0)$ are negative. So, it is claimed that there are two eigenvalues λ_5, λ_6, where

$$\lambda_5 = -\frac{1}{2}\left(\varepsilon_2 + \varepsilon_3 + \sqrt{(\varepsilon_2 - \varepsilon_3)^2 + 4\varepsilon_2 \varepsilon_3 R_0} \right), \tag{13}$$

and

$$\lambda_6 = -\frac{1}{2}\left(\varepsilon_2 + \varepsilon_3 - \sqrt{(\varepsilon_2 - \varepsilon_3)^2 + 4\varepsilon_2 \varepsilon_3 R_0} \right). \tag{14}$$

with $\varepsilon_2 = -(\alpha + \mu)$ and $\varepsilon_3 = -(\delta + \mu)$. While λ_6 is indeed smaller than 0 when $R_0 < 1$, the same does not hold true for Expression (13). More specifically, we have

$$\sqrt{(\varepsilon_2 - \varepsilon_3)^2 + 4\varepsilon_2 \varepsilon_3 R_0} < \sqrt{(\varepsilon_2 - \varepsilon_3)^2 + 4\varepsilon_2 \varepsilon_3} = |\varepsilon_2 + \varepsilon_3| = -(\varepsilon_2 + \varepsilon_3),$$

or

$$\varepsilon_2 + \varepsilon_3 + \sqrt{(\varepsilon_2 - \varepsilon_3)^2 + 4\varepsilon_2 \varepsilon_3 R_0} < 0 \ ,$$

or

$$-\frac{1}{2}\left(\varepsilon_2 + \varepsilon_3 + \sqrt{(\varepsilon_2 - \varepsilon_3)^2 + 4\varepsilon_2 \varepsilon_3 R_0} \right) > 0 \ ,$$

leading to $\lambda_5 > 0$. According to the above, the DFE becomes asymptotically unstable when $R_0 < 1$, which contradicts with the statement of Theorem 3. Moreover, this outcome opposes several analyses in literature [6,8,9,12,20–26]. On the other hand, when R_0 is greater than 1, the DFE becomes asymptotically unstable as $\lambda_5 < 0$ and $\lambda_6 > 0$.

The aforementioned issues possibly derive from the form of the Jacobin matrix $J(X^0)$, which is presented in [1] (Equation (20), Section 3.3), as there are several mistakes concerning the signs of the elements that take place on the matrix diagonal. The authors' proof for Theorem 3 does not validate the theorem's statement.

4. Existence and Uniqueness of the Endemic Equilibrium

Following the theorem that concerns the local stability of the DFE, the authors emphasize the existence and uniqueness of an endemic equilibrium, denoted by X^*. To begin with, the expression of the endemic equilibrium should be rectified to $X^* = (S^*, E^*, I^*, Q^*, R^*, V^*)$, as the number of diseased cases—and the respective differential equation—are excluded from the determination of the equilibrium.

At the first part of the proof, the authors in [1] describe the components of X^* with respect to I^* after adding the second and sixth equation of the system evaluated on the endemic equilibrium. In Section 3.4 of [1], the authors use the notations $\varepsilon_1 = \mu + \alpha$, $\varepsilon_3 = \mu + \delta$ and $\varepsilon_4 = \mu + \lambda(1 - \kappa) + \kappa \rho$, and lead to expression

$$V^* = \frac{\Lambda \beta \gamma I + \Lambda \alpha \gamma - \varepsilon_2 \varepsilon_3 (\beta I + \varepsilon_1) I}{\mu \gamma (\beta I + \varepsilon_1)} \ , \tag{15}$$

which represents the number of vaccinated cases when the system has entered the endemic equilibrium. The endemic equilibrium is obtained after setting all derivatives of system (1) to zero. After solving with respect to V^*, we reach Expression (15).

First, the I symbols should be replaced with I^*, as the system has to be evaluated at the endemic equilibrium X^* to describe V^*. Also, considering the notation in Section 3.3 of [1], where $\varepsilon_2 = -(\gamma + \mu)$, the minus sign of the numerator must be replaced with a plus sign.

Afterwards, the statement that a_2 is always positive and a_0 is negative when $R_0 > 1$ contradicts Formula (26) in that paper. It should be emphasized that the opposite behavior holds for these two quantities, namely $a_2 < 0$ and $a_0 > 0$.

Finally, we notice that an alternative, simpler formula can be derived for the number of vaccinated cases at the equilibrium. Using the sixth equation of the system evaluated at X^*, we culminate in $V^* = \frac{aS^*}{\mu + \sigma\beta I^*} = \frac{a\Lambda}{(\mu + \sigma\beta I^*)(\beta I^* + \mu + a)}$.

5. Global Stability Analysis of Epidemic Equilibria

At this point we emphasize the extension of the results concerning the stability analysis of epidemic equilibria. Global stability analysis provides information about the behavior of a system across its entire state space. Therefore, it determines the stability of the system for all initial conditions. Thus, it offers a comprehensive view of the system's behavior in contrast to the local stability analysis, which can provide insights only around the equilibria.

Theorem 1. *The DFE X^0, is globally asymptotically stable if and only if $R_0 < 1$.*

Proof of Theorem 1. Based on the LaSalle's invariance principle, we choose a Lyapunov function $L(t)$ that is positive semidefinite in the feasible region $\Omega = \{(S, E, I, Q, R, V) \mid S, E, I, Q, R, V \geq 0\} = \mathbb{R}^6_+$, while its derivative is negative definite in the same region. Let

$$L(t) = \frac{1}{2}\left[\left(S - S^0\right)^2 + E^2 + I^2 + Q^2 + R^2 + \left(V - V^0\right)^2\right] = \frac{1}{2}X^T X \geq 0, \tag{16}$$

where $X = \left(S - S^0, E, I, Q, R, V - V^0\right)^T$, as $E^0 = I^0 = Q^0 = R^0 = 0$. Function $L(t)$ becomes 0 only on X^0. For the derivate, we obtain

$$
\begin{aligned}
\frac{dL}{dt} &= \left(S - S^0\right)\frac{dS}{dt} + E\frac{dE}{dt} + I\frac{dI}{dt} + Q\frac{dQ}{dt} + R\frac{dR}{dt} + \left(V - V^0\right)\frac{dV}{dt} \\
&= \left(S - S^0\right)\left[\Lambda - \beta\left(S - S^0\right)I - \beta S^0 I - (\alpha + \mu)\left(S - S^0\right) - (\alpha + \mu)S^0\right] \\
&\quad + E\left[-(\gamma + \mu)E + \beta\left(S - S^0\right)I + \beta S^0 I + \sigma\beta\left(V - V^0\right)I + \sigma\beta V^0 I\right] \\
&\quad + I[\gamma E - (\delta + \mu)I] + Q[\delta I - ((1 - \kappa)\lambda + \kappa\rho + \mu)Q] + R[(1 - \kappa)\lambda Q - \mu R] \\
&\quad + \left(V - V^0\right)\left[a\left(S - S^0\right) + aS^0 - \mu\left(V - V^0\right) - \mu V^0 - \sigma\beta\left(V - V^0\right)I + \sigma\beta V^0 I\right] \\
&= -\beta\left(S - S^0\right)^2 I - \beta S^0\left(S - S^0\right)I - (\alpha + \mu)\left(S - S^0\right)^2 \\
&\quad - (\gamma + \mu)E^2 + \beta\left(S - S^0\right)EI + \sigma\beta\left(V - V^0\right)EI + \beta S^0 EI + \sigma\beta V^0 EI \\
&\quad + \gamma IE - (\delta + \mu)I^2 + \delta QI - ((1 - \kappa)\lambda + \kappa\rho + \mu)Q^2 + (1 - \kappa)\lambda RQ - \mu R^2 \\
&\quad + \alpha\left(V - V^0\right)\left(S - S^0\right) - \mu\left(V - V^0\right)^2 - \sigma\beta I\left(V - V^0\right)^2 + \sigma\beta V^0\left(V - V^0\right)I \\
&= X^T A X = X^T A_1 X + X^T A_2 X,
\end{aligned}
\tag{17}
$$

where

$$
A_1 = \begin{pmatrix}
-(\alpha + \mu) & 0 & -\beta S^0 & 0 & 0 & 0 \\
0 & -(\gamma + \mu) & \beta\left(S^0 + \sigma V^0\right) & 0 & 0 & 0 \\
0 & \gamma & -(\delta + \mu) & 0 & 0 & 0 \\
0 & 0 & \delta & -((1 - \kappa)\lambda + \kappa\rho + \mu) & 0 & 0 \\
0 & 0 & 0 & (1 - \kappa)\lambda & -\mu & 0 \\
\alpha & 0 & -\sigma\beta V^0 & 0 & 0 & -\mu
\end{pmatrix},
$$

and

$$
A_2 = \begin{pmatrix}
-\beta I & 0 & 0 & 0 & 0 & 0 & 0 \\
\beta I & 0 & 0 & 0 & 0 & 0 & \sigma\beta I \\
0 & 0 & 0 & 0 & 0 & 0 & 0 \\
0 & 0 & 0 & 0 & 0 & 0 & 0 \\
0 & 0 & 0 & 0 & 0 & 0 & 0 \\
0 & 0 & 0 & 0 & 0 & 0 & -\sigma\beta I
\end{pmatrix},
$$

where A_2 is a polynomial matrix. We have dropped the (t) notation for the sake of simplicity. Furthermore, we notice that $\Lambda - (\alpha + \mu)S^0 = 0$ and $aS^0 - \mu V^0 = 0$. Quantities $\beta(S - S^0)IE$, $\sigma\beta(V - V^0)IE$, $-\sigma\beta I(V - V^0)^2$ and $-\beta(S - S^0)^2 I$ are matched with A_2.

The characteristic polynomial of the 6×6 matrix A_1 is

$$
\begin{aligned}
p(x) = \det(xI_6 - A_1) &= (x + \alpha + \mu)(x + \mu)^2(x + ((1 - \kappa)\lambda + \kappa\rho + \mu)) \\
&\quad \left(x^2 + (\gamma + \delta + 2\mu)x + (\mu + \delta)(\mu + \gamma) - \beta\gamma(S^0 + \sigma V^0)\right) = 0,
\end{aligned} \tag{18}
$$

leading to 4 negative eigenvalues. Now, for the second-order polynomial in (18), we implement the 2nd-order Routh–Hurwitz criterion, where the roots of the polynomial, lay on the left-hand side of the complex plane when coefficients $(\gamma + \delta + 2\mu)$ and $(\mu + \delta)(\mu + \gamma) - \beta\gamma(S^0 + \sigma V^0)$ are both positive. Apparently, $(\gamma + \delta + 2\mu) > 0$. Then the Routh–Hurwitz criterion is satisfied when $(\mu + \delta)(\mu + \gamma) - \beta\gamma(S^0 + \sigma V^0) > 0$, and based on the R_0 formula displayed in [1], this inequality is true if and only if $R_0 < 1$.

Ultimately, the eigenvalues of A_2 are all non-positive due to $I(t)$ being non-negative, (non-negativity of system's states). In parallel, the eigenvalues of A_1 are all negative if and only if $R_0 < 1$. According to the above observations we get that $X^T A_1 X < 0$, and $X^T A_2 X \leq 0$. To summarize, $\frac{dL}{dt} = X^T A X < 0$, if and only if $R_0 < 1$, which proves the global asymptotic stability of the DFE. $\square$

Theorem 2. *The endemic equilibrium X^*, is globally asymptotically stable when $R_0 > 1$.*

Proof of Theorem 2. Following a similar approach to that of the previous theorem, we note that according to [1] the endemic equilibrium exists only when R_0 is greater than 1. We choose the quadratic Lyapunov function,

$$
L(t) = \frac{1}{2}\left[(S - S^*)^2 + (E - E^*)^2 + (I - I^*)^2 + (Q - Q^*)^2 + (R - R^*)^2 + (V - V^*)^2\right] = \frac{1}{2}Y^T Y \geq 0, \tag{19}
$$

where $Y = (S - S^*, E - E^*, I - I^*, Q - Q^*, R - R^*, V - V^*)^T$, and $L(X^*) = 0$. Employing the second equation of the proposed system of differential equations evaluated on the endemic equilibrium, we get

$$
\beta S^* I^* + \sigma\beta V^* I^* - \gamma E^* - \mu E^* = 0,
$$

or

$$
\beta(S^* + \sigma V^*) = \frac{(\gamma + \mu)E^*}{I^*} = \frac{(\gamma + \mu)(\delta + \mu)}{\gamma} \tag{20}
$$

For the derivative of the selected Lyapunov function, we have

$$
\frac{dL}{dt} = (S - S^*)\frac{dS}{dt} + (E - E^*)\frac{dE}{dt} + (I - I^*)\frac{dI}{dt} + (Q - Q^*)\frac{dQ}{dt} + (R - R^*)\frac{dR}{dt} + (V - V^*)\frac{dV}{dt}, \tag{21}
$$

and after some algebraic manipulations we obtain

$$\frac{dL}{dt} = (S - S^*)[-(a + \mu)(S - S^*) - \beta(S - S^*)I - \beta S^*(I - I^*)]$$
$$+(E - E^*)[-(a + \delta)(E - E^*) + \sigma\beta(V - V^*)I + \beta(S - S^*)I - \beta(S^* + \sigma V^*)I^*]$$
$$+(I - I^*)[\gamma(E - E^*) - (\delta + \mu)(I - I^*)]$$
$$+(Q - Q^*)[\delta(I - I^*) - ((1 - \kappa)\lambda + \kappa\rho + \mu)(Q - Q^*)] \qquad (22)$$
$$+(R - R^*)[(1 - \kappa)\lambda(Q - Q^*) - \mu(R - R^*)]$$
$$+(V - V^*)[\alpha(S - S^*) - \mu(V - V^*) - \sigma\beta(V - V^*)I - \sigma\beta V^*(I - I^*)],$$

since according to [1] it holds that $E^* = \frac{\delta + \mu}{\gamma}I^*$, $Q^* = \frac{\delta}{(1-\kappa)\lambda + \kappa\rho + \mu}I^*$, $R^* = \frac{(1-\kappa)\lambda\delta}{\mu((1-\kappa)\lambda + \kappa\rho + \mu)}I^*$, and $S^* = \frac{\Lambda}{\beta I^* + \mu + a}$. Additionally, we notice that $\Lambda - (a + \mu)S^* + \beta S^* I^* = 0$, $\beta(S^* + \sigma V^*)I^* - (\gamma + \mu)E^* = 0$, and $\alpha S^* - \sigma\beta V^* I^* - \mu V^* = 0$, which derive from Equation (22) of [1] (Section 3.4), leading to our Equation (22).

Now, Expression (22) can be represented in matrix form as

$$\frac{dL}{dt} = X^T B X = X^T B_1 X + X^T B_2 X, \qquad (23)$$

where

$$B_1 = \begin{pmatrix} -(\alpha + \mu) & 0 & -\beta S^* & 0 & 0 & 0 \\ 0 & -(\gamma + \mu) & 0 & 0 & 0 & 0 \\ 0 & \gamma & -(\delta + \mu) & 0 & 0 & 0 \\ 0 & 0 & \delta & -((1 - \kappa)\lambda + \kappa\rho + \mu) & 0 & 0 \\ 0 & 0 & 0 & \lambda(1 - \kappa) & -\mu & 0 \\ \alpha & 0 & -\sigma\beta V^* & 0 & 0 & -\mu \end{pmatrix},$$

and

$$B_2 = \begin{pmatrix} -\beta I & 0 & 0 & 0 & 0 & 0 & 0 \\ \beta I & 0 & \frac{(\gamma + \mu)(\delta + \mu)}{\gamma} & 0 & 0 & 0 & \sigma\beta I \\ 0 & 0 & 0 & 0 & 0 & 0 & 0 \\ 0 & 0 & 0 & 0 & 0 & 0 & 0 \\ 0 & 0 & 0 & 0 & 0 & 0 & 0 \\ 0 & 0 & 0 & 0 & 0 & 0 & -\sigma\beta I \end{pmatrix}.$$

Hence, the model's endemic equilibrium is globally asymptotically stable when $R_0 > 1$. The eigenvalues of B_2 are all non-positive due to $I(t)$ being non-negative, while all eigenvalues of B_1 lie on the left complex plain since they represent negative real numbers. Consequently, we obtain $X^T B_1 X < 0$, and $X^T B_2 X \leq 0$. Thus, $\frac{dL}{dt} = X^T B X < 0$, when $R_0 > 1$, proving the global stability of the endemic equilibrium. □

Theorem 3. *When $R_0 < 1$, the extended SEIR model converges exponentially to the DFE according to the maximum eigenvalue of matrix A. On the other hand, in case $R_0 > 1$, the system converges to the endemic equilibrium based on the maximum eigenvalue of matrix B.*

Proof of Theorem 3. In order to determine the convergence rate of the suggested epidemiological model to the DFE, it is necessary to find a positive value for the parameter k that fulfills the inequality

$$\frac{dL(t)}{dt} \leq -kL(t), \qquad (24)$$

where $L(t)$ still represents the Lyapunov function. Based on the above, we can lead to the epidemic system's convergence rate, which is determined by $\frac{k}{2}$. The distinction of the two cases, $R_0 < 1$ and $R_0 > 1$, is included to ensure that the existence of the two examined endemic equilibria is satisfied, before we proceed to the investigation of their convergence rates. We require the most appropriate k value that satisfies Expression

(24). After substituting the formulas for $L(t)$ and its derivate with respect to time, we obtain

$$X^T A X \leq -k\frac{1}{2}X^T X, \tag{25}$$

$$X^T \left(A + \frac{k}{2}I \right) X \leq 0, \tag{26}$$

leading to the conclusion that matrix $A + \frac{k}{2}I$ must be negative semidefinite. For $R_0 < 1$, the eigenvalues (λ_i) of A are all negative. Our goal is to determine the value of k, for which the eigenvalues $\left(\lambda_i + \frac{k}{2} \right)$ of matrix $A + \frac{k}{2}I$ are also negative.

As a result, we culminate in $\lambda_i + \frac{k}{2} \leq 0$, when $k \leq -2\lambda_i$ for $i = 1, \ldots, 6$, which leads to the selection of $k = -2\max\{\lambda_i, i = 1, \ldots, 6\} > 0$. This validates that the convergence rate to DFE is equal to $-\max\{\lambda_i, i = 1, \ldots, 6\} > 0$. Similarly, in case $R_0 > 1$ the convergence rate of the epidemiological model to the endemic equilibrium is based on the positive equivalent of the maximum eigenvalue of matrix B. □

6. Conclusions

In this paper, we have identified several issues regarding the theoretical results that are presented in [1] and accounted for the non-negativity, boundedness, existence, and local stability of epidemic equilibria. Moreover, special emphasis is placed on examining the global stability analysis of the produced equilibria based on the LaSalle's invariance principle, extending the theoretical investigation of the aforementioned paper.

It is important to underline that the global stability analysis can provide insights into the entire state space's stability, not just a neighborhood around an equilibrium point. Global stability analysis is often more robust to uncertainties and parameter variations. It can reveal whether a system remains stable under a wide range of conditions, making it particularly valuable in fields like control theory and engineering, where parameter variations are common. More importantly, it reveals the long-term behavior of the system regardless of the initial condition.

At this point, we should emphasize that despite the aforementioned issues, the statistical methodology proposed in [1], has an important role in the field of mathematical modelling in epidemiology. Kalman filtering provides the best linear unbiased estimate of a system's states in the presence of noise and uncertainty, while it optimally combines measurements and a priori system predictions [12,27,28]. It can adapt to changing system dynamics by adjusting the filter's parameters. This makes it suitable for systems with time-varying characteristics. Additionally, Kalman filters are computationally efficient, making them applicable in real-time systems. Like the traditional Kalman filter, Ensemble Kalman filtering provides estimates of state uncertainty and consistency, aiding in decision-making processes. Also, by sampling from the state space it accomplishes the capturing of complex nonlinear dynamics and avoids filter divergence.

Global stability analysis of COVID-19 models provides crucial insights that are immensely valuable for practical applications. It helps in predicting the long-term behavior of the disease spread. Understanding the stability of the model equilibria allows for projections about the disease trajectory, aiding in preparedness and resource allocation. Also, by analyzing the stability of different equilibria within the models, researchers can assess the effectiveness of various intervention strategies. This insight guides policymakers in implementing control measures such as vaccination drives, social distancing, or lockdowns. It assists in resource allocation by estimating the potential severity and duration of the outbreak. Hospitals, medical supplies, and personnel can be strategically deployed based on the projected stability of the disease dynamics. Finally, analyzing the stability of the model against real-world data allows for model validation. Insights gained from the analysis can also contribute to refining the model by identifying areas where the model might deviate from observed patterns.

There are several analyses in the literature that propose the utilization of statistical methodologies like Kalman filters, aiming to provide estimations about the future state of the COVID-19 pandemic [1,12,29–31]. The employed statistical methodology holds promise in steering decisions concerning the short-term trajectory of the pandemic. Conversely, the stability analysis provided in our study furnishes insights into the extended patterns of the phenomenon, augmenting awareness around this public health concern in the long run. Therefore, we argue that both analyses present valuable insights into the pandemic, each offering unique viewpoints.

In future work, we find it intriguing to explore a hybrid epidemiological particle filter. This approach handles the uncertainty inherent in pandemic phenomena by integrating particle filtering, which offers an alternative way to address the uncertainties present in both the equations defining the state and the observations of such phenomena. Moreover, delving into the disease's evolution using various stochastic methods like discrete or continuous time Markov chains holds significant promise aiming to examine interesting stochastic descriptors [32]. Finally, numerical methods for the computationally efficient solving of the ODE system can be investigated [33], as the establishment of methodologies of low complexity is always of interest in mathematical modelling [34–36].

Finally, in the case of COVID-19, given the ongoing circumstances, it remains difficult to curtail the transmission of the virus in the foreseeable future. The R_0 decreases during periods of lockdown, although it rises right after the easing of restrictions to values which are far higher than unity [37,38]. Also, even after the initialization of the vaccination campaigns, variants like omicron continue to spread rapidly [39,40].

Several variants have emerged even after the onset of the vaccination period, with the most widely known being the alpha, delta, and omicron variants, while the corresponding values for the delta variant ranged between 3.2 and 8 with a mean of 5.08 [41,42]. Moreover, according to the review of Liu and Rocklöv [43], the basic reproduction number for the omicron variant is 2.5 times greater than the respective reproduction number of the delta variant. Hence, according to the above comments, it becomes evident that the transmissibility of the virus will persist for quite a long-time interval. This perspective was strongly supported by many researchers even during the early stages of the pandemic [44,45]. Neither the establishment of lockdowns nor the vaccination campaigns, reduced the reproduction values less than unity for sufficiently long periods. Therefore, the eradication of the disease seems almost impossible.

As a result, public authorities may emphasize the reduction of severe infections, hospitalizations, and deaths as these are the main issues of concern for the entire population. Until now, this policy has shown a significant improvement of the confrontation against the pandemic's drawbacks. Without a doubt, the systematic and timely vaccination of the population plays a pivotal role in realizing this objective.

Author Contributions: Conceptualization, V.E.P.; methodology, V.E.P.; validation, V.E.P. and G.V.; formal analysis, V.E.P.; investigation, V.E.P.; writing—original draft preparation, V.E.P.; writing—review and editing, G.V. and G.T.; supervision, G.T. All authors have read and agreed to the published version of the manuscript.

Funding: This research received no external funding.

Data Availability Statement: Not applicable.

Conflicts of Interest: The authors declare no conflict of interest.

References

1. Ghostine, R.; Gharamti, M.; Hassrouny, S.; Hoteit, I. An extended seir model with vaccination for forecasting the COVID-19 pandemic in saudi arabia using an ensemble kalman filter. *Mathematics* **2021**, *9*, 636. [CrossRef]
2. Brauer, F.; Castillo-Chavez, C.; Feng, Z. Endemic Disease Models. In *Mathematical Models in Epidemiology*; Springer: New York, NY, USA, 2019; pp. 63–116.

3. Salman, A.M.; Ahmed, I.; Mohd, M.H.; Jamiluddin, M.S.; Dheyab, M.A. Scenario analysis of COVID-19 transmission dynamics in Malaysia with the possibility of reinfection and limited medical resources scenarios. *Comput. Biol. Med.* **2021**, *133*, 104372. [CrossRef] [PubMed]
4. Rajagopal, K.; Hasanzadeh, N.; Parastesh, F.; Hamarash, I.I.; Jafari, S.; Hussain, I. A fractional-order model for the novel coronavirus (COVID-19) outbreak. *Nonlinear Dyn.* **2020**, *101*, 711–718. [CrossRef] [PubMed]
5. Malkov, E. Simulation of coronavirus disease 2019 (COVID-19) scenarios with possibility of reinfection. *Chaos Solitons Fractals* **2020**, *139*, 110296. [CrossRef] [PubMed]
6. Lu, H.; Ding, Y.; Gong, S.; Wang, S. Mathematical modeling and dynamic analysis of SIQR model with delay for pandemic COVID-19. *Math. Biosci. Eng.* **2021**, *18*, 3197–3214. [CrossRef] [PubMed]
7. Younes, A.B.; Hasan, Z. COVID-19: Modeling, prediction, and control. *Appl. Sci.* **2020**, *10*, 3666. [CrossRef]
8. Nana-Kyere, S.; Boateng, F.A.; Jonathan, P.; Donkor, A.; Hoggar, G.K.; Titus, B.D.; Kwarteng, D.; Adu, I.K. Global Analysis and Optimal Control Model of COVID-19. *Comput. Math. Methods Med.* **2022**, *2022*, 9491847. [CrossRef]
9. Chaharborj, S.S.; Chaharborj, S.S.; Asl, J.H.; Phang, P.S. Controlling of pandemic COVID-19 using optimal control theory. *Results Phys.* **2021**, *26*, 104311. [CrossRef]
10. Zamir, M.; Abdeljawad, T.; Nadeem, F.; Wahid, A.; Yousef, A. An optimal control analysis of a COVID-19 model. *Alex. Eng. J.* **2021**, *60*, 2875–2884. [CrossRef]
11. Korolev, I. Identification and estimation of the SEIRD epidemic model for COVID-19. *J. Econ.* **2021**, *220*, 63–85. [CrossRef]
12. Papageorgiou, V.E.; Tsaklidis, G. An improved epidemiological-unscented Kalman filter (hybrid SEIHCRDV-UKF) model for the prediction of COVID-19. Application on real-time data. *Chaos Solitons Fractals* **2023**, *166*, 112914. [CrossRef] [PubMed]
13. Romeo, G. Mathematics for dynamic economic models. In *Elements of Numerical Mathematical Economics with Excel*; Elsevier: Amsterdam, The Netherlands, 2020.
14. Kalogiratou, Z.; Monovasilis, T.; Simos, T.E. Two-derivative Runge-Kutta methods with optimal phase proper-ties. *Math. Methods Appl. Sci.* **2020**, *43*, 1267–1277. [CrossRef]
15. Monovasilis, T.; Kalogiratou, Z. High Order Two-Derivative Runge-Kutta Methods with Optimized Dispersion and Dissipation Error. *Mathematics* **2021**, *9*, 232. [CrossRef]
16. Kalogiratou, Z.; Monovasilis, T.; Simos, T.E. New fifth-order two-derivative Runge-Kutta methods with constant and frequency-dependent coefficients. *Math. Methods Appl. Sci.* **2019**, *42*, 1955–1966. [CrossRef]
17. Wang, W.; Zhang, H.; Jiang, X.; Yang, X. A high-order and efficient numerical technique for the nonlocal neutron diffusion equation representing neutron transport in a nuclear reactor. *Ann. Nucl. Energy* **2024**, *195*, 110163. [CrossRef]
18. Yang, X.; Wu, L.; Zhang, H. A space-time spectral order sinc-collocation method for the fourth-order nonlocal heat model arising in viscoelasticity. *Appl. Math. Comput.* **2023**, *457*, 128192. [CrossRef]
19. Jiang, X.; Wang, J.; Wang, W.; Zhang, H. A Predictor–Corrector Compact Difference Scheme for a Nonlinear Fractional Differential Equation. *Fractal Fract.* **2023**, *7*, 521. [CrossRef]
20. Araz, S.I. Analysis of a COVID-19 model: Optimal control, stability and simulations. *Alex. Eng. J.* **2021**, *60*, 647–658. [CrossRef]
21. Bouhali, A.; Aribi, W.B.; Miled, S.B.; Kebir, A. Optimal Control applied to SIRD model of COVID 19. *arXiv* **2021**, arXiv:2109.01457.
22. Jiménez-Rodríguez, P.; Muñoz-Fernández, G.A.; Rodrigo-Chocano, J.C.; Seoane-Sepúlveda, J.B.; Weber, A. A population structure-sensitive mathematical model assessing the effects of vaccination during the third surge of COVID-19 in Italy. *J. Math. Anal. Appl.* **2022**, *514*, 125975. [CrossRef]
23. Mohsen, A.A.; Al-Husseiny, H.F.; Zhou, X.; Hattaf, K. Global stability of COVID-19 model involving the quarantine strategy and media coverage effects. *AIMS Public Health* **2020**, *7*, 587–605. [CrossRef] [PubMed]
24. Vargas-De-León, C. On the global stability of SIS, SIR and SIRS epidemic models with standard incidence. *Chaos Solitons Fractals* **2011**, *44*, 1106–1110. [CrossRef]
25. Al-Shbeil, I.; Djenina, N.; Jaradat, A.; Al-Husban, A.; Ouannas, A.; Grassi, G. A New COVID-19 Pandemic Model including the Compartment of Vaccinated Individuals: Global Stability of the Disease-Free Fixed Point. *Mathematics* **2023**, *11*, 576. [CrossRef]
26. Elaiw, A.M.; Alsaedi, A.J.; Al Agha, A.D.; Hobiny, A.D. Global Stability of a Humoral Immunity COVID-19 Model with Logistic Growth and Delays. *Mathematics* **2022**, *10*, 1857. [CrossRef]
27. Loumponias, K.; Vretos, N.; Tsaklidis, G.; Daras, P. An Improved Tobit Kalman Filter with Adaptive Censoring Limits. *Circuits, Syst. Signal Process.* **2020**, *39*, 5588–5617. [CrossRef]
28. Theodosiadou, O.; Tsaklidis, G. State space modeling with non-negativity constraints using quadratic forms. *Mathematics* **2021**, *9*, 1908. [CrossRef]
29. Sebbagh, A.; Kechida, S. EKF-SIRD model algorithm for predicting the coronavirus (COVID-19) spreading dynamics. *Sci. Rep.* **2022**, *12*, 13415. [CrossRef]
30. Zhu, X.; Gao, B.; Zhong, Y.; Gu, C.; Choi, K.-S. Extended Kalman filter based on stochastic epidemiological model for COVID-19 modelling. *Comput. Biol. Med.* **2021**, *137*, 104810. [CrossRef]
31. Song, J.; Xie, H.; Gao, B.; Zhong, Y.; Gu, C.; Choi, K.S. Maximum likelihood-based extended Kalman filter for COVID-19 pre-diction. *Chaos Solitons Fractals* **2021**, *146*, 110922. [CrossRef]
32. Papageorgiou, V.E.; Tsaklidis, G. A stochastic SIRD model with imperfect immunity for the evaluation of epidemics. *Appl. Math. Model.* **2023**, *124*, 768–790. [CrossRef]

33. Zhang, H.; Liu, Y.; Yang, X. An efficient ADI difference scheme for the nonlocal evolution problem in three-dimensional space. *J. Appl. Math. Comput.* **2023**, *69*, 651–674. [CrossRef]
34. Papageorgiou, V.E.; Dogoulis, P.; Papageorgiou, D.-P. A Convolutional Neural Network of Low Complexity for Tumor Anomaly Detection. In *Proceedings of Eighth International Congress on Information and Communication Technology, ICICT 2023, London, Volume 4*; Lecture Notes in Networks and Systems 696; Springer: Berlin/Heidelberg, Germany, 2024; pp. 973–983.
35. Papageorgiou, V. Brain tumor detection based on features extracted and classified using a low-complexity neural network. *Trait. Signal* **2021**, *38*, 547–554. [CrossRef]
36. Papageorgiou, V.E.; Zegkos, T.; Efthimiadis, G.; Tsaklidis, G. Analysis of digitalized ECG signals based on artificial intelligence and spectral analysis methods specialized in ARVC. *Int. J. Numer. Methods Biomed. Eng.* **2022**, *38*, e3644. [CrossRef] [PubMed]
37. Glass, D.H. European and US lockdowns and second waves during the COVID-19 pandemic. *Math. Biosci.* **2020**, *330*, 108472. [CrossRef] [PubMed]
38. Lonergan, M.; Chalmers, J.D. Estimates of the ongoing need for social distancing and control measures post-"lockdown" from trajectories of COVID-19 cases and mortality. *Eur. Respir. J.* **2020**, *56*, 2001483. [CrossRef] [PubMed]
39. Fan, Y.; Li, X.; Zhang, L.; Wan, S.; Zhang, L.; Zhou, F. SARS-CoV-2 Omicron variant: Recent progress and future perspectives. *Signal Transduct. Target. Ther.* **2022**, *7*, 141. [CrossRef] [PubMed]
40. Manjunath, R.; Gaonkar, S.L.; Saleh, E.A.M.; Husain, K. A comprehensive review on COVID-19 Omicron (B.1.1.529) variant. *Saudi J. Biol. Sci.* **2022**, *29*, 103372. [CrossRef] [PubMed]
41. Zhang, M.; Xiao, J.; Deng, A.; Zhang, Y.; Zhuang, Y.; Hu, T.; Li, J.; Tu, H.; Li, B.; Zhou, Y.; et al. Transmission Dynamics of an Outbreak of the COVID-19 Delta Variant B.1.617.2—Guangdong Province, China, May–June 2021. *China CDC Wkly.* **2021**, *3*, 584–586. [CrossRef]
42. Liu, Y.; Rocklöv, J. The reproductive number of the Delta variant of SARS-CoV-2 is far higher compared to the ancestral SARS-CoV-2 virus. *J. Travel Med.* **2021**, *8*, taab124. [CrossRef]
43. Liu, Y.; Rocklöv, J. The effective reproductive number of the Omicron variant of SARS-CoV-2 is several times relative to Delta. *J. Travel Med.* **2022**, *29*, taac037. [CrossRef]
44. The Lancet. The COVID-19 pandemic in 2023: Far from over. *Lancet* **2023**, *401*, 79. [CrossRef] [PubMed]
45. Torjesen, I. COVID-19 will become endemic but with decreased potency over time, scientists believe. *BMJ* **2021**, *372*, n494. [CrossRef] [PubMed]

Article

A Bilevel DEA Model for Efficiency Evaluation and Target Setting with Stochastic Conditions

Andreas C. Georgiou *, Konstantinos Kaparis, Eleni-Maria Vretta, Kyriakos Bitsis and George Paltayian

Quantitative Methods and Decision Analysis Lab, Department of Business Administration, University of Macedonia, GR-54636 Thessaloniki, Greece; k.kaparis@uom.edu.gr (K.K.); emvretta@uom.edu.gr (E.-M.V.); kmpitsis@uom.edu.gr (K.B.); gpaltag@uom.edu.gr (G.P.)
* Correspondence: acg@uom.edu.gr

Abstract: The effective allocation of limited resources and the establishment of targeted goals play a pivotal role in enhancing the overall efficiency of large enterprises and organizations. To achieve optimal organizational efficiency, managers seek dynamic strategies that adapt to the constraints of limited and uncertain historical data. This paper introduces an evaluation of organizational efficiency through a stochastic framework, employing a bilevel data envelopment analysis (DEA) approach. This decision-making process is centralized within a decision-making unit (DMU) overseeing subordinate decision-making units (subDMUs). Discrete scenarios, each associated with a realization probability, define the uncertain parameters in the bilevel DEA-based model. This stochastic approach allows for recourse actions upon scenario realization leading to an enhanced overall organizational strategy. Decision-makers acting within uncertain and dynamic environments can benefit from this research since it allows the investigation of efficiency assessment under alternative scenarios in the presence of volatility and risk. The potential impact of applying this methodology varies depending on the specific domain. Although, the context of this paper focuses on banking, in general, enhancing resource allocation and target setting under stochasticity, contributes to advancing sustainability across all its three dimensions (economic, environmental, social). As mentioned earlier, the practical application of our approach is demonstrated via a case study in the banking sector.

Keywords: DEA; bilevel optimization; stochastic conditions; resource allocation

MSC: 90-10

Citation: Georgiou, A.C.; Kaparis, K.; Vretta, E.-M.; Bitsis, K.; Paltayian, G. A Bilevel DEA Model for Efficiency Evaluation and Target Setting with Stochastic Conditions. *Mathematics* **2024**, *12*, 529. https://doi.org/10.3390/math12040529

Academic Editor: Maria C. Mariani

Received: 1 January 2024
Revised: 31 January 2024
Accepted: 3 February 2024
Published: 8 February 2024

1. Introduction

Large enterprises and organizations are the backbone of local and national economies; they generate substantial profits, contribute to economic development, and foster innovation. Their investments in human capital, productivity, and facilities contribute to technological advancements. Additionally, these entities actively promote green growth and a circular economy, aligning with sustainable development goals and the protection of natural assets. Beyond economic contributions, their impact on societal welfare is significant, providing job opportunities, healthcare coverage, and social insurance that underpin overall well-being. The ongoing changes in economic policies, prices, and market fluctuations necessitate these entities to optimally allocate resources and set targets. Such strategic decisions are paramount, influencing productivity, efficiency, future planning, and profitability. The perpetual limitation of resources underscores the critical importance of optimal resource allocation for large enterprises and organizations, facilitating their ability to achieve objectives and remain competitive in a dynamic market.

Major organizations usually comprise a central decision-making unit (DMU) and several subordinate decision-making units (subDMUs). The primary DMU, which is responsible for overseeing and managing the subDMUs, plays a pivotal role in allocating finite resources and defining appropriate output targets. Concurrently, it may also set

minimum thresholds for the *efficiency* of each subDMU. The latter term (i.e., efficiency) is quantified as the weighted ratio of the outputs generated to inputs utilized by the DMU. On the other hand, *effectiveness* in the context of a DMU is articulated in terms of profitability however in a broader spectrum, effectiveness encapsulates the extent to which an organization achieves its objectives.

The problem of resource allocation and target setting, calls for redesigning policies of organizations with multi-stage or multi-level structures, in a way that optimizes organizational efficiency and effectiveness.

Data envelopment analysis (DEA) introduced by Charnes, Cooper, and Rhodes [1] is a widely used non-parametric method for assessing the efficiency of homogeneous DMUs with multiple inputs and outputs. Traditional DEA models, treat DMUs as black boxes, disregarding internal structures, interconnections, and interactions among operational and organizational stages. On the other hand, in a *Network* DEA (NDEA) environment, each DMU comprises various stages or levels, so optimizing the performance of a DMU could theoretically result from evaluating the performance of each individual stage or level (sub-DMUs). In an NDEA scheme, intermediate outputs play a vital role in the DMU evaluation as they are generated from a sub-DMU, and act as inputs to another sub-DMU of the system, as defined by Färe and Grosskopf [2]. Kao and Hwang in [3] showed that ignoring the sub-processes of a DMU may lead to an overall efficient system, even though a DMU might be inefficient in an individual stage. Kao and Hwang in [4] showed that it is important to consider the internal structure of a DMU to identify any inefficiencies, since a DMU may have better overall efficiency compared to another DMU, although the sub-processes of the first DMU may have worse individual efficiencies. The internal structure of a DMU can be decomposed into two stages in a simple case, while in a more complex case, it may consist of multiple stages. Halkos et al. [5] provide a comprehensive classification of two-stage DEA models.

Despotis et al. [6] presented a novel definition for overall system efficiency in network DEA literature, inspired by the concept of the "weak link" in supply chains and the maximum-flow/minimum-cut problem in networks. Employing a two-phase max-min optimization technique within a multi-objective programming framework, they estimate individual stage efficiencies and overall system efficiency in two-stage processes of varying complexity. Additional research on composition and decomposition techniques in both two-stage and multi-stage environments can be found in [7–9]. In the context of assessing a parallel network structure integrated with a hierarchical one, Kremantzis et al. [10] propose a linear additive decomposition DEA model as well as a non-linear multiplicative aggregation DEA model. Both constitute alternative approaches to evaluating the performance in parallel network DEA problems.

Fukuyama and Matousek [11] studied the strengths between network and traditional DEA. Based on their research, the precision and accuracy of DEA results are better when network models are used compared to traditional DEA models. In the same manner, Kao [12] showed that it is possible for a DMU to be considered as efficient using traditional DEA and not efficient using the network DEA approach. Hence, the efficiency can be overestimated by the classical models, and this problem is perpetuated as the stages increase. More comprehensive research about NDEA models can be found in [13–18]. Typically, each DMU independently optimizes its input and output levels to maximize its efficiency. However, our study concerns the cases of major enterprises, where a central DMU governs a group of subDMUs to maximize overall organizational efficiency and profitability. DEA serves as a mathematical programming technique extensively applied to address centralized resource allocation and target-setting challenges. In most resource allocation DEA models, precise input and output data are assumed, whereas real-world data are often unavailable or inaccurate. Relying on calculated optimal solutions based on such data may lead to profit loss, planning inconsistencies, and reduced production. Therefore, acknowledging the uncertainty in achieving output targets becomes imperative. Large organizations must be capable of redesigning consumption and production processes,

and taking remedial actions to maximize overall efficiency. Uncertainty is a fundamental factor in addressing challenges related to resource allocation, production design, and output targeting. One of the most challenging issues faced by traditional optimization problems is the tendency of optimal solutions to perturbations in the values of the problem's parameters, often exhibiting a high degree of sensitivity. This characteristic underscores the crucial importance of identifying "robust solutions" in the realm of optimization theory. To mitigate such uncertainties, the optimization community employs various mathematical frameworks, including stochastic programming, chance-constrained programming, and robust optimization. Stochastic programming optimizes the expected outcome of an objective function. On the other hand, chance constraint programming ensures that the derived solution satisfies certain constraints within a given probability level. Finally, robust optimization is a risk-averse strategy, focusing on optimizing the "worst- case" scenario within a predefined uncertainty set. In the stochastic programming approach, the uncertain parameter vector is modeled using discrete probabilistic scenarios, while in the robust optimization approach, its values are defined by a continuous set [19].

The latest approaches tackle data uncertainty by incorporating methods that account for and mitigate the impact of fluctuations, or imprecisions in the input data. This is achieved by considering a range or set of possible values for the input parameters rather than relying on precise, fixed values. The robust DEA approach aims to provide reliable and stable efficiency assessments even when faced with uncertainties in the data, thus enhancing the model's resilience to variations that consider the dynamic and uncertain nature of the banking environment. Therefore, a robust solution remains optimal regardless of the stochasticity governing the problem's parameters, although this optimal performance is restricted to a specific parameter range. The latter represents a significant advantage over traditional DEA methods that do not handle data uncertainty.

In their recent work, Zhang et al. [20] addressed the challenge of allocating limited medical reserves in the context of a public health emergency. It takes into account uncertainties in both demand and donated supplies, as well as the priorities of healthcare centers. The formulation of the problem involves a two-stage stochastic program, treating donated supplies as an effective recourse action with the ultimate goal of minimizing overall losses. According to Shakouri et al. [21], in situations where uncertainties exist in the data of a problem, traditional DEA models may yield inaccurate results. For this reason, they proposed two stochastic p-robust two-stage network DEA (NDEA) models to estimate the efficiency of DMU in an uncertain environment. These models are developed within the context of a bilevel framework. Their approach facilitates more effective mitigation of the adverse impact on the objective function, addressing uncertainties often neglected in traditional NDEA models. The practical application of these models is demonstrated through an analysis of the performance of bank branches. Finally, robust and stochastic optimization techniques have been successfully applied in various DEA models, such as [22–25].

This paper introduces a stochastic bilevel DEA model aimed at optimizing overall organizational efficiency. The efficiency metric, defined as profitability (total revenues minus total input costs), is evaluated within a stochastic framework in a bilevel structure (DMU and sub DMUs and under uncertainty). Building upon Hakim et al.'s deterministic model [26], the proposed DEA model accommodates stochastic conditions for uncertain parameters by incorporating alternative scenarios with associated occurrence probabilities. Specifically, the model assumes imprecise and unknown data for output targets, requiring the decision-maker of the central unit to formulate a strategy without perfect information. The motivation is an application in the banking sector where DEA methods have been extensively applied ([11,27–33]).

Our research is driven by the recent performance evaluations conducted by Greek banking institutions, which are a response to the ongoing transformative phase within the Greek banking system. This restructuring is mandated by regulatory directives issued by European supervisory authorities and is deemed crucial due to the economic crisis of the past fifteen years and the prolonged debt crisis. At its essence, this restructuring is

guided by two principles: the reduction of operational costs and the strategic deployment of technology. Consequently, Greek banks have embarked on a new era characterized by a comprehensive overhaul of their network infrastructure. The primary aim is to enhance organizational effectiveness and branch efficiency, thereby boosting revenue generation from retail banking products while optimizing resource utilization. Additionally, in accordance with European guiding principles, banks are revamping their branch networks by introducing innovative outlets that seamlessly integrate state-of-the-art technologies to serve customers, along with augmenting their specialized staff. This transformative process is geared toward achieving key objectives, including heightened net profitability and the equitable distribution of dividends to shareholders.

The rest of the paper is organized as follows: Section 2 discusses pertinent DEA-based models, exploring various approaches to resource allocation, targeting, and uncertainty capture. We review fundamental concepts and mathematical formulations of bilevel programming and optimization under uncertainty. Section 3 provides the problem description and notation. Section 4 details the bilevel DEA-based model with stochastic conditions and outlines the proposed solution methodology. Our computational study and results are presented in Section 5, while Section 6 encapsulates concluding remarks based on the paper's findings and contributions.

2. Literature

2.1. Resource Allocation

Numerous approaches have been proposed to tackle resource allocation and target-setting challenges. Golany et al. [34] introduced a DEA-based model optimizing overall organizational profitability and technical efficiency. Athanassopoulos [35] integrated goal programming and DEA for multi-level resource allocation, applied to central fund allocation in Greek local authorities. Yu et al. [36] employed a centralized DEA model with a Russell measure for human resource reallocation in Taiwanese airports. Amirteimoori and Tabar [37] addressed fixed resource allocation in organizations with multiple DMUs, while Beasley [38] maximized average efficiency for DEA-based models, incorporating fixed-cost resources and output targets in centralized decision-making. Lozano and Villa [39] presented DEA models for centralized resource allocation, aiming to minimize input consumption, maximize output production, and enhance individual DMU efficiency. Varmaz et al. [40] incentivized subDMUs in large organizations, adapting Lozano and Villa's model [39] to compute super-efficiency. Afsharian et al. [41] proposed a DEA-based model for incentivizing DMUs under central management, addressing shortcomings in Varmaz et al. [40]. Similarly, Afsharian et al. [42] extended this approach to hierarchically structured organizations, illustrating it with data from a German retail bank. Asmild et al. [43] expanded Lozano and Villa's [39] models, suggesting modifications for inefficient DMUs and providing a procedure for alternative optimal solutions in an input-oriented BCC framework. Wu et al. [44] incorporated economic and environmental factors in DEA models for resource allocation, considering three scenarios for resource availability. Fang [45] proposed a generalized centralized resource allocation model, decomposing technical efficiency into components and illustrating the approach with a supermarket example.

Two-stage network DEA approaches addressing the resource allocation problem have been introduced by various researchers. Chen et al. [46] proposed a DEA model evaluating the efficiency of two-stage network processes with shared inputs across both stages, encompassing inputs utilized collectively and those specific to each stage. Zha and Liang [47] outlined a cooperative model allocating freely shared inputs in a series production process. This product-form model calculates the overall efficiency for the assessed DMU, illustrating collaboration between the two stages.

Wu et al. [48] presented an approach to managing undesirable intermediate outputs in a two-stage production process with shared resources. They employed additive and non-cooperative models to gauge the efficiency of each DMU and subDMU, applying these models to industrial production in thirty provincial regions in China. Yu et al. [49]

addressed the allocation of fixed costs among subDMUs, considering efficiency. They introduced a two-stage network DEA model grounded in cross-efficiency concepts.

Recent studies, particularly [50,51], have introduced notable advancements in tackling the issue of resource allocation prompted by the Internet of Things.

2.2. Bilevel Network DEA

In his seminal work, Dempe [52] describes a bilevel programming problem (BLP) as a setting where an optimization problem includes within its constraint set a second, partial optimization problem. The outer optimization task is commonly denoted as the upper level, while the inner optimization task is referred to as the lower level. The idea can be traced back to the early work of Freiherr von Stackelberg [53] in economic game theory. According to Stackelberg's conceptualization, the hierarchical structure encompasses two distinct decision-makers: the leader and the follower, corresponding to the upper and lower-level problems, respectively. The standard mathematical formulation of a bilevel problem is as follows:

$$\min_{x,y} \quad F(x,y) \tag{1}$$

$$\text{s.t.} \quad G(x,y) \leq 0 \tag{2}$$

$$H(x,y) = 0 \tag{3}$$

$$\min_{y} \quad f(x,y) \tag{4}$$

$$\text{s.t.} \quad g(x,y) \leq 0 \tag{5}$$

$$h(x,y) = 0 \tag{6}$$

where $x \in R^n$ and $y \in R^m$ are the set of upper- and lower-level variables, respectively. Moreover, the upper-level problem (leader's problem) is specified via (1)–(3) and its domain is partially specified by the optimal solutions of the lower-level problem (follower's problem) outlined by (4)–(6).

The motivation behind the employment of this optimization schema is its ability to capture the hierarchical relations between the centralized decision-maker and the multiple sub-DMUs with great accuracy.

Shafiee et al. [54] introduced a bilevel DEA model for evaluating bank branch performance, employing a mixed-integer linear programming (MILP) approach for its solution. The study incorporates internal structures and Stackelberg relationships, providing insightful information about each component of the banking chain. Zhou et al. [55] devised a bilevel DEA model tailored for systems with bilevel structures, exemplified by manufacturing supply chains with multiple distribution centers. Their approach, rooted in the Stackelberg competition game theory, features multiple followers. The case study involves a supply chain with a plant and two distribution centers. Sinha et al. [56] developed an oligopolistic market model with multiple leaders and followers over multiple time periods under Stackelberg relations. Their model, applicable to industries like aircraft manufacturing, accounts for leaders acting in a Stackelberg manner toward followers while engaging in the Cournot competition among themselves. Experimental results illustrate the impact of player entrance or exit on profits and costs, with nonlinear handling of demand and cost functions for accurate problem simulation. Hajiagha et al. [57] proposed an efficiency-based planning method, considering current DMU performance and projecting future efficiency while also considering profit performance. This bilevel approach maximizes efficiency at the upper level and optimizes inputs and outputs based on costs and profits at the lower level. Addressing the limitations of classic DEA models, the authors emphasize the simultaneous consideration of profit and technical efficiency. In recent developments, bilevel DEA-based models for resource allocation and target setting have emerged. Hakim et al. [26] proposed a deterministic bilevel DEA model for centralized resource allocation and target setting, optimizing organizational effectiveness by maximizing total profit while ensuring each

DMU operates efficiently within predefined bounds. Ang et al. [58] extended this work for organizational systems with higher-level entities and subordinate two-stage DMUs. Their bilevel model aims to maximize both organizational and two-stage DMU efficiency.

2.3. Stochastic Optimization for DEA

According to Olesen and Petersen [59], stochastic DEA extends the original idea in three different directions. First, is the deviations from the production frontier, while in the second case, DEA can handle random noise coming from measurement or specification errors. In the latter case, the production possibility set (PPS) is adjusted according to the random data.

Chance constraints were introduced by Charnes and Cooper [60] and are routinely used ever since in the context of stochastic DEA. By using this method, we can formulate a problem with stochastic constraints assuming that we may have constraints' violation within a certain probability level. Beraldi and Bruni [61] proposed a stochastic DEA method using chance constraints formulation that transformed into a deterministic equivalent under the discrete distribution assumption.

Zhou et al. [62] suggest a stochastic network DEA model to facilitate a two-stage system under data uncertainty. The model is based on a centralized control mechanism and a transformation to a deterministic equivalent linear programming model. The transformation relies on the assumption that some problem parameters, e.g., inputs/outputs are related to stochastic factors.

The conventional DEA formulations exhibit determinism and static characteristics, rendering them highly sensitive to minor parameter fluctuations. Acknowledging this susceptibility to small changes, the incorporation of robustness in DEA models becomes imperative. The objective is to maintain solution stability in the face of uncertain conditions. Marbini et al. [63] pioneered the development of novel robust non-radial DEA models, specifically designed to gauge the performance of decision-making units under conditions of data uncertainty. Their approach involves the utilization of Interval DEA, enabling the assessment of interval efficiencies based on both optimistic and pessimistic viewpoints. Ultimately, the authors introduce the concept of the "price of robustness" to comprehensively evaluate the effectiveness and robustness of the proposed models.

In their study, Tseng et al. [64] investigated the dynamics of economic efficiency and revenue sharing in the electricity market, employing a sophisticated bilevel scheme. Their primary objective was to pinpoint the Nash equilibrium while contending with capacity constraints estimated through DEA. To tackle the challenges arising from price uncertainties, the researchers introduced a cutting-edge approach by developing stochastic mixed complementarity models. These models seamlessly integrate stochastic programming and robust optimization techniques, offering a robust solution to address the intricate issue of price uncertainty in the electricity market.

As highlighted by Omrani et al. [65], the sole computation of a single efficiency metric proves insufficient in certain contexts for assessing the overall efficiency of decision-making units (DMUs). Consequently, a multi-objective DEA model has been devised to concurrently evaluate profit, operational, and transactional efficiencies within the realm of bank branches, particularly under conditions of data uncertainty. To address the challenges posed by data uncertainty, a robust approach has been employed in the formulation of the model, enhancing its capacity to provide a more comprehensive and nuanced assessment of efficiency in banking operations.

2.4. The Proposed Stochastic Framework

In traditional DEA models, such as [1], each DMU decides on its own input and output levels to maximize its own efficiency. In single-stage resource allocation DEA models, DMUs are considered as black boxes, namely the internal structures, and the interconnections and interactions among the stages of the operational and organizational structures are ignored [34–45]. However, in large enterprises and organizations, a group of subDMUs

is under the control of a central DMU, aiming to maximize overall organizational efficiency and profitability. Nonetheless, in the two-stage DEA models [46,47] where interactions and interconnections are incorporated, hierarchical relations among the departments or the organizational levels are not considered. In the majority of resource allocation DEA models, the input and output data are known and precise, while in real-world problems, these data are often unavailable or erroneous. The stochastic DEA models on resource allocation [59–65] deal with uncertainty, however, to the best of our knowledge, the DMUs under examination have no bilevel structure.

Within our proposed stochastic framework, we incorporate a bilevel approach to DEA methodology alongside stochastic conditions, aimed at capturing the uncertainty surrounding the achievement of output targets and thereby optimizing organizational efficiency. The uncertainty within our framework is delineated by discrete realizations of uncertain parameters across various scenarios. Each uncertain parameter within the model is assigned a value corresponding to a scenario, with each scenario linked to a realization probability reflecting managerial estimations. Furthermore, the decision-maker retains the ability to select a strategy either prior to or independently of knowing the exact values assumed by uncertain parameters when a scenario materializes.

3. Problem Description

Within this section, we offer a comprehensive description of the problem at hand. Firstly, in Section 3.1, we provide a detailed description of our case, pointing out all the major elements. We explain how an input, which is associated with a cost, is converted into a valuable output. Moreover, in Section 3.2, we present the notation and model assumptions to establish a clear understanding of the problem.

3.1. An Application in Banking

In general, the banking sector plays a pivotal role in conducting diverse financial transactions, aggregating funds, and financing both short- and long-term public and private investments. In particular, the Greek banking sector is further characterized by fierce competition, driven by the pursuit of increased profitability for stakeholders. In recent years, this competition has intensified as management endeavors to optimize returns. Given the paramount significance of this sector, the proposed stochastic bilevel DEA model is motivated by an application specific to banking.

In the application scenario, the central administration aims to maximize overall efficiency by optimizing profit. This necessitates strategic resource allocation among subDMUs (which actually are specific branches) and the establishment of output targets aligned with their capabilities. Concretely, the bank management defines future performance targets for each individual DMU, considering the resources available to them. The institution selected for the implementation of the proposed model is among the Greek systemic banks. It maintains an active network of more than 250 branches and significant metrics in terms of human capital, deposits, and loans, capturing an estimated 25% of the total market share. For the specific case under consideration, the implementation focuses on a network situated in one of the largest urban centers in Greece. The planning process includes ten branches (DMUs) of diverse sizes, (b)ig, (m)edium, or (s)mall, determined by factors, such as staffing levels, customer base, and the volume of deposits and loans across various categories (including mortgage loans, consumer loans, and small business loans). Additionally, the branches are geographically classified as eastern, central, or western, reflecting their specific locations in the region. The spatial planning of these branches was designed to allow coverage of geographical districts within the urban landscape under study. The data mirror typical real-world scenarios; however, they have been simulated for disclosure purposes.

In our model (Figure 1), we established five key inputs that induce expenses under typical operation circumstances for each bank branch (DMU):

X_1: Specialized personnel (relationship managers);
X_2: Supporting personnel (base officers);

X_3: ATMs;

X_4: Administrative costs (thousands of euros);

X_5: Interests for deposits (millions of euros).

In a similar manner, six outputs were selected and are outlined as follows:

Y_1: Mortgage loans (ML);

Y_2: Small business loans (SB);

Y_3: Consumer loans (CL);

Y_4: Mutual funds (MF);

Y_5: Net fee income (NFI);

Y_6: Surplus deposits (SD).

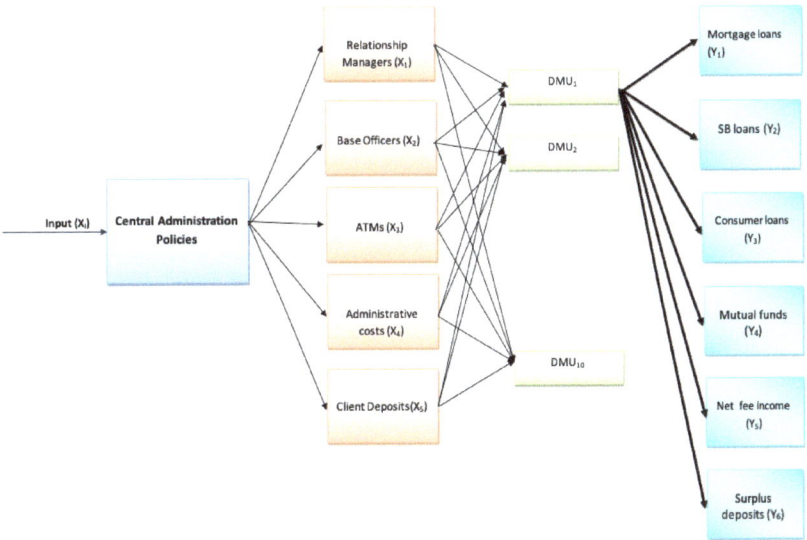

Figure 1. Input and output structures.

During the conversion of inputs into expenses, we adhered to industry-standard practices prevalent in the banking sector. For the two staff categories, namely relationship managers and base officers, we considered the average yearly salary expenses. Regarding ATMs and administrative expenses, we factored in the costs associated with installation, operation, and distribution per staff member. Regarding deposits, we accounted for the average weighted interest rate of bank deposits, set at 0.35%. All expenses are presented on an annual basis.

The bank manager's objective encompasses two primary goals: to enhance both efficiency and profitability, thus safeguarding sustainability and ensuring resilience in the face of dynamic economic and political conditions. To aid the decision-maker, we propose an optimal resource allocation strategy and establish output targets. It is important to note that the pursuit of profit maximization is tempered by an additional constraint, mandating the fulfillment of a minimum efficiency rate for each DMU. In the process, each DMU utilizes inputs X_1 to X_5 (see Table 1). Table 1 includes typical values for the above inputs for 10 DMUs.

Table 1. Input data for each DMU.

Label	DMU	X_1	X_2	X_3	X_4	X_5
East B1	1	4	12	3	16	0.788
East B2	2	3	10	2	15.6	0.525
East M	3	2	8	1	8	0.420
East S	4	1	5	1	2.4	0.280
Central B	5	4	10	4	21	0.875
Central M	6	5	13	4	36	1.225
Central S	7	1	4	2	1.4	0.350
West B	8	3	9	2	12	0.455
West M	9	2	7	1	7.2	0.385
West S	10	0	6	2	7.2	0.420
Total	10	25	84	22	126.8	5.723

One could argue that outputs ML, SB, and CL, correspond to revenues coming from loans while MF and NFI refer to commissions from banking transactions and mutual funds management. Finally, SD pertains to the revenue that stems from the surplus of deposits that a branch holds and are placed as deposits in the European Central Bank, through the Bank of Greece.

Table 2 contains the balances for each loan type (in millions of euros), the balances of mutual funds under management (in millions of euros), the surplus of deposits (in millions of euros), and the net commissions from banking activities (in thousands of euros).

Table 2. Output balances.

DMU	ML	SB	CL	MF	NFI	SD
1	30	19	9.8	40	9.1	67.5
2	40	15	4.5	35	7.56	45
3	18	6	2.3	20	4.54	36
4	10	3	1.5	8	2.25	24
5	30	12	11	50	8.81	50
6	24	10	9	35	7.58	35
7	12	8	5	15	1.85	15
8	50	10	12	20	5.4	20
9	34	5.8	8	9	4.5	9
10	15	3	5	5	1.3	5
Total	263	91.8	68.1	237	52.889	302.45

The income of each DMU is calculated as a percentage of the output balances. Moreover, these percentages are summarized in Table 3.

Table 3. Net margin rate profit for each output.

Output Income	Percentage
Mortgages income	2.00%
SB Loans income	4.00%
Consumer income	7.00%
Mutual income	0.50%
Deposit income	3.75%

Additionally, we added the net fee income for each DMU to the above balances in order to calculate the total income. Using the output balances and income rates, we can deduce the final output data recorded in Table 4.

Table 4. Output data for each DMU.

Scenario	Output	1	2	3	4	5	6	7	8	9	10
						DMU					
1	Y_1	0.42	0.56	0.25	0.14	0.42	0.34	0.17	0.70	0.48	0.21
	Y_2	0.53	0.42	0.17	0.08	0.34	0.28	0.22	0.28	0.16	0.08
	Y_3	0.48	0.22	0.11	0.07	0.54	0.44	0.25	0.59	0.39	0.25
	Y_4	0.14	0.12	0.07	0.03	0.18	0.12	0.05	0.07	0.03	0.02
	Y_5	6.37	5.29	3.18	1.58	6.17	5.31	1.3	3.78	3.15	0.91
	Y_6	1.77	1.18	0.95	0.63	1.97	2.76	0.79	1.02	0.87	0.95
2	Y_1	0.6	0.8	0.36	0.2	0.6	0.48	0.24	1	0.68	0.3
	Y_2	0.76	0.6	0.24	0.12	0.48	0.4	0.32	0.4	0.23	0.12
	Y_3	0.69	0.32	0.16	0.11	0.77	0.63	0.35	0.84	0.56	0.35
	Y_4	0.2	0.18	0.10	0.04	0.25	0.18	0.08	0.1	0.05	0.03
	Y_5	9.1	7.56	4.54	2.25	8.81	7.58	1.85	5.4	4.5	1.3
	Y_6	2.53	1.69	1.35	0.9	2.81	3.94	1.13	1.46	1.24	1.35
3	Y_1	0.69	0.92	0.41	0.23	0.69	0.55	0.28	1.15	0.78	0.35
	Y_2	0.87	0.69	0.28	0.14	0.55	0.46	0.37	0.46	0.27	0.14
	Y_3	0.79	0.36	0.19	0.12	0.89	0.72	0.4	0.97	0.64	0.4
	Y_4	0.23	0.2	0.12	0.05	0.29	0.2	0.09	0.12	0.05	0.03
	Y_5	10.47	8.69	5.22	2.59	10.13	8.72	2.13	6.21	5.18	1.5
	Y_6	2.91	1.94	1.55	1.04	3.23	4.53	1.29	1.68	1.42	1.55

3.2. Notations and Assumptions

Table 5 presents a comprehensive compilation of the notation, accompanied by brief descriptions.

Table 5. Notation summary.

Notation	Description
Indices	
n	number of DMUs
m	number of input resources
s	number of output targets
ω	scenario index
Sets	
$\mathcal{J}$	set of DMUs
$\mathcal{I}$	set of inputs
$\mathcal{O}$	set of outputs
Ω	set of scenarios
Parameters	
p_r	unit price for output r
c_i	unit cost for input i
X_{ik}	observed input i for DMU k
Y_{rk}^{ω}	observed output r for DMU k of scenario ω
Le_k	lower bound for efficiency of DMU k
Lx_{ik}	lower bound for input resource i of DMU k
Ux_{ik}	upper bound for input resource i of DMU k
Ly_{rk}	lower bound for output target r of DMU k
Uy_{rk}	upper bound for output target r of DMU k
b_i	availability for input resource i
ϵ	infinitesimal number
q^{ω}	realization probability of scenario ω

Table 5. *Cont.*

Notation	Description
Variables	
x_{ik}	input resource i for DMU k
y_{rk}^{ω}	output target r for DMU k of scenario ω
v_{ik}	weight attached to input resource i for DMU k
u_{rk}^{ω}	weight attached to output target r for DMU k of scenario ω
l_k^t	unrestricted variable
λ_{jk}^{ω}	is used for defining the possibility set of input resources or output targets of DMU k of scenario ω
e_k^*	optimal efficiency for DMU k
$e_k^{\omega*}$	optimal efficiency for DMU k of scenario ω
e_{kj}	cross-efficiency of DMU j with respect to DMU k

4. Methodology

4.1. Stochastic Bilevel DEA Model

In the context described in Section 3.1, it is apparent that the decisions for the allocation of inputs within the branches (subDMUs) are made at the beginning of the period by the central unit and then are followed by the resolution of the inherent uncertainty. It makes sense that target setting should take into account the observed outputs under the realized scenario. Thus, target setting constitutes the second-stage (aka recourse) variables in our formulation. Therefore, we extend, analogously, the deterministic bilevel model of Hakim et al. [26] to a two-stage stochastic bilevel DEA model with recourse actions.

4.1.1. The Upper-Level Model

Within a defined set of scenarios denoted as Ω, the upper-level structure follows the framework given in (7)–(15). The upper-level model includes decision variables for the input resources (x_{ik}) and the output targets (y_{rk}^{ω}). The optimization criterion involves profit maximization through optimal resource allocation, output targeting, and efficiency lower bounds of each subDMU.

$$\max_{x_{ik}, y_{rk}^{\omega}, \lambda_{jk}^{\omega}} \sum_{\omega=1}^{|\Omega|} q^{\omega} \left[\sum_{r=1}^{s} p_r \sum_{k=1}^{n} y_{rk}^{\omega} \right] - \sum_{i=1}^{m} c_i \sum_{k=1}^{n} x_{ik} \tag{7}$$

$s.t.$

$$Le_k \le e_k^{\omega*} \qquad\qquad \forall k \in \mathcal{J} \tag{8}$$

$$x_{ik} \ge \sum_{j=1}^{n} \lambda_{jk}^{\omega} X_{ij} \qquad\qquad \forall i \in \mathcal{I}, k \in \mathcal{J} \tag{9}$$

$$y_{rk}^{\omega} \le \sum_{j=1}^{n} \lambda_{jk}^{\omega} Y_{rj}^{\omega} \qquad\qquad \forall r \in \mathcal{O}, k \in \mathcal{J}, \omega \in \Omega \tag{10}$$

$$\sum_{j=1}^{n} \lambda_{jk}^{\omega} = 1 \qquad\qquad \forall k \in \mathcal{J}, \omega \in \Omega \tag{11}$$

$$\lambda_{jk}^{\omega} \ge 0 \qquad\qquad \forall k \in \mathcal{J}, \omega \in \Omega \tag{12}$$

$$\sum_{k=1}^{n} x_{ik} \le b_i \qquad\qquad \forall i \in \mathcal{I} \tag{13}$$

$$Lx_{ik} \le x_{ik} \le Ux_{ik} \qquad\qquad \forall i \in \mathcal{I}, k \in \mathcal{J} \tag{14}$$

$$Ly_{rk} \le y_{rk}^{\omega} \le Uy_{rk} \qquad\qquad \forall r \in \mathcal{O}, k \in \mathcal{J}, \omega \in \Omega \tag{15}$$

The objective function (7) maximizes the expected overall organizational profits, where c_i and p_r denote the unit input costs and the unit output prices, respectively. Constraint (8)

sets an efficiency lower bound for each subDMU decided by the central DMU. Constraints (9) and (10) ensure that the optimal allocation of resources and targeting is feasible with respect to the production possibility set constructed by the observed input and output values of the subDMUs. Constraint (11) poses the variable returns to scale (VRS) assumption for the model; nevertheless, the constant returns to scale (CRS) assumption can also be considered ignoring the latter constraint. Constraint (13) sets an upper bound for the availability of resources. Constraints (14) and (15) set upper and lower bounds for input resources and output targets decided by the central DMU.

4.1.2. The Lower-Level Model

The lower-level model is the multiplier DEA-based model under VRS assumption as presented in Beasley [38]. In the lower level, the optimal weights associated with inputs and outputs are determined. The main objective here is that each DMU tries to maximize its efficiency, given the input resources and target setting based on the upper-level decisions. For every DMU $k(k = 1, \ldots, n)$ and scenario $\omega \in \Omega$, the lower-level problem is described by (16)–(19).

$$e_k^{\omega*} = \max_{v_{ik}, u_{rk}^\omega, l_k^\omega} \frac{\sum_{r=1}^s u_{rk}^\omega y_{rk}^\omega - l_k^\omega}{\sum_{i=1}^m v_{ik} x_{ik}} \tag{16}$$

s.t.

$$0 \leq e_{kj}^\omega = \frac{\sum_{r=1}^s u_{rk}^\omega y_{rj}^\omega - l_k^\omega}{\sum_{i=1}^m v_{ik} x_{ij}} \leq 1 \qquad \forall k, j \in \mathcal{J}, \omega \in \Omega \tag{17}$$

$$v_{ik} \geq \epsilon \qquad \forall i \in \mathcal{I}, k \in \mathcal{J} \tag{18}$$

$$u_{rk}^\omega \geq \epsilon \qquad \forall r \in \mathcal{O}, k \in \mathcal{J}, \omega \in \Omega \tag{19}$$

The objective function (16) of this model calculates the optimal efficiency score $e_k^{\omega*}$ for each subDMU k and each scenario ω. The model, which runs for each subDMU k, computes the optimal input (v_{ik}) and output weights (u_{rk}^ω) for each scenario ω that maximizes the efficiency for each subDMU k. Constraint (17) restricts the values of subDMU efficiency between zero and one. Constraints (18) and (19) ensure that the weights take values larger than a nonnegative infinitesimal number for input and output respectively. The existence of the free variable l_k^ω imposes the variable returns to scale assumption for the efficiency of the subDMU k.

4.2. Solution Approach

In this section, we generalize Theorem 1 of Hakim et al. [26] in our stochastic framework.

Lemma 1. *The solution* $(x_{ik}^*, y_{rk}^{\omega*}, \lambda_{jk}^{\omega*}; \forall i, k, j, r)$ *of the upper-level model (7)–(15) is optimal, assuming that* $(u_{rk}^{\omega*}, v_{ik}^*, l_k^{\omega*}; \forall i, k, r)$ *is an optimal solution of the lower level model (16)–(19) if and only if* $(x_{ik}^*, y_{rk}^{\omega*}, \lambda_{jk}^{\omega*}, u_{rk}^{\omega*}, v_{ik}^*, l_k^{\omega*}; \forall i, k, j, r)$ *is an optimal solution of the single-level model (20)–(31).*

Proof. Let us assume that $(x_{ik}^*, y_{rk}^{\omega*}, \lambda_{jk}^{\omega*}; \forall i, k, j, r)$ is an optimal solution of the upper-level model (7)–(15) and U^* is the corresponding objective value. Moreover, let $(u_{rk}^{\omega*}, v_{ik}^*, l_k^{\omega*}; \forall i, k, r)$ be the optimal solution of the lower-level model (16)–(19), given that $(x_{ik}^*, y_{rk}^{\omega*}, \lambda_{jk}^*; \forall i, k, j, r)$ is a feasible solution of the upper-level model (7)–(15). Then, $(x_{ik}^*, y_{rk}^{\omega*}, \lambda_{jk}^{\omega*}, u_{rk}^{\omega*}, v_{ik}^*, l_k^{\omega*}; \forall i, k, j, r)$ satisfies all the constraints of the single-level model (20)–(31) since it satisfies constraints (9)–(15) and (17)–(19), which are the same with (22)–(31). Furthermore, the optimal solution of the lower-level model e_k^* equals e_{kk} when the weights are replaced with their optimal values $(u_{rk}^{\omega*}, v_{ik}^*, l_k^{\omega*}; \forall i, k, r)$; therefore, constraint (21) is also satisfied. Hence, $(x_{ik}^*, y_{rk}^{\omega*}, \lambda_{jk}^*, u_{rk}^*, v_{ik}^*, l_k^{\omega*}; \forall i, k, j, r)$ is a feasible solution for the single-level model and the corresponding objective value is equal to the optimum value U^* of the bilevel model. If A^* is the optimum value of the single-level model then it holds that $A^* \geq U^*$.

Conversely, we have to show that the optimal solution $(x_{ik}^*, y_{rk}^{\omega*}, \lambda_{jk}^{\omega*}, u_{rk}^{\omega*}, v_{ik}^*, l_k^{\omega*}; \forall i, k, j, r)$ of the single-level model (20)–(31) induces an optimal solution $(x_{ik}^*, y_{rk}^{\omega*}, \lambda_{jk}^{\omega*}; \forall i, k, j, r)$ of the upper-level model (7)–(15) and an optimal solution $(u_{rk}^{\omega*}, v_{ik}^*, l_k^{\omega*}; \forall i, k, r)$ of the lower-level model (16)–(19). The optimal solution $(x_{ik}^*, y_{rk}^{\omega*}, \lambda_{jk}^{\omega*}, u_{rk}^{\omega*}, v_{ik}^*, l_k^{\omega*}; \forall i, k, j, r)$ of the single-level model (20)–(31) satisfies constraints (9)–(15) and (17)–(19), which are the same with (22)–(31). Furthermore, e_k^* equals e_{kk} for the optimal weights, thereby constraint (8) is also satisfied. Thus, the optimal solution $(x_{ik}^*, y_{rk}^{\omega*}, \lambda_{jk}^{\omega*}, u_{rk}^{\omega*}, v_{ik}^*, l_k^{\omega*}; \forall i, k, j, r)$ of the single-level model (20)–(31) induces a feasible solution $(x_{ik}^*, y_{rk}^{\omega*}, \lambda_{jk}^{\omega*}; \forall i, k, j, r)$ of the upper-level model (7)–(15), where $(u_{rk}^{\omega*}, v_{ik}^*, l_k^{\omega*}; \forall i, k, r)$ is an optimal solution of the lower-level model (16)–(19). Assuming that U^* is the optimum value of the upper-level model and the objective value of the feasible solution $(x_{ik}^*, y_{rk}^{\omega*}, \lambda_{jk}^{\omega*}; \forall i, k, j, r)$ of the upper-level model (7)–(15) is A^*, then it holds that $A^* \leq U^*$. $\square$

By Lemma 1, the stochastic bilevel DEA programming problem is converted to a single-level as follows:

$$\max_{x_{ik}, y_{rk}^\omega, \lambda_{jk}^\omega} \sum_{\omega=1}^{|\Omega|} q^\omega \left[\sum_{r=1}^s p_r \sum_{k=1}^n y_{rk}^\omega \right] - \sum_{i=1}^m c_i \sum_{k=1}^n x_{ik} \tag{20}$$

s.t.

$$Le_k \leq e_{kk}^\omega = \frac{\sum_{r=1}^s u_{rk}^\omega y_{rk}^\omega - l_k^\omega}{\sum_{i=1}^m v_{ik} x_{ik}} \qquad \forall k \in \mathcal{J}, \omega \in \Omega \tag{21}$$

$$x_{ik} \geq \sum_{j=1}^n \lambda_{jk}^\omega X_{ij} \qquad \forall i \in \mathcal{I}, k \in \mathcal{J} \tag{22}$$

$$y_{rk}^\omega \leq \sum_{j=1}^n \lambda_{jk}^\omega Y_{rj}^\omega \qquad \forall r \in \mathcal{O}, k \in \mathcal{J}, \omega \in \Omega \tag{23}$$

$$\sum_{j=1}^n \lambda_{jk}^\omega = 1 \qquad \forall k \in \mathcal{J}, \omega \in \Omega \tag{24}$$

$$\lambda_{jk}^\omega \geq 0 \qquad \forall k \in \mathcal{J}, \omega \in \Omega \tag{25}$$

$$\sum_{k=1}^n x_{ik} \leq b_i \qquad \forall i \in \mathcal{I} \tag{26}$$

$$Lx_{ik} \leq x_{ik} \leq Ux_{ik} \qquad \forall i \in \mathcal{I}, k \in \mathcal{J} \tag{27}$$

$$Ly_{rk} \leq y_{rk}^\omega \leq Uy_{rk} \qquad \forall r \in \mathcal{O}, k \in \mathcal{J}, \omega \in \Omega \tag{28}$$

$$0 \leq e_{kj}^\omega = \frac{\sum_{r=1}^s u_{rk}^\omega y_{rj}^\omega - l_k^\omega}{\sum_{i=1}^m v_{ik} x_{ij}} \leq 1 \qquad \forall j \in \mathcal{J}, \omega \in \Omega \tag{29}$$

$$v_{ik} \geq 0 \qquad \forall i \in \mathcal{I}, k \in \mathcal{J} \tag{30}$$

$$u_{rk}^\omega \geq 0 \qquad \forall r \in \mathcal{O}, k \in \mathcal{J}, \omega \in \Omega \tag{31}$$

The above optimization problem is non-linear and can be shown to be non-convex as well by considering the Hessian matrix of constraints (21) and (29). In either case, the Hessian matrix is not positive semidefinite and, thus, the constrained set is not convex.

5. Computational Study

The proposed work was encoded in Python 3.7.0, and for the stochastic bilevel model, Pyomo 5.7.3 was used, combined with the optimization engine of Gurobi 10.0.1. This solver version can deal with quadratic non-convex constraint problems by using global optimization techniques. All the experiments were conducted on an Intel Core i5-8350 CPU @ 1.70 GHz with 16 GB of RAM, running on 64-bit Ubuntu 22.04.1 (Intel, Santa Clara, CA, USA).

Our test instance comprises three different distinct scenarios denoted by ω, where $\omega = 1, 2, 3$ and the realization probabilities are $q^1 = 0.2, q^2 = 0.5, q^3 = 0.3$, respectively. We assume that the input availabilities are independent of scenarios and are given as $b_i = (25, 84, 22, 126.8, 5.723) \quad \forall i \in \mathcal{I}$, respectively. The lower bound on each input i and DMU k is given by $Lx_{ik} = 0.8X_{ik}$, while the upper bound is calculated as $Ux_{ik} = 1.2X_{ik}$. In a similar manner, the lower and upper bound for output r and DMU k are given by $Ly_{rk} = 0.8Y_{rk}^1$, and $Uy_{rk} = 1.2Y_{rk}^3$, respectively. The output bounds are independent of the scenarios. The unit costs for each of the five inputs are $c_i = (40{,}000, 28{,}000, 27{,}500, 1000,$ and $1{,}000{,}000) \; \forall i \in \mathcal{I}$. In addition, the corresponding unit output prices are set to EUR 100,000, except the last output price, which is $p_6 = 1{,}000{,}000$. We are aligned with the VRS assumption and the efficiency lower bound is $Le_k = 0.95$ for all DMU and scenarios. Finally, we should point out that our test instance has 5 inputs, 6 outputs, and 10 DMUs.

Additionally, a sensitivity analysis is undertaken to evaluate the model's performance, with a specific emphasis on both profitability and efficiency, while maintaining all other parameters at a constant level. In the initial scenario, we systematically vary the efficiency lower bound. Subsequently, a series of test instances is executed, each characterized by distinct input resources.

Utilizing the data outlined in Tables 1 and 4, we have derived an optimal solution addressing the challenge of resource allocation and target setting, accounting for an efficiency lower bound ($LBe_k = 0.95$) across all decision-making units. Referencing Table 6, the allocation of input resources among bank branches by the central administration is depicted. Notably, all resources are fully utilized, except for AC, which exhibits a slack of 7.63 in relation to the upper availability bound of 126.8.

Table 6. Resource allocation for each DMU.

DMU	X_1	X_2	X_3	X_4	X_5
1	4.00	12.00	3.00	16.00	0.788
2	3.30	10.37	2.30	13.93	0.630
3	2.20	7.82	1.20	8.38	0.437
4	1.10	5.20	1.00	2.88	0.291
5	4.01	10.72	3.65	19.42	0.848
6	4.35	11.24	3.90	28.80	0.987
7	1.05	4.14	1.95	1.68	0.352
8	2.80	9.00	1.80	12.79	0.546
9	2.20	7.50	1.20	8.08	0.425
10	0.00	6.00	2.00	7.20	0.420
Total	25.00	84.00	22.00	119.17	5.723

In addition to managing resource allocation among DMUs, our model emphasizes a crucial aspect: the establishment of output targets designed to enhance organizational effectiveness and profit maximization. Table 7 showcases the optimal output plan for each output and DMU, considering various scenarios. The final column displays the summation of outputs for each distinct output. The probability of occurrence for each scenario reflects the economic uncertainty anticipated during the future implementation of the strategic plan. Specifically, we consider scenarios representing a pessimistic outlook ($q^1 = 0.2$), a normal economic environment ($q^2 = 0.5$), and an optimistic scenario ($q^3 = 0.3$). This probability distribution accounts for the potential economic conditions that may influence the execution of the strategic plan.

Table 7. Output targets for every DMU and scenario.

Scenario	Output	1	2	3	4	5	6	7	8	9	10	Total
						DMU						
1	Y_1	0.420	0.469	0.392	0.174	0.419	0.391	0.183	0.560	0.470	0.210	3.687
	Y_2	0.532	0.421	0.199	0.092	0.403	0.337	0.221	0.239	0.199	0.084	2.726
	Y_3	0.480	0.394	0.222	0.105	0.518	0.499	0.252	0.470	0.401	0.245	3.587
	Y_4	0.140	0.111	0.056	0.028	0.162	0.153	0.051	0.063	0.042	0.018	0.825
	Y_5	6.370	5.373	3.471	1.733	6.228	5.889	1.385	3.766	3.472	0.910	38.597
	Y_6	1.772	1.418	0.982	0.654	1.909	2.221	0.791	1.154	0.957	0.945	12.802
2	Y_1	0.600	0.669	0.497	0.248	0.599	0.558	0.261	0.648	0.672	0.300	5.053
	Y_2	0.760	0.601	0.287	0.131	0.576	0.481	0.316	0.443	0.285	0.120	4.000
	Y_3	0.686	0.435	0.222	0.145	0.740	0.713	0.360	0.610	0.573	0.350	4.833
	Y_4	0.200	0.159	0.078	0.041	0.232	0.219	0.074	0.107	0.061	0.025	1.195
	Y_5	9.100	7.676	4.973	2.475	8.897	8.413	1.978	6.340	4.960	1.300	56.112
	Y_6	2.531	2.025	1.403	0.934	2.727	3.173	1.130	1.755	1.367	1.350	18.395
3	Y_1	0.690	0.770	0.497	0.276	0.689	0.642	0.300	0.745	0.773	0.345	5.727
	Y_2	0.874	0.691	0.331	0.151	0.662	0.552	0.363	0.510	0.320	0.138	4.592
	Y_3	0.789	0.435	0.222	0.145	0.850	0.820	0.414	0.702	0.658	0.403	5.438
	Y_4	0.230	0.183	0.090	0.047	0.267	0.242	0.085	0.123	0.062	0.029	1.356
	Y_5	10.465	8.827	5.719	2.846	10.232	9.675	2.275	7.291	5.704	1.495	64.529
	Y_6	2.911	2.329	1.614	1.074	3.136	3.649	1.300	2.018	1.572	1.553	21.155

The efficiency analysis in Table 8 provides a comprehensive overview of DMU performance under varying operating scenarios. It is essential to note that $\tilde{e}_k$ represents the weighted average efficiency across all scenarios. Notably, DMU 10 consistently demonstrates high efficiency across all scenarios, whereas DMU 7 exhibits lower efficiency in the first scenario but achieves efficiency in subsequent scenarios. DMUs 3 and 6 showcase increased efficiency in scenarios 2 and 3, respectively. The primary objective of the proposed model is to maximize overall profit, and Table 9 elucidates the total revenues, costs, profits, and profitability. Notably, the input allocation remains constant across scenarios, resulting in a fixed total input cost of 9,799,166. As anticipated, revenues and, consequently, profits, vary with scenarios, with lower profitability in the worst economic scenario, moderate profitability in the moderate scenario, and high profitability in the most optimistic scenario. It is crucial to highlight that the 'Expected' row represents the *weighted* sum of revenues and profits, respectively. In reference to our benchmark instance, with an efficient lower bound, $LBe_k = 0.95$, the total expected profit amounts to EUR 15,302,644, reflecting a 60.69% profitability. This underscores the model's effectiveness in achieving optimal outcomes even in diverse operating conditions.

Table 8. Efficiencies for every DMU in each scenario.

DMU	e_k^{1*}	e_k^{2*}	e_k^{3*}	$\tilde{e}_k$
1	0.95	0.95	0.95	0.95
2	0.95	0.95	0.95	0.95
3	0.95	0.98	0.95	0.97
4	0.95	0.95	0.95	0.95
5	0.95	0.95	0.95	0.95
6	0.95	0.95	0.96	0.95
7	0.95	1	1	0.99
8	0.95	0.95	0.95	0.95
9	0.95	0.95	0.95	0.95
10	1	1	1	1

$\tilde{e}_k$ is the weighted average efficiency.

Table 9. Revenues, profits, and profitability for the three scenarios.

Scenario	Revenues	Profit	Profitability (%)
1	17,744,100	7,944,934	44.78
2	25,514,665	15,715,499	61.59
3	29,318,860	19,519,693	66.58
Expected	25,101,811	15,302,644	60.96

5.1. Sensitivity Analysis

We performed a sensitivity analysis by changing the efficiency lower bound to be achieved by the bank branches from 0.95 to 0.7 and 0, respectively. In Table 10, we can see all optimal DMU efficiencies taking into consideration the output scenarios and the enforced efficiency lower bound. We can observe that in the first case, e.g., $LBe_k = 0.7$, we do not have significant variations except for DMUs 2 and 4, which have average efficiencies of 0.78 and 0.89, respectively. More precisely, DMU 4 performs very well in the moderate and optimistic scenario. In Table 11, it appears that the organization has higher profits for $LBe_k = 0$ than for $LBe_k = 0.7$. This means that a strict policy about branch efficiency does not necessarily yield greater profitability. Another argument of the latter statement is that the relaxed problem for $LBe_k = 0.7$ seems to have an inferior solution to the one we obtain when $LBe_k = 0.95$ and a better one in the case where $LBe_k = 0$.

It is noteworthy that—during the experiments—we identified that the system can work in a completely efficient manner, having all $e_k^{\omega*} = 1 \quad \forall k \in J$ and $\omega \in \Omega$. In order to achieve this ambitious feat, we need to increase the input availability b_5 from 5.723 to 6, yielding a profit of 15,452,279.

Table 10. Efficiencies for each DMU for $LBe_k = 0.7$ and $LBe_k = 0$.

	$LBe_k = 0.7$				$LBe_k = 0$			
DMU	e_k^{1*}	e_k^{2*}	e_k^{3*}	$\tilde{e}_k$	e_k^{1*}	e_k^{2*}	e_k^{3*}	$\tilde{e}_k$
1	0.7	0.72	0.72	0.72	0.27	0.3	0.34	0.31
2	0.78	0.76	0.81	0.78	0.54	0.18	0.37	0.31
3	0.7	0.7	0.78	0.72	0.57	0.61	0.63	0.61
4	0.7	0.94	0.94	0.89	0.7	0.84	0.84	0.81
5	0.72	0.7	0.72	0.71	0.28	0.32	0.34	0.32
6	0.7	0.7	0.75	0.72	0.32	0.37	0.4	0.37
7	0.71	0.7	0.7	0.70	0.93	0.62	0.08	0.52
8	0.72	0.7	0.7	0.70	0.47	0.55	0.58	0.54
9	0.7	0.7	0.7	0.70	0.86	0.94	0.66	0.84
10	0.79	0.73	0.7	0.73	0.57	0.49	0.46	0.50

Table 11. Revenues, costs, and profits for the three scenarios for $LBe_k = 0.7$ and $LBe_k = 0$.

	$LBe_k = 0.7$			$LBe_k = 0$		
Scenario	Revenues	Profit	Yield (%)	Revenues	Profit	Yield (%)
1	17,744,100	7,945,593	44.78	17,744,100	7,945,084	44.78
2	25,514,665	15,716,158	61.60	25,514,665	15,715,649	61.59
3	29,314,435	19,515,928	66.57	29,318,946	19,519,931	66.58
Expected	25,100,483	15,301,976	60.96	25,101,836	15,302,821	60.96

Input cost = 9,798,507.

We also implemented a sensitivity analysis for the case study presented in Section 3.1, considering seven different strategies to maximize the overall organizational efficiency. In the first case, two base officers were replaced with an ATM and, therefore, the ATMs are increased by one in each bank branch. Then the overall profits of the bank are increased in contrast to the profits in the base case study (see Table 12). In this scenario, the overall

profits are even higher than the base case study. Thereby this strategy creates the highest profit for the bank. In the second case, one base officer is replaced with a relationship manager in each bank branch. Following this strategy, the overall profitability of the bank decreases in comparison to the base case study. This reduction is expected since relationship managers have a higher cost for the bank. In the third scenario, we differentiate the cost of deposits among the bank branches with respect to their location. More precisely, the cost of deposits increases to 1% from 0.35% for the West bank branches, to 1.5% for the City Center bank branches, and to 2% for the East bank branches. In the fourth scenario, we combine the replacement of a base officer with a relationship manager in each bank branch with the increase in the cost of deposits performed in the third scenario. In the third and fourth scenarios, the overall profit becomes negative. Since the cost of deposits is augmented, the costs exceed the revenues of the bank eliminating the profit. In the fifth scenario, a combination of the first and third scenarios is implemented and a loss is observed, however lower than that of scenario four. In the sixth scenario, two base officers were replaced with an ATM, and one base officer was replaced with a relationship manager in each bank branch. Thus, the tendency of the banks to replace employees with ATMs and digital services is also due to profit gain. In the seventh scenario, a combination of scenarios one, two, and three is performed, leading to a loss higher than those observed in scenarios three, four, and five. Furthermore, in conjunction with Table 12, Figure 2 illustrates the fluctuations in revenues, costs, and profits. In this sensitivity analysis, we modify input resources, noting that expected revenues remain consistent compared to input allocation costs. However, the variability in costs has a substantial impact on expected profits, resulting in losses in some scenarios.

Table 12. Sensitivity analysis for the seven scenarios assumed.

Scenario	Exp. Revenues	Total Cost	Exp. Profit
1	25,098,657	9,495,636	15,603,021
2	25,106,434	9,917,651	15,188,784
3	23,951,562	25,579,251	−1,627,688
4	23,982,217	25,693,324	−1,711,107
5	24,074,086	25,261,859	−1,187,773
6	25,103,557	9,615,635	15,487,922
7	24,117,803	25,382,135	−1,264,331

'Exp.' = 'Expected'.

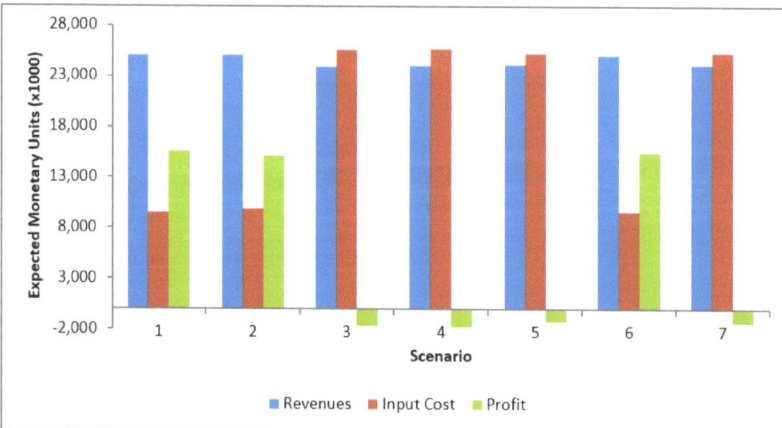

Figure 2. Revenues, costs, and profits for every scenario.

5.2. Theoretical and Managerial Implications

In a theoretical context within the exploration of bilevel modeling, decisions that need to be made at the outset of the examined time period and before any of the scenarios unfold are termed first-stage decisions. Moreover, decisions executed after a scenario materializes, known as recourse decisions, allow corrective actions and are referred to as second-stage decisions. The initial-stage solutions, implemented at the beginning, remain consistent across all scenarios. In contrast, second-stage decisions vary and are contingent on the specific scenario. The bilevel DEA model, incorporating stochastic conditions, enables recourse decisions and actions based on information obtained following the realization of a particular scenario.

As a result, managers can adjust their strategic planning in response to information revealed over time. On the other hand, the deterministic counterpart of the proposed DEA model lacks the flexibility for dynamic changes in strategy and adjustments to emerging economic conditions. For DMUs with multi-stage or multi-level structures, managers aim for optimal organizational efficiency by pursuing dynamic strategies that can adapt to the constraints of limited and uncertain historical data. To this end, the total input consumption is reduced and/or the total production is augmented and simultaneously the overall profits are maximized. Decision-makers acting within uncertain and dynamic environments can benefit from the suggested approach since it allows the investigation of efficiency assessment under alternative scenarios in the presence of volatility and risk. The potential impact of applying this methodology varies depending on the specific domain. Although, the context of this paper focuses on banking, in general, enhancing resource allocation and target setting under stochasticity, contributes to advancing sustainability across all its three dimensions (economic, environmental, social).

The bilevel DEA model, incorporating stochastic conditions, calculates the anticipated organizational profit by considering total expected income from outputs and subtracting total input costs. These computations account for various scenarios determined by the manager. In contrast, the deterministic model optimizes future organizational profits based on historical data with fixed input and output values. In both models, the central DMU must formulate a strategy before uncertain parameters are revealed, ensuring consideration of potential future outcomes for more informed predictions of organizational profits. This approach enhances the accuracy of predicting expected organizational efficiency and allows for more precise resource allocation and target setting through adjustments when new information is revealed.

6. Conclusions

The presented bilevel DEA model with stochastic conditions simultaneously optimizes resource allocation and output targeting, taking into consideration the efficiency lower bound posed by the central manager of large DMUs comprising multiple subDMUs. It considers the hierarchical relations that appear in such large organizations and enterprises that can be captured uniquely through the bilevel framework. Within this framework, objectives are optimized while simultaneously ensuring that DMU's operational efficiency aligns with the managerial strategy. The interconnections and conflicting interests inherent in this complex organizational structure involving the central administration and subordinate DMUs cannot be adequately captured by the network DEA optimization schema. In our approach, the uncertainty and unavailability of data are considered when evaluating the efficiency of large DMUs with a hierarchical structure. The proposed stochastic approach allows for the realization of uncertain parameters through discrete scenarios associated with an occurrence probability. One of the main advantages of this model is that it enables decision-makers of large DMUs to obtain an optimal economic strategy that permits readjustment to the new data upon the realization of one of the scenarios. Based on the scenario to be realized, recourse actions can be taken to adjust input consumption and output targets accordingly. To examine the performance of the stochastic approach, we

apply the proposed model to evaluate the efficiency of a bank based on data that mirror typical real-world scenarios.

One limitation of this study is its exclusive focus on for-profit organizations, particularly large enterprises, which directly influence the objective function. Alternative applications of the model could explore diverse efficiency realizations, incorporating variations of the objective function. Additionally, when addressing banking issues, our concentration was on stochastic fluctuations in output targets while assuming deterministic input values. However, in many real-world scenarios, inputs may also exhibit stochastic tendencies. Furthermore, although our analysis was based on three scenarios, there are typically numerous potential scenarios to consider. For our case study, we chose to examine only a small number of decision-making units (DMUs) and scenarios. However, increasing the dimension of the problem will substantially increase the computational resources needed. This may necessitate the use of additional methodologies rooted in machine learning, offering an intriguing avenue for further research. For instance, Hao and An [66] suggested a pre-scoring method for DMUs, referred to as the angle-index synthesis method. They performed several numerical experiments, highlighting that their algorithm demonstrates excellent performance in computational time, exhibiting a linear increase in computational time, even for a staggering case involving 1 billion DMUs.

Taking into account the above, other avenues for future research could involve introducing stochastic elements at the input level, providing a representation of a potentially more realistic economic environment. Furthermore, we are investigating the possible integration of chance constraints concerning the targeted efficiency levels for each DMU. This approach allows the central administration to specify a range of desired efficiency levels for each distinguished DMU rather than a precise value. Finally, another path for future exploration might involve substituting the lower level with a two-stage problem while preserving the bilevel hierarchy. This approach would entail addressing a stochastic bilevel network DEA problem, thus finding applications in diverse sectors beyond banking. Ultimately, an alternative approach could involve demonstrating a tighter formulation to effectively address instances with larger dimensions.

Author Contributions: Conceptualization, A.C.G., K.K., E.-M.V. and K.B.; methodology, A.C.G., K.K., E.-M.V., K.B. and G.P.; software, K.K., E.-M.V. and K.B.; validation, A.C.G., K.K., E.-M.V., K.B. and G.P.; formal analysis, A.C.G., K.K., E.-M.V., K.B. and G.P.; investigation, A.C.G., K.K., E.-M.V., K.B. and G.P.; resources, A.C.G., K.K., E.-M.V., K.B. and G.P.; data curation, A.C.G., K.K., E.-M.V., K.B. and G.P.; writing—original draft preparation, K.K., E.-M.V., K.B. and G.P.; writing—review and editing, A.C.G. and K.K.; visualization, K.K., E.-M.V. and K.B.; supervision, A.C.G. and K.K.; project administration, A.C.G.; funding acquisition, A.C.G. All authors have read and agreed to the published version of the manuscript.

Funding: The research project was funded by the Hellenic Foundation for Research and Innovation (H.F.R.I.) under the "2nd Call for H.F.R.I. Research Projects to support Faculty Members & Researchers" (Project Number: 3154).

Data Availability Statement: The data presented in this study are available in the article.

Acknowledgments: The authors are grateful to Emmanuel Thanassoulis from the Aston Business School for engaging in fruitful discussions regarding the general idea of the problem. Additionally, they would like to thank the three anonymous referees for their valuable and constructive comments and suggestions.

Conflicts of Interest: The authors declare no conflicts of interest.

References

1. Charnes, A.; Cooper, W.W.; Rhodes, E. Measuring the efficiency of decision-making units. *Eur. J. Oper. Res.* **1979**, *3*, 339. [CrossRef]
2. Färe, R.; Grosskopf, S. Intertemporal production frontiers: With dynamic DEA. *J. Oper. Res. Soc.* **1997**, *48*, 656. [CrossRef]
3. Kao, C.; Hwang, S.N. Efficiency decomposition in two-stage data envelopment analysis: An application to non-life insurance companies in Taiwan. *Eur. J. Oper. Res.* **2008**, *185*, 418–429. [CrossRef]

4. Kao, C.; Hwang, S.N. Efficiency measurement for network systems: IT impact on firm performance. *Decis. Support Syst.* **2010**, *48*, 437–446. [CrossRef]
5. Halkos, G.E.; Tzeremes, N.G.; Kourtzidis, S.A. A unified classification of two-stage DEA models. *Surv. Oper. Res. Manag. Sci.* **2014**, *19*, 1–16. [CrossRef]
6. Despotis, D.K.; Koronakos, G.; Sotiros, D. The "weak-link" approach to network DEA for two-stage processes. *Eur. J. Oper. Res.* **2016**, *254*, 481–492. [CrossRef]
7. Koronakos, G.; Sotiros, D.; Despotis, D.K.; Kritikos, M.N. Fair efficiency decomposition in network DEA: A compromise programming approach. *Socio-Econ. Plan. Sci.* **2022**, *79*, 101100. [CrossRef]
8. Despotis, D.K.; Sotiros, D.; Koronakos, G. A network DEA approach for series multi-stage processes. *Omega* **2016**, *61*, 35–48. [CrossRef]
9. Despotis, D.K.; Koronakos, G.; Sotiros, D. Composition versus decomposition in two-stage network DEA: A reverse approach. *J. Product. Anal.* **2016**, *45*, 71–87. [CrossRef]
10. Kremantzis, M.D.; Beullens, P.; Kyrgiakos, L.S.; Klein, J. Measurement and evaluation of multi-function parallel network hierarchical DEA systems. *Socio-Econ. Plan. Sci.* **2022**, *84*, 101428. [CrossRef]
11. Fukuyama, H.; Matousek, R. Efficiency of Turkish banking: Two-stage network system. Variable returns to scale model. *J. Int. Financ. Mark. Inst. Money* **2011**, *21*, 75–91. [CrossRef]
12. Kao, C. *Network Data Envelopment Analysis: Foundations and Extensions*; Springer: Berlin/Heidelberg, Germany, 2016; Volume 240.
13. Kourtzidis, S.; Tzeremes, N. Measuring Banking Performance in a Network DEA context: A General Weight Assurance Region Model. In Proceedings of the European Workshop on Efficiency and Productivity Analysis XVII, Porto, Portugal, 27–29 June 2022.
14. Kao, C. Network data envelopment analysis: A review. *Eur. J. Oper. Res.* **2014**, *239*, 1–16. [CrossRef]
15. Henriques, I.C.; Sobreiro, V.A.; Kimura, H.; Mariano, E.B. Two-stage DEA in banks: Terminological controversies and future directions. *Expert Syst. Appl.* **2020**, *161*, 113632. [CrossRef] [PubMed]
16. Omrani, H.; Oveysi, Z.; Emrouznejad, A.; Teplova, T. A mixed-integer network DEA with shared inputs and undesirable outputs for performance evaluation: Efficiency measurement of bank branches. *J. Oper. Res. Soc.* **2023**, *74*, 1150–1165. [CrossRef]
17. Tsaples, G.; Papathanasiou, J. Multi-level DEA for the construction of multi-dimensional indices. *MethodsX* **2020**, *7*, 101169. [CrossRef] [PubMed]
18. Roudabr, N.; Najafi, S.E.; Moghaddas, Z.; Movahedi Sobhani, F. Overall Efficiency of Four-Stage Structure with Undesirable Outputs: A New SBM Network DEA Model. *Complexity* **2022**, *2022*, 9577175. [CrossRef]
19. Kazemzadeh, N.; Ryan, S.M.; Hamzeei, M. Robust optimization vs. stochastic programming incorporating risk measures for unit commitment with uncertain variable renewable generation. *Energy Syst.* **2019**, *10*, 517–541. [CrossRef]
20. Zhang, Y.; Li, Z.; Jiao, P.; Zhu, S. Two-stage stochastic programming approach for limited medical reserves allocation under uncertainties. *Complex Intell. Syst.* **2021**, *7*, 3003–3013. [CrossRef]
21. Shakouri, R.; Salahi, M.; Kordrostami, S. Stochastic p-robust approach to two-stage network DEA model. *Quant. Financ. Econ.* **2019**, *3*, 315–346. [CrossRef]
22. Sadjadi, S.J.; Omrani, H.; Makui, A.; Shahanaghi, K. An interactive robust data envelopment analysis model for determining alternative targets in Iranian electricity distribution companies. *Expert Syst. Appl.* **2011**, *38*, 9830–9839. [CrossRef]
23. Wang, K.; Wei, F. Robust data envelopment analysis based MCDM with the consideration of uncertain data. *J. Syst. Eng. Electron.* **2010**, *21*, 981–989. [CrossRef]
24. Landete, M.; Monge, J.F.; Ruiz, J.L. Robust DEA efficiency scores: A probabilistic/combinatorial approach. *Expert Syst. Appl.* **2017**, *86*, 145–154. [CrossRef]
25. Charles, V.; Cornillier, F. Value of the stochastic efficiency in data envelopment analysis. *Expert Syst. Appl.* **2017**, *81*, 349–357. [CrossRef]
26. Hakim, S.; Seifi, A.; Ghaemi, A. A bi-level formulation for DEA-based centralized resource allocation under efficiency constraints. *Comput. Ind. Eng.* **2016**, *93*, 28–35. [CrossRef]
27. Seiford, L.M.; Zhu, J. Profitability and marketability of the top 55 US commercial banks. *Manag. Sci.* **1999**, *45*, 1270–1288. [CrossRef]
28. Portela, M.C.A.S.; Thanassoulis, E. Comparative efficiency analysis of Portuguese bank branches. *Eur. J. Oper. Res.* **2007**, *177*, 1275–1288. [CrossRef]
29. Akther, S.; Fukuyama, H.; Weber, W.L. Estimating two-stage network slacks-based inefficiency: An application to Bangladesh banking. *Omega* **2013**, *41*, 88–96. [CrossRef]
30. Wanke, P.; Barros, C. Two-stage DEA: An application to major Brazilian banks. *Expert Syst. Appl.* **2014**, *41*, 2337–2344. [CrossRef]
31. Wang, K.; Huang, W.; Wu, J.; Liu, Y.N. Efficiency measures of the Chinese commercial banking system using an additive two-stage DEA. *Omega* **2014**, *44*, 5–20. [CrossRef]
32. Hafsal, K.; Suvvari, A.; Durai, S.R.S. Efficiency of Indian banks with non-performing assets: Evidence from two-stage network DEA. *Future Bus. J.* **2020**, *6*, 1–9. [CrossRef]
33. Fukuyama, H.; Matousek, R.; Tzeremes, N.G. A Nerlovian cost inefficiency two-stage DEA model for modeling banks' production process: Evidence from the Turkish banking system. *Omega* **2020**, *95*, 102198. [CrossRef]
34. Golany, B.; Phillips, F.; Rousseau, J. Models for improved effectiveness based on DEA efficiency results. *IIE Trans.* **1993**, *25*, 2–10. [CrossRef]

35. Athanassopoulos, A.D. Goal programming & data envelopment analysis (GoDEA) for target-based multi-level planning: Allocating central grants to the Greek local authorities. *Eur. J. Oper. Res.* **1995**, *87*, 535–550.
36. Yu, M.M.; Chern, C.C.; Hsiao, B. Human resource rightsizing using centralized data envelopment analysis: Evidence from Taiwan's Airports. *Omega* **2013**, *41*, 119–130. [CrossRef]
37. Amirteimoori, A.; Tabar, M.M. Resource allocation and target setting in data envelopment analysis. *Expert Syst. Appl.* **2010**, *37*, 3036–3039. [CrossRef]
38. Beasley, J.E. Allocating fixed costs and resources via data envelopment analysis. *Eur. J. Oper. Res.* **2003**, *147*, 198–216. [CrossRef]
39. Lozano, S.; Villa, G. Centralized resource allocation using data envelopment analysis. *J. Product. Anal.* **2004**, *22*, 143–161. [CrossRef]
40. Varmaz, A.; Varwig, A.; Poddig, T. Centralized resource planning and Yardstick competition. *Omega* **2013**, *41*, 112–118. [CrossRef]
41. Afsharian, M.; Ahn, H.; Thanassoulis, E. A DEA-based incentives system for centrally managed multi-unit organisations. *Eur. J. Oper. Res.* **2017**, *259*, 587–598. [CrossRef]
42. Afsharian, M.; Ahn, H.; Thanassoulis, E. A frontier-based system of incentives for units in organisations with varying degrees of decentralisation. *Eur. J. Oper. Res.* **2019**, *275*, 224–237. [CrossRef]
43. Asmild, M.; Paradi, J.C.; Pastor, J.T. Centralized resource allocation BCC models. *Omega* **2009**, *37*, 40–49. [CrossRef]
44. Wu, J.; An, Q.; Ali, S.; Liang, L. DEA based resource allocation considering environmental factors. *Math. Comput. Model.* **2013**, *58*, 1128–1137. [CrossRef]
45. Fang, L. A generalized DEA model for centralized resource allocation. *Eur. J. Oper. Res.* **2013**, *228*, 405–412. [CrossRef]
46. Chen, Y.; Du, J.; Sherman, H.D.; Zhu, J. DEA model with shared resources and efficiency decomposition. *Eur. J. Oper. Res.* **2010**, *207*, 339–349. [CrossRef]
47. Zha, Y.; Liang, L. Two-stage cooperation model with input freely distributed among the stages. *Eur. J. Oper. Res.* **2010**, *205*, 332–338. [CrossRef]
48. Wu, J.; Zhu, Q.; Ji, X.; Chu, J.; Liang, L. Two-stage network processes with shared resources and resources recovered from undesirable outputs. *Eur. J. Oper. Res.* **2016**, *251*, 182–197. [CrossRef]
49. Yu, M.M.; Chen, L.H.; Hsiao, B. A fixed cost allocation based on the two-stage network data envelopment approach. *J. Bus. Res.* **2016**, *69*, 1817–1822. [CrossRef]
50. Li, X.; Da Xu, L. A review of Internet of Things—Resource allocation. *IEEE Internet Things J.* **2020**, *8*, 8657–8666. [CrossRef]
51. Qiu, Q.; Cui, L.; Gao, H.; Yi, H. Optimal allocation of units in sequential probability series systems. *Reliab. Eng. Syst. Saf.* **2018**, *169*, 351–363. [CrossRef]
52. Dempe, S. *Foundations of Bilevel Programming*; Springer Science & Business Media: Berlin/Heidelberg, Germany, 2002.
53. Von Stackelberg, H. *Market Structure and Equilibrium*; Springer Science & Business Media: Berlin/Heidelberg, Germany, 2010.
54. Shafiee, M.; Lotfi, F.H.; Saleh, H.; Ghaderi, M. A mixed integer bi-level DEA model for bank branch performance evaluation by Stackelberg approach. *J. Ind. Eng. Int.* **2016**, *12*, 81–91. [CrossRef]
55. Zhou, X.; Luo, R.; Tu, Y.; Lev, B.; Pedrycz, W. Data envelopment analysis for bi-level systems with multiple followers. *Omega* **2018**, *77*, 180–188. [CrossRef]
56. Sinha, A.; Malo, P.; Frantsev, A.; Deb, K. Finding optimal strategies in a multi-period multi-leader–follower Stackelberg game using an evolutionary algorithm. *Comput. Oper. Res.* **2014**, *41*, 374–385. [CrossRef]
57. Hajiagha, S.H.R.; Mahdiraji, H.A.; Tavana, M. A new bi-level data envelopment analysis model for efficiency measurement and target setting. *Measurement* **2019**, *147*, 106877. [CrossRef]
58. Ang, S.; Liu, P.; Yang, F. Intra-organizational and inter-organizational resource allocation in two-stage network systems. *Omega* **2020**, *91*, 102009. [CrossRef]
59. Olesen, O.B.; Petersen, N.C. Stochastic data envelopment analysis—A review. *Eur. J. Oper. Res.* **2016**, *251*, 2–21. [CrossRef]
60. Charnes, A.; Cooper, W.W. Chance-constrained programming. *Manag. Sci.* **1959**, *6*, 73–79. [CrossRef]
61. Beraldi, P.; Bruni, M. Efficiency evaluation under uncertainty: A stochastic DEA approach. *Decis. Econ. Financ.* **2020**, *43*, 519–538. [CrossRef]
62. Zhou, Z.; Lin, L.; Xiao, H.; Ma, C.; Wu, S. Stochastic network DEA models for two-stage systems under the centralized control organization mechanism. *Comput. Ind. Eng.* **2017**, *110*, 404–412. [CrossRef]
63. Hatami-Marbini, A.; Arabmaldar, A.; Toloo, M.; Nehrani, A.M. Robust non-radial data envelopment analysis models under data uncertainty. *Expert Syst. Appl.* **2022**, *207*, 118023. [CrossRef]
64. Tseng, C.Y.; Lee, C.Y.; Wang, Q.; Wu, C. Data envelopment analysis and stochastic equilibrium analysis for market power investigation in a bi-level market. *Transp. Res. Part E Logist. Transp. Rev.* **2022**, *161*, 102705. [CrossRef]
65. Omrani, H.; Shamsi, M.; Emrouznejad, A.; Teplova, T. A robust DEA model under discrete scenarios for assessing bank branches. *Expert Syst. Appl.* **2023**, *219*, 119694. [CrossRef]
66. Muren; Hao, L.; An, Q. Efficiency evaluation of very large-scale samples: Data envelopment analysis with angle-index synthesis. *Comput. Oper. Res.* **2024**, *161*, 106457. [CrossRef]

Article

Strong Ergodicity in Nonhomogeneous Markov Systems with Chronological Order

P.-C.G. Vassiliou

Department of Statistical Sciences, University College London, Gower St., London WC1E 6BT, UK;
vasiliou@math.auth.gr

Abstract: In the present, we study the problem of strong ergodicity in nonhomogeneous Markov systems. In the first basic theorem, we relax the fundamental assumption present in all studies of asymptotic behavior. That is, the assumption that the inherent inhomogeneous Markov chain converges to a homogeneous Markov chain with a regular transition probability matrix. In addition, we study the practically important problem of the rate of convergence to strong ergodicity for a nonhomogeneous Markov system (NHMS). In a second basic theorem, we provide conditions under which the rate of convergence to strong ergodicity is geometric. With these conditions, we in fact relax the basic assumption present in all previous studies, that is, that the inherent inhomogeneous Markov chain converges to a homogeneous Markov chain with a regular transition probability matrix geometrically fast. Finally, we provide an illustrative application from the area of manpower planning.

Keywords: strong ergodicity; nonhomogeneous Markov systems; rate of convergence

MSC: 60J10; 60J20

Citation: Vassiliou, P.-C.G. Strong Ergodicity in Nonhomogeneous Markov Systems with Chronological Order. *Mathematics* **2024**, *12*, 660. https://doi.org/10.3390/math12050660

Academic Editor: Michael Voskoglou

Received: 11 January 2024
Revised: 5 February 2024
Accepted: 18 February 2024
Published: 23 February 2024

1. Introductory Notes

Consider a stochastic system that has a population of members categorized in different states. Three types of movements are possible in the system. Firstly, movements of members are probable among the states of the system; secondly, members are leaving the system from the various states; and thirdly, new members are entering the system to replace leavers and to expand the population. When the various movements of the system are modeled by a nonhomogeneous Markov chain, we call such a system a nonhomogeneous Markov system (NHMS).

An NHMS is actually a generalization of the classical Markov chain where we have one particle moving among the states without the possibility of leaving the system and probably being replaced by another with possibly different characteristics. Of great importance is the vector of absolute probabilities which consists of the probabilities of the particle to be in any state of the Markov chain. On the other hand, in an NHMS, we have a population of particles categorized according to their characteristics in the various states. Particles are leaving the population from all the states, and new particles are entering the population to replace them and to expand the population. Of great importance is the vector of the expected relative population structure. Hence, the problems to be solved are a lot harder, and new strategies and tools are used other than the simple Markov chain. The roots of the motive for the development of the theory of NHMS, which was first introduced in Vassiliou [1], could be summarized in the use of Markov models in manpower systems. This started with the work of Young and Almond [2], Young [3,4], and Bartholomew [5,6], and it was extended in the works of Young and Vassiliou [7], Vassiliou [8,9], and McClean [10,11]. In the book by Vassiliou [12], one can find the evolution of the theory of NHMS and the large diversity of its developments in various directions, that is, NHMS in discrete and continuous time, stochastic control in NHMS, Laws of Large Numbers for NHMS, Perturbations theory, NHMS in a stochastic environment, Markov systems, and others.

In Section 5.4 of [12], there is a synopsis of real and potential applications of NHMS which illustrates the breadth of applications and some of the reasons why the entire theory is central to these processes. Work on manpower planning using results from NHMS and new areas has continued throughout the years up to nowadays, for example, Garg, et al. [13–15], Ugwugo and McClean [16], Vassiliadis [17,18], Georgiou, et al. [19], Guerry [20,21], Pollard [22], Esquivel, et al. [23–25].

In Section 2 of the present study, we define and describe the NHMS in discrete time and space in a compact but hopefully readable way for the reader who comes in contact for the first time with these processes. We also state the expected relative population structure in the various states as a function of the parameters of the population that could be estimated from the available data. In Section 3, we start with some basic definitions of concepts and mathematical tools, as well as useful known results that will be used in what follows. The novel part of this section is Theorem 1, where we study strong ergodicity for NHMS by relaxing the basic assumption present in all studies of strong ergodicity for NHMS. That is, we will not assume that the inherent inhomogeneous Markov chain converges as time goes to infinity to a homogeneous Markov chain with a regular (it consists of one communicating class of states, which is aperiodic) transition probability matrix or, equivalently, that the inhomogeneous Markov chain is strongly ergodic. In Section 3, we start with some basic definitions of concepts and mathematical tools, as well as useful known results that will be used in what follows. The novel part of this section is Theorem 4, where we prove under what conditions the rate of convergence of strong ergodicity in a NHMS is geometrically fast. This is an important question in NHMS due to its large practical value. In Theorem 4, we relax the basic assumption present in all studies of the rate of convergence to its asymptotic behavior for a NHMS. That is, we will not assume that the inherent inhomogeneous Markov chain converge as time goes to infinity to a homogeneous Markov chain with a regular transition probability matrix geometrically fast. Finally, in Section 5, we provide an illustrative application from the area of manpower planning.

2. The NHMS in Discrete Time and Space

Let a population consist of any kind of entities and let us denote by $T(t)$ for $t = 1, 2, \ldots$, the total number of memberships at time t, that is, at the end of the interval $(t - 1, t]$, which are being held by its members. At every point of time that a member leaves the population, the membership is being transferred to a new member. For example, members could be patients in a hospital and memberships the beds they occupy. It is assumed that the total number of memberships are known or the sequence $\{T(t)\}_{t=0}^{\infty}$ is a realization of a known stochastic process depending on the application. The memberships are distributed in a finite number of states and let $S = \{1, 2, \ldots, k\}$ be the state space. Important aspect of an NHMS (see Vassiliou [12], Section 5.2) is the *population structure*, that is, the vector of random variables

$$\mathbf{N}(t) = [N_1(t), N_2(t), \ldots, N_k(t)],$$

where $N_i(t)$ is the number of memberships in state i at time t. Also, very important is the *relative population structure*, which is the vector of random variables $\mathbf{q}(t) = \mathbf{N}(t)/T(t)$. We denote by $\mathbf{P}(t)$ the transition probability matrix of the internal transitions of the members of the population during the interval $(t - 1, t]$, that is, the t-th interval. Also, we have probable leavers from the states in S in every time interval t and let us denote by

$$\mathbf{p}_{k+1}(t) = [p_{1,k+1}(t), p_{2,k+1}(t), \ldots, p_{k,k+1}(t)],$$

where the state $k + 1$ represents the external environment. Finally, we have new entrants of memberships to the population in order to replace leavers and to expand the population. Let us collect the probabilities of allocation of the memberships to the various states in the t-th interval in the following stochastic vector

$$\mathbf{p}_0(t) = [p_{01}(t), p_{02}(t), \ldots, p_{0k}(t)],$$

where the state 0 represents the new entrants with their memberships waiting to be allocated in the various states. Note that in what follows we assume that $\Delta T(t) = T(t) - T(t-1) \geq 0$.

The transition probability matrix of the memberships $\mathbf{Q}(t)$ in the t-th interval can be shown (Vassiliou [12], p. 193), and it is given by

$$\mathbf{Q}(t) = \mathbf{P}(t) + \mathbf{p}_{k+1}(t)\mathbf{p}_0(t). \tag{1}$$

We call the inhomogeneous Markov chain defined uniquely by the sequence of transition probability matrices $\{\mathbf{Q}(t)\}_{t=0}^{\infty}$ the *embedded or inherent nonhomogeneous Markov chain of NHMS*. A population or any physical phenomenon that could be modeled in the above described way is defined to be a *nonhomogeneous Markov system*.

Now, as previously, we define the relative population structure for a population which started at time s and is at time t to be $\mathbf{q}(s,t) = \mathbf{N}(s,t)/T(t)$, where $\mathbf{N}(s,t)$ is the population structure for the population. It could be proved that (Georgiou and Vassiliou [26] and Vassiliou [12], p. 195)

$$\mathbb{E}[\mathbf{q}(s,t)] = \mathbb{E}[\mathbf{q}(s,t-1)]\alpha(t-1)\mathbf{Q}(t) + b(t-1)\mathbf{p}_0(t), \tag{2}$$

where s is the initial time and, therefore, $\mathbf{q}(s)$ is the initial relative population structure which is known and

$$\alpha(t-1) = \frac{T(t-1)}{T(t)} \quad \text{and} \quad b(t-1) = \frac{T(t) - T(t-1)}{T(t)}, \tag{3}$$

and where $\mathbf{q}(s,t)$ is the relative population structure at time t for the system that started with initial relative population structure $\mathbf{q}(s)$, which apparently is a random variable, and we denote by $\mathbb{E}[\mathbf{q}(s,t)]$ its expected value.

From (2), recursively, we obtain

$$\mathbb{E}[\mathbf{q}(s,t)] = \mathbf{q}(s)\frac{T(s)}{T(t)}\mathbf{Q}(s,t) + \frac{1}{T(t)}\sum_{\tau=1}^{t}\Delta T(s+t)\mathbf{p}_0(s+t)\mathbf{Q}(s+\tau,t), \tag{4}$$

where

$$\mathbf{Q}(s,t) = \mathbf{Q}(s+1)\mathbf{Q}(s+2)\ldots\mathbf{Q}(t).$$

3. Strong Ergodicity in NHMS with Chronological Order

The asymptotic behavior of NHMS and of nonhomogeneous Markov chains, as well as of homogeneous Markov chains, has been one of the central problems for many years, as can be seen in Refs. [12,27–31]. The asymptotic behavior of NHMS started with Vassiliou [1,32], and an updated evolution of these theorems and their variants could be found in Vassiliou [12]. In the present section, we provide and prove a basic theorem for strong ergodicity in NHMS when the transition probabilities matrices of the inherent Markov chain $\{\mathbf{Q}(t)\}_{t=0}^{\infty}$ are given in chronological order; that is, it is assumed that the time order of the elements of the sequence $\{\mathbf{Q}(t)\}_{t=0}^{\infty}$ is given and will not be changed. In Theorem 1 we relax the basic assumption present in all studies of asymptotic behavior for NHMS. That is, we will not assume that the inherent inhomogeneous Markov chain converge as time goes to infinity to a homogeneous Markov chain with a regular (it consists of one communicating class of states which is aperiodic) transition probability matrix or, equivalently, that the inhomogeneous Markov chain is strongly ergodic. We start with some basic definitions and results, which will be useful in what follows.

For what follows, we assume a complete probability space $(\Omega, \mathcal{F}, \mathbb{P})$ and consider an NHMS in discrete time and space. Therefore, we will not repeat this in every Definition, Lemma, Proposition, or Theorem.

Definition 1. *We say that the NHMS is strongly ergodic if and only if there exists a stochastic vector $\boldsymbol{\psi}$ such that*

$$\lim_{\nu \to \infty} \|\mathbb{E}[\mathbf{q}(t, t+\nu)] - \boldsymbol{\psi}\| = 0. \text{ for } t = 0, 1, 2, \ldots, \tag{5}$$

where $\|.\|$ from now on is any vector norm, except if it is otherwise stated.

Definition 2. *If $\mathbf{Q}$ is any finite stochastic matrix with state space $S = \{1, 2, \ldots, k\}$, then the Dobrushin ergodicity coefficient that is known is given by*

$$\tau_1(\mathbf{Q}) = \frac{1}{2} \max_{i,r} \sum_{j=1}^{k} \left| q_{ij} - q_{kj} \right|. \tag{6}$$

We now define another class of ergodicity coefficients which will be generated by different norms.

Definition 3 (Seneta [27]). *Let the set*

$$D^n = \left\{ \mathbf{x} : \mathbf{x} \in \mathbb{R}^n, \mathbf{x} \geq \mathbf{0}, \mathbf{x}\mathbf{1}^\top = 1 \right\},$$

and by $d(\ldots)$ any metric on this set. Then, the quantity

$$\tau(\mathbf{P}) = \sup_{\mathbf{x}, \mathbf{y} \in D^n} \frac{d(\mathbf{x}\mathbf{P}, \mathbf{y}\mathbf{P})}{d(\mathbf{x}, \mathbf{y})} \text{ with } \mathbf{x} \neq \mathbf{y}, \tag{7}$$

for any stochastic matrix, $\mathbf{P}$ is called a coefficient of ergodicity.

Remark 1. *All matrix norms on $\mathbb{R}^n$ provide an appropriate metric on D^n via $d(\mathbf{x}, \mathbf{y}) = \|\mathbf{x} - \mathbf{y}\|$. Then for any stochastic matrix $\mathbf{P}$ we get*

$$\tau_{\|.\|}(\mathbf{P}) = \sup_{\mathbf{x}, \mathbf{y} \in D^n} \frac{\|(\mathbf{x} - \mathbf{y})\mathbf{P}\|}{\|\mathbf{x} - \mathbf{y}\|} \text{ with } \mathbf{x} \neq \mathbf{y}. \tag{8}$$

We call $\tau_{\|.\|}(\mathbf{P})$ the coefficient of ergodicity induced by the norm $\|.\|$. It is proved that (8) can be written equivalently (Vassiliou [12], p. 118) as follows:

$$\tau_{\|.\|}(\mathbf{P}) = \sup_{\substack{\|z\|=1 \\ \mathbf{z}\mathbf{1}^\top=1}} \|\mathbf{z}\mathbf{P}\| \text{ over all } \mathbf{z} \in \mathbb{R}^n. \tag{9}$$

When the L_1 norm is used, that is, for an $n \times n$ matrix $\mathbf{A}$ with elements from $\mathbb{C}$, we obtain that

$$\|\mathbf{A}\|_1 = \sum_{i,j=1}^{n} |a_{ij}|, \tag{10}$$

then

$$\tau_1(\mathbf{P}) = \sup_{\substack{\|z\|_1=1 \\ \mathbf{z}\mathbf{1}^\top=1}} \|\mathbf{z}\mathbf{P}\|_1 \text{ over all } \mathbf{z} \in \mathbb{R}^n. \tag{11}$$

We now give the definitions of strong and weak ergodicity for a nonhomogeneous Markov chain:

Definition 4. *Consider an inhomogeneous Markov chain $\{X_t\}_{t=0}^{\infty}$ in discrete time and space. We say that $\{X_t\}_{t=0}^{\infty}$ with a sequence of transition probability matrices $\{\mathbf{Q}(t)\}_{t=0}^{\infty}$ is strongly ergodic if there exists a stable stochastic matrix $\mathbf{Q}$ such that for every t*

$$\lim_{\nu \to \infty} \|\mathbf{Q}(t, t+\nu) - \mathbf{Q}\| = 0. \tag{12}$$

If the limit is zero uniformly in t we say that $\{X_t\}_{t=0}^{\infty}$ or equivalently $\{\mathbf{Q}(t)\}_{t=0}^{\infty}$ is uniformly strongly ergodic.

Definition 5. *Consider an inhomogeneous Markov chain $\{X_t\}_{t=0}^{\infty}$ in discrete time and space. We say that $\{X_t\}_{t=0}^{\infty}$ with sequence of transition probability matrices $\{\mathbf{Q}(t)\}_{t=0}^{\infty}$ is weakly ergodic if for all states i, j, r, t*

$$q_{ir}(t, t+v) - q_{jr}(t, t+v) \to 0 \text{ as } v \to \infty. \tag{13}$$

Note that in (13), $\lim_{v \to \infty} q_{ij}(t, t+v)$ is not actually necessary to exist.

Remark 2. *Note that equivalently a non-homogeneous Markov chain is weakly ergodic if $\tau_1(\mathbf{Q}(t, t+v)) < 1$ for every t.*

We now state the following Lemma the proof of which exists in Vassiliou ([12], p. 119).

Lemma 1. *The coefficient of ergodicity generated by any metric as in (7) or induced by any vector norm on $\mathbb{R}^n$ has the following properties:*

(1) $\tau(\mathbf{P}_1\mathbf{P}_2) \leq \tau(\mathbf{P}_1)\tau(\mathbf{P}_2)$ *for any $\mathbf{P}_1, \mathbf{P}_2$ stochastic matrices.*
(2)   *For any stochastic matrix $\mathbf{P}$, $\tau(\mathbf{P}) = 0$ if and only if $\text{rank}(\mathbf{P}) = 1$.*

The following Lemma proof, which can be found in Paz [33], is useful in what follows:

Lemma 2. *If $\mathbf{P}$ is a stochastic matrix and if $\mathbf{R}$ is any real matrix such that $\mathbf{R}\mathbf{1}^{\top} = \mathbf{0}$ and in addition $\|\mathbf{R}\| < \infty$, then*

$$\|\mathbf{R}\mathbf{P}\| \leq \|\mathbf{R}\|\tau_1(\mathbf{P}).$$

We now state and prove one of the basic theorems of the present paper.

Theorem 1. *Let there be the complete probability space $(\Omega, \mathcal{F}, \mathbb{P})$ and consider an NHMS in discrete time and space. We assume that*

$$\lim_{t \to \infty} T(t) = T \text{ with } \Delta T(t) \geq 0. \tag{14}$$

Let $\{Y(t)\}_{t=0}^{\infty}$ be the inherent nonhomogeneous Markov chain of the movement of memberships. If $\{Y(t)\}_{t=0}^{\infty}$ is weakly ergodic with $\{\mathbf{Q}(t)\}_{t=0}^{\infty}$, the sequence of transition probabilities, and in addition, there exists a stochastic vector

$$\boldsymbol{\psi}(t) = [\psi_1(t), \psi_2(t), \dots, \psi_k(t)], \tag{15}$$

which is the left eigenvector of $\mathbf{Q}(t)$ for $t = 0, 1, 2, \dots$, that is

$$\boldsymbol{\psi}(t) = \boldsymbol{\psi}(t)\mathbf{Q}(t) \text{ for } t = 0, 1, 2, \dots, \tag{16}$$

and

$$\sum_{t=0}^{\infty} \|\boldsymbol{\psi}(t+1) - \boldsymbol{\psi}(t)\| < \infty, \tag{17}$$

then the NHMS is strongly ergodic.

Proof. From (17) we obtain that there exists a stochastic vector $\boldsymbol{\psi}$ such that

$$\lim_{t \to \infty} \|\boldsymbol{\psi}(t) - \boldsymbol{\psi}\| = 0. \tag{18}$$

From (16) and (18), we obtain that there exists a stochastic matrix $\mathbf{Q}$ such that

$$\lim_{t \to \infty} \|\mathbf{Q}(t) - \mathbf{Q}\| = 0 \text{ with } \mathbf{Q}\mathbf{1}^{\top} = \mathbf{1}^{\top}. \tag{19}$$

Denote by $\mathbf{\Psi}(t)$ to be the stable matrix with row the stochastic vector $\boldsymbol{\psi}(t)$ and $\mathbf{\Psi}$ the stable matrix with row $\boldsymbol{\psi}$. Then, we have

$$\|\mathbf{\Psi}(t+1) - \mathbf{\Psi}(t)\| = \|\boldsymbol{\psi}(t+1) - \boldsymbol{\psi}(t)\| \text{ and } \|\mathbf{\Psi}(t) - \mathbf{\Psi}\| = \|\boldsymbol{\psi}(t) - \boldsymbol{\psi}\|. \tag{20}$$

We now show that

$$\lim_{\nu \to \infty} \|\mathbf{Q}(t, t+\nu) - \mathbf{\Psi}\| = 0. \tag{21}$$

We have that

$$\mathbf{Q}(t, t+\nu) - \mathbf{\Psi} = \mathbf{Q}(t, t+r)\mathbf{Q}(t+r, t+\nu) - \mathbf{\Psi}(t+r)\mathbf{Q}(t+r, t+\nu)+$$

$$\mathbf{\Psi}(t+r)\mathbf{Q}(t+r, t+\nu) - \mathbf{\Psi}(t+\nu-1) + \mathbf{\Psi}(t+\nu-1) - \mathbf{\Psi}. \tag{22}$$

Taking norms on (22) we obtain that

$$\|\mathbf{Q}(t, t+\nu) - \mathbf{\Psi}\| \leq \|\mathbf{Q}(t, t+r)\mathbf{Q}(t+r, t+\nu) - \mathbf{\Psi}(t+r)\mathbf{Q}(t+r, t+\nu)\|$$

$$+\|\mathbf{\Psi}(t+r)\mathbf{Q}(t+r, t+\nu) - \mathbf{\Psi}(t+\nu-1)\| + \|\mathbf{\Psi}(t+\nu-1) - \mathbf{\Psi}\|. \tag{23}$$

We now have

$$N_1(t, \nu) = \|\mathbf{Q}(t, t+r)\mathbf{Q}(t+r, t+\nu) - \mathbf{\Psi}(t+r)\mathbf{Q}(t+r, t+\nu)\| \leq$$

$$\|[\mathbf{Q}(t, t+r) - \mathbf{\Psi}(t+r)]\mathbf{Q}(t+r, t+\nu)\| \leq (\text{Due to Lemma 2}) \leq$$

$$\|\mathbf{Q}(t, t+r) - \mathbf{\Psi}(t+r)\|\tau_1(\mathbf{Q}(t+r, t+\nu)) \leq 2\tau_1(\mathbf{Q}(t+r, t+\nu)), \tag{24}$$

where $\tau_1(\mathbf{Q}(t+r, t+\nu))$ is less than one due to weak ergodicity of $\{Y(t)\}_{t=0}^{\infty}$ the inherent nonhomogeneous Markov chain. Also for fixed r, we can always choose ν such that

$$N_1(t, \nu) \leq \frac{\varepsilon}{3}, \text{ with } \varepsilon > 0 \text{ a small number.} \tag{25}$$

We now have that

$$\mathbf{\Psi}(t+r)\mathbf{Q}(t+r, t+\nu) = (\text{due to Equation (16)}) =$$

$$[\mathbf{\Psi}(t+r) - \mathbf{\Psi}(t+r+1)]\mathbf{Q}(t+r+1, t+\nu)+$$

$$+\mathbf{\Psi}(t+r+1)\mathbf{Q}(t+r+1, t+\nu). \tag{26}$$

Now, similarly, we obtain

$$\mathbf{\Psi}(t+r+1)\mathbf{Q}(t+r+1, t+\nu) =$$

$$[\mathbf{\Psi}(t+r+1) - \mathbf{\Psi}(t+r+2)]\mathbf{Q}(t+r+2, t+\nu)$$

$$+\mathbf{\Psi}(t+r+2)\mathbf{Q}(t+r+2, t+\nu), \tag{27}$$

and using this equation recursively, we obtain

$$\mathbf{\Psi}(t+r)\mathbf{Q}(t+r, t+\nu) = \sum_{j=t+r+1}^{t+\nu-1} [\mathbf{\Psi}(j-1) - \mathbf{\Psi}(j)]\mathbf{Q}(j, t+\nu)$$

$$+\mathbf{\Psi}(t+\nu-1)\mathbf{Q}(t+\nu-1, t+\nu). \tag{28}$$

From condition (16), we obtain that

$$\boldsymbol{\Psi}(t+v-1) = \boldsymbol{\Psi}(t+v-1)\mathbf{Q}(t+v-1), \tag{29}$$

and

$$\boldsymbol{\psi}(t+v-1) = \boldsymbol{\psi}\boldsymbol{\Psi}(t+v-1). \tag{30}$$

Therefore, from (28)–(30), as well as, Lemma 2, we have that

$$N_2(t,v) = \|\boldsymbol{\Psi}(t+r)\mathbf{Q}(t+r,t+v) - \boldsymbol{\Psi}\boldsymbol{\Psi}(t+v-1)\| \leq$$

$$\left\|\sum_{j=t+r+1}^{t+v-1}[\boldsymbol{\Psi}(j-1) - \boldsymbol{\Psi}(j)]\tau_1(\mathbf{Q}(j,t+v))\right\| \leq$$

$$\sum_{j=t+r+1}^{t+v-1}\|\boldsymbol{\psi}(j-1) - \boldsymbol{\psi}(j)\|\tau_1(\mathbf{Q}(j,t+v)) \leq$$

$$\leq \quad (\tau_1(\mathbf{Q}(t+r,t+v)) < 1 \text{ due to weak ergodicity of } \{Y(t)\}_{t=0}^{\infty};$$
see also Remark 2).

$$\leq \sum_{j=t+r+1}^{t+v-1}\|\boldsymbol{\psi}(j-1) - \boldsymbol{\psi}(j)\| < \infty, \tag{31}$$

due to condition (17). Since $N_2(t,v) < \infty$ for every r and v and it is a sum of positive numbers, we have that its tail goes to zero. Hence, we could, for every $\varepsilon > 0$, fix $t+r$ such that $N_2(t,v) < \varepsilon/3$ for $v-1 \geq r$ and we can always take a v large enough so that $N_1(t,v) < \varepsilon/3$ and

$$N_3(t,v) = \|\boldsymbol{\Psi}(t+v-1) - \boldsymbol{\Psi}\| \leq \frac{\varepsilon}{3}, \tag{32}$$

therefore, we obtain that

$$\lim_{v\to\infty}\|\mathbf{Q}(t,t+v) - \boldsymbol{\Psi}\| = 0. \tag{33}$$

Now, from (4), we have that

$$\|\mathbb{E}[\mathbf{q}(t,t+v)] - \boldsymbol{\psi}\| =$$

$$\left\|\mathbf{q}(t)\frac{T(t)}{T(t+v)}\mathbf{Q}(t,t+v) + \frac{1}{T(t+v)}\sum_{\tau=t}^{t+v}\Delta T(\tau)\mathbf{Q}(\tau,t+v) - \boldsymbol{\psi}\right\| \leq$$

$$\frac{1}{T(t+v)}\left\|\mathbf{q}(t)T(t)\mathbf{Q}(t,t+v) + \sum_{\tau=t}^{t+v}\Delta T(\tau)\mathbf{Q}(\tau,t+v) - T(t+v)\boldsymbol{\psi}\right\| \leq$$

$$\|\mathbf{q}(t)T(t)\mathbf{Q}(t,t+v) - T(t)\boldsymbol{\psi}\| +$$

$$\left\|\sum_{\tau=t}^{t+v}\Delta T(\tau)\mathbf{p}_0(\tau)\mathbf{Q}(\tau,t+v) - [T(t+v) - T(t)]\boldsymbol{\psi}\right\|. \tag{34}$$

Now, we have

$$\mathcal{A}(t,t+v) = \|\mathbf{q}(t)T(t)\mathbf{Q}(t,t+v) - T(t)\boldsymbol{\psi}\| \leq$$

$$T(t)\|\mathbf{q}(t)\|\|\mathbf{Q}(t,t+v) - \boldsymbol{\psi}\|. \tag{35}$$

By fixing $\varepsilon > 0$, we can always find ν_0 such that

$$\mathcal{A}(t, t+\nu) \leq \frac{\varepsilon}{2} \text{ for } \nu \geq \nu_0. \tag{36}$$

$$\mathcal{B}(t, t+\nu) = \left\| \sum_{\tau=t}^{t+\nu} \Delta T(\tau) \mathbf{p}_0(\tau) \mathbf{Q}(\tau, t+\nu) - [T(t+\nu) - T(t)]\boldsymbol{\psi} \right\| =$$

$$= (\text{since } \mathbf{p}_0(\tau)\boldsymbol{\Psi} = \mathbf{p}_0\boldsymbol{\Psi} = \boldsymbol{\psi}) =$$

$$\left\| \sum_{\tau=t}^{t+\nu} \Delta T(\tau) \mathbf{p}_0(\tau) \mathbf{Q}(\tau, t+\nu) - \sum_{\tau=t}^{t+\nu} \Delta T(\tau) \mathbf{p}_0\boldsymbol{\Psi} \right\| =$$

$$\left\| \sum_{\tau=t}^{t+\nu} \Delta T(\tau) [\mathbf{p}_0(\tau) \mathbf{Q}(\tau, t+\nu) - \mathbf{p}_0\boldsymbol{\Psi}] \right\| \leq$$

$$\sum_{\tau=t}^{t+\nu} \Delta T(\tau) \| \mathbf{p}_0(\tau) \mathbf{Q}(\tau, t+\nu) - \mathbf{p}_0\boldsymbol{\Psi} \| \leq$$

$$\sum_{\tau=t}^{t+\nu} \Delta T(\tau) \| \mathbf{p}_0(\tau) [\mathbf{Q}(\tau, t+\nu) - \boldsymbol{\Psi}] + \mathbf{p}_0(\tau)\boldsymbol{\Psi} - \mathbf{p}_0\boldsymbol{\Psi} \|$$

$$\leq \sum_{\tau=t}^{t+\nu} \Delta T(\tau) \| \mathbf{Q}(\tau, t+\nu) - \boldsymbol{\Psi} \| \tag{37}$$

Now, for $\nu > \nu_0$ from (37), we have that

$$\mathcal{B}(t, t+\nu) \leq \sum_{\tau=t}^{t+\nu-\nu_0} \Delta T(\tau) \| \mathbf{Q}(\tau, t+\nu) - \boldsymbol{\Psi} \| + \sum_{\tau=t+\nu-\nu_0}^{t+\nu} \Delta T(\tau) \| \mathbf{Q}(\tau, t+\nu) - \boldsymbol{\Psi} \|$$

$$\leq \sum_{\tau=t}^{t+\nu-\nu_0} \Delta T(\tau)\frac{\varepsilon}{2} + 2|T(t+\nu) - T(t+\nu - \nu_0 + 1)|, \tag{38}$$

where the second part of (38) for $\nu \gg \nu_0$ is less than $\varepsilon/2$ due to condition (14). The first part is also for, $\nu \gg \nu_0$, less than $\varepsilon/2$ since $\Delta T(t) \to_{t\to\infty} 0$ due to condition (14). From (34) and (36), and a $\nu > \nu_0$ large enough ($\nu \gg \nu_0$), we easily see that

$$\| \mathbb{E}[\mathbf{q}(t, t+\nu)] - \boldsymbol{\psi} \| \leq \varepsilon \text{ for every } \nu \gg \nu_0,$$

hence, the NHMS is strongly ergodic. $\quad\square$

4. Rate of Convergence in NHMS with Chronological Order

An important question in nonhomogeneous Markov chains and NHMS, due to its very large practical value, is the rate of convergence to their asymptotic structure. In fact, it is important to find the necessary conditions under which the rate of convergence is geometric because then the value of the asymptotic result is greater. The roots of the study of finding conditions under which the rate of convergence is geometric for nonhomogeneous Markov chains are in Huang, et al. [34,35] and Seneta [31]. The study of the geometric rate of convergence in NHMS started in Vassiliou and Tsaklidis [36] and Georgiou and Vassiliou [26], and an updated evolution of these theorems and their variants could be found in Vassiliou [12]. The importance of answering this problem for practical purposes is apparent in Bartholomew [37] for the homogeneous Markov system, which is a very special case of an NHMS. In the present section, we provide and prove a basic theorem for the rate of convergence to strong ergodicity in NHMS when the transition probabilities matrices of the inherent Markov chain $\{\mathbf{Q}(t)\}_{t=0}^{\infty}$ are given in chronological order. In Theorem 4, we relax the basic assumption present in all studies of the rate of convergence to its asymptotic behavior for an NHMS. That is, we will not assume that the inherent

inhomogeneous Markov chain converges as time goes to infinity to a homogeneous Markov chain with a regular transition probability matrix geometrically fast. We start with some basic definitions and results which will be useful in what follows.

Definition 6. *We say that a sequence of matrices $\{\mathbf{A}_n\}_{n=0}^{\infty}$ converges with geometrical rate to a matrix $\mathbf{A}$ if there exists constants $c > 0$ and $0 < b < 1$ such that*

$$\|\mathbf{A}_n - \mathbf{A}\| \le cb^n \text{ for } n = 1, 2, \dots. \tag{39}$$

Lemma 3 (Vassiliou and Tsaklidis [36]). *The following statements are equivalent:*

(i)   *The sequence $\{\Delta T(t)\}_{t=0}^{\infty}$ converges to zero geometrically fast.*
(ii)   *The sequence $\{T(t)\}_{t=0}^{\infty}$ converges to T geometrically fast.*

Definition 7. (i) *A stochastic matrix $\mathbf{P}$ is called Markov if at least one column of $\mathbf{P}$ is entirely positive. Let $\mathcal{M}$ be the set of all Markov matrices. (ii) We say that the stochastic matrix $\mathbf{P} \in \mathcal{G}_2$ if (a) $\mathbf{P} \in \mathcal{G}_1$ the set of all regular matrices; (b) $\mathbf{QP} \in \mathcal{G}_1$ for any $\mathbf{Q} \in \mathcal{G}_1$. (iii) We say that the stochastic matrix $\mathbf{P} \in \mathcal{G}_3$ the set of all scrambling matrices if $\tau_{\|.\|_1}(\mathbf{P}) < 1$.*

Remark 3. *The distinction of the set $\mathcal{G}_2$ from all stochastic regular matrices is due to the fact that the product of two regular matrices is not always regular. In addition, the product of two nonregular stochastic matrices could be regular. A practical way to check if a stochastic matrix of small dimension is scrambling is the following: given any two rows i, j, there is at least one column k such that $p_{ik} > 0$ and $p_{jk} > 0$.*

Definition 8. *The incidence matrix of a stochastic matrix $\mathbf{P}$ is a matrix where in the positions of positive elements we put the number 1. Therefore, two stochastic matrices $\mathbf{P}$ and $\mathbf{Q}$ of the same dimension have the same incidence matrix if they have the positive elements in the same positions. Then, we write $\mathbf{P} \sim \mathbf{Q}$.*

We now state some known Lemmas and Theorems, the proofs of which can be found in Vassiliou ([12], p. 143).

Theorem 2. *For all stochastic matrices, we have $\mathcal{M} \subset \mathcal{G}_3 \subset \mathcal{G}_2 \subset \mathcal{G}_1$.*

Lemma 4. *If $\mathbf{P}(t, t + v) \in \mathcal{G}_1$ with $t \ge 0, n \ge 1$, then $\mathbf{P}(t, t + v) \in \mathcal{M}$ for $t + v \ge \mu$ the number of distinct incidence matrices corresponding to $\mathcal{G}_1$ with the same dimension as $\mathbf{P}(t, t + v)$.*

Theorem 3. *Let there be a complete probability space $(\Omega, \mathcal{F}, \mathbb{P})$, and consider a nonhomogeneous Markov chain $\{X_t\}_{t=0}^{\infty}$ in discrete time and space with a sequence of transition probabilities matrices $\{\mathbf{P}(t)\}_{t=0}^{\infty}$. If $\mathbf{P}(t) \in \mathcal{G}_2$ for every $t = 1, 2, \dots$ and*

$$\min_{i,j} \left(p_{ij}(t), 0 \right)^+ \ge \gamma > 0, \tag{40}$$

uniformly for all $t \ge 1$, then weak ergodicity obtains at a uniform geometric rate.

We now define the geometrically strongly ergodic NHMS, which is a central concept in the present section.

Definition 9. *Let there be a complete probability space $(\Omega, \mathcal{F}, \mathbb{P})$, and consider an NHMS in discrete time and space. We say that the NHMS is strongly ergodic if there exists a stochastic vector $\boldsymbol{\psi}$ and constants $c > 0$ and $0 < b < 1$ such that*

$$\|\mathbb{E}[\mathbf{q}(t, t + v) - \boldsymbol{\psi}]\| \le cb^v \text{ for } c > 0 \text{ and } 0 < b < 1.$$

We now state and prove the basic theorem of this section.

Theorem 4. *Let there be a complete probability space* $(\Omega, \mathcal{F}, \mathbb{P})$, *and consider an NHMS in discrete time and space. We assume that the total number of memberships is increasing* $(\Delta T(t) \geq 0)$, *and it converges geometrically fast to T. That is,*

$$\lim_{t \to \infty} T(t) = T \ \text{geometrically fast with } \Delta T(t) \geq 0. \tag{41}$$

Let $\{Y(t)\}_{t=0}^{\infty}$ *be the inherent nonhomogeneous Markov chain of the movement of memberships. If* $\{Y(t)\}_{t=0}^{\infty}$ *is weakly ergodic with* $\{\mathbf{Q}(t)\}_{t=0}^{\infty}$ *the sequence of transition probabilities to be such that*

$$(i) \ \mathbf{Q}(t) \in \mathcal{G}_2 \text{ for every } t = 1, 2, \ldots, \tag{42}$$

$$(ii) \ \min_{i,j} (q_{ij}(t), 0)^+ \geq \gamma > 0, \tag{43}$$

and if in addition there exists a stochastic vector

$$\boldsymbol{\psi}(t) = [\psi_1(t), \psi_2(t), \ldots, \psi_k(t)], \tag{44}$$

which is the left eigenvector for $t = 1, 2, \ldots$ *of* $\mathbf{Q}(t)$, *that is,*

$$\boldsymbol{\psi}(t) = \boldsymbol{\psi}(t)\mathbf{Q}(t) \text{ for every } t, \tag{45}$$

and in addition

$$\lim_{\nu \to \infty} \|\boldsymbol{\psi}(t + \nu) - \boldsymbol{\psi}(t + \nu - 1)\| = 0 \ \text{geometrically fast}, \tag{46}$$

then the NHMS is geometrically strongly ergodic.

Proof. In order to prove that the NHMS is geometrically strongly ergodic, we must show that the expected relative structure satisfies Definition 9.

From (46), we have that there exists a vector $\boldsymbol{\psi}$ and constants $c_1 > 0$ and $0 < b_1 < 1$ such that

$$\|\boldsymbol{\psi}(t + \nu) - \boldsymbol{\psi}\| \leq c_1 b_1^{t+\nu}. \tag{47}$$

We define $\boldsymbol{\Psi}(t)$ and $\boldsymbol{\Psi}$ as the stable matrices with rows $\boldsymbol{\psi}(t)$ and $\boldsymbol{\psi}$, respectively.

We now show that the inherent nonhomogeneous Markov chain $\{Y(t)\}_{t=0}^{\infty}$ is geometrically strongly ergodic. That is, we need to show that there exists constants $c_2 > 0$ and $0 < b_2 < 1$ such that

$$\|\mathbf{Q}(t, t + \nu) - \boldsymbol{\Psi}\| \leq c_2 b_2^{\nu} \text{ for every } t. \tag{48}$$

Let us denote by μ the number of distinct incidence matrices corresponding to $\mathcal{G}_1$ with the same dimension as $\mathbf{P}(t, t + \nu)$. Then, for $\nu > \mu$, we have that

$$\|\mathbf{Q}(t, t + \nu) - \boldsymbol{\Psi}\| \leq \|\mathbf{Q}(t, t + \mu)\mathbf{Q}(t + \mu, t + \nu) - \boldsymbol{\Psi}(t + \mu)\mathbf{Q}(t + \mu, t + \nu)\|$$

$$+ \|\boldsymbol{\Psi}(t + \mu)\mathbf{Q}(t + \mu, t + \nu) - \boldsymbol{\Psi}(t + \nu - 1)\| + \|\boldsymbol{\Psi}(t + \nu - 1) - \boldsymbol{\Psi}\|. \tag{49}$$

Now, we have that

$$\mathcal{D}_1(t, \nu, \mu) = \|\mathbf{Q}(t, t + \mu)\mathbf{Q}(t + \mu, t + \nu) - \boldsymbol{\Psi}(t + \mu)\mathbf{Q}(t + \mu, t + \nu)\|$$

$$\leq \|[\mathbf{Q}(t, t + \mu) - \boldsymbol{\Psi}(t + \mu)]\mathbf{Q}(t + \mu, t + \nu)\|$$

$$\leq \|\mathbf{Q}(t, t + \mu) - \boldsymbol{\Psi}(t + \mu)\|\tau_1(\mathbf{Q}(t + \mu, t + \nu))$$

$$\leq 2\tau_1(\mathbf{Q}(t + \mu, t + \nu)). \tag{50}$$

For arbitrary but fixed t and ν with $m\mu \leq \nu$ with m, the largest such integer from (50), we have that

$$\mathcal{D}_1(t, \nu, \mu) \leq 2\tau_1(\mathbf{Q}(t+\mu, t+2\mu))\tau_1(\mathbf{Q}(t+\mu, t+2\mu))\ldots$$

$$\tau_1(\mathbf{Q}(t+(m-1)\mu, t+m\mu))\tau_1(\mathbf{Q}(t+m\mu, t+\nu)). \tag{51}$$

Since $\mathbf{Q}(t) \in \mathcal{G}_2$ and by Lemma 4 we have that $\tau_1(\mathbf{Q}(t+(i-1)\mu, t+i\mu)) \in \mathcal{M}$ and

$$\tau_1(\mathbf{Q}(t+(i-1)\mu, t+i\mu)) \leq 1 - \gamma^\mu \text{ with } 0 < \gamma < 1 \text{ for } i = 2, 3, \ldots, m. \tag{52}$$

From the weak ergodicity of the inherent nonhomogeneous Markov chain $\{Y(t)\}_{t=0}^{\infty}$, we have that

$$\tau_1(\mathbf{Q}(t+m\mu, t+\nu)) \leq 1. \tag{53}$$

From (51)–(53), we arrive at

$$\mathcal{D}_1(t, \nu, \mu) \leq (1-\gamma^\mu)^m, \tag{54}$$

which as $\nu \to \infty$ goes to zero at a uniform geometric rate.

Following the steps of arriving at relation (31), we straightforwardly obtain that

$$\mathcal{D}_2(t, \nu, \mu) = \|\mathbf{\Psi}(t+\mu)\mathbf{Q}(t+\mu, t+\nu) - \mathbf{\Psi}(t+\nu-1)\|$$

$$\leq \|\mathbf{\Psi}(t+\mu)\mathbf{Q}(t+\mu, t+\nu) - \mathbf{\Psi}\mathbf{\Psi}(t+\nu-1)\|$$

$$\leq \sum_{j=t+\mu+1}^{t+\nu-1} \|\boldsymbol{\psi}(j-1) - \boldsymbol{\psi}(j)\|\tau_1(\mathbf{Q}(j, t+\nu)). \tag{55}$$

We now have the largest integer for m, such that $m\mu \leq \nu$

$$\tau_1(\mathbf{Q}(t+\mu, t+\nu)) = \tau_1(\mathbf{Q}(t+\mu, t+2\mu)\mathbf{Q}(t+2\mu, t+3\mu)\ldots$$

$$\mathbf{Q}(t+(m-1)\mu, t+m\mu)\mathbf{Q}(t+m\mu, t+\nu\mu))$$

$$= \text{(by Lemma 1)}$$

$$\leq \tau_1(\mathbf{Q}(t+\mu, t+2\mu))\tau_1(\mathbf{Q}(t+2\mu, t+3\mu))\ldots$$

$$\tau_1(t+(m-1)\mu, t+m\mu)\tau_1(t+m\mu, t+\nu) \leq$$

$$\leq \text{(using (52))}$$

$$\leq (1-\gamma^\mu)(1-\gamma^\mu)\ldots(1-\gamma^\mu) = (1-\gamma^\mu)^m. \tag{56}$$

From (56), we have that

$$\tau_1(\mathbf{Q}(t+\mu, t+\nu)) \to_{\nu\to\infty} 0 \text{ uniformly geometrically fast.} \tag{57}$$

From (55), we have that

$$\mathcal{D}_2(t, \nu, \mu) \leq \|\boldsymbol{\psi}(t+\mu-1) - \boldsymbol{\psi}(t+\mu)\|(1-\gamma^\mu)^m+$$

$$\|\boldsymbol{\psi}(t+\mu) - \boldsymbol{\psi}(t+\mu+1)\|(1-\gamma^\mu)^{m-1} + \|\boldsymbol{\psi}(t+\mu) - \boldsymbol{\psi}(t+\mu+1)\|(1-\gamma^\mu)^{m-1}$$

$$+\ldots+ \|\boldsymbol{\psi}(t+\mu(m-1)-1) - \boldsymbol{\psi}(t+\mu(m-1))\|(1-\gamma^\mu)$$

$$+\|\boldsymbol{\psi}(t+\mu m-1) - \boldsymbol{\psi}(t+\mu m)\|. \tag{58}$$

Now, we have that

$$(1-\gamma^\mu)^m \to_{m\to\infty} 0 \text{ geometrically fast,}$$

since $(1 - \gamma^\mu) < 1$. Also, from condition (46), we have that

$$\|\boldsymbol{\psi}(t + \mu m - 1) - \boldsymbol{\psi}(t + \mu m)\| \to_{m \to \infty} 0 \text{ geometrically fast,}$$

Therefore,

$$\mathcal{D}_2(t, \nu, \mu) \to_{\nu \to \infty} 0 \text{ geometrically fast.} \tag{59}$$

Now, from (49), (54) and (59), and condition (46), we easily have that

$$\|\mathbf{Q}(t, t + \nu) - \boldsymbol{\Psi}\| \to_{\nu \to \infty} 0 \text{ geometrically fast;} \tag{60}$$

hence, there exist constants $c > 0$ and $0 < b < 1$ such that

$$\|\mathbf{Q}(t, t + \nu) - \boldsymbol{\Psi}\| \le cb^\nu \text{ for every } t, \text{ and } c > 0, 0 < b < 1. \tag{61}$$

What remains, according to Definition 9, is to show that the expected relative population structure $\mathbb{E}[\mathbf{q}(t, t + \nu)]$ converges for every t to the vector $\boldsymbol{\psi}$ as ν goes to infinity geometrically fast.

From (35), we have that

$$\mathcal{A}(t, t + \nu) = \|\mathbf{q}(t)T(t)\mathbf{Q}(t, t + \nu) - T(t)\boldsymbol{\psi}\| \le$$

$$T(t)\|\mathbf{q}(t)\|\|\mathbf{Q}(t, t + \nu) - \boldsymbol{\psi}\|. \tag{62}$$

From (61), we have that

$$\mathcal{A}(t, t + \nu) \le T(t)\|\mathbf{q}(t)\|\|\mathbf{Q}(t, t + \nu) - \boldsymbol{\psi}\| \le c_1 b^\nu, \tag{63}$$

with $c_1 > 0$ and $0 < b < 1$.

From Lemma 3, we have that since $T(t)$ converges geometrically fast to T, then $\Delta T(t)$ converges geometrically fast to zero. Hence,

$$\Delta T(t) \le c_2 b_2^t \text{ with } c_2 > 0 \text{ and } 0 < b_2 < 1. \tag{64}$$

Now, from (37), we have that

$$\mathcal{B}(t, t + \nu) \le \sum_{\tau=t}^{t+\nu} \Delta T(\tau)\|\mathbf{Q}(\tau, t + \nu) - \boldsymbol{\Psi}\|. \tag{65}$$

With no loss of generality, we may assume that $b > b_2$, and then, from (63) and (64), we have that

$$\mathcal{B}(t, t + \nu) \le c_1 c_2 \sum_{\tau=t}^{t+\nu} \left(\frac{b_2}{b}\right)^\tau b^{t+\nu} = c_3 b^{t+\nu} \sum_{\tau=t}^{t+\nu} \left(\frac{b_2}{b}\right)^\tau$$

$$\le c_3 b^{t+\nu} \left(1 - \frac{b_2}{b}\right)^\nu \left(1 - \frac{b_2}{b}\right)^{-1} \le c_4 b_3^\nu. \tag{66}$$

From (63) and (66), we easily arrive at the proof of the theorem. $\square$

5. An Illustrative Application

We will illustrate the results in the previous section with an example from a population of manpower. To possibly better visualize, the reader may have in mind a University system with three grades. That is, grade one is those with the level of Professors, grade two belongs to the Associate Professors, and finally, in grade three, there are the Assistant Professors. The University has a plan for funding $T(t)$ for $t = 0, 1, 2, \ldots$ memberships for the next few years. When a member of staff is leaving, their membership remains with the University, that is, the funding of their position is not lost but remains, and the University could go

on to appoint someone at any grade. The external environment to which the leavers go and their membership is retained by the University and it is the population of members of academic staff from Universities almost all over the world, as practices have shown. Hence, it is from this external environment that the new members will obtain the memberships available from the organization of the University.

A fundamental question for the practitioner is the estimation of the transition probabilities from the historical records. The way to estimate the transition probabilities of the memberships is a small extension of the way it is performed in manpower planning, which is well documented in Bartholomew [38]. Another quite similar problem is that of the competing risk model in the medical literature, as it was presented by Kalbfleisch and Prentice ([39], Chapter 8), Lee [40], and Cox and Oakes [41]. Also, similar problems exist in the study of reliability models and various actuarial studies as discussed in Elandt–Johnson and Johnson ([42], Chapter 7).

Now define by

$N_{ij}(t)$: the number of memberships moving from grade i to grade j in the t-th interval.

$N_i(t-1)$: the number of memberships in state i at the beginning of the t-th interval.

Assume that the number of years available in the historical data of the University is n. Then, the maximum likelihood estimate of the probability $q_{ij}(t)$ is the following:

$$\hat{q}_{ij}(t) = \frac{N_{ij}(t)}{N_i(t-1)} \text{ for any } t. \tag{67}$$

It is an apparent advantage that the probabilities $\hat{q}_{ij}(t)$ are separately estimated for every (i,j). In this way, the number of years of historical records necessary are significantly reduced. At this point, it is useful to test the hypothesis that the probabilities $\hat{q}_{ij}(t)$ are indeed functions of time. That is,

$$H_0: \hat{q}_{ij}(t) = \hat{q}_{ij} \text{ for every } t. \tag{68}$$

Considering the flow of memberships which move from grade i to grade j as a multinomial random variable, then (see Andersen and Goodman [43]) hypothesis (68) is tested by the statistic:

$$\chi^2(i,j) = \sum_{t=1}^{n} N_i(t-1) \frac{(\hat{q}_{ij}(t) - \hat{q}_{ij})}{\hat{q}_{ij}}, \tag{69}$$

where

$$\hat{q}_{ij} = \frac{\sum_{t=0}^{n} N_{ij}(t)}{\sum_{t=1}^{n} N_i(t-1)}, \tag{70}$$

is the maximum likelihood estimate under the null hypothesis and is chi-square distributed with $n-1$ degrees of freedom.

Now, let that the $\chi^2(i,j)$ showed that the probabilities $\hat{q}_{ij}(t)$ are functions of time. Then, there is a need to predict their values as functions of time. For a specific pair (i,j), let that

$$x_{1ij}(t), x_{2ij}(t), \ldots, x_{mij}(t), \tag{71}$$

are probable covariates for the specific application. Then, logistic stepwise regression is an appropriate model for these probabilities. Let us define by

$$\log it(x) = \log\left(\frac{x}{1-x}\right), \tag{72}$$

then we obtain

$$\log it(\hat{q}_{ij}(t)) = a_0 + a_1 x_{1ij}(t) + a_2 x_{2ij}(t) + \ldots + a_m x_{mij}(t). \tag{73}$$

Now, it is obvious that stepwise regression will show what are the important covariates to predict $\hat{q}_{ij}(t)$ (see also Vassiliou [44]).

Let that following the above-described steps, we ended with the matrix:

$$\mathbf{Q}(t) = \begin{pmatrix} 0.2 + \frac{1}{4+t^3} & 0.8 - \frac{1}{4+t^3} & 0 \\ 0.3 & 0.5 - \frac{1}{8+t^4} & 0.2 + \frac{1}{8+t^4} \\ 0 & 0.2 + \frac{2}{10+t^8} & 0.8 - \frac{2}{10+t^8} \end{pmatrix} \text{ for } t = 1,2,\dots. \tag{74}$$

The total population of memberships was planned according to the following sequence

$$T(0) = 400, \ T(1) = 430, \ T(2) = 450,$$

$$T(3) = 475, \ T(4) = 500 \text{ and } T(t) = 500 \text{ for } t = 5,6,\dots, \tag{75}$$

that is, the total number of memberships converge geometrically fast with $\Delta T(t) \geq 0$, satisfying the condition (41) in Theorem 4.

It is not difficult to check that the sequence (74) satisfies condition (42), that is, $\mathbf{Q}(t) \in \mathcal{G}_2$ for $t = 1,2,\dots$. Also, it satisfies condition (43) since

$$\min_{i,j}\left(q_{ij}(t),0\right)^+ \geq \gamma = 0.2 > 0. \tag{76}$$

For the sequence of transition probability matrices for the memberships (74), we find for the condition (45) that the vectors $\boldsymbol{\psi}(t)$ that satisfy it were the following:

$$\text{For } t = 1 \ \ \boldsymbol{\psi}(1) = [0.216, 0.432, 0.352], \tag{77}$$

$$\text{for } t = 2 \ \ \boldsymbol{\psi}(2) = [0.166, 0.390, 0.444], \tag{78}$$

$$\text{for } t = 3 \ \ \boldsymbol{\psi}(3) = [0.164, 0.416, 0.420], \tag{79}$$

$$\text{for } t = 4 \ \ \boldsymbol{\psi}(4) = [0.164, 0.424, 0.412], \tag{80}$$

$$\text{for } t = 5 \ \ \boldsymbol{\psi}(5) = [0.163, 0.426, 0.411], \tag{81}$$

$$\text{for } t = 6 \ \ \boldsymbol{\psi}(6) = [0.163, 0.427, 0.410], \tag{82}$$

$$\text{for } t = 7 \ \ \boldsymbol{\psi}(7) = [0.163, 0.427, 0.410]. \tag{83}$$

We observe that already for t = 6 in (82) and (83) we have convergence of $\boldsymbol{\psi}(t)$ which satisfies condition (45) of Theorem 4, that is the convergence is geometrically fast. Hence, we conclude that

$$\boldsymbol{\psi} = [0.16, 0.43, 0.41].$$

Calculating using the transition probability matrices given in (74) the matrix product $\mathbf{Q}(t, t + v)$ we find that for $v \geq 9$ it converges to $\boldsymbol{\psi} = [0.16, 0.43, 0.41]$. Hence, we conclude that $\mathbf{Q}(t, t + v)$ as $v \to \infty$ converges geometrically fast as was expected from Theorem 4 relation (48).

Now, given the convergence of $\mathbf{Q}(t, t + v)$ as $v \to \infty$ it is straight forward to find from Equation (2) applying it recursively or equivalently from Theorem 1 that $\mathbb{E}[\mathbf{q}(s, t)]$ converges geometrically fast (in fact in 9 time steps) to

$$\boldsymbol{\psi} = [0.16, 0.43, 0.41].$$

Hence, the NHMS is geometrically strongly ergodic.

6. Conclusions and Further Research

Two fundamental theorems have been founded that relax previous assumptions and provide conditions for ergodicity and for the convergence rate of the relative population structure in an NHMS. More specifically, in Theorem 1 the strong ergodicity of an NHMS is studied without assuming the convergence of the inherent inhomogeneous Markov chain to infinity to a homogeneous Markov chain with a regular transition probability matrix. In Theorem 4, it is proved under what conditions the rate of convergence of strong ergodicity in a NHMS is geometrically fast. This is done by departing from the basic assumption in which the inherent inhomogeneous Markov chain converges after a large time to a homogeneous Markov chain with a regular transition probability matrix. The proved theorems are expanding the understanding of the dynamics and behavior of an NHMS. The paper concludes with an illustrative application from the field of Manpower Planning, showcasing the vital practical relevance of the discussed concepts. Further research paths may include the relaxation of relative assumptions in the many variant models of the NHMS in diverse populations. Of particular interest may be the theorems of Laws of Large numbers in an NHMS.

Funding: This research received no external funding.

Data Availability Statement: No new data were created or analyzed in this study. Data sharing is not applicable to this article.

Conflicts of Interest: The author declare no conflict of interest.

References

1. Vassiliou, P.-C.G. Asymptotic behavior of Markov systems. *J. Appl. Prob.* **1982**, *19*, 433–438. [CrossRef]
2. Young, A.; Almond, G. Predicting distributions of staff. *Comput. J.* **1961**, *3*, 144–153. [CrossRef]
3. Young, A. Models for planning recruitment and promotion of staff. *Brit. J. Indust. Rel.* **1965**, *3*, 301–310. [CrossRef]
4. Young, A. Demographic and ecological models for manpower planning. In *Aspects of Manpower Planning*; Bartholomew, D.J., Morris, B.R., Eds.; English University Press: London, UK, 1971.
5. Bartholomew, D.J. A multistage renewal processes. *J. R. Stat. Soc. B* **1963**, *25*, 150–168.
6. Bartholomew, D.J. *Stochastic Models for Social Processes*, 1st ed.; Wiley: New York, NY, USA, 1967.
7. Young, A.; Vassiliou, P.-C.G. A non-linear model on the promotion of staff. *J. R. Stat. Soc. A* **1974**, *138*, 584–595. [CrossRef]
8. Vassiliou, P.-C.G. A Markov model for wastage in manpower systems. *Oper. Res. Quart.* **1976**, *27*, 57–70. [CrossRef]
9. Vassiliou, P.-C.G. A high order non-linear Markovian model for promotion in manpower systems. *J. R. Stat. Soc. A* **1978**, *141*, 86–94. [CrossRef]
10. McClean, S.I. A continuous-time population model with Poisson recruitment. *J. Appl. Prob.* **1976**, *13*, 348–354. [CrossRef]
11. McClean, S.I. Continuous-time stochastic models for multigrade population. *J. Appl. Prob.* **1978**, *15*, 26–37. [CrossRef]
12. Vassiliou, P.-C.G. *Non-Homogeneous Markov Chains and Systems, Theory and Applications*; Chapman and Hall: London, UK; CRC Press: Boca Raton, FL, USA, 2023.
13. Garg, L.; McClean, S.I.; Meenan, B.; Millard, P. A non-homogeneous discrete time Markov model for admission scheduling and resource planning in a cost capacity constaint healthcare system. *Health Care Manag. Sci.* **2010**, *13*, 155–169. [CrossRef]
14. Garg, L.; McClean, S.I.; Meenan, B.; Millard, P. Non-homogeneous Markov models for sequential pattern mining of healthcare data. *Ima J. Manag. Math.* **2009**, *20*, 327–344. [CrossRef]
15. Garg, L.; McClean, S.I.; Meenan, B.; Millard, P. Phase-Type survival trees and mixed distribution syrvival trees for clustering patient's hospital length of stay. *Informatika* **2011**, *22*, 57–72.
16. Ugwuogo, F.I.; McClean, S.I. Modelling heterogeneity in manpower systems: A review. *Appl. Stoch. Models Bus. Ind.* **2000**, *2*, 99–110. [CrossRef]
17. Vassiliadis, G. Transient analysis of the M/M/k/N/N queue using a continuous time homogeneous Markov chain system with finite state capacity. *Commun. Stat. Theory Methods* **2014**, *43*, 1548–1562. [CrossRef]
18. Vassiliadis, G. Transient analysis of a finite source discrete-time queueing system using homogeneous Markov system with state size capacities. *Commun. Stat. Theory Methods* **2014**, *45*, 1403–1423. [CrossRef]
19. Georgiou, A.C.; Thanassoulis, E.; Papdopoulou, A. Using data envelopment analysis in markovian decision making. *Eur. J. Oper. Res.* **2022**, *298*, 276–292. [CrossRef]
20. Guerry, M.A. On the evolution of stock vectors in a deterministic integer-valued Markov system. *Linear Algebra Its Appl.* **2008**, *429*, 1944–1953. [CrossRef]

21. Guerry, M.A. Some results on the embeddable problem for discrete time Markov models in manpower planning. *Commun. Stat. Theory Methods* **2014**, *43*, 1575–1584. [CrossRef]
22. Pollard, B.S. Open Markov processes: A compositional perspective on a non-equilibrium steady state in biology. *Entropy* **2016**, *18*, 140. [CrossRef]
23. Esquivel, M.L.; Fernandes, J.M.; Guerriero, G.R. On the evolution and asymptotic analysis of open Markov populations: Application to consumption credit. *Stoch. Model.* **2014**, *30*, 365–389. [CrossRef]
24. Esquivel, M.L.; Guerriero, G.R.; Fernandes, J.M. Open Markov chain scheme models fed by second order stationary and non stationary processes. *Revstat-Stat. J.* **2017**, *15*, 277.
25. Esquivel, M.L.; Krasil, N.P.; Guerriero, G.R. Open type population models: From discrete to continuous time. *Mathematics* **2021**, *9*, 1496. [CrossRef]
26. Georgiou, A.C.; Vassiliou, P.-C.G. Periodicity of asymptotically attainable stuctures in non-homogeneous Markov systems. *Linear Algebra Its Appl.* **1992**, *176*, 137–174. [CrossRef]
27. Seneta, E. *Non-Negative Matrices and Markov Chains*, 2nd ed.; Springer: Berlin/Heidelberg, Germany, 1981.
28. Brémaud, P. Markov Chains. In *Gibbs Fields, Monte Carlo Simulation and Queues*, 2nd ed.; Springer: Berlin/Heidelberg, Germany, 2020.
29. Tweedie, R.L. Sufficient conditions for ergodicity and recurrence of Markov chains on a general state space. *Stoch. Proc. Appl.* **1975**, *3*, 385–403. [CrossRef]
30. Mitrophanov, A.Y. Sensitivity and convergence of uniformly ergodic Markov chains. *J. Appl. Prob.* **2005**, *42*, 1003–1014. [CrossRef]
31. Seneta, E. Inhomogeneous Markov chains and Ergodicity Coefficients: John Hajnal (1924–2008). *Commun. Stat. Theory Methods* **2014**, *43*, 1575–1584. [CrossRef]
32. Vassiliou, P.-C.G. On the limiting behavior of a non-homogeneous Markov model in manpower systems. *Biometrika* **1981**, *68*, 557–561.
33. Paz, A. *Introduction to Probabilistic Automata*; Academic Press: Cambridge, MA, USA, 1971.
34. Huang, C.; Isaacson, D.; Vinograde, B. The rate of convergence of certain non-homogeneous Markov chains. *Zeitsh. Wahrsch. Geb.* **1976**, *35*, 141–146. [CrossRef]
35. Huang, C.; Isaacson, D. Ergodicity using mean visit times. *J. London Math. Soc.* **1976**, *14*, 570–576. [CrossRef]
36. Vassiliou, P.-C.G.; Tsaklidis, G. The rate of convergence of the vector of variances and covariances in non-homogeneous Markov systems. *J. Appl. Prob.* **1989**, *27*, 776–783. [CrossRef]
37. Bartholomew, D.J. *Stochastic Models for Social Processes*, 3rd ed.; Wiley: New York, NY, USA, 1981.
38. Bartholomew, D.J.; Forbes, A.F.; McClean, S. *Statistical Techniques for Manpower Planning*; John Wiley: Chichester, UK, 1991.
39. Kalbfleisch, J.D.; Prentice, R.L. *The Statistical Analysis of Failure Time Data*, 2nd ed.; John Wiley: New York, NY, USA, 2002.
40. Lee, E.T. *Statistical Methods for Survival Data Analysis*, 2nd ed.; John Wiley: New York, NY, USA, 1992.
41. Cox, D.R.; Oakes, D. *Analysis of Survival Data*; Chapman and Hall: London, UK, 1984.
42. Elandt-Johnson, R.C.; Johnson, N.L. *Survival Models and Data Analysis*; John Wiley: New York, NY, USA, 1980.
43. Anderson, T.W.; Goodman, L.A. Statistical Inference about Markov chains. *Ann. Math. Statist.* **1957**, *28*, 89–110. [CrossRef]
44. Vasileiou, A.; Vassiliou, P.-C.G. An inhomogeneous semi-Markov model for the term structure of credit risk spreads. *Adv. Appl. Prob.* **2006**, *38*, 171–198. [CrossRef]

mathematics

MDPI

Article

Estimation–Calibration of Continuous-Time Non-Homogeneous Markov Chains with Finite State Space

Manuel L. Esquível [1,*], **Nadezhda P. Krasii** [2] and **Gracinda R. Guerreiro** [1]

[1] Department of Mathematics, NOVA FCT, and NOVA Math, Universidade Nova de Lisboa, Quinta da Torre, 2829-516 Monte de Caparica, Portugal; grg@fct.unl.pt

[2] Department of Higher Mathematics, Don State Technical University, Gagarin Square 1, Rostov-on-Don 344000, Russia; spu-46.3@donstu.ru

* Correspondence: mle@fct.unl.pt; Tel.: +351-212-948-388

Abstract: We propose a method for fitting transition intensities to a sufficiently large set of trajectories of a continuous-time non-homogeneous Markov chain with a finite state space. Starting with simulated data computed with Gompertz–Makeham transition intensities, we apply the proposed method to fit piecewise linear intensities and then compare the transition probabilities corresponding to both the Gompertz–Makeham transition intensities and the fitted piecewise linear intensities; the main comparison result is that the order of magnitude of the average fitting error per unit time—chosen as a year—is always less than 1%, thus validating the methodology proposed.

Keywords: Markov chains; non homogeneous; continuous time; regime switching processes; estimation; calibration; health insurance; long-term care

MSC: 60J27; 65C40; 60J28; 62M05

Citation: Esquível, M.L.; Krasii, N.P.; Guerreiro, G.R. Estimation–Calibration of Continuous-Time Non-Homogeneous Markov Chains with Finite State Space. *Mathematics* 2024, *12*, 668. https://doi.org/10.3390/math12050668

Academic Editors: Panagiotis-Christos Vassiliou and Andreas C. Georgiou

Received: 2 January 2024
Revised: 20 February 2024
Accepted: 21 February 2024
Published: 24 February 2024

1. Introduction with a Literature Review

This study follows on from a previous article (see [1]) in which we developed a way to calibrate a Markov chain model in continuous time using data obtained from Portuguese National Network of Continuing Care. The calibration methodology used in that work, although very effective, is not completely satisfactory as it rests on a series of ad hoc processes with reduced guarantees of reproducibility and robustness.

In the present work, we intend to develop simpler and more robust means of estimating and calibrating intensities for non-homogenous continuous-time Markov chains (see [2] for a recent introduction to these processes and their applications). For this purpose, we first develop the two following subjects. The first subject deals with Markov chain regime switching achieved by considering an abrupt change in the intensities, for instance, having intensities with jumps. The second subject complements the first one if we suppose that we replace regular intensities by irregular ones—like piecewise linear—in principle with more easily estimable parameters; we study the effect on the transition probabilities of a replacement of the original intensities by sufficiently close alternative intensities. These two different streams of ideas are connected not only to one another but also to the estimation–calibration techniques to be studied.

We now present a review of the literature, mainly covering the subject of estimation and calibration of continuous-time non-homogeneous Markov chains with finite state space relevant for health insurance and long-term care (LTC), existing results for the Kolmogorov ordinary differential equations, as well as works where one can find some similarities between non-homogeneous Markov chains and semi-Markov jump linear systems.

A consecrated approach in the study of continuous-time Markov chains for applications, namely, in the multiple state models—the transition intensity approach (see [3] p. 126 or [4] p. 189)—consists of giving the intensities, solving the Kolmogorov ODE and using

the transition probabilities obtained for computations. The intensities should be estimated from the data. This is the approach that we assume in this work.

The statistics of homogeneous Markov chains has already received several very thorough analyses. A very well organised and complete one is provided in Billingsley's monograph [5] that treats, in the first part, the discrete-time homogeneous Markov chains and in the second part the continuous-time chains by resorting to the canonical embedded process. A companion reference is article [6] that provides a very complete set of references on the subject until 1961. In order to obtain consistency and asymptotic normality results for the maximum likelihood estimators, the author assumes, as usual, stringent regularity assumptions in particular on the intensities.

The statistics of Markov chain models for multiple state models is usually performed under simplifying assumptions on the model. For instance, in [7], the intensities are supposed to be constant in selected time intervals, and observations are chosen for which the exact age belongs to a given selected time interval. Another set of simplifying assumptions is proposed in [8] (pp. 126–128); at first, the transition functions are approximated in a one-year period interval by a one-sided Stieltjes interval. and then, using these approximations the transition intensities, with adequate analytical properties, are obtained as a result of a minimisation of a sum of squares objective function. The method proposed in [4] (pp. 147–169) has also two steps; in the first step, the transitions intensities are supposed to be constant in one-year period intervals and are estimated with a maximum likelihood approach. Subsequently, there is a second step of denominated graduation—a method generally described in [9]—that fits parameters of exponential functional intensity using generalised linear models. The method is applied to real data, and it becomes clear that several adequate particular ad hoc assumptions in the method are inevitable in order to deal with specific properties of the data. The simplifying assumption of transition intensities constant in each one-year period is also taken in [10] (pp. 683–690), where a detailed treatment of an example is also presented; in a commentary, the authors also refer the need of a graduated procedure to obtain the final intensities.

The excellent review work [11] illustrates the manner in which multiple-state Markov and semi-Markov models can be used for the actuarial modelling of health insurance policies. The bivariate character of the Markov process naturally associated with a semi-Markov model is useful whenever the durational effects are not negligible but in contrast is technically much more difficult to handle than the univariate Markov process. Considering discrete-time semi-Markov processes, the authors in [12] study semi-Markov jump linear systems—which is a hybrid dynamical system that consists of a family of subsystem modes and a semi-Markov process that orchestrates switching between them—with bounded sojourn times, in order to provide sufficient criteria for the stability and stabilisation problems with respect to a specified approximation error. The companion work [13] enlarges the previous model by considering delay, and by means of a novel Lyapunov–Krasovskill functional and using the probability structure of semi-Markov switching signal, the sufficient stability conditions for the considered systems are presented in terms of a set of linear matrix inequalities and a proper semi-Markov switching condition. It now becomes clear that a natural extension of our work would be to consider semi-Markov models instead of Markov chains.

The estimation–calibration methodology we propose in this work is applied to continuous piecewise linear intensities. Since in health insurance and long-term-care multiple-state models, the intensities are usually of Gompertz–Makeham type (see [4] pp. 21, 24, 101), we previously showed that the distance between two transition probability matrices—in the sense of some matrix norm—is bounded by the same distance between the correspondent intensity matrices, thus showing that the Gompertz–Makeham functional form for the intensities is not really necessary.

We now refer to some works with contributions to the topic of estimation calibration of multiple state models, also called multi-state models. The work [14] proposes a review of multiple-state models via continuous-time Markov chains, signalling the usual approach for the non-homogeneous case of considering piecewise constant intensities. It is at first reading, a most interesting review paper with applications to real data comparing different model analyses. Ref. [15] deals with a nonparametric approach to statistical inference in non-homogeneous Markov processes based on counting processes for transition intensities—namely using the so-called Nelson–Aalen estimator or the kernel smoothing estimator of Ramlau–Ahnsen—presenting a case study using this methodology. Ref. [16] can be seen as a continuation of the previously referred to work. Besides reviewing methods for non-parametric estimation of transition probabilities, the authors study the case where semi-parametric Cox type regression models are specified for the transition intensities whenever there is specification of the development of the time-dependent covariates. An illustration of the methods with data from a randomised clinical trial in patients with liver cirrhosis is also presented. Ref. [17] is an ancillary reference for graduating the transition intensities in a multiple-state model for permanent health insurance applications based on generalised linear models—with a random component based on independent Poisson response variables—in the case that the intensities are supposed to depend on some secondary variables. The work in [18] follows the preceding paper in the main intent of proposing a graduation method for the transition intensities of a non-homogeneous continuous-time Markov chain model. In the work [19], a comparison between a discrete-time and continuous-time homogeneous Markov chain models is presented in order to assess the effect of unevenly spaced observations. Since the authors want to incorporate covariates in the model, this study also deals with a series of multinomial logit regressions for the discrete-time model and proportional hazard regressions for the covariates through transition intensity functions for the continuous-time model. Ref. [20] is a simplified multiple-state model that develops a generic estimation method for calculating the transition probabilities in a one-year multiple-state model based on disability prevalence rates; multiple logistic regression models are employed to estimate disability prevalence rates and the one-year recovery rates. In doing so, the authors assume three conditions of the ratio between the mortality rate of inactive and active people—and several other conditions used in the literature—that allow the necessary computations in the case treated which concerns cross-sectional data measuring the disabled status of an individual at one point in time. The work [21] introduces a semi-parametric model that employs a logit function to capture the treatment intensities across two groups, aiming to estimate transition intensity rates within the framework of an illness–death model. Parameter estimation is conducted through an EM algorithm coupled with profile likelihood. Simulation studies presented in the text indicate that the proposed method is straightforward to apply and produces results comparable to those of the parametric model. The study [22] examines the impact of part-time and full-time employment on health by employing a Markov three state model—using piecewise constant forces, where the transition intensities are graduated using generalised linear models and assumed, at the start, to be equal per age level—and generalised linear models to refine the initial raw rates. Integration of the corresponding Chapman–Kolmogorov equations allow us to derive a comprehensive solution. As an application of the model, the effectiveness of a partial early-retirement incentive in the Netherlands is evaluated. The refined rates obtained indicate that working part-time does not necessarily correlate with improved health among the elderly.

In the present work, we also establish a result with regime-switching Markov chains exploring the possibility of having, in the whole time period under study, intensities with several different functional forms (linear, exponential, etc.) in different subintervals of the whole time period. Our study of ordinary differential Equations (ODE) with regimes that began with the work [23] and was exploited in [24] is based on general results of existence and uniqueness of solutions of ODE—due to Caratheodory and Wintner for existence and Osgood for uniqueness, among others—with a non-regular second member. In the case of

a second member of the non-regular ODE, the regimes appear clearly in the solutions of the Kolmogorov equations due, for example, to possible discontinuities in the entries of the intensity matrix.

The general theory of existence of solutions of Kolmogorov equations is exhaustively treated in the works of Feinberg, Shiryaev and Mandala (see [25–27]). Their powerful results apply to jump processes with values in a general Borel space and so are also transferable to non-homogeneous Markov chains with a finite state space. Since we are dealing with this finite state space—due to our interest in health insurance and long-term-care multiple-state models—we chose to present a more simple approach that requires only classical existence theorems for ordinary differential equations, namely Caratheodory's existence theorem and Osgood's uniqueness theorem.

We now succinctly describe the contents of this work.

- In Section 2, we develop the subject of regime-switching Markov chains. The results obtained can be applied to the consideration of discontinuous intensity matrices.
- In Section 3, we deal with the approximation of matrices of transition probabilities given an approximation of the correspondent matrices of intensities.
- Sections 4–6 detail, with an example, the methodology for estimation–calibration proposed and present an analysis of the results obtained.
- In Section 7, we provide a discussion of the results obtained in the example treated, and in Section 8, we summarise all the results obtained in this work.

There are three main contributions of this work. The first is the proposal of a method to estimate the parameters of a set of transition intensities from ideal observed data. The second is a result on regime-switching Markov chains that establishes the possibility of considering transition intensities made up of different sorts of functional forms, with each one of the functional forms depending on different sets of parameters. Finally, the third contribution is a result that quantifies the norm of the difference of two probability transition matrices in terms of the norm of the corresponding matrices of transition intensities; this last result justifies the choice of arbitrary functional forms for the transition intensities in ways more adequate for parameter estimation.

2. Regime Switching Markov Chains

In this section, we develop the formalism of regime switching for Markov chains, in which the transition probabilities are derived from intensities that, at a certain point in time, can change either in functional form or in the parameters. The consideration of discontinuous piecewise linear intensities suggests the study of Markov chains in continuous time with regimes. Let us state some preliminary notations and results for context purposes (see [28]). Firstly, we recall the definition of an intensity matrix $Q(t, \theta)$.

Definition 1. *Let $\mathcal{L}(\mathbb{R}^{d \times d})$ be the space of $d \times d$ square matrices with coefficients in $\mathbb{R}$. A function $Q : [0, +\infty[\to \mathcal{L}(\mathbb{R}^{d \times d})$ denoted by*

$$Q(t, \theta) = \left[\mu_{ij}^{\theta}(t) \right]_{i,j=1,\dots,d},$$

with $\theta \in \Theta \subset \mathbb{R}^p$ a parameter is a transition intensity matrix if, for almost all $t \geq 0$, it verifies

(i) $\forall i = 1, \dots, d,\ t \geq 0,\ \mu_{ii}^{\theta}(t) \leq 0;$

(ii) $\forall i = 1, \dots, d,\ \forall j = 1, \dots, d,\ t \geq 0,\ i \neq j \Rightarrow \mu_{ij}^{\theta}(t) \geq 0;$

(iii) $\forall i = 1, \dots, d,\ t \geq 0,\ \sum_{j=1,\dots,d} \mu_{ij}^{\theta}(t) = 0.$

Secondly, we recall the Kolmogorov ordinary differential Equations (ODE) for non-homogeneous continuous-time Markov chains. These equations, upon integration, give the matrix of transition probabilities $P(x, t, \theta)$ as a function of the matrix of intensities $Q(t, \theta)$, where $\theta \in \Theta$ is a parameter. The forward Kolmogorov ODE can be represented in the following form:

$$\begin{cases} P'_t(x, t, \theta) = P(x, t, \theta) Q(t, \theta) \\ \\ P(x, x) = I, \end{cases} \tag{1}$$

or, in integrated form, by

$$P(x, t, \theta) = I + \int_{[x,t]} P(x, s, \theta) Q(s, \theta) ds. \tag{2}$$

Finally, let us now deal with regime-switching Markov chains.

The general motivation for the study of regime switching in ODE can be seen in [23,24]. Let us elaborate on the motivation to study regime-switching Markov chains. Suppose that we have two continuous-time Markov chains, having the same state space, with intensities of different functional forms—such as piecewise constant or affine of the Gompertz-Makeham type, etc.—depending on two sets of parameters, say Θ_1 and Θ_2, respectively, defined in two contiguous-time intervals, say $[0, t_1]$ and $[t_1, t_2]$. The result we proof shows that there exists a well-defined Markov chain in the interval $[0, t_2]$ with intensities depending on a set of parameters $\Theta := \Theta_1 \cup \Theta_2$ such that the transition probabilities of this Markov chain—obtained by the solution of the Kolmogorov equations—coincide with the transition probabilities of the first initial Markov chain in $[0, t_1]$ and also coincide with the transition probabilities of the second initial Markov chain in $[t_1, t_2]$. This result will grant us a greater latitude in the choice of the functional forms of the intensities for estimation purposes since it will be possible to partition a time interval of interest in two or more disjoint intervals and to have intensities, in each one of the intervals, possibly of different functional forms and different sets of parameters. In Theorem 4, we consider extended solutions of an ODE in the sense of Carathéodory. For that, following [29] (pp. 41–44), we consider the definition of an extended solution of a differential equation.

Definition 2 (Extended solution of an ODE). *For* $f(t, y) : I \times \mathcal{D} \to \mathbb{R}^{d \times d}$ *a non necessarily continuous function, with* $I \subset [0, +\infty[$ *and* $\mathcal{D} \subset \mathbb{R}^{d \times d}$ *and a differential equation given by*

$$Y'(t) = f(t, Y(t)), \ Y(0) = y_0 \in \mathbb{R}^{d \times d}, \tag{3}$$

or in the equivalent integral form, with the appropriate Lebesgue measure du in $\mathbb{R}$,

$$Y(t) = y_0 + \int_0^t f(u, Y(u)) du, \tag{4}$$

an extended solution $Y(t)$ *of the ODE in Formula (3) is an absolutely continuous function* $Y(t)$, *such that* $f(t, Y(t)) \in \mathcal{D}$ *for* $t \in I$ *and Formula (3)—or equivalently, Formula (4)—is verified for all* $t \in I$ *almost everywhere (a.e), that is, possibly with the exception of a set of null Lebesgue measure in* $[0, +\infty[$.

We now recall Caratheodory's existence theorem—see [29] (p. 43) for the unidimensional result and [30] (pp. 28–29) for the multidimensional result, with a proof via Schauder's fixed point theorem—in the context of the model we are studying, a theorem that ensures the existence of an extended solution under general conditions.

Theorem 1 (Caratheodory's existence theorem). *Suppose that $f(t, \boldsymbol{y}) : I \times \mathcal{D} \to \mathbb{R}^{d \times d}$, with $I = [0, u[$ an open set of $[0, +\infty[$ and $\mathcal{D}$ an open set of $\mathbb{R}^{d \times d}$, verifies that*

(i) *$f(t, \boldsymbol{y})$ is measurable in the variable t, for fixed $\boldsymbol{y}$, and continuous in the variable $\boldsymbol{y}$, for fixed t, for $(t, \boldsymbol{y}) \in I \times \mathcal{D}$.*

(ii) *For each compact set $K \Subset \mathcal{D}$ and $T > 0$, there exists a Lebesgue integrable function $\lambda(t)$, such that $\|f(t, \boldsymbol{y})\| \leq \lambda(t)$ for $(t, \boldsymbol{y}) \in [0, T] \times K$.*

Then, for every $(t_0, \boldsymbol{y}_0) \in I \times \mathcal{D}$ such that $Y(t_0) = \boldsymbol{y}_0$, that is, a given initial condition of equation in Formula (3), there exists an extended solution according to Definition 2, defined in a neighbourhood of $(t_0, \boldsymbol{y}_0)$.

Despite the fact that Theorem 1 guaranties the local existence of an extended solution, it is always possible to consider a maximal extension of this solution, possibly, to a larger time interval (see [30] pp. 29–30).

Theorem 2 (Maximal time interval for existence). *With the notations and under the hypothesis of Theorem 1, any existing solution Y admits a continuation $\widetilde{Y}$ to a maximal time interval of existence, let it be $[a, b]$ such that, $\partial \mathcal{D}$ being the boundary of $\mathcal{D}$:*

$$\lim_{t \to a} \widetilde{Y}(t) \in \partial \mathcal{D} \text{ and } \lim_{t \to b} \widetilde{Y}(t) \in \partial \mathcal{D} \ .$$

Remark 1 (Applying Caratheodory theorem to the Kolmogorov ODE). *Kolmogorov ODE for continuous time Markov chains, in Formula (1), falls under this formalism in the following way:*

$$f(t, \boldsymbol{y}, \boldsymbol{\theta}) = Q(t, \boldsymbol{\theta}) \cdot \boldsymbol{y} \tag{5}$$

which is essentially the equation in Formula (3) with the possibility of dependence on a parameter $\boldsymbol{\theta} \in \Theta$. Consider a matrix norm $\|\cdot\|$ in the sense of [31] (p. 340), that is, a submultiplicative norm—such as the l^1 norm and l^2 norm, also known as the Frobenius norm—and observe that since

$$\|f(t, \boldsymbol{y}, \boldsymbol{\theta})\| = \|Q(t, \boldsymbol{\theta}) \cdot \boldsymbol{y}\| \leq \|Q(t, \boldsymbol{\theta})\| \|\boldsymbol{y}\| \ , \tag{6}$$

and since any norm of a probability intensity matrix is bounded, we can apply Caratheodory's theorem to the Kolmogorov ODE under the condition that there exists a Lebesgue integrable function $\lambda(t)$ such that

$$\sup_{\boldsymbol{\theta} \in \Theta} \|Q(t, \boldsymbol{\theta})\| \leq \lambda(t) \ , \tag{7}$$

for all $t \in [0, T]$. We will see in Remark 3 that the condition in Formula (7) is also sufficient to ensure the unicity of the extended solutions.

Remark 2 (Existence of extended solutions alternative proof). *We could also quote Wintner's theorem, referred to in [32], a theorem that states that if $\|f(t, \boldsymbol{y})\| \leq N(t) L(\|\boldsymbol{y}\|)$ with N and L piecewise continuous, positive and L non-decreasing, such that for some $c > 0$*

$$\int_c^{+\infty} \frac{1}{L(s)} ds = +\infty \ ,$$

then the ODE in Formula (3) has a solution for a given initial condition. We observe that the quoted theorem is valid, under the assumption that $f(t, \boldsymbol{y})$ is continuous with the possible exception of points of a null Lebesgue set of the time variable, by considering extended solutions instead of usual solutions, which have a continuous derivative, and as $L(t)$ and $N(t)$ both satisfy the hypotheses of Wintner's theorem for parameters of the intensity functions and taking each, two (or several) distinct values in two (or several) complementary intervals of the time domain.

We now quote an unicity result—from [30] p. 30—applicable whenever there is existence of an extended solution in the Caratheodory sense.

Theorem 3 (Unicity of extended solutions). *Suppose that $f(t, \mathbf{y}) : I \times \mathcal{D} \to \mathbb{R}^{d \times d}$, with $I = [0, u[$ an open set of $[0, +\infty[$ and $\mathcal{D}$ an open set of $\mathbb{R}^{d \times d}$, verifies the conditions in Theorem 1, and moreover, that for each compact set $K \Subset \mathcal{D}$ and $T > 0$, there exists a Lebesgue integrable function $\lambda_K(t)$, such that*

$$\|f(t, \mathbf{y}_1) - f(t, \mathbf{y}_2)\| \leq \lambda_K(t) \|\mathbf{y}_1 - \mathbf{y}_2\| , \tag{8}$$

for $(t, \mathbf{y}_1)$, $(t, \mathbf{y}_2) \in [0, T] \times K$. Then, for every $(t_0, \mathbf{y}_0) \in I \times \mathcal{D}$ such that $\mathbf{Y}(t_0) = \mathbf{y}_0$, that is, a given initial condition of equation in Formula (3), there exists an unique extended solution $\mathbf{Y}$ according to Definition 2, defined in a neighbourhood of $(t_0, \mathbf{y}_0)$. The domain of definition of $\mathbf{Y}$ is open, and $\mathbf{Y}$ is continuous in this domain.

Remark 3 (Applying the unicity result to the Kolmogorov ODE). *With the interpretation given in Formula (5) and if the norm is a matrix norm, similarly to what we had in Formula (6), we now have that a sufficient condition for the unicity of the extended solutions of Kolmogorov ODE is for each compact set $K \Subset \mathcal{D}$ and $T > 0$, there exists a Lebesgue integrable function $\lambda_K(t)$ such that $\|\mathbf{Q}(t, \boldsymbol{\theta})\| \leq \lambda_K(t)$, thus implying that*

$$\|f(t, \mathbf{y}_1, \boldsymbol{\theta}) - f(t, \mathbf{y}_2, \boldsymbol{\theta})\| = \|\mathbf{Q}(t, \boldsymbol{\theta}) \cdot (\mathbf{y}_1 - \mathbf{y}_2)\| \leq \|\mathbf{Q}(t, \boldsymbol{\theta})\| \|\mathbf{y}_1 - \mathbf{y}_2\| \leq$$
$$\leq \lambda_K(t) \|\mathbf{y}_1 - \mathbf{y}_2\| , \tag{9}$$

which is the hypothesis bound in Formula (8) for Theorem 3.

Remark 4 (On the unicity of the extended solutions). *Either directly using Theorem 18.4.13 in [33] (p. 337) or using Osgood's uniqueness theorem—as presented for instance, in [34] (p. 58) or in [35] (pp. 149–151)—we may also conclude that the extended solution, that we know to exist, is unique, in the sense that two solutions may only differ on a set of Lebesgue measures equal to zero.*

Remark 5 (On the numerical computation of extended solutions). *We observe that these existence and uniqueness results are essential for a numerical integration of the ODE, but that no result on numerical convergence is implied—in the existence and uniqueness results above—for the regime switching ODE with discontinuous coefficients. Nevertheless, the Lipschitz condition with respect to the $\mathbf{y}$ variable—such as the one in Formula (8)—is sufficient for the convergence of the Euler method (see [36] p. 74).*

The next theorem is a simple example of a regime-switching result for continuous-time Markov chains. The extension of this result to more than two regimes is straightforward. We consider the Kolmogorov ODE in a time interval $[0, T]$.

Theorem 4 (Regime switching continuous-time Markov chains). *Let $\|\cdot\|$ denote a matrix norm, let $\boldsymbol{\Theta}$ denote a parameter set and let $\mathbf{Q}_1(t, \boldsymbol{\theta})$ defined for $t \in [0, t_1]$ and $\mathbf{Q}_2(t, \boldsymbol{\theta})$ defined for $t \in [t_1, T]$ be two intensity matrices such that for $\lambda(t)$, an integrable function defined in $[0, T]$, we have for $t \in [0, T]$*

$$\max \left(\sup_{\boldsymbol{\theta} \in \boldsymbol{\Theta}} \|\mathbf{Q}_1(t, \boldsymbol{\theta})\|, \sup_{\boldsymbol{\theta} \in \boldsymbol{\Theta}} \|\mathbf{Q}_2(t, \boldsymbol{\theta})\| \right) \leq \lambda(t) . \tag{10}$$

Then, there exists $\widetilde{\mathbf{P}}(t, \boldsymbol{\theta})$ such that

1. *In $[0, t_1]$, we have that $\widetilde{\mathbf{P}} \equiv \mathbf{P}_1$, a.e. in t, where $\mathbf{P}_1$ is a solution of the Cauchy problem $(\mathbf{P}_1)'_t(t, \boldsymbol{\theta}) = \mathbf{P}_1 \mathbf{Q}_1(t, \boldsymbol{\theta})$ with the usual initial conditions;*
2. *In $[t_1, T]$, we have that $\widetilde{\mathbf{P}} \equiv \mathbf{P}_2$ a.e. in t, where $\mathbf{P}_2$ is a solution of the Cauchy problem $(\mathbf{P}_2)'_t(t, \boldsymbol{\theta}) = \mathbf{P}_2 \mathbf{Q}_2(t, \boldsymbol{\theta})$ with the initial conditions given by $\mathbf{P}_1(t_1, \boldsymbol{\theta})$;*
3. *$\widetilde{\mathbf{P}}$ is a transition probability matrix.*

Proof. Let $Q_1(t, \theta) = \left[\mu_{ij}^{1,\theta}(t)\right]_{i,j=1,\dots,d}$ and $Q_2(t, \theta) = \left[\mu_{ij}^{2,\theta}(t)\right]_{i,j=1,\dots,d}$. If we define

$$Q(t, \theta) = \left[\mu_{ij}^{\theta}(t)\right]_{i,j=1,\dots,d} := Q_1(t, \theta)\mathbb{1}_{[0,t_1]}(t) + Q_2(t, \theta)\mathbb{1}_{]t_1,T]}(t), \tag{11}$$

we will have that:

$$\mu_{ij}^{\theta}(t) = \mu_{ij}^{1,\theta}(t)\mathbb{1}_{[0,t_1]}(t) + \mu_{ij}^{2,\theta}(t)\mathbb{1}_{]t_1,T]}(t),$$

and we can, immediately, verify that $Q(t, \theta)$ is an intensity matrix on $[0, T]$ according to Definition 1. Moreover, since by Formula (10) and the definition in Formula (11), we have that

$$\|Q(t, \theta)\| \le \lambda(t),$$

we can let $\widetilde{P}(t, \theta)$ be the unique solution of the Kolmogorov equation $\widetilde{P}'_t = \widetilde{P}Q$ on $[0, T]$ with the usual conditions. It is then clear that $\widetilde{P}(t, \theta)$ is a transition probability matrix. Furthermore, if we define

$$\widehat{P}(t, \theta) := P_1(t, \theta)\mathbb{1}_{]0,t_1[}(t) + P_2(t, \theta)\mathbb{1}_{]t_1,T[}(t)$$

and we will then have, using the hypothesis that

$$\frac{\partial \widehat{P}(t, \theta)}{\partial t} \stackrel{=}{_{\text{a.e.}}} \frac{\partial \widehat{P}_1(t, \theta)}{\partial t}\mathbb{1}_{]0,t_1[}(t) + \frac{\partial \widehat{P}_2(t, \theta)}{\partial t}\mathbb{1}_{]t_1,T[}(t) \stackrel{=}{_{\text{a.e.}}}$$

$$\stackrel{=}{_{\text{a.e.}}} P_1 Q_1(t, \theta)\mathbb{1}_{]0,t_1[}(t) + P_2 Q_2(t, \theta)\mathbb{1}_{]t_1,T[}(t) \stackrel{=}{_{\text{a.e.}}}$$

$$\stackrel{=}{_{\text{a.e.}}} \left(P_1(t, \theta)\mathbb{1}_{]0,t_1[}(t) + P_2(t, \theta)\mathbb{1}_{]t_1,T[}(t)\right)\left(Q_1(t, \theta)\mathbb{1}_{[0,t_1]}(t) + Q_2(t, \theta)\mathbb{1}_{]t_1,T]}(t)\right) \stackrel{=}{_{\text{a.e.}}}$$

$$\stackrel{=}{_{\text{a.e.}}} \widehat{P}(t, \theta)Q(t, \theta),$$

which shows that $\widehat{P}(t, \theta) \equiv \widetilde{P}(t, \theta)$ a.e. in t and, as a consequence, that $\widetilde{P}(t, \theta) \equiv \widehat{P}(t, \theta) \equiv P_1$ in $[0, t_1]$ a.e. and $\widetilde{P}(t, \theta) \equiv \widehat{P}(t, \theta) \equiv P_2$ in $[t_1, T]$ a.e. $\square$

We present in Figure 1 graphical representations of transition probabilities obtained by numerical integration of Kolmogorov equations with discontinuous piecewise linear intensities for a four-state Markov chain with intensity matrix given in Formula (16).

State one is the healthy state, state four is an absorbing state corresponding to death and states two and three are intermediate dependent states. This representation, aside from being an illustration of a regime switching Markov chain, also illustrates the possible extreme effects of a regime switching of discontinuous-intensity matrix entries. The subject of Markov chains with regimes has, as can easily be observed, an interest independent of the objective that motivates us to study it. However, in the context of the present work, it can be a way to justify a more efficient and robust parameter estimation (or calibration) process by an adequate choice of functional forms for the intensities.

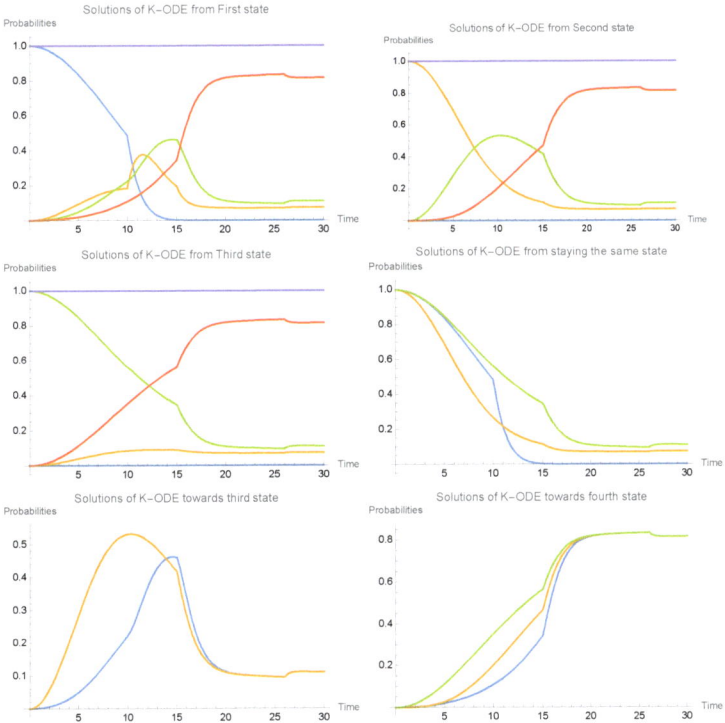

Figure 1. Solutions of Kolmogorov ODE for discontinuous linear intensities. p_{ij}: $j = 1$ (blue); $j = 2$ (orange); $j = 3$ (green); $j = 4$ (red). $\sum_{j=1}^{4} p_{ij}$ (purple). Lower left p_{i3}: $i = 1$ (blue); $i = 2$ (orange); Lower right p_{i4}: $i = 1$ (blue); $i = 2$ (orange); $i = 3$ (green).

3. On the Approximation of Intensities and Corresponding Transition Probabilities

One way to simplify the estimation of intensities of Markov chain models in continuous time—relevant for health insurance and long-term-care models—is to replace the usual Gompertz–Makeham type intensities—containing exponential and linear terms and therefore being difficult to estimate—by continuous piecewise linear intensities. In this sense, it is important to have a result that controls the distance between two matrices of transition probabilities resulting from the integration of the Kolmogorov equations for the correspondent two matrices of intensities.

It is known (see, for example, [37] p. 264 and [1]) that we can represent the transition probabilities in the Hostinsky form:

$$
\begin{aligned}
\boldsymbol{P}(x, t, \boldsymbol{\theta}) = \\
= \boldsymbol{I} + \sum_{n=1}^{+\infty} \int_{[x,t]} \int_{[t_1,t]} \cdots \int_{[t_{n-1},t]} \boldsymbol{Q}(t_1, \boldsymbol{\theta}) \boldsymbol{Q}(t_2, \boldsymbol{\theta}) \cdots \boldsymbol{Q}(t_n, \boldsymbol{\theta}) dt_n \cdots dt_1 ,
\end{aligned}
\tag{12}
$$

where the right-hand member only depends on the intensities and where the series converges uniformly. The following theorem—akin to a multidimensional Gronwall-type inequality—is a natural result.

Theorem 5 (Dependence of the transition probabilities on the intensities). *Let $\|\cdot\|$ be a matrix norm and let $\boldsymbol{Q}_1(t, \boldsymbol{\theta})$ and $\boldsymbol{Q}_2(t, \boldsymbol{\theta})$ be two matrices of intensities norm bounded by $M > 0$ in $[0, T]$. Define*

$$
\epsilon(\boldsymbol{Q}_1, \boldsymbol{Q}_2) := \sup_{t \in [0,T], \, \boldsymbol{\theta} \in \boldsymbol{\Theta}} \|\boldsymbol{Q}_1(t, \boldsymbol{\theta}) - \boldsymbol{Q}_2(t, \boldsymbol{\theta})\| .
\tag{13}
$$

Then, we have that

$$\sup_{t\in[x,T],\,\theta\in\Theta} \|\boldsymbol{P}_1(x,t,\theta) - \boldsymbol{P}_2(x,t,\theta)\| \le \epsilon(\boldsymbol{Q}_1,\boldsymbol{Q}_2)\frac{e^{M|T-x|}-1}{M}, \tag{14}$$

where $\boldsymbol{P}_1(x,u,\theta)$ and $\boldsymbol{P}_2(x,u,\theta)$ are the solutions of the Kolmogorov equations—given in Formula (1)—with matrices of intensities $\boldsymbol{Q}_1(t,\theta)$ and $\boldsymbol{Q}_2(t,\theta)$, respectively.

Proof. The proof of a result of this type for an ordinary differential equation $y'(t) = f(t,y(t))$, satisfying the condition

$$|f(t,y_1(t)) - f(t,y_2(t))| \le \lambda(t)|y_1(t) - y_2(t)|,$$

where λ is integrable and is immediate from the integral representation of the differential equation. So we will use the integral representation given by Formula (12). The following well-known result (see [38] p. 217 and, for a proof, [28] p. 348) will be instrumental.

Lemma 1. *Let $q: \mathbb{R}_+ \mapsto \mathbb{R}$ a measurable function integrable over every bounded interval of $\mathbb{R}_+$. Then, we have that*

$$\int_s^t \int_{s_1}^t \cdots \int_{s_{n-1}}^t q(s_1)q(s_2)\ldots q(s_n)ds_n\ldots ds_2 ds_1 = \frac{\left(\int_s^t q(u)du\right)^n}{n!},$$

for all $0 \le s \le t, n \ge 1$.

Let us show, by induction, that if $\|\boldsymbol{Q}_1(t,\theta)\| \le M$ and $\|\boldsymbol{Q}_2(t,\theta)\| \le M$ for some $0 < M < +\infty$ then, using hypothesis in Formula (13), we have that

$$\left\|\prod_{k=1}^n \boldsymbol{Q}_1(t_k,\theta) - \prod_{k=1}^n \boldsymbol{Q}_2(t_k,\theta)\right\| \le \max_{k=1,\ldots,n}\|\boldsymbol{Q}_1(t_k,\theta) - \boldsymbol{Q}_2(t_k,\theta)\| \cdot M^{n-1} \le \tag{15}$$
$$\le \epsilon(\boldsymbol{Q}_1,\boldsymbol{Q}_2)M^{n-1}$$

In fact, for the first order bound we have that

$$\boldsymbol{Q}_1(t_1,\theta)\boldsymbol{Q}_1(t_2,\theta) - \boldsymbol{Q}_2(t_1,\theta)\boldsymbol{Q}_2(t_2,\theta) =$$
$$= \boldsymbol{Q}_1(t_1,\theta)\boldsymbol{Q}_1(t_2,\theta) - \boldsymbol{Q}_1(t_1,\theta)\boldsymbol{Q}_2(t_2,\theta) + \boldsymbol{Q}_1(t_1,\theta)\boldsymbol{Q}_2(t_2,\theta) - \boldsymbol{Q}_2(t_1,\theta)\boldsymbol{Q}_2(t_2,\theta) =$$
$$= \boldsymbol{Q}_1(t_1,\theta)(\boldsymbol{Q}_1(t_2,\theta) - \boldsymbol{Q}_2(t_2,\theta)) + (\boldsymbol{Q}_1(t_1,\theta) - \boldsymbol{Q}_2(t_1,\theta))\boldsymbol{Q}_2(t_2,\theta),$$

and then it follows, using the matrix norm hypothesis, that

$$\|\boldsymbol{Q}_1(t_1,\theta)\boldsymbol{Q}_1(t_2,\theta) - \boldsymbol{Q}_2(t_1,\theta)\boldsymbol{Q}_2(t_2,\theta)\| \le$$
$$\le M\|\boldsymbol{Q}_1(t_2,\theta) - \boldsymbol{Q}_2(t_2,\theta)\| + M\|\boldsymbol{Q}_1(t_1,\theta) - \boldsymbol{Q}_2(t_1,\theta)\| \le$$
$$\le M \cdot \max_{k=1,2}\|\boldsymbol{Q}_1(t_k,\theta) - \boldsymbol{Q}_2(t_k,\theta)\|.$$

Consider now, for clarity, the next induction step, the second order bound.

$$\boldsymbol{Q}_1(t_1,\theta)[\boldsymbol{Q}_1(t_2,\theta)\boldsymbol{Q}_1(t_3,\theta)] - \boldsymbol{Q}_2(t_1,\theta)[\boldsymbol{Q}_2(t_2,\theta)\boldsymbol{Q}_2(t_3,\theta)] =$$
$$= \boldsymbol{Q}_1(t_1,\theta)[\boldsymbol{Q}_1(t_2,\theta)\boldsymbol{Q}_1(t_3,\theta)] - \boldsymbol{Q}_1(t_1,\theta)[\boldsymbol{Q}_2(t_2,\theta)\boldsymbol{Q}_2(t_3,\theta)] +$$
$$+ \boldsymbol{Q}_1(t_1,\theta)[\boldsymbol{Q}_2(t_2,\theta)\boldsymbol{Q}_2(t_3,\theta)] - \boldsymbol{Q}_2(t_1,\theta)[\boldsymbol{Q}_2(t_2,\theta)\boldsymbol{Q}_2(t_3,\theta)] =$$
$$= \boldsymbol{Q}_1(t_1,\theta)([\boldsymbol{Q}_1(t_2,\theta)\boldsymbol{Q}_1(t_3,\theta)] - [\boldsymbol{Q}_2(t_2,\theta)\boldsymbol{Q}_2(t_3,\theta)]) +$$
$$+ (\boldsymbol{Q}_1(t_1,\theta) - \boldsymbol{Q}_2(t_1,\theta))[\boldsymbol{Q}_2(t_2,\theta)\boldsymbol{Q}_2(t_3,\theta)].$$

Again it follows, from the matrix norm hypothesis and using the previous order one bound, that

$$\|Q_1(t_1,\theta)Q_1(t_2,\theta)Q_1(t_3,\theta) - Q_2(t_1,\theta)Q_2(t_2,\theta)Q_2(t_3,\theta)\| \leq$$
$$\leq M\|[Q_1(t_2,\theta)Q_1(t_3,\theta)] - [Q_2(t_2,\theta)Q_2(t_3,\theta)]\| + M^2\|Q_1(t_1,\theta) - Q_2(t_1,\theta)\| \leq$$
$$\leq M^2 \cdot \max_{k=1,2,3} \|Q_1(t_k,\theta) - Q_2(t_k,\theta)\|.$$

The induction proof is now cleared. Now, by using Formulas (12) and (15) and Lemma 1, we have the following bound for the norm of the difference of the two transition probability matrices.

$$\|P_1(x,t,\theta) - P_2(x,t,\theta)\| \leq$$
$$\leq \sum_{n=1}^{+\infty} \int_{[x,t]} \int_{[t_1,t]} \cdots \int_{[t_{n-1},t]} \left\| \prod_{k=1}^{n} Q_1(t_k,\theta) - \prod_{k=1}^{n} Q_2(t_k,\theta) \right\| dt_n \cdots dt_1 \leq$$
$$\leq \frac{1}{M} \sum_{n=1}^{+\infty} \int_{[x,t]} \int_{[t_1,t]} \cdots \int_{[t_{n-1},t]} \epsilon(Q_1,Q_2) M^n \, dt_n \cdots dt_1 \leq$$
$$\leq \frac{1}{M} \sum_{n=1}^{+\infty} \int_{[x,t]} \int_{[t_1,t]} \cdots \int_{[t_{n-1},t]} \epsilon(Q_1,Q_2)^{1/n} M \times \cdots \times \epsilon(Q_1,Q_2)^{1/n} M \, dt_n \cdots dt_1 =$$
$$= \frac{1}{M} \epsilon(Q_1,Q_2) \sum_{n=1}^{+\infty} \frac{M^n |t-x|^n}{n!} = \epsilon(Q_1,Q_2) \frac{e^{M|T-x|} - 1}{M},$$

thus proving the result, in Formula (14). □

A result like the one given by Theorem 5 is expected to simplify the estimation of the parameters $\theta \in \Theta$ that allow the fitting of a Markov chain model to real data coming, for example, from multi-state models for health insurance or long-term care, which was the case discussed in [1].

Remark 6 (Applying Theorem 5). *The applicability of Formula (14) requires that $M|T - x| \ll 1$; if not, the result is of no use. The usefulness of the result relies on the possibility of localising the computation of the solutions of Kolmogorov ODE. Once time units are chosen—let us say, one year— this is achieved by solving, successively, the Kolmogorov differential equations in time intervals $[x_k, x_{k+1}]$ of length $|x_{k+1} - x_k| \ll 1$. In doing so, the final values of the transition probability matrix in one interval must be the initial values of the transition probability matrix Kolmogorov ODE in the immediately following time interval. Supposing the adequate hypothesis for the existence and unicity of solutions of the Kolmogorov forward equations, we may then conclude that two matrix intensity matrices are close to one another in some small time interval, the correspondent probability transition matrices will be close to one another in the same small time interval.*

An illustrative example of the usefulness of this result is given in Figure 2 for which the intensity matrix considered is the following.

$$\begin{pmatrix} \mu_{11}(t) & 1.20135 \times 10^{-5} e^{0.117(t+50)} + \frac{1}{200} & 1.2 \cdot \mu_{12}(t) & 0.05 \cdot \mu_{34}(t) \\ 0.7 \cdot \mu_{12}(t) & \mu_{22}(t) & 5.49958 \times 10^{-6} e^{0.128(t+50)} + \frac{3}{500} & 0.5 \cdot \mu_{34}(t) \\ 0.36 \cdot \mu_{12}(t) & 0.3 \cdot \mu_{23}(t) & \mu_{33}(t) & 4.08902 \times 10^{-6} e^{0.139(t+50)} + \frac{7}{1000} \\ 0. & 0 & 0 & 1 \end{pmatrix} \quad (16)$$

That is all the intensities are of Gompertz–Makeham type; moreover, $\mu_{12}(t)$, $\mu_{23}(t)$ and $\mu_{34}(t)$ were first defined, and then, all the others were defined proportional to these three; the determinations of the parameters of these intensities from the data is the goal of an estimation calibration procedure. The coefficients of $\mu_{12}(t)$, $\mu_{23}(t)$ and $\mu_{34}(t)$ were chosen having in mind a unit time of one year and a LTC model starting at the age of 50 years and

going on until 100 years of age. The proportions between $\mu_{12}(t)$, $\mu_{23}(t)$ and $\mu_{34}(t)$ and all the others can be calibrated using a discrete-time transition matrix if available. The linear interpolations of the intensities were given at the six following points $t = 0, 15, 30, 40, 45, 50$. The differences of the linear interpolated intensities and the original Gompertz–Makeham intensities $\mu_{12}(t)$, $\mu_{23}(t)$ and $\mu_{34}(t)$ are shown in Figure 3.

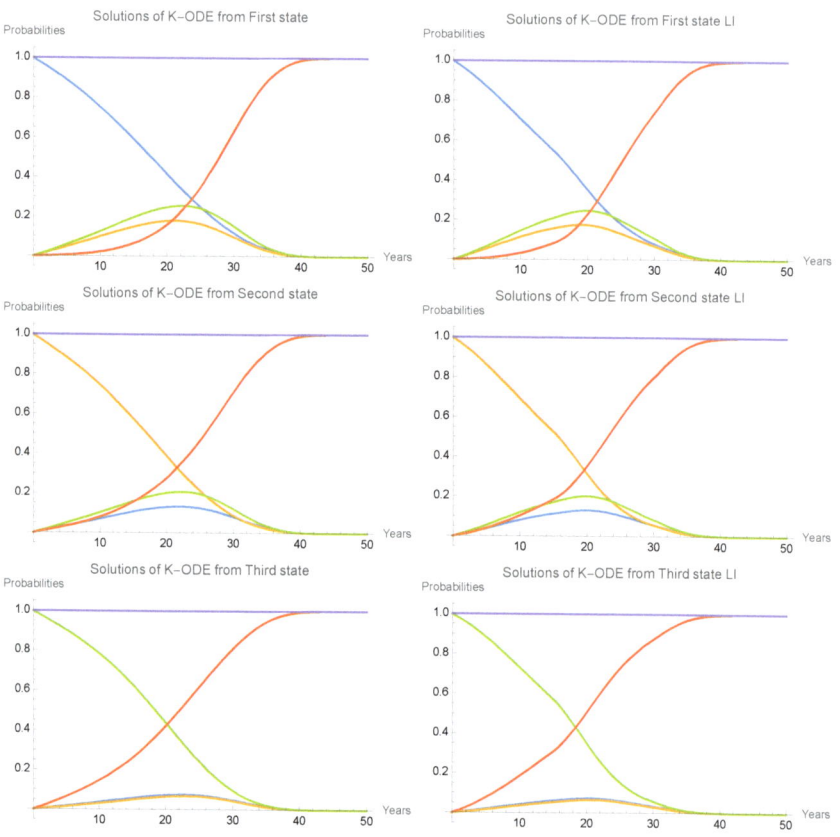

Figure 2. Comparing transition probabilities from Gompertz–Makeham intensities (left-hand side) and corresponding six-point linear interpolations (right-hand side). p_{ij}: $j = 1$ (blue); $j = 2$ (orange); $j = 3$ (green); $j = 4$ (red). $\sum_{j=1}^{4} p_{ij}$ (purple).

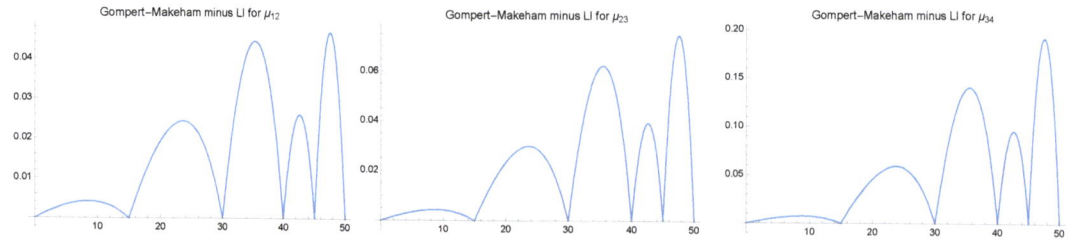

Figure 3. The symmetric of the differences between Gompertz–Makeham intensities and corresponding six-point linear interpolations for $\mu_{12}(t)$, $\mu_{23}(t)$ and $\mu_{34}(t)$.

The analysis of Figure 3 together with Figure 2 conveys an illustration of Theorem 5 and Remark 6 in the particular case of the approximation of Gompertz–Makeham intensities by linear interpolated ones.

4. Constructive Definition of CT-MC

The existence of a non-homogenous continuous-time Markov chain can also be guaranteed by a known constructive procedure that we now present, for completeness, and that is most useful for simulation and that we will use for defining the estimation calibration procedure proposed in this work. A reference for the following algorithmic definition of a Markov chain in continuous time is [37] (p. 266). For a proof of Theorem 6 below, see [38] (pp. 221–233). Let $\theta \in \Theta$ be a parameter.

Definition 3 (Constructive definition). *Given a transition intensity matrix,*

$$Q(t, \theta) = \left[\mu_{ij}^{\theta}(t) \right]_{i,j=1,\ldots,d},$$

define

$$p^{\star}(t, i, j) = \begin{cases} \frac{1 - \delta_i^j}{-\mu_{ii}^{\theta}(t)} \mu_{ij}^{\theta}(t) & \mu_{ii}^{\theta}(t) \neq 0 \\ \delta_i^j & \mu_{ii}^{\theta}(t) = 0, \end{cases} \tag{17}$$

with δ_i^j Kronecker's delta. Let $X_0 = i$, according to some initial distribution on $\{1, 2, \ldots, d\}$.

1. *The jump sequence $(\tau_n)_{n \geq 0}$ of stopping times is defined by induction as follows; $\tau_0 \equiv 0$.*
2. *τ_1, the sojourn time in state i which is also the time of first jump, has an exponential distribution function given by*

$$F_{\tau_1}(t) = \mathbb{P}[\tau_1 \leq t] = 1 - \exp\left(\int_0^t \mu_{ii}^{\theta}(t) du \right). \tag{18}$$

We note that this distribution of the stopping time is mandatory as a consequence of a general result on the distribution of sojourn times of a continuous-time Markov chain (see Theorem 2.3.15 in [38] p. 221).

3. *Given that the process is in state i, it may jump to state j at time $\tau_1 = s_1$ with probability $p^{\star}(t, i, j)$ defined in Formula (3), that is*

$$\mathbb{P}[X_{s_1} = j \mid \tau_1 = s_1, X_0 = i] = p^{\star}(s_1, i, j), \tag{19}$$

and so $X_t = i$ for $0 \equiv \tau_0 \leq t < \tau_1$.

4. *Given that $\tau_1 = s_1$ and $X_{s_1} = j$, τ_2 time of the second jump with an exponential distribution function,*

$$F_{\tau_2|\tau_1 = s_1}(t) = \mathbb{P}[\tau_2 \leq t \mid \tau_1 = s_1] = 1 - \exp\left(\int_0^t \mu_{jj}^{\theta}(u + s_1) du \right)$$

and

$$\mathbb{P}[X_{s_2} = k \mid \tau_1 = s_1, X_0 = i, \tau_2 = s_2, X_{s_1} = j] = p^{\star}(s_1 + s_2, j, k),$$

and so $X_t = j$ for $\tau_1 \leq t < \tau_2$.

The following theorem ensures that the preceding construction yields the desired result.

Theorem 6 (The continuous-time Markov chain). *Let the intensity matrix be norm bounded by a Lebesgue integrable function in $[0, T]$. Then, given the times $(\tau_0)_{n \geq 1}$, we have that with the sequence $(Y_n)_{n \geq 1}$ defined by $Y_n = X_{\tau_n}$, the process defined by*

$$X_t = \sum_{n=0}^{+\infty} Y_n \mathbb{1}_{[\tau_n, \tau_{n+1}[}(t) = \sum_{n=0}^{+\infty} X_{\tau_n} \mathbb{1}_{[\tau_n, \tau_{n+1}[}(t) \tag{20}$$

which is a continuous-time Markov chain with transition probabilities P and transition intensities Q.

Proof. This theorem is stated and proved, in the general case of continuous-time Markov processes in [38] (p. 229). □

5. Estimation–Calibration Procedure

In the following, we consider the set of procedures that allow us to obtain transition intensities from simulated data and then, by integration of the forward Kolmogorov ODE, the transition probabilities; these so-called estimated transition probabilities will be compared to the original transition probabilities that were used to generate the simulated data. The procedures comprehend both non-parametric statistical estimation by kernel methods and fitting piecewise linear functions to data with additional constraints, a procedure more akin to calibration.

We will consider an ideal sample of complete data represented in Figure 4; each line represents a *trajectory* and we have on the left-hand side the initial state, following it, we have the time spent in that state then the new state and the time spent in that state an so on and so forth...

$$
\begin{pmatrix}
\{1,\ 5.10729,\ 1,\ 11.2061,\ 4\} \\
\{1,\ 8.94734,\ 1,\ 13.8573,\ 3,\ 24.6617,\ 4\} \\
\{1,\ 6.87776,\ 4\} \\
\{1,\ 6.98515,\ 1,\ 13.3962,\ 4\} \\
\{1,\ 4.71123,\ 1,\ 9.89146,\ 3,\ 18.109,\ 4\} \\
\{2,\ 7.70894,\ 4\} \\
\{1,\ 6.84374,\ 1,\ 13.6126,\ 4\} \\
\{1,\ 6.04099,\ 1,\ 10.3816,\ 4\} \\
\{2,\ 6.33596,\ 4\} \\
\{3,\ 9.85956,\ 4\} \\
\{2,\ 4.69848,\ 3,\ 12.0129,\ 4\} \\
\{3,\ 5.10992,\ 4\} \\
\{1,\ 8.59185,\ 1,\ 15.0347,\ 1,\ 25.448,\ 4\} \\
\{1,\ 6.32415,\ 1,\ 12.4971,\ 4\} \\
\{1,\ 4.45355,\ 1,\ 9.13481,\ 4\} \\
\{1,\ 8.64611,\ 4\}
\end{pmatrix}
$$

Figure 4. A set of simulated trajectories of a 4-state continuous-time Markov chain.

Using the procedure detailed in Section 4, these data were generated with a full intensity matrix, that is a matrix of the form,

$$
\begin{pmatrix}
-(\mu_{12}+\mu_{13}+\mu_{14}) & \mu_{12} & \mu_{13} & \mu_{14} \\
\mu_{21} & -(\mu_{21}+\mu_{23}+\mu_{24}) & \mu_{23} & \mu_{24} \\
\mu_{31} & \mu_{32} & -(\mu_{31}+\mu_{32}+\mu_{34}) & \mu_{34} \\
0 & 0 & 0 & 0
\end{pmatrix}
\tag{21}
$$

with the intensities given by

$$
\begin{cases}
\mu_{12} = 3.47 \cdot 10^{-6}\, e^{0.138(t+65)} + \frac{1}{2500} = \mu_{21} & \mu_{13} = 0.5 \cdot \mu_{12} \quad \mu_{23} = 1.5 \cdot \mu_{12} \\
\mu_{14} = 0.0000758\, e^{0.087(t+65)} + \frac{1}{2000} & \mu_{24} = 1.4 \cdot \mu_{14} \quad \mu_{34} = 1.8 \cdot \mu_{14} \\
\mu_{21} = \mu_{12} & \mu_{31} = 0.1 \cdot \mu_{21} \quad \mu_{32} = 0.4 \cdot \mu_{21}
\end{cases}
\tag{22}
$$

This set of intensities used to generate the full data sample was supposed to determine a model for LTC with four states; the relations between the intensities reflect the qualitative relations describing the force of transitions that we suppose are held in this particular model.

For estimation–calibration purposes—following the results on the distance of transition probabilities—we will suppose that is has given the most tractable functional form of

the intensities depending on some parameters to be estimated. For instance, a continuous piecewise linear functional form for which we can have, for $i \neq j$,

$$\mu_{ij}^{\theta}(t) = \sum_{k=1}^{r} \left(\theta_{ij}^{k,1} + \theta_{ij}^{k,2} t \right) \mathbb{1}_{[t_k, t_{k+1}[}(t) \,, \tag{23}$$

with $0 = t_0 < t_1 < \cdots < t_{r+1} = T$, and possibly some conditions on the parameters $\theta_{ij}^{k,1}$ and $\theta_{ij}^{k,2}$ if the intensity $\mu_{ij}^{\theta}(t)$ is supposed to be piecewise linear and continuous.

We stress again that the values in Figure 4 were simulated. For LTC, for example, real data will be given, possibly, with time stamps of a day, at best; being so, the order of approximation will have to be chosen looking for precision with a balance between a sufficiently narrow interval around a given time and having enough observations to perform the estimation.

Let us detail a methodology to identify the parameter $\theta \in \Theta$ inspired by the constructive definition of the Markov chain in Remark 3. The general idea of the methodology is as follows.

(i)   Given a state i, we have to find a fitting for the distribution of random times of $i \rightarrow i$ jumps. According to Formula (18), these times have an exponential distribution with density $\mu_{ii}^{\theta}(t)$.

(ii) For every other state j, by using $\mathbb{P}[X_{s_1} = j | \tau_1 = s_1, X_0 = i]$, possibly with an approximation, by Formula (19), we can obtain an approximation of $p^{\star}(s_1, i, j)$.

(iii) By using Formula (17) and the approximation obtained for $p^{\star}(s_1, i, j)$, we can obtain an approximation for $\mu_{ij}^{\theta}(t)$.

(iv) Finally, we will fit a linear continuous piecewise intensity to $\mu_{ij}^{\theta}(t)$.

Let us detail the procedures for applying the methodology just described.

1.   Recall that an observed trajectory has the following structure: (first state, time spent in state, second state, time spent in state, third state ...). The maximum length of a trajectory in our sample is 11. Select all the trajectories of length greater than 3 that start at state $i = 1$. If the next state is also $i = 1$, the time spent in state—in this case, in state $i = 1$—is the first part of the sample for obtaining $\mu_{11}^{\theta}(t)$. Select all the trajectories of length greater than 5 for which the second state is $i = 1$; this set of trajectories already contains the previous considered set of trajectories and so, if the third state is also $i = 1$, the sum of the time spent in the first state and the time spent in the second state will be the second part of the sample for obtaining $\mu_{ii}^{\theta}(t)$. Repeat, successively, the procedure for all trajectories of length greater than 7, then of length greater than 9 and finally of length greater than 11 to obtain the full sample for the intensity $\mu_{11}^{\theta}(t)$.

2.   Fit a smooth kernel distribution to the sample obtaining the intensity $\mu_{11}^{\theta}(t)$.

3.   Repeat the procedure used for obtaining the sample for $\mu_{11}^{\theta}(t)$, but this time, select the transitions $1 \rightarrow 2$, that is, the transitions from state $i = 1$ to state $i = 2$. Fit a smooth kernel distribution to these data.

4.   Now, we look for an estimate of $p^{\star}(t, i, j)$ given by Formulas (17) and (19). For that, we will consider rounding the sojourn times—say to the unity, in order to have enough observations—and then group all observations of jumps from the first state according to this rounding. Consider then the observations towards state $i = 2$. We will then have that

$$
\begin{aligned}
p^{\star}(s_1, 1, 2) = \mathbb{P}[X_{s_1} = 2 | \tau_1 = s_1, X_0 = 1] &\approx \frac{\mathbb{P}[X_{s_1} = 2, s_1 - 0.5 \leq \tau_1 < s_1 + 0.5]}{\mathbb{P}[s_1 - 0.5 \leq \tau_1 < s_1 + 0.5]} = \\
&= \frac{\mathbb{P}[s_1 - 0.5 \leq \tau_1 < s_1 + 0.5 | X_{s_1} = 2] \cdot \mathbb{P}[X_{s_1} = 2]}{\mathbb{P}[s_1 - 0.5 \leq \tau_1 < s_1 + 0.5]}
\end{aligned} \tag{24}
$$

and most of the left-hand side of the formula will be estimable with the observations by using the smooth kernel distributions.

5. Resorting to Formula (17), we can compute values for $\mu_{12}^{\theta}(t)$ and fit a piecewise linear density. That is, using again Formula (17), since $\mu_{11}^{\theta}(s_1) \neq 0$, we have that for an arbitrary time $t = s_1$,

$$\mu_{12}^{\theta}(s_1) \approx \frac{-\mu_{11}^{\theta}(s_1)}{1 - \delta_1^2} p^{\star}(s_1, 1, 2) = -\mu_{11}^{\theta}(s_1) \cdot p^{\star}(s_1, 1, 2) \, .$$

6. We consider a set of values of $\mu_{12}^{\theta}(s_1), \mu_{12}^{\theta}(s_2), \ldots, \mu_{12}^{\theta}(s_k)$ and then fit the multidimensional parameter $\boldsymbol{\theta} \in \boldsymbol{\Theta}$ to these values (see Formula (23) for the case of a continuous piecewise linear intensity functional form).

7. These procedures are to be repeated in order to obtain the parameters μ_{2j}^{θ} for $j \neq 2$ and μ_{3j}^{θ} for $j \neq 3$.

8. The intensities μ_{jj}^{θ} for $j = 1, 2, 3$ are obtained in the usual form and are forcible continuous piecewise linear since they are the sum of continuous piecewise linear functions.

6. Results of the Estimation–Calibration Procedure

We present the results from the estimation procedure developed in accordance with the methodology proposed in Section 5.

The estimated matrix structure is a full matrix such as the one given in Formula (21) but with piecewise linear intensities which are not very elucidative in themselves. It is preferable to look at a graphical representation of these intensities. In Figure 5, we have the estimated intensities (in blue colour) and the fitted piecewise linear intensities (in red colour). We can observe that despite observable differences the fitting is reasonably good with the exception of the intensity μ_{21}. This may be due to the fact that we only had seven observations in the sample, and they are consistent with LTC data. We also observe that the fitting with an exponential-type density will give a non satisfactory result. In order to evaluate the quality of this fitting, we present in Table 1 the maximum distance between the computed approximate intensities and the fitted piecewise linear intensities.

Table 1. (1)—Maximum distance between the values of the computed approximate intensities; and (2)—the fitted piecewise linear intensities and the maximum distance normalised by the maximum value of the estimated intensities.

	μ_{12}	μ_{13}	μ_{14}
(1)	0.025381	0.159100	1.165812
(2)	0.000667	0.004186	0.030679
	μ_{21}	μ_{23}	μ_{24}
(1)	0.003661	0.020507	0.397256
(2)	0.000963	0.005396	0.104541
	μ_{31}	μ_{32}	μ_{34}
(1)	7.398272	0.000024	0.086817
(2)	3.52299	0.000011	0.04134

We observe that the error for μ_{31} is quite large compared to the other errors; this could be due to the fact that the estimation was performed with only 20 observations, again consistent with LTC data.

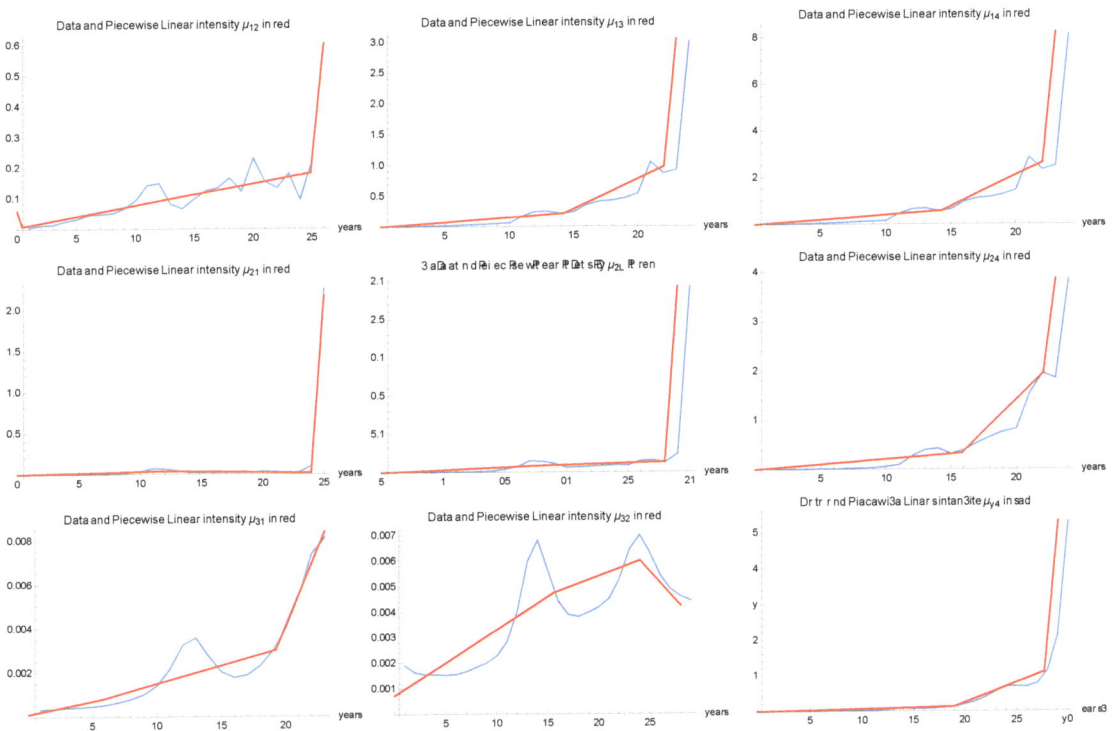

Figure 5. Data recovered from the simulated results (blue) and the piecewise linear intensities fitted (red).

In Figure 6, we can compare qualitatively the original transition probabilities with the ones obtained as the solution of the forward Kolmogorov ODE with the estimated piecewise linear intensities. A first qualitative observation is that the general behaviour of the estimated and fitted intensities is similar. In order to compare quantitatively the original transition probabilities with the ones obtained as the solution of the Kolmogorov ODE with the estimated piecewise linear intensities, we present, in Figure 7, the difference between the original transition probabilities and the estimated transition probabilities for each of the three transient states. It is clear that there are substantial differences. To justify these differences we have at least two cumulative sources of error. The first error source is induced by the fact that there was a estimation–calibration procedure applied to 5000 trajectories generated from the original transition probabilities; the second error source comes from the fact that while the original transition probabilities are produced from intensities of the Gompertz–Makeham type, the estimated transition probabilities are produced by continuous piecewise linear intensities fitted to the simulated data.

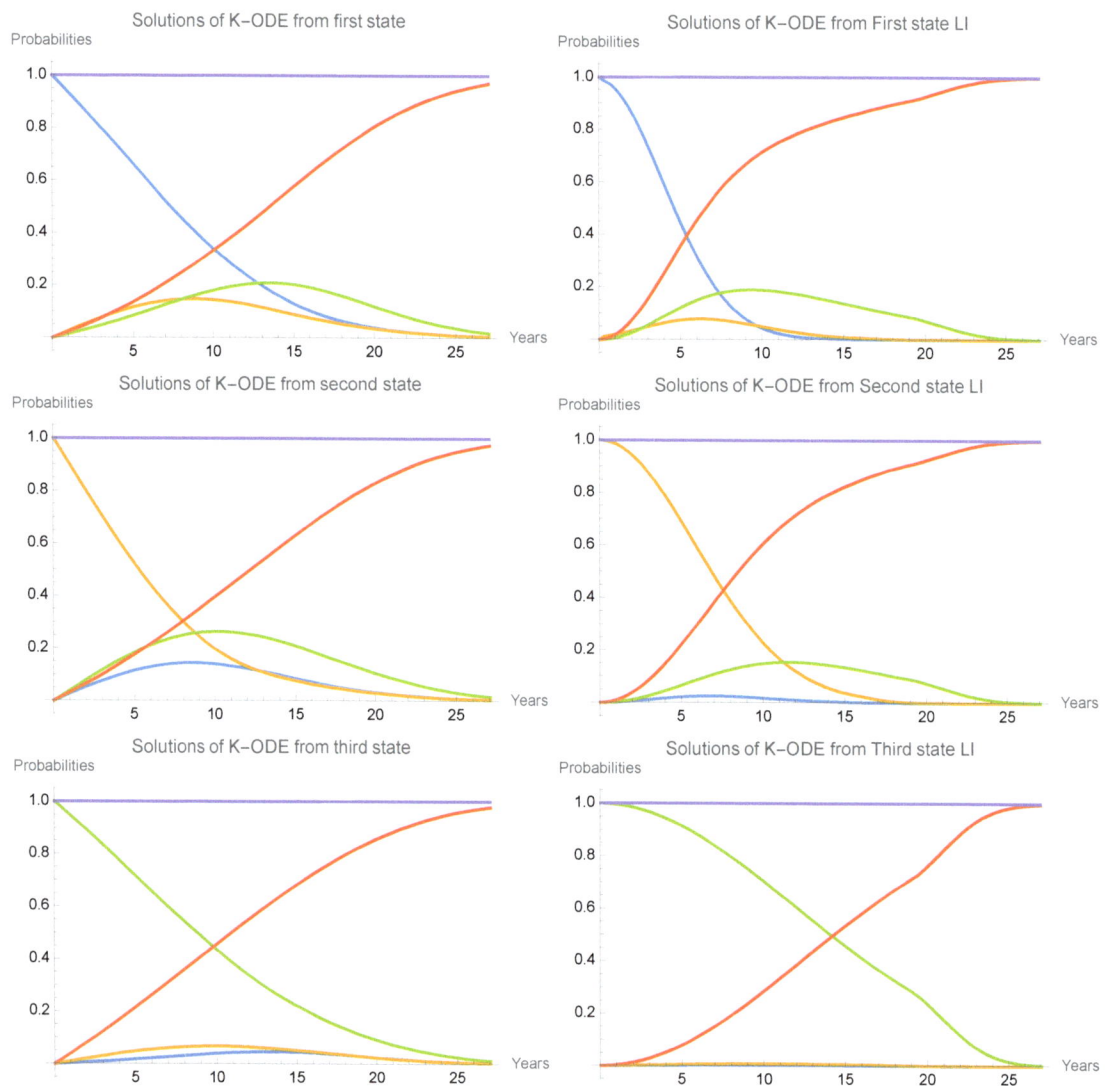

Figure 6. Comparing original transition probabilities used for simulation (left) with the estimated piecewise linear transition probabilities (right). p_{ij}: $j = 1$ (blue); $j = 2$ (orange); $j = 3$ (green); $j = 4$ (red). $\sum_{j=1}^{4} p_{ij}$ (purple).

In order to detail the average error per year coming from the estimation procedure we can compute

$$\Delta_{ij} := \frac{1}{27} \int_0^{27} \left| p_{ij}(t) - \widetilde{p}_{ij}(t) \right| dt \qquad (25)$$

with $p_{ij}(t)$ the original transition probabilities and $\widetilde{p}_{ij}(t)$ the estimated transition probabilities. The results are presented in Table 2.

Table 2. Average error per year between the estimated and the original probability transitions.

Δ_{11}	Δ_{12}	Δ_{13}	Δ_{14}
0.004647	0.001806	0.000896	0.007118
Δ_{21}	Δ_{22}	Δ_{23}	Δ_{24}
0.002394	0.002140	0.002624	0.004081
Δ_{31}	Δ_{32}	Δ_{33}	Δ_{34}
0.000896	0.001258	0.005907	0.003898

The main conclusion is that the order of magnitude of the average error per unit time—chosen as a year since it is the time duration of an interval where transition probabilities in health insurance and long-term-care models can have a significant impact—is always less than 1%. Of course, we have to be careful of the extremes of these errors that are visible in Figure 7.

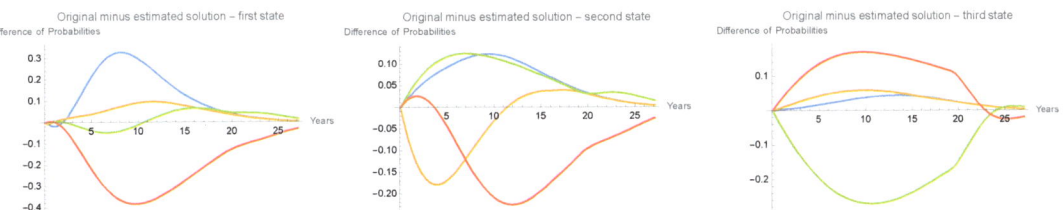

Figure 7. The difference between the original transition probabilities and the estimated ones. $p_{ij} - \tilde{p}_{ij}$: $j = 1$ (blue); $j = 2$ (orange); $j = 3$ (green); $j = 4$ (red).

All computations and graphic representations were created with a Mac mini (M1 2020) equipped with macOS Monterey 12.5.1 with Wolfram Mathematica 12, version 12.3.1.0. The estimation–calibration procedures use either native functions or small routines that require reasonable execution times of the order of a second.

7. Discussion

The methodology proposed in this work gave us the continuous piecewise linear intensities depicted in Figure 5. The use of the continuous piecewise linear functional form was intentional although not necessary; a better fit to the data, most possibly with a larger number of parameters, could be computed and possibly could provide a better final result, qualitatively, in Figure 6 and quantitatively with metrics given by both the average error per year, as in Table 2 and as in Figure 7, showing the analysis of local discrepancies between the original transition probabilities and the transition probabilities resulting from the estimation methodology. The intention of using the continuous piecewise linear functional form for the intensities was to illustrate the possibility of an estimation–calibration procedure relying on a small number of parameters. Whenever faced with the estimation–calibration of intensities for real-data modelling, a situation where there are no known determined intensities generating the data, the choice of the functional form is secondary with respect to the quality of the model fitting.

8. Conclusions

In this work, we proposed a methodology for estimation–calibration of continuous-time non-homogeneous Markov chains with finite state space. We presented an application of the methodology to a Monte Carlo simulated set of trajectories generated from intensities of Gompertz-Makeham type, and we obtained, by the methodology, estimated continuous piecewise linear intensities. We compared the correspondent transition probabilities—obtained by solving the forward Kolmogorov ODE for the original

Gompertz–Makeham intensities and for the continuous piecewise linear intensities—obtaining an average error per year of always less than 1%.

In order to justify the methodology, we presented a result on regime-switching Markov chains, proving the existence of a Markov chain process, in a given time interval, obtained by glueing together different intensities matrices defined in the different intervals of a partition of the time interval of the Markov chain process; this result shows that it is possible to consider intensities of different functional forms for different sub intervals of the time interval where the whole Markov chain process is defined.

We also presented a result that shows that it is possible to bound the distance between the matrix of transition probabilities corresponding to different matrix intensities by the distance between these matrix intensities. This result shows that, with respect to the transition probabilities, we can consider changes in functional form of the intensities—in an intensity matrix—as long as the distance between the original intensity matrix and the altered one is small enough.

In future work, we intend to improve the methodology in order to control the quality of the process by adequate tests and to improve the algorithm used.

Author Contributions: Conceptualization, M.L.E.; methodology, M.L.E., N.P.K. and G.R.G.; software, M.L.E., N.P.K. and G.R.G.; validation, M.L.E., N.P.K. and G.R.G.; formal analysis, M.L.E., N.P.K. and G.R.G.; investigation, M.L.E., N.P.K. and G.R.G.; data curation, M.L.E., N.P.K. and G.R.G.; writing—original draft preparation, M.L.E.; writing—review and editing, M.L.E., N.P.K. and G.R.G.; supervision, M.L.E. All authors have read and agreed to the published version of the manuscript.

Funding: This research was partially funded by national funds through the FCT—Fundação para a Ciência e Tecnologia, I.P., under the scope of the projects UIDB/00297/2020 and UIDP/00297/2020—Center for Mathematics and Applications.

Data Availability Statement: Data are contained within the article.

Acknowledgments: The authors are indebted to Albert N. Shiryaev for drawing attention to very important work on the subject and to the referees for the improvement seggestions.

Conflicts of Interest: The authors declare no conflicts of interest.

Abbreviations

The following abbreviations are used in this manuscript:

MCCT	Markov chain in continuous time
ODE	ordinary differential equations

References

1. Esquível, M.; Guerreiro, G.; Oliveira, M.; Real, P. Calibration of Transition Intensities for a Multistate Model: Application to Long-Term Care. *Risks* **2021**, *9*, 37. [CrossRef]
2. Vassiliou, P.C.G. *Non-Homogeneous Markov Chains and Systems—Theory and Applications*; CRC Press: Boca Raton, FL, USA, 2023; pp. xxi+450. [CrossRef]
3. Pitacco, E. *Health Insurance*; European Actuarial Academy (EAA) Series; Basic Actuarial Models; Springer: Cham, Switzerland, 2014; pp. xii+162. [CrossRef]
4. Haberman, S.; Pitacco, E. *Actuarial Models for Disability Insurance*; Chapman & Hall/CRC: Boca Raton, FL, USA, 1999; pp. xx+280.
5. Billingsley, P. *Statistical inference for Markov Processes*; Volume II, *Statistical Research Monographs*; University of Chicago Press: Chicago, IL, USA, 1961; pp. vii+75.
6. Billingsley, P. Statistical methods in Markov chains. *Ann. Math. Statist.* **1961**, *32*, 12–40. [CrossRef]
7. Waters, H.R. An Approach to the Study of Multiple State Models. *J. Inst. Actuar. (1886–1994)* **1984**, *111*, 363–374. [CrossRef]
8. Wolthuis, H. *Life Insurance Mathematics (The Markovian Model)*; CAIRE: Brussels, Belgium, 1994.
9. Forfar, D.O.; McCutcheon, J.J.; Wilkie, A.D. On Graduation by Mathematical Formula. *J. Inst. Actuar. (1886–1994)* **1988**, *115*, 1–149. [CrossRef]
10. Dickson, D.C.M.; Hardy, M.R.; Waters, H.R. *Actuarial Mathematics for Life Contingent Risks*, 3rd ed.; International Series on Actuarial Science; Cambridge University Press: Cambridge, UK, 2020; pp. xxiv+759. [CrossRef]
11. Christiansen, M.C. Multistate models in health insurance. *AStA Adv. Stat. Anal.* **2012**, *96*, 155–186. [CrossRef]

12. Wang, B.; Zhu, Q. Stability Analysis of Discrete-Time Semi-Markov Jump Linear Systems. *IEEE Trans. Autom. Control.* **2020**, *65*, 5415–5421. [CrossRef]
13. Wang, B.; Zhu, Q.; Li, S. Stability Analysis of Discrete-Time Semi-Markov Jump Linear Systems with Time Delay. *IEEE Trans. Autom. Control.* **2023**, *68*, 6758–6765. [CrossRef]
14. Meira–Machado, L.; de Uña Álvarez, J.; Cadarso-Suárez, C.; Andersen, P.K. Multi-state models for the analysis of time-to-event data. *Stat. Methods Med. Res.* **2009**, *18*, 195–222. [CrossRef]
15. Keiding, N.; Andersen, P.K. Nonparametric estimation of transition intensities and transition probabilities: A case study of a two-state Markov process. *J. R. Statist. Soc. Ser. C* **1989**, *38*, 319–329. [CrossRef]
16. Andersen, P.K.; Hansen, L.S.; Keiding, N. Non- and semi-parametric estimation of transition probabilities from censored observation of a nonhomogeneous Markov process. *Scand. J. Statist.* **1991**, *18*, 153–167.
17. Renshaw, A.E.; Haberman, S. On the graduations associated with a multiple state model for permanent health insurance. *Insur. Math. Econ.* **1995**, *17*, 1–17. [CrossRef]
18. Fong, J.H.; Shao, A.W.; Sherris, M. Multistate actuarial models of functional disability. *N. Am. Actuar. J.* **2015**, *19*, 41–59. [CrossRef]
19. Wan, L.; Lou, W.; Abner, E.; Kryscio, R.J. A comparison of time-homogeneous Markov chain and Markov process multi-state models. *Commun. Stat. Case Stud. Data Anal. Appl.* **2016**, *2*, 92–100. [CrossRef] [PubMed]
20. Naka, P.; Boado-Penas, M.d.C.; Lanot, G. A multiple state model for the working-age disabled population using cross-sectional data. *Scand. Actuar. J.* **2020**, *2020*, 700–717. [CrossRef]
21. Qian, C.; Srivastava, D.K.; Pan, J.; Hudson, M.M.; Rai, S.N. Estimating transition intensity rate on interval-censored data using semi-parametric with EM algorithm approach. In *Communications in Statistics—Theory and Methods*; Taylor and Francis: Abingdon, UK, 2023; pp. 1–17. [CrossRef]
22. de Mol van Otterloo, S.; Alonso-García, J. A multi-state model for sick leave and its impact on partial early retirement incentives: The case of the Netherlands. *Scand. Actuar. J.* **2023**, *2023*, 244–268. [CrossRef]
23. Esquível, M.; Patrício, P.; Guerreiro, G. From ODE to Open Markov Chains, via SDE: An application to models for infections in individuals and populations. *Comput. Math. Biophys.* **2020**, *8*, 180–197. [CrossRef]
24. Esquível, M.; Krasii, N.; Guerreiro, G.; Patricio, P. The Multi-Compartment SI(RD) Model with Regime Switching: An Application to COVID-19 Pandemic. *Symmetry* **2021**, *13*, 2427. [CrossRef]
25. Feinberg, E.A.; Mandava, M.; Shiryaev, A.N. On solutions of Kolmogorov's equations for nonhomogeneous jump Markov processes. *J. Math. Anal. Appl.* **2014**, *411*, 261–270. [CrossRef]
26. Feinberg, E.; Mandava, M.; Shiryaev, A.N. Kolmogorov's equations for jump Markov processes with unbounded jump rates. *Ann. Oper. Res.* **2022**, *317*, 587–604. [CrossRef]
27. Feinberg, E.A.; Shiryaev, A.N. Kolmogorov's equations for jump Markov processes and their applications to control problems. *Theory Probab. Appl.* **2022**, *66*, 582–600. *Transl. Teor. Veroyatn. Primen.* **2021**, *66*, 734–759. [CrossRef]
28. Rolski, T.; Schmidli, H.; Schmidt, V.; Teugels, J. *Stochastic Processes for Insurance and Finance*; Wiley Series in Probability and Statistics; John Wiley & Sons, Ltd.: Chichester, UK, 1999; pp. xviii+654. [CrossRef]
29. Coddington, E.A.; Levinson, N. *Theory of Ordinary Differential Equations*; McGraw-Hill Book Co., Inc.: New York, NY, USA, 1955; pp. xii+429.
30. Hale, J.K. *Ordinary Differential Equations*, 2nd ed.; Robert E. Krieger Publishing Co., Inc.: Huntington, NY, USA, 1980; pp. xvi+361.
31. Horn, R.A.; Johnson, C.R. *Matrix Analysis*, 2nd ed.; Cambridge University Press: Cambridge, UK, 2013; pp. xviii+643.
32. Stokes, A. The application of a fixed-point theorem to a variety of nonlinear stability problems. *Proc. Nat. Acad. Sci. USA* **1959**, *45*, 231–235. [CrossRef] [PubMed]
33. Kurzweil, J. Ordinary differential equations. In *Studies in Applied Mechanics*; Elsevier Scientific Publishing Co.: Amsterdam, The Netherlands, 1986; Volume 13, 440p.
34. Teschl, G. *Ordinary Differential Equations and Dynamical Systems*; Graduate Studies in Mathematics; American Mathematical Society: Providence, RI, USA, 2012; Volume 140, pp. xii+356. [CrossRef]
35. Nevanlinna, F.; Nevanlinna, R. *Absolute Analysis*; Springer: New York, NY, USA, 1973; Volume 102, pp. vi+270.
36. Butcher, J.C. *Numerical Methods for Ordinary Differential Equations*, 3rd ed.; John Wiley & Sons, Ltd.: Chichester, UK, 2016; pp. xxiii+513. [CrossRef]
37. Iosifescu, M. *Finite Markov Processes and Their Applications*; (Wiley Series in Probability and Mathematical Statistics); John Wiley & Sons, Ltd.: Chichester, UK; Editura Tehnică: Bucharest, Romania, 1980; p. 295.
38. Iosifescu, M.; Tăutu, P. *Stochastic Processes and Applications in Biology and Medicine. I: Theory*; Editura Academiei RSR: Bucharest, Romania; Springer: Berlin/Heidelbeerg, Germany, 1973; Volume 3, p. 331.

mathematics

MDPI

Article

A Class of Power Series q-Distributions

Charalambos A. Charalambides

Department of Mathematics, University of Athens, Panepistemiopolis, GR-15784 Athens, Greece; ccharal@math.uoa.gr

Abstract: A class of power series q-distributions, generated by considering a q-Taylor expansion of a parametric function into powers of the parameter, is discussed. Its q-factorial moments are obtained in terms of q-derivatives of its series (parametric) function. Also, it is shown that the convolution of power series q-distributions is also a power series q-distribution. Furthermore, the q-Poisson (Heine and Euler), q-binomial of the first kind, negative q-binomial of the second kind, and q-logarithmic distributions are shown to be members of this class of distributions and their q-factorial moments are deduced. In addition, the convolution properties of these distributions are examined.

Keywords: Euler distribution; Heine distribution; negative q-binomial distribution; q-binomial distribution; q-factorial moments; q-logarithmic distribution; q-poisson distribution

MSC: 60C05; 05A30

Citation: Charalambides, C.A. A Class of Power Series q-Distributions. *Mathematics* **2024**, *12*, 712. https://doi.org/10.3390/math12050712

Academic Editors: Panagiotis-Christos Vassiliou, Andreas C. Georgiou and Antonio Di Crescenzo

Received: 12 November 2023
Revised: 23 February 2024
Accepted: 24 February 2024
Published: 28 February 2024

1. Introduction

Benkherouf and Bather (1988) [1] derived the Heine and Euler distributions, which constitute the q-analogs of the Poisson distribution, as feasible priors in a simple Bayesian model for oil exploration. The probability (mass) function of the q-Poisson distributions is given by (Charalambides (2016), p. 107) [2]

$$p_x(\lambda; q) = E_q(-\lambda) \frac{\lambda^x}{[x]_q!}, \quad x = 0, 1, \ldots, \tag{1}$$

where $0 < \lambda < 1/(1-q)$ and $0 < q < 1$ (Euler distribution) or $0 < \lambda < \infty$ and $1 < q < \infty$ (Heine distribution). Also, $E_q(t) = \prod_{i=1}^{\infty}(1 + t(1-q)q^{i-1})$ is a q-exponential function, satisfying the relation $E_q(t)E_{q^{-1}}(-t) = 1$, where $|t| < b(q)$ and $|q| < 1$ or $|q| > 1$, with the bound $b(q) \leq \infty$ depending on q. It should be noted that $e_q(t) = \prod_{i=1}^{\infty}(1 - t(1-q)q^{i-1})^{-1}$ is another q-exponential function, connected to the first one by $e_q(t) = E_{q^{-1}}(t)$.

Kemp and Kemp (1991) [3], in their study of Weldon's classical dice data, introduced a q-binomial distribution. It is the distribution of the number of successes in a sequence of n independent Bernoulli trials, with the odds of success at a trial varying geometrically with the number of trials. Kemp and Newton (1990) [4] further studied it as a stationary distribution of a birth and death process. The probability function of this q-binomial distribution of the first kind is given by

$$p_x(\theta; q) = \begin{bmatrix} n \\ x \end{bmatrix}_q \frac{\theta^x q^{\binom{x}{2}}}{\prod_{i=1}^{n}(1 + \theta q^{i-1})}, \quad x = 0, 1, \ldots, n, \tag{2}$$

where $0 < \theta < \infty$ and $0 < q < 1$ or $1 < q < \infty$.

Charalambides (2010) [5] in his study of the q-Bernstein polynomials as a q-binomial distribution of the second kind, introduced the negative q-binomial distribution of the second kind. It is the distribution of the number of failures until the occurrence of the nth success in a sequence of independent Bernoulli trials, with the probability of success at a

trial varying geometrically with the number of successes. The probability function of this negative q-binomial distribution of the second kind is given by

$$p_x(\theta;q) = \begin{bmatrix} n+x-1 \\ x \end{bmatrix}_q \theta^x \prod_{i=1}^{n}(1-\theta q^{i-1}), \quad x = 0,1,\ldots, \tag{3}$$

where $0 < \theta < 1$ and $0 < q < 1$.

A q-logarithmic distribution was studied byC. D. Kemp (1997) [6] as a group size distribution. Its probability function is given by

$$p_x(\theta;q) = [-l_q(1-\theta)]^{-1}\frac{\theta^x}{[x]_q}, \quad x = 1,2,\ldots, \tag{4}$$

where $0 < \theta < 1, 0 < q < 1$, and

$$-l_q(1-\theta) = \lim_{t \to 0}\frac{1}{[t]_q}\left(\prod_{i=1}^{\infty}\frac{1-\theta q^{t+i-1}}{1-\theta q^{i-1}} - 1\right) = \sum_{j=1}^{\infty}\frac{\theta^j}{[j]_q}$$

is a q-logarithmic function.

A class of power series q-distributions, which is introduced in Section 2 by considering a q-Taylor expansion of a parametric function, provides a unified approach to the study of these distributions. Its q-factorial moments, for $0 < q < 1$ and $1 < q < \infty$, are obtained in terms of q-derivatives of its series function. As essentially noted by Dunkl (1981) [7] and formally expressed in Charalambides and Papadatos (2005) [8] and Charalambides (2016) [2], the usual factorial (and binomial) moments are given in terms of the q-factorial (and q-binomial) moments through the q-Stirling numbers of the first kind. Moreover, it is proved that a power series q-distribution is completely determined from its first two q-cumulants (or q-moments). Also, the convolution of power series q-distributions, using probability-generating functions, is shown to be a power series q-distribution. Furthermore, in Section 3, demonstrating this approach, the q-factorial moments for $0 < q < 1$ and $1 < q < \infty$ of the q-Poisson (Heine and Euler) distributions, q-binomial distribution of the first kind, negative q-binomial distribution of the second kind, and q-logarithmic distribution are obtained as members of this class of distributions. In addition, interesting and useful structural information about these distributions is obtained through their probability-generating functions.

2. Power Series q-Distributions

Consider a positive function $g(\theta)$ of a positive parameter θ and assume that it is analytic with a q-Taylor expansion about zero (Jackson (1909) [9], Ernst (2012) [10], p. 103)

$$g(\theta) = \sum_{x=0}^{\infty}a_{x,q}\theta^x, \quad 0 < \theta < \rho, \quad \rho > 0, \tag{5}$$

where the coefficient

$$a_{x,q} = \frac{1}{[x]_q!}[D_q^x g(t)]_{t=0} \geq 0, \quad x = 0,1,\ldots, \quad 0 < q < 1, \quad \text{or} \quad 1 < q < \infty, \tag{6}$$

with $D_q = d_q/d_q t$ the q-derivative operator (Ernst (2012) [10], p. 200),

$$D_q g(t) = \frac{d_q g(t)}{d_q t} = \begin{cases} \dfrac{g(t)-g(qt)}{(1-q)t}, & q \neq 1, \ t \neq 0, \\[2mm] Dg(t) = \dfrac{dg(t)}{dt}, & q = 1, \\[2mm] Dg(0) = \dfrac{dg(0)}{dt}, & t = 0, \end{cases}$$

does not involve the parameter θ. Clearly, the function

$$p_x(\theta; q) = \frac{a_{x,q}\theta^x}{g(\theta)}, \quad x = 0, 1, \ldots,$$ (7)

with $0 < \theta < \rho$ and $0 < q < 1$ or $1 < q < \infty$, satisfies the properties of a probability (mass) function.

Definition 1. *A family of discrete q-distributions $p_x(\theta; q)$, $\theta \in \Theta$, $q \in Q$, is said to be a class of power series q-distributions, with parameters θ and q and series function $g(\theta)$ if it has the representation (7), with series function satisfying condition (5).*

Remark 1. *The q-Taylor expansion (5) may be equivalently expressed as expressed as Jackson (1942) [11], Ernst (2012) [10], p. 103*

$$g(\theta) = \sum_{x=0}^{\infty} b_{x,q}\theta^x, \quad 0 < \theta < \rho, \quad \rho > 0,$$

where the coefficient

$$b_{x,q} = \frac{q^{\binom{x}{2}}}{[x]_q!}[D_q^x g(qt)]_{t=0} \geq 0, \quad x = 0, 1, \ldots, \quad 0 < q < 1, \quad or \quad 1 < q < \infty,$$

and does not involve the parameter θ. Indeed, replacing q by q^{-1} in (5) and (6) and since $[x]_{q^{-1}}! = q^{-\binom{x}{2}}[x]_q!$ and $[D_{q^{-1}}^x g(t)]_{t=0} = [D_q^x g(qt)]_{t=0}$, the equivalent expression is readily deduced.

Remark 2. *The class of power series q-distributions, for $q \to 1$, reduces to the class of (usual) power series distributions, which was introduced by Noack (1950) [12] and further studied by Khatri (1959) [13] and Patil (1962) [14]. Furthermore, it should be noted that the range of x in (7), as in the case of the power series distributions, need not be the entire set of nonnegative integers; it can be an arbitrary non-null subset of nonnegative integers. Also, note that a truncated version of a power series q-distribution is itself a power series q-distribution in its own right; hence, the properties that hold for a power series q-distribution continue to hold for its truncated forms.*

The basic properties of a power series q-distribution are established in the following propositions. Its q-factorial moments are derived first, in terms of the q-derivatives of the series function.

Proposition 1. *The mth q-factorial moment of the power series q-distribution (7) is given by*

$$E([X]_{m,q}) = \frac{\theta^m}{g(\theta)} \cdot \frac{d_q^m g(\theta)}{d_q\theta^m}, \quad m = 1, 2, \ldots.$$ (8)

In particular, the q-mean and q-variance are given by

$$E([X]_q) = \frac{\theta}{g(\theta)} \cdot \frac{d_q g(\theta)}{d_q\theta}$$ (9)

and

$$V([X]_q) = \frac{\theta^2 q}{g(\theta)} \cdot \frac{d_q^2 g(\theta)}{d_q\theta^2} - \frac{\theta}{g(\theta)} \cdot \frac{d_q g(\theta)}{d_q\theta}\left(\frac{\theta}{g(\theta)} \cdot \frac{d_q g(\theta)}{d_q\theta} - 1\right),$$ (10)

respectively.

Proof. The mth q-factorial moment,

$$E([X]_{m,q}) = \sum_{x=m}^{\infty} [x]_{m,q} \frac{a_{x,q}\theta^x}{g(\theta)} = \frac{\theta^m}{g(\theta)} \sum_{x=m}^{\infty} a_{x,q} [x]_{m,q}\theta^{x-m},$$

on using the mth q-derivative of the series function (5),

$$\frac{d_q^m g(\theta)}{d_q\theta^m} = \sum_{x=m}^{\infty} a_{x,q}[x]_{m,q}\theta^{x-m},$$

is readily deduced as (8). In particular, for $m = 1$, the q-mean is given by (9). Also, using the expression (Charalambides (2016), p. 43)

$$V([X]_q) = qE([X]_{2,q}) - E([X]_q)\big(E([X]_q) - 1\big),$$

the q-variance is obtained in the form (10). $\square$

The derivation of the q^{-1}-factorial moments, $E([X]_{m,q^{-1}})$, $m = 1, 2, \ldots$, of several power series q-distributions, in addition to their own interest, are shown to be useful in the study of limiting distributions (Kyriakoussis and Vamvakari (2013) [15] and Charalambides (2016) [2], chapter 4). These moments are given, in terms of the q^{-1}-derivatives of the series function, by (8) with q replaced by q^{-1}. An alternative expression, in terms of the q-derivatives of the series function, is obtained in the next proposition.

Proposition 2. *The mth q^{-1}-factorial moment of the power series q-distribution (7) is given by*

$$E([X]_{m,q^{-1}}) = \frac{\theta^m q^{\binom{m+1}{2}}}{g(\theta)} \frac{d_q^m g(q^{-m}\theta)}{d_q\theta^m}, \quad m = 1, 2, \ldots. \tag{11}$$

In particular, the q^{-1}-mean and q^{-1}-variance are given by

$$E([X]_{q^{-1}}) = \frac{\theta q}{g(\theta)} \cdot \frac{d_q g(q^{-1}\theta)}{d_q\theta} \tag{12}$$

and

$$V([X]_{q^{-1}}) = \frac{\theta^2 q^2}{g(\theta)} \cdot \frac{d_q^2 g(q^{-2}\theta)}{d_q\theta^2} - \frac{\theta q}{g(\theta)} \cdot \frac{d_q g(q^{-1}\theta)}{d_q\theta} \left(\frac{\theta q}{g(\theta)} \cdot \frac{d_q g(q^{-1}\theta)}{d_q\theta} - 1 \right), \tag{13}$$

respectively.

Proof. The mth q^{-1}-factorial moment, since $[x]_{m,q^{-1}} = q^{\binom{m+1}{2}-mx}[x]_{m,q}$, may be expressed as

$$E([X]_{m,q^{-1}}) = \sum_{x=m}^{\infty} [x]_{m,q^{-1}} \frac{a_{x,q}\theta^x}{g(\theta)} = \frac{\theta^m q^{\binom{m+1}{2}}}{g(\theta)} \sum_{x=m}^{\infty} a_{x,q}[x]_{m,q}q^{-mx}\theta^{x-m}.$$

Also, the mth q-derivative of the series function $g(q^{-m}\theta)$, with respect to θ, can be written as

$$\frac{d_q^m g(q^{-m}\theta)}{d_q\theta^m} = q^{-m^2} \left[\frac{d_q^m g(u)}{d_q u^m} \right]_{u=q^{-m}\theta} = \sum_{x=m}^{\infty} a_{x,q}[x]_{m,q}q^{-mx}\theta^{x-m}.$$

Introducing it into the last expression of the mth q^{-1}-factorial moment, (11) is obtained. In particular, for $m = 1$, the q^{-1}-mean is given by (12). Also, using the expression

$$V([X]_{q^{-1}}) = q^{-1}E([X]_{2,q^{-1}}) - E([X]_{q^{-1}})\big(E([X]_{q^{-1}}) - 1\big),$$

the q^{-1}-variance is obtained in the form (13). □

The convolution of power series q-distributions is also a power q-series distribution, according to the following proposition.

Proposition 3. *(a) The probability generating function $P(t) = E(t^X)$ of the power series q-distribution (7) is given, in terms of the series function (5), by*

$$P(t) = \frac{g(\theta t)}{g(\theta)}, \quad |t| < \rho/\theta. \tag{14}$$

(b) Suppose that $X_j, j = 1, 2, \ldots, n$, is a sequence of n independent random variables obeying a power series q-distribution, with series function $g_j(\theta), j = 1, 2, \ldots, n$. Then, the sum $S_n = \sum_{j=1}^n X_j$ obeys a power series q-distribution, with series function

$$g(\theta) = \prod_{j=1}^n g_j(\theta). \tag{15}$$

Proof. (a) The probability generating function $P(t) = \sum_{x=0}^{\infty} p_x(\theta; q) t^x$, on using (5) and (7), is readily obtained as (14).

(b) The probability generating function $P_{S_n}(t)$, of the sum $S_n = \sum_{j=1}^n X_j$, is the product of the generating functions $P_{X_j}(t), j = 1, 2, \ldots, n$, of the summands, $P_{S_n}(t) = \prod_{j=1}^n P_{X_j}(t)$, and so by (14) is deduced in the form

$$P_{S_n}(t) = \prod_{j=1}^n \frac{g_j(\theta t)}{g_j(\theta)} = \frac{\prod_{j=1}^n g_j(\theta t)}{\prod_{j=1}^n g_j(\theta)}.$$

Using again (14), the last expression implies (15). □

The second part of Proposition 3 can be directly extended to an infinite series of random variables according to the following corollary.

Corollary 1. *Suppose that $X_j, j = 1, 2, \ldots$, is a sequence of independent random variables obeying a power series q-distribution, with series function $g_j(\theta), j = 1, 2, \ldots$. Then, the sum $S = \sum_{j=1}^{\infty} X_j$ obeys a power series q-distribution, with series function*

$$g(\theta) = \prod_{j=1}^{\infty} g_j(\theta), \tag{16}$$

provided $\prod_{j=1}^{\infty} g_j(\theta) < \infty$.

3. Particular Power Series q-Distributions

Particular power series q-distributions, which are obtained by specifying the series function, are discussed; their q-factorial moments are deduced and convolution properties are examined.

3.1. q-Poisson Distributions

The q-Poisson distributions, with probability function (1), belong in the family of power series q-distributions, with series function $g(\lambda) = e_q(\lambda) = 1/E_q(-\lambda)$, where $0 < \lambda < 1/(1-q)$ and $0 < q < 1$ (Euler distribution) or $0 < \lambda < \infty$ and $1 < q < \infty$ (Heine distribution). Indeed, since $D_q e_q(t) = e_q(t)$ and $e_q(0) = 1$, it follows from (6) that

$$a_{x,q} = \frac{1}{[x]_q!} [D_q^x e_q(t)]_{t=0} = \frac{1}{[x]_q!}, \quad x = 0, 1, \ldots,$$

and the probability function (7) reduces to (1).

The q-factorial moments, by (8) and since $d_q^m e_q(\lambda)/d_q \lambda^m = e_q(\lambda)$, are readily deduced as

$$E([X]_{m,q}) = \lambda^m, \quad m = 1, 2, \ldots,$$

where $0 < \lambda < 1/(1-q)$ and $0 < q < 1$ (Euler distribution) or $0 < \lambda < \infty$ and $1 < q < \infty$ (Heine distribution). In particular, the q-mean is given by

$$E([X]_q) = \lambda.$$

Furthermore, using (10), the q-variance is obtained as

$$V([X]_q) = q\lambda^2 - \lambda(\lambda - 1) = \lambda(1 + (q-1)\lambda).$$

The q^{-1}-factorial moments, by (11) and since

$$\frac{d_q^m e_q(q^{-m}\lambda)}{d_q \lambda^m} = q^{-m^2} e_q(q^{-m}\lambda),$$

are obtained as

$$E([X]_{m,q^{-1}}) = \frac{\lambda^m q^{\binom{m+1}{2}}}{e_q(\lambda)} \cdot q^{-m^2} e_q(q^{-m}\lambda) = \frac{\lambda^m q^{-\binom{m}{2}} \prod_{i=1}^{\infty}\left(1 - \lambda(1-q)q^{i-1}\right)}{\prod_{i=1}^{\infty}\left(1 - \lambda(1-q)q^{-m+i-1}\right)},$$

which on using

$$\prod_{i=1}^{\infty}\left(1 - \lambda(1-q)q^{-m+i-1}\right) = \prod_{j=1}^{m}\left(1 + \lambda(1-q^{-1})q^{-(j-1)}\right) \prod_{i=1}^{\infty}\left(1 - \lambda(1-q)q^{i-1}\right),$$

reduces to

$$E([X]_{m,q^{-1}}) = \frac{\lambda^m q^{-\binom{m}{2}}}{\prod_{j=1}^{m}\left(1 + \lambda(1-q^{-1})q^{-(j-1)}\right)}, \quad m = 1, 2, \ldots,$$

where $0 < \lambda < 1/(1-q)$ and $0 < q < 1$ (Euler distribution) or $0 < \lambda < \infty$ and $1 < q < \infty$ (Heine distribution). In particular, the q^{-1}-mean is

$$E([X]_{q^{-1}}) = \frac{\lambda}{1 + \lambda(1-q^{-1})}.$$

Also, by (13), the q^{-1}-variance is obtained as

$$
\begin{aligned}
V([X]_{q^{-1}}) &= \frac{\lambda^2 q^{-2}}{\left(1 + \lambda(1-q^{-1})\right)\left(1 + \lambda(1-q^{-1})q^{-1}\right)} + \frac{\lambda + \lambda^2(1-q^{-1}) - \lambda^2}{\left(1 + \lambda(1-q^{-1})\right)^2} \\
&= \frac{\lambda^2 q^{-2} + \lambda^3 q^{-2} - \lambda^3 q^{-3} + \lambda - \lambda^2 q^{-1} + \lambda^2 q^{-2} - \lambda^2 q^{-2} - \lambda^3 q^{-2} + \lambda^3 q^{-3}}{\left(1 + \lambda(1-q^{-1})\right)^2 \left(1 + \lambda(1-q^{-1})q^{-1}\right)},
\end{aligned}
$$

which reduces to

$$V([X]_{q^{-1}}) = \frac{\lambda}{\left(1 + \lambda(1-q^{-1})\right)^2 \left(1 + \lambda(1-q^{-1})q^{-1}\right)}.$$

A characterization of a q-Poisson distribution through a relation between the first two q-factorial moments is worth mentioning. Clearly,

$$E([X]_{2,q}) = \left(E([X]_q)\right)^2,$$

for $0 < \lambda < 1/(1-q)$ and $0 < q < 1$ (Euler distribution) or $0 < \lambda < \infty$ and $1 < q < \infty$ (Heine distribution). Charalambides and Papadatos (2005) [8] showed that a family of nonnegative integer-valued random variables X_λ, for $0 < \lambda < \rho$ and $0 < q < 1$, with a power series q-distribution, obeys a Euler distribution, if and only if

$$E([X_\lambda]_{2,q}) = \big(E([X_\lambda]_q)\big)^2,$$

for $0 < \lambda < \rho$ and $0 < q < 1$. Without any change in the proof, the last relation holds true for $0 < \lambda < \rho$ and $0 < q < 1$ or $1 < q < \infty$ if and only if the probability function of X_λ is given by

$$p_x(a\lambda; q) = E_q(-a\lambda) \frac{(a\lambda)^x}{[x]_q!}, \quad x = 0, 1, \ldots,$$

where $0 < a\lambda < 1/(1-q)$ and $0 < q < 1$ or $0 < a\lambda < \infty$ and $1 < q < \infty$, with $a > 0$ an arbitrary constant. The additional characterization provided by this extension may be rephrased as follows. A family of nonnegative integer-valued random variables X_λ, for $0 < \lambda < \rho$ and $0 < q < 1$, with a power series q-distribution, obeys a Heine distribution, if and only if

$$E([X_\lambda]_{2,q^{-1}}) = \big(E([X_\lambda]_{q^{-1}})\big)^2,$$

for $0 < \lambda < \rho$ and $0 < q < 1$.

A close examination of the probability generating function of a q-Poisson distribution reveals interesting and useful structural information about the probability distribution. Specifically, from expression (14), with series function $g(\lambda) = E_q(\lambda) = \prod_{i=1}^{\infty}\big(1 + \lambda(1-q)q^{i-1}\big)$, and setting $\theta = \lambda(1-q)$, the probability generating function of the Heine distribution is deduced as

$$P(t) = \frac{E_q(\lambda t)}{E_q(\lambda)} = \prod_{i=1}^{\infty} \frac{1 + \theta t q^{i-1}}{1 + \theta q^{i-1}}, \quad -\infty < t < \infty, \quad 0 < \theta < \infty, \quad 0 < q < 1,$$

where $P_{X_i}(t) = \big(1 + \theta t q^{i-1}\big)/\big(1 + \theta q^{i-1}\big)$ is the probability generating function of a Bernoulli distribution. Therefore, according to Corollary 1, the Heine distribution may be expressed as an infinite convolution of independent (and not identically distributed) Bernoulli distributions. This representation of the Heine distribution was first noticed by Benkherouf and Bather (1988).

Also, from (14), with $g(\lambda) = e_q(\lambda) = \prod_{j=1}^{\infty}\big(1 - \lambda(1-q)q^{j-1}\big)^{-1}$, and setting $\theta = \lambda(1-q)$, the probability generating function of the Euler distribution is obtained as

$$P(t) = \frac{e_q(\lambda t)}{e_q(\lambda)} = \prod_{j=1}^{\infty} \frac{1 - \theta q^{j-1}}{1 - \theta t q^{j-1}}, \quad |t| < 1/\theta, \quad 0 < \theta < 1, \quad 0 < q < 1,$$

where $P_{X_j}(t) = \big(1 - \theta q^{j-1}\big)/\big(1 - \theta t q^{j-1}\big)$ is the probability generating function of a geometric distribution. Therefore, according to Corollary 1, the Euler distribution may be expressed as an infinite convolution of independent (and not identically distributed) geometric distributions. It should be noted that this expression of the Euler distribution was derived by Kemp (1992) [16].

3.2. q-Binomial Distribution of the First Kind

The q-binomial distribution of the first kind, with probability function (2), is a power series q-distribution, with series function $g(\theta) = \prod_{i=1}^{n}(1 + \theta q^{i-1})$, where $0 < \theta < \infty$ and $0 < q < 1$ or $1 < q < \infty$. Indeed, since

$$D_q g(\theta) = \frac{\prod_{i=1}^n (1 + \theta q^{i-1}) - \prod_{i=1}^n (1 + \theta q^i)}{(1-q)\theta}$$

$$= \frac{[(1+\theta) - (1+\theta q^n)] \prod_{i=1}^{n-1} (1+\theta q^i)}{(1-q)\theta} = [n]_q \prod_{i=1}^{n-1} (1 + (\theta q)q^{i-1}),$$

it follows successively that

$$D_q^x g(\theta) = [n]_{x,q} q^{1+2+\cdots+(x-1)} \prod_{i=1}^{n-x} (1 + (\theta q^x)q^{i-1}) = [n]_{x,q} q^{\binom{x}{2}} \prod_{i=1}^{n-x} (1 + (\theta q^x)q^{i-1}),$$

for $x = 1, 2, \ldots, n$, and, by (6), that

$$a_{x,q} = \frac{1}{[x]_q!} [D_q^x g(t)]_{t=0} = \begin{bmatrix} n \\ x \end{bmatrix}_q q^{\binom{x}{2}}, \quad x = 0, 1, \ldots, n,$$

and the probability function (7) reduces to (2).

The q-factorial moments, by (8) and since

$$\frac{d_q^m g(\theta)}{d_q \theta^m} = [n]_{m,q} q^{\binom{m}{2}} \prod_{i=1}^{n-m} (1 + (\theta q^m)q^{i-1}) = [n]_{m,q} q^{\binom{m}{2}} \prod_{i=m+1}^{n} (1 + \theta q^{i-1}),$$

are obtained as

$$E([X]_{m,q}) = \frac{[n]_{m,q} \theta^m q^{\binom{m}{2}}}{\prod_{i=1}^m (1 + \theta q^{i-1})}, \quad m = 1, 2, \ldots,$$

where $0 < \theta < \infty$ and $0 < q < 1$ or $1 < q < \infty$. In particular, the q-mean is

$$E([X]_q) = \frac{[n]_q \theta}{(1+\theta)}.$$

Also, by (10), the q-variance is obtained as

$$V([X]_q) = \frac{[n]_q [n-1]_q \theta^2 q^2}{(1+\theta)(1+\theta q)} + \frac{[n]_q \theta}{1+\theta} \left(1 - \frac{[n]_q \theta}{1+\theta} \right),$$

which, on using the expression $q[n-1]_q = [n]_q - 1$, reduces to

$$V([X]_q) = \frac{[n]_q \theta}{(1+\theta)(1+\theta q)} \left(1 + \frac{[n]_q \theta (q-1)}{1+\theta} \right).$$

The q^{-1}-factorial moments, on using (11) with

$$\frac{d_q^m g(q^{-m}\theta)}{d_q \theta^m} = [n]_{m,q} q^{\binom{m}{2} - m^2} \prod_{i=1}^{n-m} (1 + \theta q^{i-1}) = [n]_{m,q} q^{-\binom{m+1}{2}} \prod_{i=1}^{n-m} (1 + \theta q^{i-1}),$$

and since

$$\prod_{i=1}^{n} (1 + \theta q^{i-1}) = \prod_{i=1}^{n-m} (1 + \theta q^{i-1}) \prod_{i=n-m+1}^{n} (1 + \theta q^{i-1})$$

$$= \prod_{i=1}^{n-m} (1 + \theta q^{i-1}) \prod_{i=1}^{n} (1 + \theta q^{n-m+i-1}),$$

are obtained as

$$E([X]_{m,q^{-1}}) = \frac{[n]_{m,q}\theta^m}{\prod_{i=1}^m(1+\theta q^{n-m+i-1})}, \quad m = 1,2,\ldots,$$

where $0 < \theta < \infty$ and $0 < q < 1$ or $1 < q < \infty$. In particular, the q^{-1}-mean is

$$E([X]_{q^{-1}}) = \frac{[n]_q\theta}{1+\theta q^{n-1}}.$$

Also, by (13) and using the expression $[n-1]_q = [n]_q - q^{n-1}$, the q^{-1}-variance is obtained as

$$V([X]_{q^{-1}}) = \frac{[n]_q\theta}{1+\theta q^{n-1}} - \frac{[n]_q\theta^2 q^{n-2}}{(1+\theta q^{n-1})(1+\theta q^{n-2})}$$
$$+ \frac{[n]_q^2\theta^2 q^{-1}}{(1+\theta q^{n-1})(1+\theta q^{n-2})} - \frac{[n]_q^2\theta^2}{(1+\theta q^{n-1})^2},$$

which after some algebra reduces to

$$V([X]_{q^{-1}}) = \frac{[n]_q\theta}{(1+\theta q^{n-1})(1+\theta q^{n-2})}\left(1 + \frac{[n]_q\theta(q^{-1}-1)}{1+\theta q^{n-1}}\right).$$

The probability generating function of the q-binomial distribution of the first kind, on using (14), is deduced as

$$P(t) = \prod_{i=1}^n \frac{1+\theta t q^{i-1}}{1+\theta q^{i-1}}, \quad |t| < \infty, \ 0 < \theta < \infty, \ 0 < q < 1 \text{ or } 1 < q < \infty,$$

where $P_{X_i}(t) = (1+\theta t q^{i-1})/(1+\theta q^{i-1})$ is the probability generating function of a Bernoulli distribution. Therefore, according to Proposition 3(b), the q-binomial distribution of the first kind, may be expressed as a convolution of n independent (and not identically distributed) Bernoulli distributions.

More generally, the q-binomial distribution of the first kind may be expressed as a convolution of n independent q-binomial distributions of the first kind. Specifically, let $X_j, j = 1,2,\ldots,n$, be a sequence of n independent random variables and assume that X_j follows a q-binomial distribution of the first kind with parameters $r_j, \theta q^{s_{j-1}}$, and q, where $s_j = \sum_{i=1}^j r_i$, for $j = 1,2,\ldots,n$ and $s_0 = 0$. Clearly, the probability-generating function of X_j is given by

$$P_{X_j}(t) = \prod_{i=1}^{r_j} \frac{1+\theta t q^{s_{j-1}+i-1}}{1+\theta q^{s_{j-1}+i-1}}, \quad |t| < \infty, 0 < \theta < \infty, 0 < q < 1 \text{ or } 1 < q < \infty.$$

Consequently, the probability-generating function of the sum $S_n = \sum_{j=1}^n X_j$, is deduced as

$$P_{S_n}(t) = \prod_{j=1}^n \prod_{i=1}^{r_j} \frac{1+\theta t q^{s_{j-1}+i-1}}{1+\theta q^{s_{j-1}+i-1}} = \prod_{j=1}^n \prod_{i=s_{j-1}+1}^{s_j} \frac{1+\theta t q^{i-1}}{1+\theta q^{i-1}},$$

which, for $s_n \equiv m$, simplifies to

$$P_{S_n}(t) = \prod_{i=1}^m \frac{1+\theta t q^{i-1}}{1+\theta q^{i-1}}, \quad |t| < \infty, \ 0 < \theta < \infty, \ 0 < q < 1 \text{ or } 1 < q < \infty.$$

Therefore, the distribution of S_n is a q-binomial distribution of the first kind with parameters m, θ, and q.

Finally, it is worth noticing that the probability-generating function of the Heine distribution, with parameters λ and q,

$$P_X(t) = \prod_{i=1}^{\infty} \frac{1 + \theta t q^{i-1}}{1 + \theta q^{i-1}}, \quad -\infty < t < \infty, \ 0 < \theta < \infty, \ 0 < q < 1,$$

where $\theta = \lambda(1-q)$, may be expressed as product, $P_X(t) = P_{X_n}(t)P_{Y_n}(t)$, of the probability generating function of the q-binomial distribution of the first kind, with parameters n, θ, and q,

$$P_{X_n}(t) = \prod_{i=1}^{n} \frac{1 + \theta t q^{i-1}}{1 + \theta q^{i-1}}, \quad -\infty < t < \infty, \ 0 < \theta < \infty, \ 0 < q < 1,$$

and the probability generating function of the Heine distribution, with parameters λq^n and q,

$$P_{Y_n}(t) = \prod_{i=1}^{\infty} \frac{1 + \theta t q^{n+i-1}}{1 + \theta q^{n+j-1}}, \quad -\infty < t < \infty, \ 0 < \theta < \infty, \ 0 < q < 1.$$

Therefore, a Heine distribution may be expressed as a convolution of a q-binomial distribution of the first kind and an independent Heine distribution.

3.3. Negative q-Binomial Distribution of the Second Kind

The negative q-binomial distribution of the second kind with probability function (3) is a power series q-distribution, with series function $g(\theta) = \prod_{i=1}^{n}(1 - \theta q^{i-1})^{-1}$, where $0 < \theta < 1$ and $0 < q < 1$. Indeed, since

$$D_q g(\theta) = \frac{\prod_{i=1}^{n}(1 - \theta q^{i-1})^{-1} - \prod_{i=1}^{n}(1 - \theta q^i)^{-1}}{(1-q)\theta}$$

$$= \frac{[(1 - \theta q^n) - (1 - \theta)]\prod_{i=1}^{n+1}(1 - \theta q^{i-1})}{(1-q)\theta} = [n]_q \prod_{i=1}^{n+1}(1 - \theta q^{i-1}),$$

it follows successively that

$$D_q^x g(\theta) = [n]_q[n+1]_q \cdots [n+x-1]_q \prod_{i=1}^{n+x}(1 - \theta q^{i-1}) = [n+x-1]_{x,q} \prod_{i=1}^{n+x}(1 - \theta q^{i-1}),$$

for $x = 1, 2, \ldots$, and, by (6), that

$$a_{x,q} = \frac{1}{[x]_q!}[D_q^x g(t)]_{t=0} = \begin{bmatrix} n+x-1 \\ x \end{bmatrix}_q, \quad x = 0, 1, \ldots,$$

and the probability function (7) reduces to (3).

The q-factorial moments, by (8) and since

$$D_q^m g(\theta) = [n+m-1]_{m,q} \prod_{i=1}^{n+m}(1 - \theta q^{i-1})^{-1}$$

$$= [n+m-1]_{m,q} \prod_{i=1}^{n}(1 - \theta q^{i-1})^{-1} \prod_{i=1}^{m}(1 - \theta q^{n+i-1})^{-1},$$

are obtained as

$$E([X]_{m,q}) = \frac{[n+m-1]_{m,q}\theta^m}{\prod_{i=1}^{m}(1 - \theta q^{n+i-1})}, \quad m = 1, 2, \ldots,$$

where $0 < \theta < 1$ and $0 < q < 1$. In particular, the q-expected value is

$$E([X]_q) = \frac{[n]_q \theta}{1 - \theta q^n}.$$

Also, by (10), the q-variance is obtained as

$$V([X]_q) = \frac{[n]_q[n+1]_q\theta^2 q}{(1-\theta q^n)(1-\theta q^{n+1})} + \frac{[n]_q\theta}{1-\theta q^n}\left(1 - \frac{[n]_q\theta}{1-\theta q^n}\right)$$

which, on using the expression $[n+1]_q = [n]_q + q^n$, reduces to

$$V([X]_q) = \frac{[n]_q\theta}{(1-\theta q^n)(1-\theta q^{n+1})}\left(1 + \frac{[n]_q\theta(q-1)}{1-\theta q^n}\right).$$

The q^{-1}-factorial moments, on using (11) with

$$\frac{d_q^m g(q^{-m}\theta)}{d_q\theta^m} = q^{-m^2}[n+m-1]_{m,q}\prod_{i=1}^{n+m}(1-\theta q^{-m+i-1})^{-1},$$

and since

$$\prod_{i=1}^{n+m}(1-\theta q^{-m+i-1})^{-1} = \prod_{i=1}^{m}(1-\theta q^{-m+i-1})^{-1}\prod_{i=m+1}^{m+n}(1-\theta q^{-m+i-1})^{-1}$$

$$= \prod_{j=1}^{m}(1-\theta q^{-j})^{-1}\prod_{j=1}^{n}(1-\theta q^{j-1})^{-1},$$

are obtained as

$$E([X]_{m,q^{-1}}) = \frac{[n+m-1]_{m,q}\theta^m q^{-\binom{m}{2}}}{\prod_{i=1}^{m}(1-\theta q^{-j})}, \quad m = 1, 2, \ldots,$$

where $0 < \theta < 1$ and $0 < q < 1$. In particular, the q^{-1}-mean is

$$E([X]_{q^{-1}}) = \frac{[n]_q\theta}{1-\theta q^{-1}}.$$

Also, by (13), the q^{-1}-variance is obtained as

$$V([X]_{q^{-1}}) = \frac{[n]_q[n+1]_q\theta^2 q^{-2}}{(1-\theta q^{-1})(1-\theta q^{-2})} + \frac{[n]_q\theta}{1-\theta q^{-1}}\left(1 - \frac{[n]_q\theta}{1-\theta q^{-1}}\right)$$

which, on using the expression $[n+1]_q = q[n]_q + 1$, reduces to

$$V([X]_{q^{-1}}) = \frac{[n]_q\theta}{(1-\theta q^{-1})(1-\theta q^{-2})}\left(1 + \frac{[n]_q\theta(q^{-1}-1)}{1-\theta q^{-1}}\right).$$

The probability generating function of the negative q-binomial distribution of the second kind, on using (14), is deduced as

$$P(t) = \prod_{i=1}^{n}\frac{1-\theta q^{i-1}}{1-\theta t q^{i-1}}, \quad |t| < 1/\theta, \ 0 < \theta < 1, \ 0 < q < 1,$$

where $P_{X_i}(t) = (1-\theta q^{i-1})(1-\theta t q^{i-1})$ is the probability generating function of a geometric distribution. Therefore, according to Proposition 3(b), the negative q-binomial distribution of the second kind may be expressed as a convolution of n independent (and not identically distributed) geometric distributions.

More generally, the negative q-binomial distribution of the second kind may be expressed as a convolution of n independent negative q-binomial distributions of the second kind. Specifically, let X_j, $j = 1, 2, \ldots, n$, be a sequence of n independent random variables

and assume that X_j, follows a negative q-binomial distribution of the second kind with parameters r_j, $\theta q^{s_{j-1}}$, and q, where $s_j = \sum_{i=1}^{j} r_i$, for $j = 1, 2, \ldots, n$ and $s_0 = 0$. Clearly, the probability-generating function of X_j is given by

$$P_{X_j}(t) = \prod_{i=1}^{r_j} \frac{1 - \theta q^{s_{j-1}+i-1}}{1 - \theta t q^{s_{j-1}+i-1}}, \quad |t| < 1/\theta, \ 0 < \theta < 1, \ 0 < q < 1.$$

Consequently, the probability-generating function of the sum $S_n = \sum_{j=1}^{n} X_j$, is deduced as

$$P_{S_n}(t) = \prod_{j=1}^{n} \prod_{i=1}^{r_j} \frac{1 - \theta q^{s_{j-1}+i-1}}{1 - \theta t q^{s_{j-1}+i-1}} = \prod_{j=1}^{n} \prod_{i=s_{j-1}+1}^{s_j} \frac{1 - \theta q^{i-1}}{1 - \theta t q^{i-1}},$$

which, for $s_n \equiv m$, simplifies to

$$P_{S_n}(t) = \prod_{i=1}^{m} \frac{1 - \theta q^{i-1}}{1 - \theta t q^{i-1}}, \quad |t| < 1/\theta, \ 0 < \theta < 1, \ 0 < q < 1.$$

Therefore, the distribution of S_n is a negative q-binomial distribution of the second kind with parameters m, θ, and q.

Finally, it is worth noticing that the probability-generating function of the Euler distribution, with parameters λ and q,

$$P_X(t) = \prod_{i=1}^{\infty} \frac{1 - \theta q^{i-1}}{1 - \theta t q^{i-1}}, \quad |t| < 1/\theta, \ 0 < \theta < 1, \ 0 < q < 1,$$

where $\theta = \lambda(1 - q)$ may be expressed as product, $P_X(t) = P_{X_n}(t) P_{Y_n}(t)$, of the probability generating function of the negative q-binomial distribution of the second kind, with parameters n, θ, and q,

$$P_{X_n}(t) = \prod_{i=1}^{n} \frac{1 - \theta q^{i-1}}{1 - \theta t q^{i-1}}, \quad |t| < 1/\theta, \ 0 < \theta < 1, \ 0 < q < 1,$$

and the probability generating function of the Euler distribution, with parameters λq^n and q,

$$P_{Y_n}(t) = \prod_{i=1}^{\infty} \frac{1 - \theta q^{n+i-1}}{1 - \theta t q^{n+j-1}}, \quad |t| < 1/\theta, \ 0 < \theta < 1, \ 0 < q < 1.$$

Therefore, an Euler distribution may be expressed as a convolution of a negative q-binomial distribution of the second kind and an independent Euler distribution.

3.4. q-Logarithmic Distribution

The q-logarithmic distribution, with probability distribution (4), is a power series q-distribution with a series function

$$g(\theta) = -l_q(1 - \theta) = \sum_{j=1}^{\infty} \frac{\theta^j}{[j]_q}, \quad 0 < \theta < 1, \quad 0 < q < 1.$$

Indeed, taking successively q-derivatives of the series function,

$$D_q^x g(\theta) = \sum_{j=x}^{\infty} [j-1]_{x-1,q} \theta^{j-x} = [x-1]_q! \sum_{j=x}^{\infty} \begin{bmatrix} j-1 \\ j-x \end{bmatrix}_q \theta^{j-x},$$

and using the negative q-binomial formula

$$\sum_{k=0}^{\infty} \begin{bmatrix} x+k-1 \\ k \end{bmatrix}_q \theta^k = \prod_{i=1}^{x}(1-\theta q^{i-1})^{-1},$$

we find

$$D_q^x g(\theta) = [x-1]_q! \prod_{i=1}^{x}(1-\theta q^{i-1})^{-1}$$

and, by (6),

$$a_{x,q} = \frac{1}{[x]_q!}[D_q^x g(t)]_{t=0} = \frac{1}{[x]_q}, \quad x = 1, 2, \ldots,$$

and the probability function (7) reduces to (4).

The q-factorial moments, by (8) and since

$$\frac{d_q^m g(\theta)}{d\theta^m} = [m-1]_q! \prod_{i=1}^{m}(1-\theta q^{i-1})^{-1},$$

are obtained as

$$E([X]_{m,q}) = \frac{[-l_q(1-\theta)]^{-1}[m-1]_q!\theta^m}{\prod_{i=1}^{m}(1-\theta q^{i-1})}, \quad m = 1, 2, \ldots.$$

In particular, the q-mean value is

$$E([X]_q) = \frac{[-l_q(1-\theta)]^{-1}\theta}{1-\theta}.$$

Also, using (11), the q-variance is obtained as

$$V([X]_q) = \frac{[-l_q(1-\theta)]^{-1}\theta}{1-\theta}\left(\frac{1}{1-\theta q} - \frac{[-l_q(1-\theta)]^{-1}\theta}{1-\theta}\right).$$

The q^{-1}-factorial moments, on using (11) with

$$\frac{d_q^m g(q^{-m}\theta)}{d_q\theta^m} = [m-1]_q!q^{-m^2}\prod_{i=1}^{m}(1-\theta q^{-m+i-1})^{-1},$$

are obtained as

$$E([X]_{m,q^{-1}}) = \frac{[-l_q(1-\theta)]^{-1}[m-1]_q!\theta^m q^{-\binom{m}{2}}}{\prod_{i=1}^{m}(1-\theta q^{-m+i-1})}, \quad m = 1, 2, \ldots.$$

In particular, the q^{-1}-mean value is

$$E([X]_{q^{-1}}) = \frac{[-l_q(1-\theta)]^{-1}\theta}{1-\theta q^{-1}}.$$

Also, using (13), the q^{-1}-variance is obtained as

$$V([X]_{q^{-1}}) = \frac{[-l_q(1-\theta)]^{-1}\theta}{1-\theta q^{-1}}\left(1 + \frac{\theta q^{-1}}{1-\theta q^{-2}} - \frac{[-l_q(1-\theta)]^{-1}\theta}{1-\theta}\right).$$

The probability generating function of the q-logarithmic distribution, using (14) is deduced

$$P_X(t) = \frac{-l_q(1-\theta t)}{-l_q(1-\theta)}, \quad |t| < 1/\theta, \quad 0 < \theta < 1, \quad 0 < q < 1.$$

Funding: This research received no external funding.

Data Availability Statement: Data is contained within the article.

Acknowledgments: The author is very grateful to the referees for their valuable comments towards revising this paper.

Conflicts of Interest: The author declares no conflicts of interest.

References

1. Benkherouf, L.; Bather, J.A. Oil exploration: Sequential decisions in the face of uncertainty. *J. Appl. Probab.* **1988**, *25*, 529–543. [CrossRef]
2. Charalambides, C.A. *Discrete q-Distributions*; John Wiley & Sons: Hoboken, NJ, USA, 2016
3. Kemp, A.; Kemp, C.D. Weldon's dice data revisited. *Am. Stat.* **1991**, *45*, 216–222.
4. Kemp, A.; Newton, J. Certain state-dependent processes for dichotomized parasite population. *J. Appl. Probab.* **1990**, *27*, 251–258. [CrossRef]
5. Charalambides, C.A. The *q*-Bernstein basis as a *q*-binomial distribution. *J. Statist. Plann. Inference* **2010**, *140*, 2184–2190. [CrossRef]
6. Kemp, C.D. A *q*-logarithmic distribution. In *Advances in Combinatorial Methods and Applications to Probability and Statistics*; Balakrishnan, N., Ed.; Birkhäuser: Boston, MA, USA, 1997; pp. 465–470.
7. Dunkl, C.F. The absorption distribution and the *q*-binomial theorem. *Commun. Statist. Theory Methods* **1981**, *10*, 1915–1920. [CrossRef]
8. Charalambides, C.A.; Papadatos, N. The *q*-factorial moments of discrete *q*-distributions and a characterization of the Euler distribution. In *Advances on Models, Characterization and Applications*; Balakrishnan, N., Bairamov, I.G., Gebizlioglu, G.L., Eds.; Chapman & Hall/CRC: Boca Raton, FL, USA, 2005; pp. 57–71.
9. Jackson, F.H. A *q*-form of Taylor's theorem. *Messenger Math.* **1909**, *38*, 62–64.
10. Ernst, T. *A Comprehensive Treatment of q-Caluclus*; Birkhäuser: Basel, Switzerland; Springer: Basel, Switzerland, 2012.
11. Jackson, F.H. On basic double hypergeometric functions. *Q. J. Math.* **1942**, *13*, 69–82. [CrossRef]
12. Noack, A. A class of random variables with discrete distributions. *Ann. Math. Stat.* **1950**, *21*, 127–132. [CrossRef]
13. Khatri, C.G. On certain properties of power-series distributions. *Biometrika* **1959**, *46*, 486–490. [CrossRef]
14. Patil, G.P. Certain properties of the generalized power series distribution. *Ann. Inst. Stat. Math.* **1962**, *14*, 179–182. [CrossRef]
15. Kyriakoussis, A.; Vamvakari, M. A *q*-analogue of the Stirling formula and a continuous limiting behaviour of the *q*-binomial distribution-Numerical calculations. *Methodol. Comput. Appl. Probab.* **2013**, *15*, 187–213. [CrossRef]
16. Kemp, A. Heine and Euler extensions of the Poisson distribution. *Commun. Statist. Theory Methods* **1992**, *21*, 791–798. [CrossRef]

Article

Educational Status as a Mediator of Intergenerational Social Mobility in Europe: A Positional Analysis Approach

Glykeria Stamatopoulou, Eva Tsouparopoulou and Maria Symeonaki *

Department of Social Policy, Panteion University of Social and Political Sciences, 176 71 Athens, Greece;
gl.stamatopoulou@panteion.gr (G.S.); etsouparopoulou@panteion.gr (E.T.)
* Correspondence: msymeon@panteion.gr

Abstract: This paper investigates the transmission of educational attainment from parents to offspring as a mediator of intergenerational class mobility in Europe. The study covers the last two decades with data drawn from a cross-national large-scale sample survey, namely the European Social Survey (ESS), for the years 2002–2018. Interest has focused on the question of the persistence of inequality of educational opportunities by examining the attainment of nominal levels of education and the association between the educational attainment of the parent with the highest level of education and their descendants. The study also covers new trends in social mobility that consider education as a "positional good", and a novel method of incorporating educational expansion into the transition probabilities is proposed, providing answers to whether the rising accessibility of educational qualifications attenuates the association between social origin and educational attainment. Therefore, the concept of positionality is taken into account in the estimation of intergenerational transition probabilities, and to complement the analysis, mobility measures are provided for both methods, nominal and positional. The proposed positional method is validated through a correlation analysis between the upward mobility scores (nominal and positional) with the Education Expansion Index (EEI) for the respective years. The upward mobility scores estimated via the positional method are more highly correlated with the EEI for all years, indicating a better alignment with the broader trends in educational participation and achievement.

Keywords: intergenerational social mobility; Markov processes; ESS

MSC: 60J20; 60G35; 62-07

Citation: Stamatopoulou, G.; Tsouparopoulou, E.; Symeonaki, M. Educational Status as a Mediator of Intergenerational Social Mobility in Europe: A Positional Analysis Approach. *Mathematics* **2024**, *12*, 966. https://doi.org/10.3390/math12070966

Academic Editors: Panagiotis-Christos Vassiliou and Andreas C. Georgiou

Received: 1 December 2023
Revised: 19 March 2024
Accepted: 20 March 2024
Published: 25 March 2024

1. Introduction

Intergenerational mobility encapsulates societal transitions spanning generations and diverse socio-economic strata. It delineates individuals' progressions and achievements in comparison to the family's social, occupational, educational, and economic heritage, serving as a gauge for evaluating social justice and equal opportunities. Education stands as a pivotal factor in measuring social mobility and is key in curbing the perpetuation of disparities through the generations and acting as a mediator between socio-economic classes. The literature has substantiated the prominence of education in understanding and quantifying intergenerational mobility. Education is considered a significant factor due to its enduring impact on subsequent generations, in contrast to income or occupation, which can be more transient [1]. Moreover, the consistent data collection on education in various studies enables a more comprehensive analysis of intergenerational mobility. The association of education with concepts of social justice and equal opportunity further amplifies its significance in societal structures [2]. Many years of research on class mobility [3–5] and intergenerational mobility in relation to other indicators [6,7] have demonstrated that a major moderator of the relationship between origin and destination classes is educational achievement. Notably, studies such as those by Breen and Goldthorpe [8] and Blanden

et al. [9] examine the persistent influence of education across generations and its role in shaping social mobility. Such studies emphasise the importance of education in understanding and measuring intergenerational mobility or even the function of academic establishments in influencing the movement of generations [10,11]. Moreover, Blanden et al. [9] draw attention to the relationship between education and social mobility, highlighting the enduring impact of educational opportunities on upward mobility, while Corak [12] explores intergenerational mobility from a multidimensional perspective, acknowledging the significance of education among other factors. Cunha and Heckman [13] examine the intergenerational transmission of both cognitive and noncognitive skills, illustrating how education acts as a channel for their transfer across generations. Blanden and Machin [14] investigate the relationship between education and intergenerational mobility, discussing the role of education in either facilitating or impeding social mobility. Moreover, Symeonaki and Stamatopoulou [15], Symeonaki et al. [16], Stamatopoulou et al. [17], and Stamatopoulou and Symeonaki [18] estimate intergenerational educational mobility across European countries, allowing for a comparative study of discrepancies among countries in social mobility, leveraging diverse large-scale European databases, while Symeonaki and Tsinaslanidou [19] studied intergenerational educational mobility across countries with different welfare regimes.

In most studies concerning intergenerational educational mobility, the focal point has long been on the relationship between individuals' social backgrounds and their educational achievements, estimating intergenerational educational mobility in absolute terms, i.e., measuring education with the same nominal categories across all cohorts (e.g., using the International Standard Classification of Education (ISCED) levels and distinguishing categories of low (ISCED levels 0–2), medium (ISCED levels 3–4), and high (ISCED levels 5–8) for both parents and offsprings), with the following outcomes indicating a diminishing influence of social backgrounds on educational achievement across multiple nations [18,20,21]. However, Goldthorpe [22] raises a pertinent question regarding the extent to which the observation of a diminishing impact of social origins, as inferred from nominal categories of educational qualifications, truly signifies a reduction in class disparities within education. He posits that in societies where education is esteemed as a positional good, individuals strive to outperform their peers in the pursuit of higher relative educational attainment. The notion of positionality revolves around the concept that the value of educational credentials is partly attributed to their relative scarcity within the population, a concept originating from Hirsch [23]. With fiercer competition for educational achievement, the influence of resources available to affluent and educated social strata becomes more pronounced. Consequently, disparities in educational attainment between social strata may persist even if the inequality of educational opportunities has ostensibly declined in nominal terms. In essence, whether education is perceived as a positional (relative) or nominal (absolute) good holds significant ramifications for understanding temporal trends in inequality in educational opportunity. Recent studies have examined intergenerational educational mobility, considering education as a positional good that captures the effect of educational expansion. Rotman et al. [24] present evidence suggesting divergent conclusions in Israel regarding trends in educational stratification between relative and absolute measures. The analysis of nominal education and years of schooling suggests consistent or decreased educational inequality, while positional measures show an increase in educational disparity. Fujihara and Ishida's [25] research in Japan reveals differing trends in educational inequality based on whether education is measured in relative or absolute terms. Using absolute measures, they note a reduced disparity between respondents with fathers of different educational levels. However, with relative measures, they observe a widening gap between respondents from distinct paternal education backgrounds. Both studies consider position in the educational distribution or economic returns for their assessments. Triventi et al. [26] present a consistent trend of declining educational inequality in Italy, irrespective of the measurement—absolute or relative—used for education. Unlike studies in Britain, Israel, and Japan, their findings indicate a consistent

decrease in educational disparity over time. While their measures of relative education differ from those of other studies, the overarching theme of assessing education in relative terms sparks inquiry into the differing trends among these countries. Moreover, Di Stasio et al. [27] analyse education as a positional good, contrasting country contexts to identify where education holds positional value. They find that strong vocational systems relate to lower overeducation instances, suggesting reduced positional value in these settings. Their study categorises countries based on overeducation and its returns, connecting these groupings to various models of the education–occupation relationship.

The present study aims to investigate both nominal (absolute) and relative (positional) patterns of intergenerational educational mobility in Europe by analysing transitions across the educational levels of respondents and their parents in Europe using raw data drawn from the European Social Survey (ESS) from the year 2002 and onwards. The objective is to reveal challenges faced by particular social strata in progressing upward within the educational framework using and comparing both nominal and positional methods. To our knowledge, this is the first attempt to incorporate positionality in the estimation process of the transition probabilities. To validate the proposed methodology for measuring mobility, we compare the correlations of upward probability measures, both nominal and positional, with the Educational Expansion Index (EEI) used in Araki [28]. Correlation coefficients are examined, and the positional approach is identified as superior, as it consistently exhibits higher correlations for all years.

The paper is outlined as follows. Section 2 reveals all the necessary information concerning the proposed methodology and the ESS data that are utilised in order to estimate intergenerational educational mobility in absolute and relative terms. Section 3 presents the measurement results of intergenerational educational mobility, nominal and positional, and the validation tests performed. Section 4 gives the conclusions of the study and provides the reader with a discussion concerning the comparison of absolute and positional intergenerational mobility and aspects of future work.

2. Materials and Methods

In the present analysis, data were drawn from the European Social Survey (ESS), a survey spanning over 40 countries since 2002, designed to track European public attitudes and values and furnish European social and attitudinal indicators. The data was analysed using IBM SPSS Statistics, Version 28.0. (IBM Corp, Armonk, NY, USA). The present study measures nominal and positional intergenerational educational mobility in Europe, making use of 5 rounds of ESS spanning a period of over 16 years (i.e., ESS1, ESS3, ESS5, ESS7, ESS9). To ensure comparability, the work specifically includes European countries that have participated in all rounds of the ESS, i.e., Belgium, Finland, France, Germany, Hungary, Ireland, the Netherlands, Norway, Poland, Portugal, Spain, Sweden, Switzerland, Slovenia, and the UK. Due to the different data collection methods used in ESS10 (face-to-face interviews, self-completion questionnaire), the variable of parental education was not measured; consequently, the most recent trends of mobility are not included in this analysis. The study also aims to provide aggregated measures for these European countries.

Table 1 presents the socio-demographic characteristics of the respondents per round. The realised sample sizes and basic socio-demographic characteristics of the samples are presented in Table 1. As shown, most of the respondents for all the countries under investigation were women, with a mean age from 41.90 (Ireland, ESS1) to 49.14 (Portugal, ESS7) years, at least 39.03% (Ireland, ESS5) to 61.36% (Sweden, ESS3) were in a paid job, while the percentage for participants in education, as the main activity within the last seven days, ranged from 7.46% (UK, ESS1) to 15.33% (Slovenia, ESS1).

Table 1. Socio-demographic characteristics of the sample, per ESS round (2002, 2006, 2010, 2014, and 2018).

Round	Characteristics		BE	CH	DE	ES	FI	FR	HU	IE	NL	NO	PL	PT	SE	SI	UK
										Country							
ESS1	N		1899	2040	2919	1729	2000	1503	1685	2046	2364	2036	2110	1511	1999	1519	2052
(2002)	Mean age (SD)		46.01	44.85	47.22	45.29	45.75	45.32	45.03	41.90	44.10	45.33	43.08	44.98	45.85	44.23	45.60
			(19.07)	(18.28)	(18.72)	(19.02)	(18.35)	(18.72)	(18.46)	(17.59)	(17.15)	(17.81)	(18.52)	(18.81)	(18.13)	(18.61)	(18.41)
	Male (%)		48.39	48.34	48.34	48.83	48.22	47.94	47.13	49.19	49.54	49.14	47.72	47.17	49.08	48.50	48.48
	In paid job * (%)		45.25	54.24	43.98	45.19	52.97	44.32	43.57	53.09	50.19	59.77	40.10	51.75	60.11	42.00	54.83
	In education * (%)		7.70	10.51	10.15	8.44	13.30	12.23	10.15	11.73	10.12	9.20	13.05	11.12	12.95	15.33	7.46
ESS3	N		1798	1804	2916	1876	1896	1986	1518	1800	1889	1750	1721	2222	1927	1476	2394
(2006)	Mean age (SD)		46.19	46.47	47.39	46.06	46.75	46.19	46.08	42.67	45.81	45.79	43.53	46.63	46.56	45.41	45.90
			(19.09)	(18.62)	(18.95)	(18.90)	(18.98)	(18.52)	(18.55)	(17.83)	(17.48)	(18.68)	(18.44)	(18.91)	(18.51)	(18.65)	(18.80)
	Male (%)		48.51	48.56	48.31	49.21	48.28	47.67	46.50	49.54	49.14	49.06	47.62	47.93	49.22	48.84	48.51
	In paid job * (%)		45.98	54.49	45.09	55.00	52.30	50.34	46.54	52.63	52.97	59.14	45.27	50.95	61.36	44.71	55.70
	In education * (%)		9.89	8.81	10.57	7.56	12.90	10.14	8.82	10.53	8.04	11.29	12.59	10.10	12.08	14.12	7.55
ESS5	N		1704	1506	3031	1885	1878	1728	1561	2576	1829	1548	1751	2150	1497	1403	2422
(2010)	Mean age (SD)		46.85	48.55	48.31	45.91	47.51	46.98	46.39	42.68	46.34	45.90	44.81	47.39	46.86	46.30	45.42
			(19.26)	(19.03)	(18.68)	(19.14)	(19.29)	(19.31)	(18.69)	(18.13)	(17.78)	(18.98)	(18.77)	(19.27)	(19.27)	(18.39)	(18.91)
	Male		48.61	48.11	48.86	48.93	48.43	47.64	46.60	49.15	49.16	49.24	47.51	47.45	49.55	49.43	49.60
	In paid job * (%)		46.67	55.32	48.48	47.54	47.64	48.51	46.89	39.03	54.77	55.73	48.81	44.24	55.86	47.76	51.70
	In education * (%)		10.11	8.36	9.26	10.13	14.16	10.98	9.03	14.53	9.47	13.99	11.40	10.42	14.29	13.06	8.77
ESS7	N		1769	1532	3045	1925	2087	1917	1698	2390	1919	1436	1615	1265	1791	1224	2264
(2014)	Mean age (SD)		47.48	46.95	48.88	47.94	48.65	47.46	47.72	44.30	46.80	45.80	46.29	49.14	47.78	47.67	46.96
			(19.34)	(18.86)	(19.92)	(18.53)	(19.56)	(18.93)	(18.91)	(17.81)	(18.42)	(19.05)	(18.61)	(19.36)	(20.14)	(18.51)	(18.70)
	Male		48.49	49.06	48.82	48.78	48.68	47.77	46.86	49.03	49.21	51.56	47.88	46.99	50.25	49.43	48.72
	In paid job * (%)		46.55	55.99	48.63	46.78	46.93	47.69	51.80	47.08	50.22	55.98	49.92	45.18	53.51	45.98	52.62
	In education * (%)		8.94	9.24	11.41	10.31	12.72	9.88	8.51	12.26	12.05	15.31	9.16	9.35	14.04	10.34	7.51
ESS9	N		1767	1542	2358	1668	1755	2010	1661	2216	1673	1406	1500	1055	1539	1318	2204
(2018)	Mean age (SD)		47.69	47.71	49.10	48.8	49.06	48.50	48.64	45.57	46.41	45.92	47.44	49.44	45.46	49.08	47.45
			(19.35)	(18.98)	(19.21)	(18.54)	(19.86)	(19.58)	(19.03)	(18.13)	(19.15)	(19.26)	(18.58)	(18.90)	(19.15)	(18.83)	(18.57)
	Male (%)		49.05	49.17	49.26	48.61	48.92	47.82	47.13	49.09	49.31	51.95	47.75	46.67	50.78	49.43	48.95
	In paid job * (%)		49.36	58.10	48.85	50.33	48.59	49.14	56.95	49.74	51.36	54.61	53.56	49.21	58.14	50.57	57.67
	In education * (%)		7.73	8.10	10.18	9.67	12.36	10.23	8.15	12.89	13.01	15.90	8.53	10.18	15.32	9.66	6.33

* The reference period is during the last seven (7) days.

Within the ESS, cross-national educational attainment variables for both parents and individuals were generated from country-specific variables in order to be standardised and to align with the latest International Standard Classification of Education (ISCED11). (The production of the generated harmonised educational variable is particularly dependent on the availability of sufficiently detailed country-specific education variables. For rounds ESS 5–9, the 7-category variable "es-isced" is used in the analysis for both respondents and parents. For rounds ESS 1–4, the same variable has not been produced for all parents and/or for all countries. Thus, for these rounds, we used the previous harmonised 5-category variable "edulvlva" in order to classify both respondents and parents into the educational categories). To facilitate the analysis, educational attainment was transformed into three educational categories using the transformation utilised by EUROSTAT, i.e., ISCED levels 0–2 = Low, ISCED levels 3–4 = Medium, and ISCED levels 5–8 = High. For parents, the maximum educational level was taken into consideration for the analysis, assuming that the highest educational level between parents will positively affect children's educational attainments. Because of the lack of a harmonised variable for the highest level of education for specific counties in the datasets of ESS1 and ESS7, we do not display results for Norway (2002) and for Hungary (2014). Table 2 outlines the ISCED levels and the categorisation to three educational levels, indicated by the color shading of the cells.

Table 2. ISCED levels and educational categories.

ISCED Levels	Description	Recoded Educational Levels
ISCED level 0	Early childhood education (Primary education not completed)	
ISCED level 1	Less than lower secondary	
ISCED level 2	Lower secondary	
ISCED level 3	Lower tier upper secondary/Upper tier upper secondary	
ISCED level 4	Advanced vocational, sub-degree	Medium
ISCED level 5	Short-cycle tertiary education (lower tertiary education)	
ISCED level 6	Bachelor's degree or equivalent	
ISCED level 7	Master's degree or equivalent	
ISCED level 8	PhD degree or equivalent	

Data weighting was performed using analysis weight (anweight). This specific weight is suitable for all types of analysis as it corrects for differential selection probabilities within each country as specified by sample design, for nonresponse, for noncoverage, and for sampling error related to the four post-stratification variables and takes into account differences in population size across countries (https://www.europeansocialsurvey.org/methodology/ess-methodology/data-processing-and-archiving/weighting, accessed on 10 November 2023).

Using raw data drawn from the ESS, we first measure intergenerational educational mobility in absolute terms, using the same educational levels both for parents and offspring. We define parental education as the educational level of either the father or the mother, based on the higher educational attainment between them. We employ Markov stochastic models to quantify educational mobility across various European countries. A Markov stochastic model describes a dynamic population system that evolves over time according to probability laws [29]. The Markov property is used in the sense that each state depends only on the previous one in time. In our case, a state represents the educational level of parents and individuals at a given time t. In more detail, we begin by stratifying the population into distinct categories according to their educational status. Let $S = \{1, 2, \ldots, k\}$ be the state space of the proposed closed model (in our case $k = 3$), where no members enter or leave the system. For each t, we estimate the transition probability matrices, the elements of which depict the transitions occurring between educational states and across generations. Each element $p_{ij}(t)$, $\forall i, j = 1, 2, 3$ of the matrix $P(t)$ describes the probability of an individual to move from state i (parental educational level) to state j (individual's educational level). The off-diagonal elements of the $P(t)$ matrix signify the shifts or movements of individuals, while p_{ii} indicates the probability of individuals remaining static over time in relation to

their parental educational status (see also [15,16]). The above model describes a closed Non-Homogeneous Markov System, since our transition probabilities are estimated for each time step t. For a comprehensive description of the theoretical background of the Markov systems, see [29–37]. Figure 1 provides a graphical representation of the proposed model.

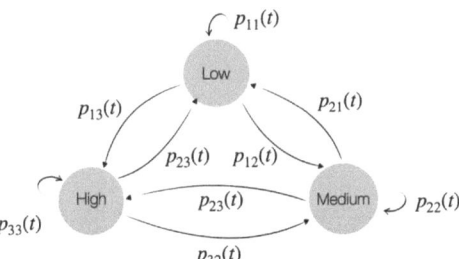

Figure 1. Transition diagram of the proposed closed Markov system.

Based on the transition probabilities of each transition matrix, mobility measures are estimated for the selected years of the ESS data for each country. Hence, we calculate indices for upward and downward mobility, as well as the immobility index [38,39] and the Prais–Shorrocks index [40,41]. Equations (1)–(4) give the mathematical expressions of the computed indices:

$$M_{PS}(t) = \left(\frac{1}{k-1}\right)(k - tr(\mathbf{P}(t))) \tag{1}$$

$$IM(t) = \frac{tr(\mathbf{P}(t))}{k} \tag{2}$$

$$UM(t) = \frac{1}{k}\sum_{j>i} p_{ij}(t) \tag{3}$$

$$DM(t) = \frac{1}{k}\sum_{j<i} p_{ij}(t) \tag{4}$$

Shifting from an absolute to a relative perspective in the evaluation of educational attainment presents a notable challenge since "there is no obvious 'one best way' of producing a relative measure" [42]. We aim to incorporate positionality into the measurement of transition probabilities following the subsequent methodology.

The proposed method is comparable to that implemented by Triventi et al. [26] for calculating the cumulative advantage associated with each educational level. To understand how positionality has influenced educational attainment, we estimated the proportions of individuals at all educational levels using EUROSTAT's data available for the last two decades and the classification described in Table 2. A logarithmic transformation of the proportions is equal to the Educational Competitive Advantage Score (ECAS) used in Triventi et al. [26], which "attributes to each educational level a measure of its competitive advantage on the basis of how many individuals attained at least that qualification in a given year". Rather than employing the actual ECAS for a specific year t, we opt for using the proportions of individuals in various educational levels as weights, denoted by $w_1(t)$, $w_2(t)$, and $w_3(t)$, to maintain the stochastic properties of the transition probability matrices. Thus, the proportion of individuals with low, medium, and high education at the time of the survey is treated as a set of weights reflecting the relative prevalence or importance of each educational category in the population. The transition probabilities are then calculated by considering not only the likelihood of moving from one educational level to another but also by incorporating the prevalence of individuals in each category as a weight. The weights act as a scaling factor, influencing the contribution of each educational category to the overall transition probabilities, and serve as a normalisation assigned to each (absolute)

transition probability based on the factor of competitive advantage. Thus, we applied proportional scaling to adjust the transition probabilities based on the proportions, using the following equation to estimate the positional transition probabilities $p_{ij}(t)$:

$$pp_{ij}(t) = \frac{w_j(t)p_{ij}(t)}{\sum_j w_j(t)p_{ij}(t)} \tag{5}$$

The applied weights stem from the proportional representation of individuals within various educational tiers across distinct time frames. These adjustments accommodate the transition probabilities, ensuring alignment with the evolving educational landscape over recent years. Through these weights, the impact of current educational distributions on projected transitions is highlighted, preserving the overall structure of transition probabilities. Accounting for these educational distribution shifts can substantially refine the precision of the analysis, enabling a more accurate and positional representation of intergenerational educational mobility.

Having estimated both nominal and positional mobility rates, we undertake cluster analysis, an exploratory method that categorises cases with akin characteristics into clusters. The classification of surveyed countries utilises both nominal and positional upward mobility. Initially, the agglomerative hierarchical method determines the optimal number of clusters that best characterises the data. Subsequently, building on the outcomes of this approach, a K-means analysis is applied to classify the countries into the suggested distinct, mutually exclusive clusters.

To substantiate the proposed methodology, the upward mobility scores were subjected to correlation analysis with the Education Expansion Index (EEI) for the corresponding years, as computed using EUROSTAT's data. The Educational Expansion Index is defined as the percentage of individuals aged between 15 and 64 that possess tertiary degrees [28] and serves as a metric encompassing the comprehensive expansion of educational attainment across a population, offering insights into alterations in educational participation and achievement. Examining the correlation between the upward mobility scores, calculated using both absolute and relational approaches, and the Educational Expansion Index (EEI) facilitates an evaluation of the extent to which the proposed measure aligns with the broader shifts in educational participation and achievement over the specified timeframe. The expectation is that the two upward mobility scores, nominal and positional, will exhibit a strong correlation. The preferred methodology would be the one generating a higher correlation coefficient between the upward mobility scores and the Education Expansion Index (EEI) for the respective years.

3. Results

3.1. Nominal/Absolute Transition Probabilities

In this section, we estimate the transition probability matrices to portray the shifts between educational categories for both parents and respondents, encapsulating the movement between the same educational stages. Table A1 in the Appendix A presents the nominal transition probability matrices for all countries and ESS rounds, as well as the respective mobility indices. From the results, it is obvious that individuals from low-educated backgrounds tend to gain better education than their parents, although they have considerably fewer chances to complete tertiary education compared to those originating from medium- or highly educated origins. Indeed, the access to tertiary education seems unequal between people from different educational backgrounds in the majority of the sample, as parents' educational profile seems to matter in all countries. However, it is notable that the upward movements predominate over the downward mobility, while the immobility rates decrease over time.

Figure 2 provides a more comprehensive overview of the transitions between educational categories, illustrating the percentages of individuals moving upward, downward, or remaining in the same educational category as their parents across all surveyed countries

from 2002 to 2018. The figure reveals variations in educational flows across countries, with Finland and Belgium displaying a steady trend of upward movement through ESS. Furthermore, a noticeable increase in percentages of upwardly mobile individuals over time is detected in the majority of the countries, especially in Ireland and Slovenia, where the values of the upward mobility index rose sharply from 2002 to 2018. Some exceptions also exist, such as Switzerland and Hungary, where a decrease in the overall mobility is recorded from 2002 to 2018.

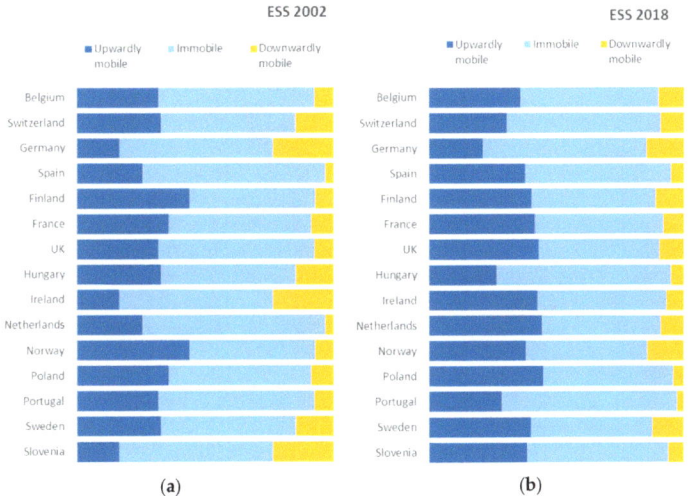

Figure 2. The percentages of people who moved upward or downward or had the same education as their parents, by country, according to the (**a**) ESS1 dataset and the (**b**) ESS9 dataset.

The values of both the Prais–Shorrocks and immobility indices validate the observed trend from 2002 to 2018 depicted in Figure 3, showing variations between countries and years. In particular, Norway and the Netherlands seem to be steadily the most mobile in the sample, while Hungary, Portugal and Switzerland show higher values of immobility, even though a notable decrease is indicated from 2002 to 2018.

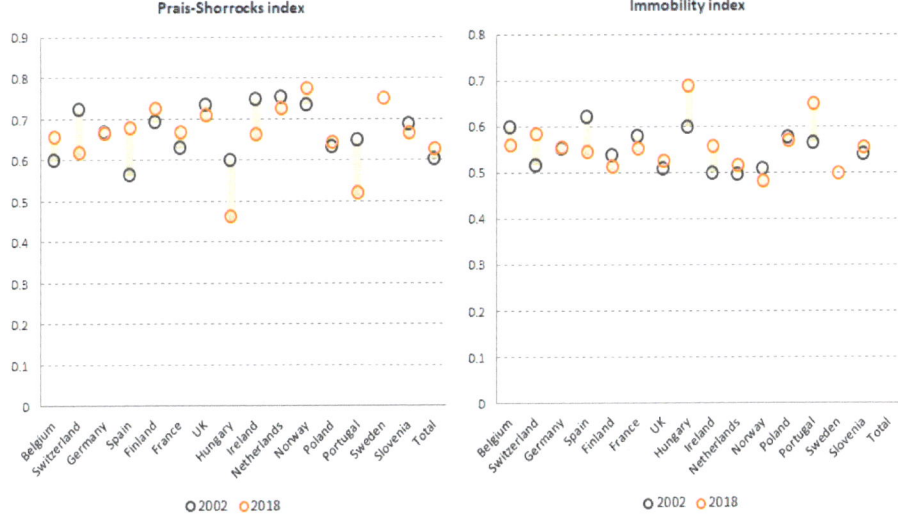

Figure 3. Changes in mobility rates by country: 2002 and 2018 (nominal mobility).

3.2. Education as a "Positional Good": Estimating Positional Transition Probabilities

In order to estimate the positional transition probabilities, the respective weights were estimated. Figure 4 depicts the proportions of individuals belonging to the three educational levels based on the data provided by EUROSTAT with the use of the EU-Labour Force Survey (EU-LFS). The depicted trend in the proportions highlights intriguing shifts in educational categories over this period (2002–2018). The proportions of low-educated individuals (ISCED 0–2) display a steady fall, which suggests a decline in the prevalence of lower educational levels over time and a diminishing number of individuals with lower educational qualifications. On the contrary, the proportions of medium-educated individuals (ISCED 3–4) exhibit relatively modest changes, suggesting stability rather than cumulative advantages. Meanwhile, the rising trend in the proportions of highly educated individuals (ISCED 5–8) implies a diminishing competitive advantage associated with higher educational levels and a decreasing prominence or influence of higher educational qualifications over the observed period.

Since transition probability matrices need to maintain their stochastic property, we opted for the incorporation of proportions in the weighting scheme adhering to this principle. Using Equation (1), the respective weights presented in Figure 4, and the nominal transition probability matrices (Table A1), the positional transition probability matrices $P(t) = [p_{ij}(t)]$, $\forall i, j = 1, 2, 3$ were estimated for the participating countries and years. Based on these positional transition probabilities, the upward and downward mobility indices were reconstructed and calculated in order to be compared with the nominal results. The rest of the mobility indices are estimated as aforementioned [38–41]. The respective matrices are exhibited in Table A1 in the Appendix A. In general, from the results, it is evident that concerning the transition probabilities, the relative measure of mobility is more robust than the absolute counterpart. In particular, for the majority of the countries, p_{12} takes higher values in the positional matrices compared to the nominal ones, and p_{11} seems to be overrated in the nominal results. Thus, shifting from a nominal to a relative perspective, people with low educational backgrounds appear to have greater chances of moving upwards and attaining a medium level of education. However, a reversed pattern is detected in Spain and Portugal. Likewise, the observed mobility appears to overestimate the chances of people from highly educated backgrounds attaining tertiary education since transition probabilities p_{33} are considerably lower after the weights are applied. A noticeable example of this trend is the case of Hungary, where p_{33} falls from 0.569 to 0.292 (ESS3) after the adjustment. However, Belgium and Ireland show no significant differences between nominal and positional transition matrices.

Figure A1 presents the differences in upward mobility indices before and after the adjustment. As shown, in all countries (except Germany), this difference between nominal and positional results takes positive values, which indicates that the nominal measure seems to exaggerate the upward movements compared to each relative measure. Between the countries, the Netherlands and France show greater differences when nominal and positional upward rates are compared, while the results for Switzerland, Norway and UK show no significant variations between the rates. On the other hand, smaller differences are observed for the case of the Prais–Shorrocks and immobility indices, in the comparison of nominal and positional mobility (Figure A2). This trend might be attributed to the fact that both M_{PS} and IM have been constructed based on the chances of people moving upwards or downwards in the social space and not on the actual flows, and for that reason, it better reflects the relative mobility. However, Poland, Hungary, and Slovenia seem to be exceptions to this trend, as the difference in M_{PS} takes significant higher values for these countries. Also, an interesting trend was detected for Portugal, where the difference in mobility rates decreased over time, reaching convergence, probably because of the changes that occurred in the participation of Portuguese in the different levels of education through the years 2002–2018 (as shown also in Figure 3).

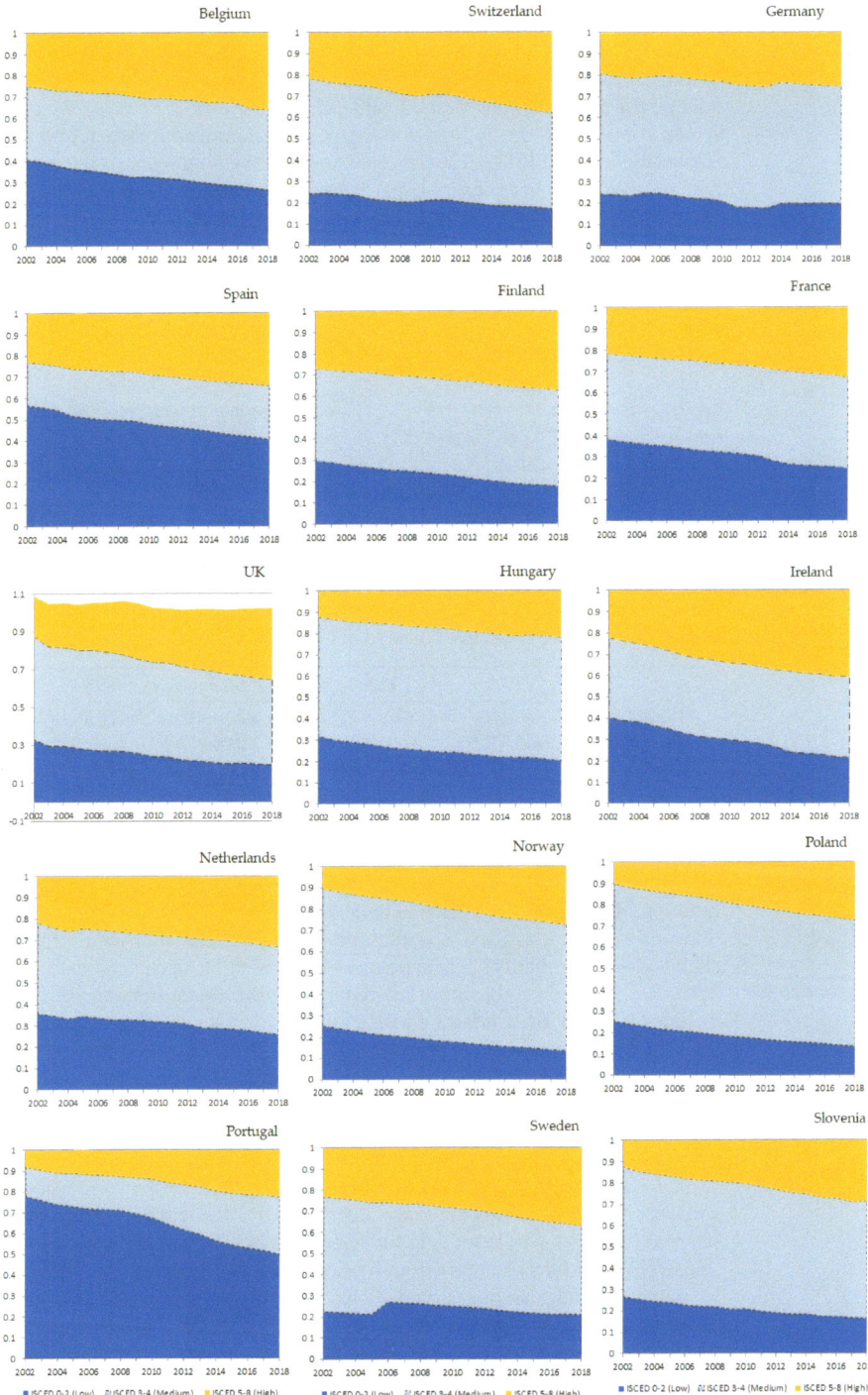

Figure 4. Country-wise distribution of proportions in educational attainment levels, 2002–2020 (EUROSTAT, based on the EU-LFS data).

3.3. Validation

To validate the proposed methodology, the upward mobility scores underwent correlation analysis, with the Education Expansion Index (EEI) calculated using EUROSTAT's data for the corresponding years. Evaluating the correlation between the upward mobility scores, computed through both nominal and positional approaches, and the Educational Expansion Index (EEI) enables an assessment of the alignment of the proposed measure with broader shifts in educational participation and achievement over the specified period. Table 3 presents Pearson's correlation coefficient between nominal and positional upward mobility, and Table 4 shows the respective correlations among nominal and positional upward mobility and EEI for the respective year. The two upward mobility indices exhibit a strong correlation, as anticipated. Notably, positional upward mobility demonstrates a higher correlation with EEI, indicating a better alignment with the broader trends in educational participation and achievement.

Table 3. Pearson's correlations coefficients among nominal upward mobility UP_N and positional upward mobility UP_P per ESS round.

ESS 1	ESS 3	ESS 5	ESS 7	ESS 9
$r = 0.650$ **, $p = 0.006$	$r = 0.715$ **, $p = 0.003$	$r = 0.604$ *, $p = 0.013$	$r = 0.599$ *, $p = 0.018$	$r = 0.846$ **, $p < 0.001$

** Correlation significant at the 0.001 level. * Correlation significant at the 0.05 level.

Table 4. Pearson's correlations coefficients among nominal upward mobility UP_N, positional upward mobility UP_P and the respective Educational Expansion Index (EEI) per ESS round.

	ESS 1	ESS 3	ESS 5	ESS 7	ESS 9
$UP_N \times EEI$	$r = 0.373$	$r = 0.580$ *	$r = 0.593$ *	$r = 0.516$ *	$r = 0.718$ **
$UP_P \times EEI$	$r = 0.521$ *	$r = 0.707$ **	$r = 0.604$ *	$r = 0.697$ **	$r = 0.773$ **

** Correlation significant at the 0.001 level. * Correlation significant at the 0.05 level.

To enhance the credibility of the proposed methodology, we conducted a cluster analysis utilising both hierarchical clustering and the K-means method and using both absolute and positional upward mobility scores across countries. Presented here are the findings from the most recent ESS data. The hierarchical process identified four clusters of counties when considering both nominal and positional upward mobility rates. This aligns with the welfare regime typology observed in European countries to a great extent. Specifically, based on the latest ESS data, the resulting clusters are as follows: Cluster 1 includes Belgium, Switzerland, Spain, France, and Slovenia; Cluster 2 comprises Germany and Hungary; Cluster 3 encompasses Finland, Norway, Ireland, Netherlands, Poland, Sweden, and the UK; and Cluster 4 consists of Portugal, a standalone cluster, distinguished by its exceptionally low values of the variables in comparison to the others (Figure 5).

The simulation conducted for both upward positional mobility scores and absolute scores stands as a robust validation of the theoretical framework outlined in the paper. The variables used were the educational levels of the father, mother, and respondent, and the simulation spanned across the examined year, 2018. The simulation was conducted for the selected countries—Ireland, Belgium, Germany, and Portugal—which emerged as representatives of distinct clusters through prior clustering analysis. By aligning the simulated outcomes with our theoretical predictions, this comprehensive approach provides evidence of the consistency and applicability of the proposed model. The convergence of theoretical insights with simulated results in these representative countries enhances the credibility of the findings, emphasising the robustness of the approach in capturing the nuances of upward mobility dynamics.

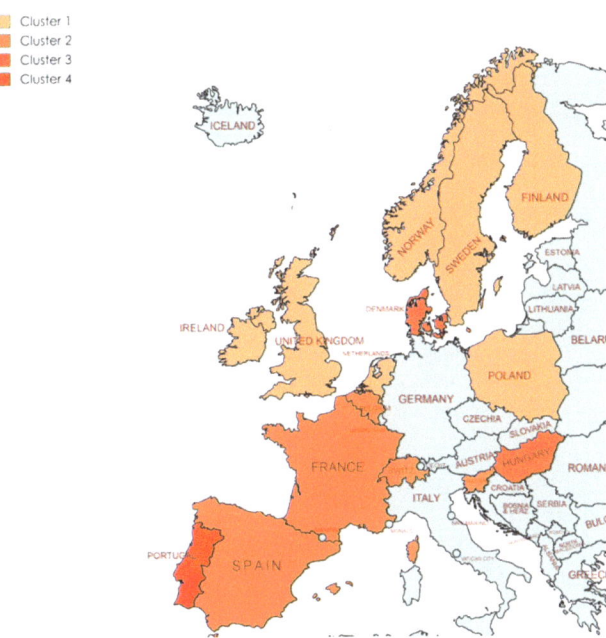

Figure 5. Clusters of countries based on nominal and positional upward mobility, ESS, 2018.

4. Discussion

The present section interprets the presented results and provides insights into the patterns of intergenerational educational mobility, considering both nominal and positional perspectives. The aim was to examine the relationship between parental and individuals' educational outcome in relative terms in order to better understand the influence of education across generations. In this context, the proposed methodology is based on the concept of positionality, where the educational expansion and the rising accessibility of educational qualifications are taken into account. It is assumed that this novel additional element in the measurement of mobility would produce a more reliable picture of educational inequalities. In order to explore this hypothesis, raw data were drawn from the European Social Survey for the 15 participated in all rounds of the surveyed countries to capture trends in educational transitions from 2002 to 2018.

The analysis of nominal transition probability matrices reveals distinct tendencies in educational mobility across European countries. More specifically, individuals from lower-educated backgrounds show a propensity to attain higher education than their parents, although access to tertiary education appears unequal. As upward mobility surpasses downward movements, a decline in immobility rates over time suggests a notable enhancement in educational opportunities. This trend signifies a propensity for individuals to progressively distance themselves from their parents' educational level. Notable exceptions, such as Switzerland and Hungary, exhibit a decrease in overall mobility. The examination of specific countries, including Finland and Belgium, underscores diverse trends in upward mobility.

The novel approach of incorporating positionality in transition probabilities enhances the understanding of mobility patterns. Weighted positional matrices demonstrate the robustness of relative measures compared to absolute ones. Low-educated individuals exhibit greater chances for upward mobility, challenging conventional findings. However, Spain and Portugal deviate from this trend. Discrepancies in the likelihood of highly educated individuals attaining tertiary education emerge after adjustment, exemplified by Hungary's notable shift.

To validate the proposed methodology, correlations between upward mobility indices and the Educational Expansion Index (EEI) were examined. The positional approach exhibits stronger alignment with broader trends in educational participation and achievement, as indicated by higher correlations with EEI for all examined ESS rounds. Differences between nominal and positional measures vary across countries, emphasising the need for a nuanced understanding of mobility patterns.

Apparently, the observed trends hold implications for policymakers and researchers. Acknowledging education as a positional good necessitates tailored policy interventions to address relative mobility. Future research should investigate the subtle dynamics driving educational shifts, considering socio-economic, cultural, and policy-related factors. Furthermore, longitudinal analyses can offer a more profound insight into the changing patterns of mobility, complementing the aforementioned findings with new results deriving from the intermediate ESS rounds (e.g., ESS round 2). The presented findings contribute to the discourse on intergenerational educational mobility, offering valuable insights for policymakers, aiming to foster equitable educational opportunities.

Author Contributions: Conceptualisation, G.S., E.T. and M.S.; methodology, G.S., E.T. and M.S.; statistical analysis with IBM SPSS v.29, G.S., E.T. and M.S.; validation, G.S., E.T. and M.S.; formal analysis, G.S., E.T. and M.S.; investigation, G.S., E.T. and M.S.; data curation, G.S., E.T. and M.S.; writing—original draft preparation, G.S. and M.S.; writing—review and editing, G.S., E.T. and M.S.; visualisation, G.S. and E.T.; supervision, M.S. All authors have read and agreed to the published version of the manuscript.

Funding: This research received no external funding.

Data Availability Statement: Raw data that support the findings of this study are available from the European Social Survey at https://ess-search.nsd.no/en/study/bdc7c350-1029-4cb3-9d5e-53f668b8 fa74, accessed on 12 November 2023.

Acknowledgments: We acknowledge use of raw data from: ESS Round 1: European Social Survey Round 1 Data (2002). Data file edition 6.6. Sikt—Norwegian Agency for Shared Services in Education and Research, Norway—Data Archive and distributor of ESS data for ESS ERIC. https://doi.org/10.21338/NSD-ESS1-2002, ESS Round 3: European Social Survey Round 3 Data (2006). Data file edition 3.7. Sikt—Norwegian Agency for Shared Services in Education and Research, Norway-Data Archive and distributor of ESS data for ESS ERIC. https://doi.org/10.21338/NSD-ESS3-2006, ESS Round 5: European Social Survey Round 5 Data (2010). Data file edition 3.4. Sikt—Norwegian Agency for Shared Services in Education and Research, Norway—Data Archive and distributor of ESS data for ESS ERIC. https://doi.org/10.21338/NSD-ESS5-2010, ESS Round 7: European Social Survey Round 7 Data (2014). Data file edition 2.2. Sikt—Norwegian Agency for Shared Services in Education and Research, Norway—Data Archive and distributor of ESS data for ESS ERIC. https://doi.org/10.21338/NSD-ESS7-2014, European Social Survey European Research Infrastructure (ESS ERIC). (2023), ESS9—integrated file, edition 3.2 [Data set]. Sikt—Norwegian Agency for Shared Services in Education and Research. https://doi.org/10.21338/ess9e03_2. The study also makes use of the EUROSTAT's data Population by educational attainment level, sex and age (%)—main indicators: Online data code: edat_lfse_03.

Conflicts of Interest: The authors declare no conflicts of interest.

Appendix A

Table A1. Transition probabilities and mobility indices for both nominal and positional mobility by country and ESS1(2002), ESS3(2006), ESS5(2010), ESS7(2014), and ESS9(2015) rounds.

Each cell shows the 3×3 transition matrix; the row below each matrix lists the summary indices M_{PS}, IM, UM, DM.

Belgium

Nominal Mobility Transition Probabilities

$P_{(YEAR)}$	Matrix	M_{PS}	IM	UM	DM
$P_{(2002)}$	[0.630 0.251 0.118; 0.176 0.462 0.361; 0.073 0.220 0.707]	0.600	0.599	0.319	0.073
$P_{(2006)}$	[0.562 0.300 0.138; 0.184 0.463 0.354; 0.029 0.183 0.788]	0.594	0.604	0.354	0.071
$P_{(2010)}$	[0.554 0.300 0.146; 0.151 0.436 0.413; 0.038 0.221 0.740]	0.635	0.577	0.356	0.084
$P_{(2014)}$	[0.504 0.385 0.112; 0.152 0.544 0.304; 0.065 0.259 0.676]	0.638	0.574	0.365	0.093
$P_{(2018)}$	[0.486 0.341 0.173; 0.103 0.461 0.436; 0.075 0.189 0.736]	0.659	0.561	0.356	0.099

Positional Mobility Transition Probabilities

$P_{(YEAR)}$	Matrix	M_{PS}	IM	UM	DM
$P_{(2002)}$	[0.687 0.234 0.079; 0.222 0.498 0.80; 0105 0.270 0.625]	0.595	0.603	0.198	0.199
$P_{(2006)}$	[0.576 0.314 0.110; 0.197 0.506 0.297; 0.035 0.224 0.741]	0.588	0.608	0.240	0.152
$P_{(2010)}$	[0.538 0.328 0.134; 0.147 0.476 0.377; 0.039 0.253 0.708]	0.639	0.574	0.280	0.146
$P_{(2014)}$	[0.450 0.440 0.110; 0.128 0.588 0.284; 0.057 0.290 0.653]	0.655	0.564	0.278	0.158
$P_{(2018)}$	[0.401 0.403 0.196; 0.076 0.485 0.439; 0.055 0.200 0.745]	0.685	0.544	0.346	0.110

Finland

Nominal Mobility Transition Probabilities

$P_{(YEAR)}$	Matrix	M_{PS}	IM	UM	DM
$P_{(2002)}$	[0.456 0.333 0.211; 0.125 0.531 0.344; 0.047 0.326 0.628]	0.693	0.538	0.439	0.070
$P_{(2006)}$	[0.430 0.364 0.206; 0.107 0.533 0.360; 0.052 0.310 0.638]	0.699	0.534	0.435	0.080
$P_{(2010)}$	[0.409 0.478 0.113; 0.118 0.614 0.268; 0.049 0.415 0.537]	0.720	0.520	0.415	0.092
$P_{(2014)}$	[0.365 0.505 0.130; 0.114 0.568 0.318; 0.035 0.368 0.596]	0.735	0.510	0.430	0.100
$P_{(2018)}$	[0.369 0.500 0.131; 0.108 0.554 0.338; 0.014 0.362 0.623]	0.727	0.515	0.399	0.111

Positional Mobility Transition Probabilities

$P_{(YEAR)}$	Matrix	M_{PS}	IM	UM	DM
$P_{(2002)}$	[0.404 0.427 0.168; 0.104 0.639 0.257; 0.043 0.435 0.522]	0.717	0.522	0.284	0.194
$P_{(2006)}$	[0.336 0.486 0.178; 0.075 0.644 0.281; 0.040 0.412 0.548]	0.736	0.509	0.315	0.176
$P_{(2010)}$	[0.279 0.618 0.103; 0.072 0.710 0.218; 0.031 0.506 0.462]	0.775	0.483	0.313	0.203
$P_{(2014)}$	[0.211 0.658 0.130; 0.059 0.658 0.283; 0.019 0.438 0.544]	0.793	0.471	0.357	0.172
$P_{(2018)}$	[0.192 0.664 0.144; 0.049 0.633 0.319; 0.006 0.410 0.583]	0.796	0.469	0.376	0.155

France

Nominal Mobility Transition Probabilities

$P_{(YEAR)}$	Matrix	M_{PS}	IM	UM	DM
$P_{(2002)}$	[0.568 0.316 0.116; 0.260 0.468 0.272; 0.095 0.202 0.703]	0.630	0.580	0.359	0.085
$P_{(2006)}$	[0.528 0.356 0.116; 0.205 0.423 0.371; 0.070 0.231 0.700]	0.675	0.550	0.404	0.077
$P_{(2010)}$	[0.511 0.418 0.071; 0.129 0.650 0.221; 0.032 0.314 0.654]	0.593	0.605	0.378	0.061
$P_{(2014)}$	[0.435 0.493 0.072; 0.129 0.634 0.237; 0.025 0.291 0.684]	0.623	0.584	0.399	0.074
$P_{(2018)}$	[0.400 0.494 0.107; 0.106 0.650 0.244; 0.042 0.345 0.613]	0.623	0.584	0.399	0.074

Positional Mobility Transition Probabilities

$P_{(YEAR)}$	Matrix	M_{PS}	IM	UM	DM
$P_{(2002)}$	[0.520 0.389 0.091; 0.231 0.560 0.209; 0.097 0.279 0.624]	0.648	0.568	0.230	0.202
$P_{(2006)}$	[0.515 0.408 0.077; 0.215 0.519 0.266; 0.085 0.330 0.585]	0.691	0.540	0.251	0.210
$P_{(2010)}$	[0.457 0.491 0.052; 0.111 0.733 0.156; 0.032 0.421 0.547]	0.632	0.579	0.233	0.188
$P_{(2014)}$	[0.327 0.611 0.061; 0.090 0.726 0.185; 0.020 0.376 0.604]	0.672	0.552	0.286	0.162
$P_{(2018)}$	[0.284 0.615 0.102; 0.068 0.724 0.208; 0.029 0.411 0.560]	0.716	0.523	0.308	0.010

Germany

Nominal Mobility Transition Probabilities

$P_{(YEAR)}$	Matrix	M_{PS}	IM	UM	DM
$P_{(2002)}$	[0.553 0.389 0.058; 0.179 0.662 0.158; 0.069 0.485 0.446]	0.669	0.554	0.165	0.233
$P_{(2006)}$	[0.520 0.409 0.071; 0.155 0.664 0.181; 0.038 0.359 0.603]	0.669	0.554	0.195	0.201
$P_{(2010)}$	[0.444 0.495 0.061; 0.113 0.732 0.155; 0.031 0.392 0.576]	0.624	0.584	0.219	0.120

Positional Mobility Transition Probabilities

$P_{(YEAR)}$	Matrix	M_{PS}	IM	UM	DM
$P_{(2002)}$	[0.365 0.605 0.030; 0.096 0.838 0.066; 0044 0.732 0.224]	0.787	0.475	0.234	0.291
$P_{(2006)}$	[0.347 0.614 0.039; 0.087 0.831 0.082; 0.051 0.682 0.267]	0.778	0.482	0.245	0.273
$P_{(2010)}$	[0.249 0.716 0.035; 0.052 0.873 0.075; 0.019 0.616 0.365]	0.757	0.496	0.275	0.229

Hungary

Nominal Mobility Transition Probabilities

$P_{(YEAR)}$	Matrix	M_{PS}	IM	UM	DM
$P_{(2002)}$	[0.538 0.403 0.058; 0.149 0.698 0.153; 0.060 0.380 0.560]	0.602	0.599	0.312	0.088
$P_{(2006)}$	[0.532 0.399 0.069; 0.131 0.701 0.169; 0.038 0.400 0.563]	0.603	0.598	0.294	0.101
$P_{(2010)}$	[0.503 0.450 0.047; 0.093 0.725 0.182; 0.015 0.415 0.569]	0.601	0.599	0.305	0.082

Positional Mobility Transition Probabilities

$P_{(YEAR)}$	Matrix	M_{PS}	IM	UM	DM
$P_{(2002)}$	[0.426 0.557 0.017; 0.104 0.855 0.041; 0.064 0.710 0.226]	0.746	0.502	0.205	0.293
$P_{(2006)}$	[0.376 0.597 0.027; 0.077 0.869 0.054; 0.031 0.709 0.259]	0.748	0.502	0.226	0.272
$P_{(2010)}$	[0.322 0.657 0.021; 0.049 0.883 0.068; 0.011 0.696 0.292]	0.752	0.499	0.249	0.252

Ireland

Nominal Mobility Transition Probabilities

$P_{(YEAR)}$	Matrix	M_{PS}	IM	UM	DM
$P_{(2002)}$	[0.549 0.228 0.222; 0.147 0.265 0.588; 0.094 0.219 0.688]	0.749	0.501	0.408	0.066
$P_{(2006)}$	[0.476 0.217 0.307; 0.130 0.261 0.609; 0.044 0.178 0.778]	0.743	0.505	0.447	0.062
$P_{(2010)}$	[0.511 0.385 0.103; 0.070 0.577 0.352; 0.050 0.300 0.650]	0.631	0.580	0.415	0.045

Positional Mobility Transition Probabilities

$P_{(YEAR)}$	Matrix	M_{PS}	IM	UM	DM
$P_{(2002)}$	[0.622 0.241 0.137; 0.206 0.345 0.449; 0.139 0.303 0.558]	0.738	0.508	0.276	0.216
$P_{(2006)}$	[0.500 0.241 0.260; 0.146 0.308 0.547; 0.052 0.219 0.729]	0.732	0.512	0.349	0.139
$P_{(2010)}$	[0.467 0.426 0.107; 0.060 0.598 0.342; 0.043 0.316 0.641]	0.647	0.569	0.291	0.140

Table A1. *Cont.*

(continued — left strip)

P(YEAR)	Nom M_PS	Nom IM	Nom UM	Nom DM	Pos M_PS	Pos IM	Pos UM	Pos DM
P(2014)		0.443	0.494	0.063		0.227	0.735	0.038
		0.119	0.725	0.156		0.050	0.874	0.076
		0.042	0.528	0.430		0.020	0.736	0.244
	0.701	0.533	0.200	0.158	0.828	0.448	0.283	0.269
P(2018)		0.452	0.499	0.049		0.235	0.732	0.033
		0.101	0.723	0.175		0.043	0.862	0.095
		0.027	0.481	0.492		0.013	0.673	0.314
	0.666	0.556	0.211	0.145	0.794	0.470	0.287	0.243

The Netherlands

P(YEAR)	Nom M_PS	Nom IM	Nom UM	Nom DM	Pos M_PS	Pos IM	Pos UM	Pos DM
P(2002)		0.481	0.382	0.137		0.471	0.448	0.081
		0.196	0.472	0.332		0.204	0.588	0.209
		0.107	0.356	0.537		0.125	0.496	0.379
	0.755	0.497	0.410	0.102	0.781	0.479	0.246	0.275
P(2006)		0.446	0.371	0.183		0.430	0.440	0.130
		0.199	0.482	0.319		0.194	0.578	0.228
		0.093	0.327	0.580		0.100	0.437	0.463
	0.746	0.503	0.427	0.101	0.765	0.490	0.266	0.244
P(2010)		0.441	0.420	0.138		0.402	0.488	0.110
		0.126	0.533	0.341		0.114	0.616	0.270
		0.056	0.364	0.580		0.055	0.452	0.493
	0.723	0.518	0.445	0.078	0.703	0.504	0.289	0.207
P(2014)		0.394	0.448	0.158		0.328	0.536	0.136
		0.108	0.432	0.460		0.090	0.516	0.394
		0.071	0.336	0.593		0.061	0.414	0.525
	0.791	0.473	0.502	0.072	0.816	0.456	0.355	0.188
P(2018)		0.403	0.425	0.172		0.313	0.519	0.169
		0.103	0.502	0.394		0.074	0.567	0.359
		0.036	0.321	0.643		0.026	0.373	0.601
	0.726	0.516	0.439	0.091	0.760	0.494	0.349	0.158

(continued — middle strip)

P(YEAR)	Nom M_PS	Nom IM	Nom UM	Nom DM	Pos M_PS	Pos IM	Pos UM	Pos DM
P(2014)		NA	NA	NA		NA	NA	NA
P(2018)		0.546	0.392	0.062		NA	NA	NA
		0.051	0.751	0.198		NA	NA	NA
		0.016	0.210	0.774		NA	NA	NA
	0.464	0.691	0.263	0.050	NA	NA	NA	NA

Norway

P(YEAR)	Nom M_PS	Nom IM	Nom UM	Nom DM	Pos M_PS	Pos IM	Pos UM	Pos DM
P(2002)		0.384	0.491	0.125		0.188	0.708	0.104
		0.143	0.546	0.311		0.063	0.705	0.233
		0.075	0.328	0.597		0.036	0.469	0.495
	0.736	0.509	0.356	0.148	0.806	0.462	0.348	0.189
P(2006)		0.371	0.510	0.119		0.303	0.604	0.093
		0.105	0.648	0.248		0.082	0.732	0.186
		0.034	0.379	0.586		0.030	0.478	0.492
	0.698	0.535	0.379	0.114	0.737	0.509	0.294	0.197
P(2010)		0.396	0.448	0.157		0.296	0.560	0.143
		0.121	0.560	0.319		0.083	0.647	0.270
		0.029	0.261	0.710		0.022	0.327	0.651
	0.667	0.555	0.370	0.107	0.703	0.532	0.324	0.144
P(2014)		0.311	0.508	0.182		0.224	0.584	0.192
		0.115	0.607	0.279		0.077	0.649	0.274
		0.025	0.325	0.650		0.017	0.347	0.637
	0.716	0.522	0.374	0.126	0.745	0.503	0.350	0.147
P(2018)		0.259	0.536	0.205		0.179	0.598	0.223
		0.105	0.564	0.331		0.069	0.593	0.338
		0.054	0.323	0.624		0.035	0.335	0.630
	0.777	0.482	0.376	0.145	0.799	0.467	0.386	0.146

(continued — right strip)

P(YEAR)	Nom M_PS	Nom IM	Nom UM	Nom DM	Pos M_PS	Pos IM	Pos UM	Pos DM
P(2014)		0.485	0.426	0.089		0.373	0.519	0.108
		0.089	0.557	0.354		0.058	0.576	0.366
		0.048	0.190	0.762		0.031	0.194	0.775
	0.598	0.601	0.428	0.045	0.638	0.575	0.331	0.094
P(2018)		0.425	0.425	0.150		0.291	0.515	0.194
		0.068	0.534	0.398		0.039	0.536	0.426
		0.041	0.245	0.714		0.022	0.238	0.740
	0.663	0.558	0.423	0.069	0.717	0.522	0.378	0.100

Poland

P(YEAR)	Nom M_PS	Nom IM	Nom UM	Nom DM	Pos M_PS	Pos IM	Pos UM	Pos DM
P(2002)		0.386	0.550	0.064		0.213	0.773	0.014
		0.103	0.715	0.182		0.052	0.912	0.037
		0.019	0.352	0.629		0.016	0.767	0.217
	0.635	0.577	0.437	0.052	0.874	0.447	0.275	0.278
P(2006)		0.403	0.561	0.036		0.188	0.800	0.012
		0.073	0.713	0.214		0.030	0.906	0.063
		0.017	0.542	0.441		0.009	0.834	0.157
	0.722	0.519	0.412	0.057	0.874	0.417	0.292	0.291
P(2010)		0.561	0.333	0.107		0.306	0.631	0.063
		0.141	0.450	0.409		0.066	0.729	0.205
		0.045	0.153	0.802		0.031	0.369	0.600
	0.594	0.604	0.392	0.048	0.683	0.545	0.300	0.155
P(2014)		0.552	0.354	0.094		0.265	0.666	0.069
		0.149	0.471	0.380		0.058	0.716	0.227
		0.030	0.187	0.783		0.015	0.373	0.612
	0.597	0.602	0.403	0.047	0.704	0.531	0.320	0.149
P(2018)		0.500	0.347	0.154		0.214	0.653	0.133
		0.092	0.442	0.466		0.031	0.653	0.316
		0.016	0.217	0.767		0.006	0.379	0.615
	0.646	0.570	0.446	0.041	0.759	0.494	0.367	0.139

Portugal

P(YEAR)	Nom M_PS	Nom IM	Nom UM	Nom DM	Pos M_PS	Pos IM	Pos UM	Pos DM
P(2002)		0.867	0.074	0.059		0.978	0.015	0.007
		0.444	0.333	0.222		0.842	0.114	0.044
		0.222	0.278	0.500		0.685	0.155	0.160
	0.650	0.567	0.132	0.025	0.650	0.418	0.022	0.560
P(2006)		0.813	0.110	0.076		0.955	0.030	0.015
		0.118	0.353	0.529		0.411	0.287	0.302
		0.208	0.208	0.583		0.592	0.138	0.270
	0.625	0.583	0.188	0.016	0.744	0.504	0.116	0.380

Slovenia

P(YEAR)	Nom M_PS	Nom IM	Nom UM	Nom DM	Pos M_PS	Pos IM	Pos UM	Pos DM
P(2002)		0.484	0.468	0.048		0.305	0.681	0.014
		0.140	0.684	0.175		0.078	0.877	0.045
		0.091	0.455	0.455		0.067	0.777	0.156
	0.689	0.541	0.323	0.108	0.831	0.446	0.247	0.307
P(2006)		0.426	0.492	0.082		0.241	0.723	0.036
		0.121	0.652	0.227		0.061	0.850	0.089
		0.000	0.471	0.529		0.000	0.748	0.252
	0.696	0.536	0.347	0.111	0.828	0.448	0.283	0.270

Spain

P(YEAR)	Nom M_PS	Nom IM	Nom UM	Nom DM	Pos M_PS	Pos IM	Pos UM	Pos DM
P(2002)		0.737	0.126	0.137		0.859	0.076	0.065
		0.251	0.318	0.430		0.425	0.279	0.295
		0.036	0.149	0.814		0.081	0.175	0.744
	0.565	0.623	0.256	0.029	0.559	0.627	0.145	0.227
P(2006)		0.651	0.168	0.181		0.793	0.092	0.115
		0.155	0.280	0.564		0.271	0.219	0.510
		0.056	0.260	0.684		0.105	0.221	0.673
	0.693	0.538	0.335	0.042	0.657	0.562	0.239	0.199

Column groups: **Nominal Mobility Transition Probabilities** (M_PS, IM, UM, DM) and **Positional Mobility Transition Probabilities** (M_PS, IM, UM, DM).

Table A1. Cont.

The table is laid out in two physical columns. Each country-year entry gives, for both the **Nominal Mobility** and **Positional Mobility** transition-probability matrices: a 3×3 matrix, the scalar M_{PS} (bottom-left), and the summary triple (IM, UM, DM) below the matrix.

Left column

$P_{(2010)}$ — (continuation)

Nominal Mobility — $M_{PS}=0.683$; summary (IM,UM,DM) = (0.545, 0.212, 0.026)

0.791	0.126	0.083
0.222	0.389	0.389
0.136	0.409	0.455

Positional Mobility — $M_{PS}=0.763$; summary = (0.491, 0.086, 0.423)

0.938	0.042	0.020
0.540	0.264	0.195
0.396	0.332	0.272

$P_{(2014)}$

Nominal — $M_{PS}=0.684$; summary = (0.544, 0.269, 0.041)

0.732	0.168	0.100
0.239	0.283	0.478
0.088	0.294	0.618

Positional — $M_{PS}=0.698$; summary = (0.535, 0.148, 0.317)

0.873	0.085	0.042
0.454	0.229	0.318
0.205	0.292	0.503

$P_{(2018)}$

Nominal — $M_{PS}=0.522$; summary = (0.652, 0.284, 0.024)

0.711	0.162	0.127
0.082	0.479	0.438
0.000	0.235	0.765

Positional — $M_{PS}=0.479$; summary = (0.680, 0.178, 0.142)

0.829	0.105	0.067
0.151	0.487	0.363
0.000	0.274	0.726

Sweden

$P_{(2002)}$ — Nominal: NA; Positional: NA

$P_{(2006)}$

Nominal — $M_{PS}=0.789$; summary = (0.474, 0.464, 0.117)

0.352	0.444	0.205
0.125	0.529	0.346
0.055	0.404	0.541

Positional — $M_{PS}=0.803$; summary = (0.447, 0.325, 0.228)

0.265	0.587	0.148
0.090	0.669	0.240
0.043	0.552	0.405

$P_{(2010)}$

Nominal — $M_{PS}=0.732$; summary = (0.512, 0.446, 0.098)

0.329	0.525	0.145
0.118	0.624	0.258
0.044	0.374	0.582

Positional — $M_{PS}=0.784$; summary = (0.478, 0.321, 0.202)

0.223	0.666	0.111
0.075	0.740	0.185
0.031	0.499	0.469

$P_{(2014)}$

Nominal — $M_{PS}=0.758$; summary = (0.495, 0.420, 0.112)

0.325	0.556	0.119
0.078	0.609	0.313
0.025	0.425	0.550

Positional — $M_{PS}=0.814$; summary = (0.458, 0.354, 0.188)

0.199	0.693	0.108
0.044	0.695	0.261
0.015	0.507	0.478

$P_{(2018)}$

Nominal — $M_{PS}=0.751$; summary = (0.499, 0.397, 0.123)

0.290	0.543	0.167
0.100	0.568	0.332
0.033	0.327	0.641

Positional — $M_{PS}=0.791$; summary = (0.473, 0.383, 0.144)

0.173	0.650	0.177
0.055	0.623	0.322
0.018	0.359	0.622

Right column

$P_{(2010)}$ — (continuation)

Nominal — $M_{PS}=0.672$; summary = (0.552, 0.322, 0.041)

0.653	0.193	0.154
0.173	0.271	0.556
0.049	0.219	0.732

Positional — $M_{PS}=0.646$; summary = (0.570, 0.245, 0.185)

0.758	0.137	0.106
0.259	0.248	0.492
0.080	0.217	0.703

$P_{(2014)}$

Nominal — $M_{PS}=0.703$; summary = (0.531, 0.350, 0.055)

0.618	0.202	0.180
0.151	0.354	0.495
0.098	0.279	0.622

Positional — $M_{PS}=0.681$; summary = (0.546, 0.357, 0.192)

0.723	0.127	0.150
0.217	0.274	0.508
0.142	0.217	0.641

$P_{(2018)}$

Nominal — $M_{PS}=0.681$; summary = (0.546, 0.374, 0.050)

0.582	0.224	0.194
0.172	0.333	0.495
0.091	0.186	0.723

Positional — $M_{PS}=0.667$; summary = (0.555, 0.287, 0.157)

0.660	0.157	0.183
0.217	0.261	0.522
0.112	0.142	0.745

Switzerland

$P_{(2002)}$

Nominal — $M_{PS}=0.723$; summary = (0.518, 0.329, 0.146)

0.377	0.474	0.149
0.118	0.611	0.271
0.061	0.374	0.566

Positional — $M_{PS}=0.839$; summary = (0.440, 0.291, 0.269)

0.209	0.775	0.016
0.030	0.890	0.080
0.000	0.777	0.223

$P_{(2006)}$

Nominal — $M_{PS}=0.676$; summary = (0.549, 0.345, 0.110)

0.426	0.467	0.108
0.107	0.619	0.274
0.038	0.359	0.603

Positional — $M_{PS}=0.742$; summary = (0.505, 0.315, 0.180)

0.175	0.794	0.031
0.032	0.845	0.123
0.000	0.617	0.383

$P_{(2010)}$

Nominal — $M_{PS}=0.644$; summary = (0.571, 0.306, 0.096)

0.375	0.554	0.071
0.102	0.726	0.172
0.037	0.352	0.611

Positional — $M_{PS}=0.731$; summary = (0.512, 0.301, 0.187)

0.212	0.734	0.054
0.050	0.836	0.114
0.022	0.488	0.490

$P_{(2014)}$

Nominal — $M_{PS}=0.650$; summary = (0.567, 0.314, 0.105)

0.358	0.570	0.073
0.115	0.692	0.193
0.048	0.302	0.651

Positional — $M_{PS}=0.720$; summary = (0.520, 0.323, 0.157)

0.183	0.752	0.065
0.051	0.797	0.152
0.024	0.395	0.581

$P_{(2018)}$

Nominal — $M_{PS}=0.621$; summary = (0.586, 0.305, 0.091)

0.441	0.487	0.072
0.075	0.697	0.228
0.063	0.316	0.620

Positional — $M_{PS}=0.700$; summary = (0.533, 0.324, 0.142)

0.235	0.681	0.084
0.031	0.760	0.209
0.028	0.368	0.604

UK

$P_{(2002)}$

Nominal — $M_{PS}=0.736$; summary = (0.510, 0.298, 0.077)

0.639	0.101	0.260
0.285	0.203	0.512
0.167	0.146	0.687

Positional — $M_{PS}=0.732$; summary = (0.512, 0.260, 0.228)

0.658	0.126	0.215
0.302	0.261	0.437
0.186	0.197	0.617

$P_{(2006)}$

Nominal — $M_{PS}=0.754$; summary = (0.497, 0.328, 0.078)

0.568	0.108	0.325
0.265	0.178	0.557
0.156	0.099	0.745

Positional — $M_{PS}=0.753$; summary = (0.498, 0.323, 0.179)

0.531	0.164	0.305
0.238	0.261	0.501
0.147	0.151	0.702

$P_{(2010)}$

Nominal — $M_{PS}=0.731$; summary = (0.513, 0.358, 0.113)

0.555	0.330	0.116
0.218	0.465	0.317
0.082	0.399	0.519

Positional — $M_{PS}=0.774$; summary = (0.484, 0.286, 0.230)

0.423	0.461	0.116
0.147	0.574	0.280
0.055	0.490	0.455

$P_{(2014)}$

Nominal — $M_{PS}=0.698$; summary = (0.535, 0.390, 0.101)

0.476	0.343	0.181
0.134	0.498	0.368
0.081	0.289	0.630

Positional — $M_{PS}=0.753$; summary = (0.498, 0.335, 0.167)

0.306	0.510	0.183
0.072	0.617	0.310
0.046	0.384	0.570

$P_{(2018)}$

Nominal — $M_{PS}=0.710$; summary = (0.527, 0.427, 0.096)

0.381	0.422	0.197
0.125	0.508	0.366
0.048	0.261	0.691

Positional — $M_{PS}=0.759$; summary = (0.494, 0.384, 0.122)

0.230	0.531	0.238
0.065	0.553	0.382
0.025	0.275	0.700

Table A1. *Cont.*

$P_{(YEAR)}$	Nominal Mobility Transition Probabilities				Positional Mobility Transition Probabilities				Nominal Mobility Transition Probabilities				Positional Mobility Transition Probabilities			
	M_{PS}	IM	UM	DM	M_{PS}	IM	UM	DM	M_{PS}	IM	UM	DM	M_{PS}	IM	UM	DM
	Total				**Total**											
$P_{(2002)}$		0.600	0.252	0.148		0.596	0.318	0.087								
		0.182	0.605	0.213		0.169	0.714	0.117								
		0.097	0.314	0.589		0.115	0.472	0.413								
	0.603	0.598	0.290	0.110	0.603	0.574	0.174	0.252								
$P_{(2006)}$		0.547	0.280	0.173		0.596	0.318	0.087								
		0.151	0.595	0.253		0.169	0.714	0.117								
		0.093	0.282	0.625		0.115	0.472	0.413								
	0.616	0.589	0.326	0.101	0.642	0.572	0.212	0.216								
$P_{(2010)}$		0.549	0.343	0.108		0.475	0.443	0.082								
		0.128	0.648	0.225		0.099	0.748	0.153								
		0.047	0.320	0.633		0.043	0.443	0.514								
	0.585	0.610	0.327	0.081	0.631	0.579	0.226	0.195								
$P_{(2014)}$		0.505	0.368	0.126		0.553	0.355	0.093								
		0.125	0.630	0.245		0.148	0.658	0.194								
		0.056	0.349	0.595		0.073	0.403	0.523								
	0.635	0.577	0.345	0.094	0.633	0.578	0.214	0.208								
$P_{(2018)}$		0.400	0.494	0.107		0.344	0.505	0.151								
		0.106	0.650	0.244		0.064	0.712	0.224								
		0.042	0.345	0.613		0.029	0.384	0.587								
	0.669	0.554	0.411	0.081	0.678	0.548	0.293	0.159								

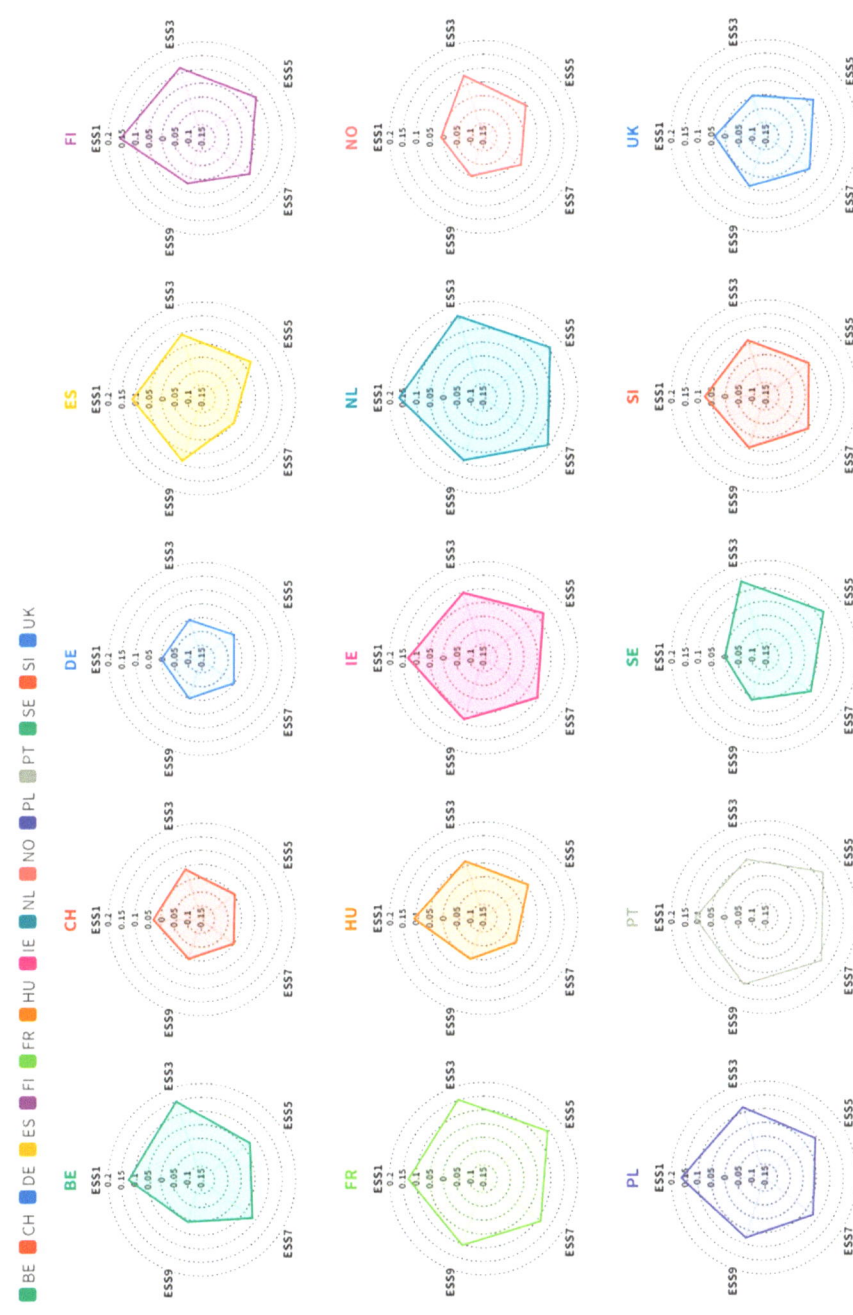

Figure A1. The differences in upward mobility index between nominal and positional mobility by country and ESS round (ESS1, ESS3, ESS5, ESS7, and ESS9).

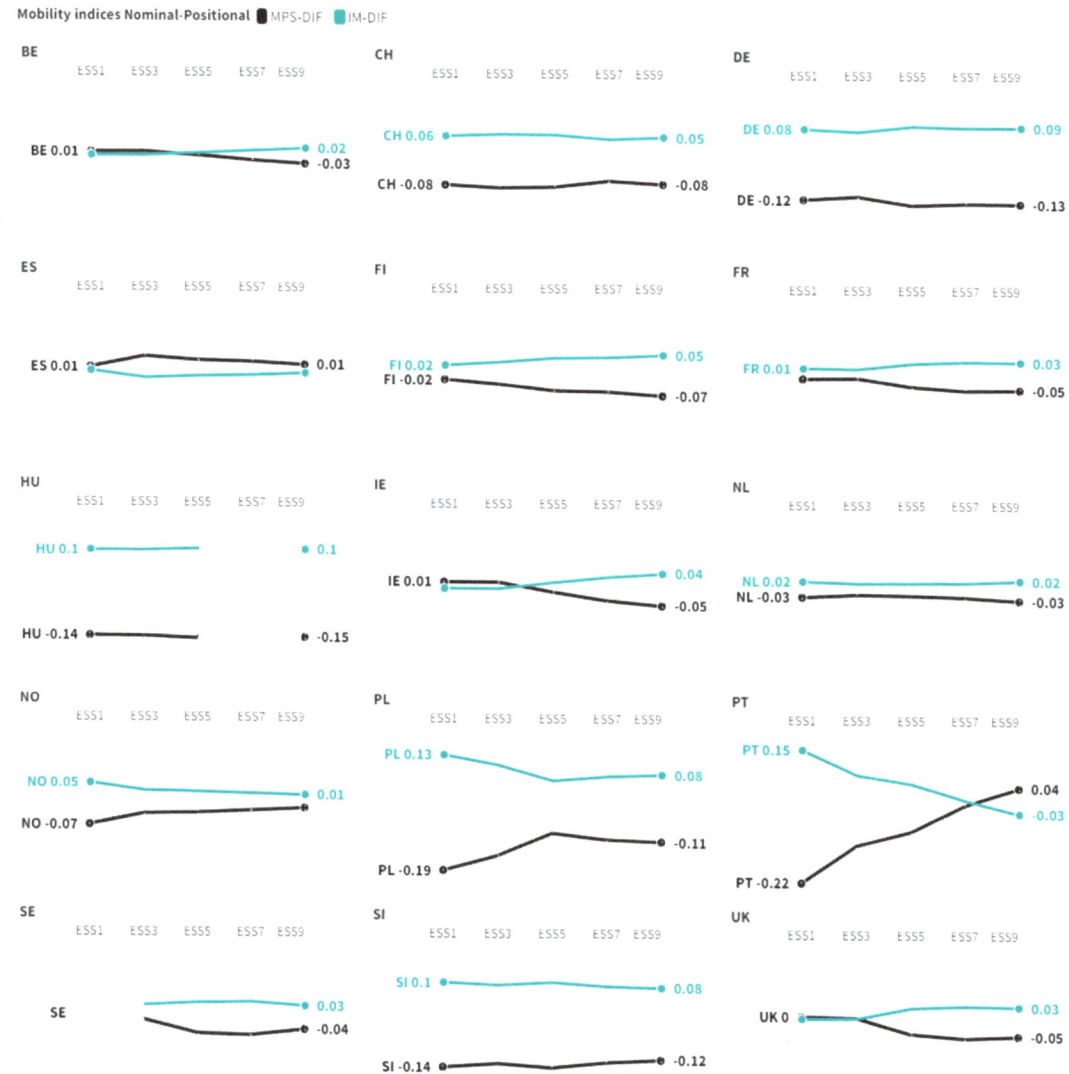

Figure A2. The differences in M_{PS} and IM between nominal and positional mobility by country and ESS round (ESS1, ESS3, ESS5, ESS7, ESS9).

References

1. Hout, M.; DiPrete, T. What we have learned: RC28's contributions to knowledge about social stratification. *Res. Soc. Stratif. Mobil.* **2006**, *24*, 1–20. [CrossRef]
2. Sensoy, O.; DiAngelo, R. *Is Everyone Really Equal?: An Introduction to Key Concepts in Social Justice Education*; Teachers College Press: New York, NY, USA, 2017.
3. Breen, R. (Ed.) *Social Mobility in Europe*; Oxford University Press: Oxford, UK, 2005.
4. Breen, R.; Muller, W. (Eds.) *Education and Intergenerational Mobility in Europe and the United States*; Stanford University Press: Stanford, CA, USA, 2020.
5. Erikson, R.; Goldthorpe, J. *The Constant Flux*; Oxford University Press: Oxford, UK, 1992.
6. Blanden, J. Cross-Country Ranking in Intergenerational Mobility: A Comparison of Approaches from Economics and Sociology. *J. Econ. Surv.* **2011**, *63*, 38–73. [CrossRef]

7. Torche, F. Analyses of Intergenerational Mobility: An Interdisciplinary Review. *Ann. Am. Acad. Political Soc. Sci.* **2015**, *657*, 37–62. [CrossRef]
8. Breen, R.; Goldthorpe, J.H. Explaining Educational Differentials: Towards a formal rational action theory. *Ration. Soc.* **1997**, *9*, 275–305. [CrossRef]
9. Blanden, J.; Gregg, P.; Machin, S. *Intergenerational Mobility in Europe and North America*; A Report Supported by the Sutton Trust; Centre for Economic Performance: London, UK, 2005.
10. Bukodi, E.; Goldthorpe, J.H. *Social Mobility and Education in Britain: Research, Politics and Policy*; Cambridge University Press: Cambridge, UK, 2018.
11. Salvanes, K.G. What Drives Intergenerational Mobility? The Role of Family, Neighborhood, Education, and Social Class: A Review of Bukodi and Goldthorpe's Social Mobility and Education in Britain. *J. Econ. Lit.* **2023**, *61*, 1540–1578. [CrossRef]
12. Corak, M. Income Inequality, Equality of Opportunity, and Intergenerational Mobility. *J. Econ. Perspect.* **2013**, *27*, 79–102. [CrossRef]
13. Cunha, F.; Heckman, J. The Technology of Skill Formation. *Am. Econ. Rev.* **2007**, *97*, 31–47. [CrossRef]
14. Blanden, J.; Machin, S. *Recent Changes in Intergenerational Mobility in Britain*; Sutton Trust: London, UK, 2007; pp. 1–34.
15. Symeonaki, M.; Stamatopoulou, G. Exploring the transition to Higher Education in Greece: Issues of intergenerational educational mobility. *Policy Futures Educ.* **2014**, *12*, 681–694. [CrossRef]
16. Symeonaki, M.; Stamatopoulou, G.; Michalopoulou, C. Intergenerational educational mobility in Greece: Transitions and social distances. *Commun. Stat.—Theory Methods* **2015**, *45*, 1710–1722. [CrossRef]
17. Stamatopoulou, G.; Symeonaki, M.; Michalopoulou, C. Occupational and educational gender segregation in southern Europe. In *Stochastic and Data Analysis Methods and Applications in Statistics and Demography*; Bozeman, J.R., Oliveira, T., Skiadas, C.H., Eds.; Springer: Berlin/Heidelberg, Germany, 2016; pp. 611–619.
18. Stamatopoulou, G.; Symeonaki, M. Intergenerational social mobility in Europe: Findings from the European Social Survey. In *The Springer Series on Demographic Methods and Population Analysis*; Springer: Berlin/Heidelberg, Germany, 2023.
19. Symeonaki, M.; Tsinaslanidou, P. *Assessing the Intergenerational Educational Mobility in European Countries Based on ESS Data: 2002–2016*; The Springer Series on Demographic Methods and Population Analysis Quantitative Methods in Demography; Springer: Cham, Switzerland, 2022; pp. 359–372. [CrossRef]
20. Breen, R.; Luijkx, R.; Müller, W.; Pollak, R. Nonpersistent inequality in educational attainment: Evidence from eight European countries. *Am. J. Sociol.* **2009**, *114*, 1475–1521. [CrossRef]
21. Breen, R.; Luijkx, R.; Müller, W.; Pollak, R. Long-term trends in educational inequality in Europe: Class inequalities and gender differences. *Eur. Sociol. Rev.* **2010**, *26*, 31–48. [CrossRef]
22. Goldthorpe, J.H. Analysing Social Inequality: A Critique of Two Recent Contributions from Economics and Epidemiology. *Eur. Sociol. Rev.* **2009**, *26*, 731–744. [CrossRef]
23. Hirsch, F. *Social Limits to Growth*; Harvard University Press: Cambridge, MA, USA, 1976.
24. Rotman, A.; Shavit, Y.; Shalev, M. Nominal and positional perspectives on educational stratification in Israel. *Res. Soc. Stratif. Mobil.* **2016**, *43*, 17–24. [CrossRef]
25. Fujihara, S.; Ishida, H. The absolute and relative values of education and the inequality of educational opportunity: Trends in access to education in postwar Japan. *Res. Soc. Stratif. Mobil.* **2016**, *43*, 25–37. [CrossRef]
26. Triventi, M.; Panichella, N.; Ballarino, G.; Barone, C.; Bernardi, F. Education as a positional good: Implications for social inequalities in educational attainment in Italy. *Res. Soc. Stratif. Mobil.* **2016**, *43*, 39–52. [CrossRef]
27. Di Stasio, V.; Bol, T.; Van de Werfhorst, H.G. What makes education positional? Institutions, overeducation and the competition for jobs. *Res. Soc. Stratif. Mobil.* **2016**, *43*, 53–63. [CrossRef]
28. Araki, S. Educational Expansion, Skills Diffusion, and the Economic Value of Credentials and Skills. *Am. Sociol. Rev.* **2020**, *85*, 128–175. [CrossRef]
29. Bartholomew, D.J. *Stochastic Models for Social Processes*, 3rd ed.; John Wiley: New York, NY, USA, 1982.
30. Bartholomew, D.J.; Forbes, A.F.; McClean, S.I. *Statistical Techniques for Manpower Planning*, 2nd ed.; Wiley: Hoboken, NJ, USA, 1991.
31. McClean, S. Semi-Markov models for manpower planning. In *Semi-Markov Models*; Janssen, J., Ed.; Springer: Boston, MA, USA, 1986.
32. McClean, S. Manpower planning models and their estimation. *Eur. J. Oper. Res.* **1991**, *51*, 179–187. [CrossRef]
33. McClean, S.; Montgomery, E. Estimation for Semi-Markov Manpower Models in a Stochastic Environment. In *Semi-Markov Models and Applications*; Janssen, J., Limnios, N., Eds.; Springer: Boston, MA, USA, 1999.
34. Vassiliou, P.-C.G. Asymptotic behavior of Markov systems. *J. Appl. Probab.* **1982**, *19*, 851–857. [CrossRef]
35. Vassiliou, P.-C.G.; Symeonaki, M. The perturbed non-homogeneous Markov system. *Linear Algebra Appl.* **1999**, *289*, 319–332. [CrossRef]
36. Vassiliou, P.-C.G. Non-Homogeneous Markov Set Systems. *Mathematics* **2021**, *9*, 471. [CrossRef]
37. Vassiliou, P.-C.G. *Non-Homogeneous Markov Chains and Systems: Theory and Applications*, 1st ed.; Chapman and Hall/CRC: Boca Raton, FL, USA, 2023.
38. Bibby, J. Methods of measuring mobility. In *Quality & Quantity: International Journal of Methodology*; Springer: Berlin/Heidelberg, Germany, 1975; Volume 9, pp. 107–136.

39. Goldthorpe, J.H.; Jackson, M. Intergenerational class mobility in contemporary Britain: Political concerns and empirical findings. *Br. J. Sociol.* **2007**, *58*, 525–546. [CrossRef] [PubMed]
40. Prais, S. Measuring social mobility. *J. R. Stat. Soc. Ser. A* **1955**, *118*, 56–66. [CrossRef]
41. Shorrocks, A. The measurement of social mobility. *Econometrica* **1978**, *46*, 1013–1024. [CrossRef]
42. Bukodi, E.; Goldthorpe, J.H. Educational attainment—Relative or absolute—As a mediator of intergenerational class mobility in Britain. *Res. Soc. Stratif. Mobil.* **2016**, *43*, 5–15. [CrossRef]

Article

Attainability for Markov and Semi-Markov Chains

Brecht Verbeken [1,2,*] and Marie-Anne Guerry [1,2]

[1] Department of Business Technology and Operations, Vrije Universiteit Brussel, Pleinlaan 2, 1050 Brussels, Belgium; marie-anne.guerry@vub.be
[2] Data Analytics Laboratory, Vrije Universiteit Brussel, Pleinlaan 2, 1050 Brussels, Belgium
* Correspondence: brecht.verbeken@vub.be

Abstract: When studying Markov chain models and semi-Markov chain models, it is useful to know which state vectors $\mathbf{n}$, where each component n_i represents the number of entities in the state S_i, can be maintained or attained. This question leads to the definitions of maintainability and attainability for (time-homogeneous) Markov chain models. Recently, the definition of maintainability was extended to the concept of state reunion maintainability (SR-maintainability) for semi-Markov chains. Within the framework of semi-Markov chains, the states are subdivided further into seniority-based states. State reunion maintainability assesses the maintainability of the distribution across states. Following this idea, we introduce the concept of state reunion attainability, which encompasses the potential of a system to attain a specific distribution across the states after uniting the seniority-based states into the underlying states. In this paper, we start by extending the concept of attainability for constant-sized Markov chain models to systems that are subject to growth or contraction. Afterwards, we introduce the concepts of attainability and state reunion attainability for semi-Markov chain models, using SR-maintainability as a starting point. The attainable region, as well as the state reunion attainable region, are described as the convex hull of their respective vertices, and properties of these regions are investigated.

Keywords: semi-Markov model; Markov model; attainability; maintainability; state reunion; manpower planning

MSC: 60K15; 91D35; 60J20

Citation: Verbeken, B.; Guerry, M.-A. Attainability for Markov and Semi-Markov Chains. *Mathematics* **2024**, *12*, 1227. https://doi.org/10.3390/math12081227

Academic Editors: Panagiotis-Christos Vassiliou and Andreas C. Georgiou

Received: 15 March 2024
Revised: 11 April 2024
Accepted: 13 April 2024
Published: 19 April 2024

1. Introduction

The notion of attainability first took root in the context of manpower planning [1,2]. While it is possible to study attainability in any (semi-)Markov chain model that allows for inflow, outflow, and internal transitions, our discussion will conform to the established norms and use the language typically linked to the context of manpower planning. In a Markov model, the system's states represent homogeneous groups that are characterised by intra-group homogeneity with similar likelihoods of transitioning from one state to another. For more context regarding population models and Markov chains we refer the reader to [3,4].

In this domain, the system's states are often aligned with hierarchical levels in the organisation, which we call the "organisational states". Let us denote the organisational states as $\mathbf{S} = \{S_1, \ldots, S_l\}$. The distribution of personnel across these states is captured by a vector $\mathbf{s} = (s_i)$, which we call the personnel structure. The central question in control theory within this context is whether a desired distribution of personnel across these states can be sustained (maintainability) or attained (attainability) through strategic adjustments to manageable parameters. When investigating maintainability and attainability, one has to start by precisely defining what should be maintained or attained and how this can be accomplished. Note, however, that the concepts of maintainability and attainability can be

used for every discrete-time Markov process that allows for leaving the system, for entering the system, and for making transitions within the system.

Regarding the means of control, control theory typically considers three primary types of personnel movements, as outlined in [5]: wastage, internal transitions, and recruitment. An employee in the organisation at time t is either still in one of the organisational states or has left the organisation through wastage at time $t + 1$. The wastage probability from state S_i is denoted as w_i, and the wastage probabilities are gathered in the wastage vector **w**. Internal transitions account for movements within the organisation, such as promotions or demotions, and are represented by a transition matrix $\mathbf{P}^I$. Recruitment reflects the process of recruiting new members into the organisation, with a recruitment vector **r**. In this paper, only systems with a finite number of states are considered.

The field of control theory is well established and has a significant history within the engineering domain, as highlighted in [6,7], among others, while the foundations for control theory in Markov models were first explored in the context of manpower planning in [5,8–11].

While there are three main approaches to influencing the personnel structure within organisations, recruitment control is often preferred. Controlling through recruitment is viewed as a more ethical alternative compared to using wastage, which involves dismissing employees and can negatively affect morale and job satisfaction. Adjusting promotion and demotion rates can also lead to dissatisfaction, particularly among those who perceive it as a hindrance to their career advancement [12]. Such adjustments may also result in promoting underqualified individuals or demoting competent ones. Therefore, recruitment control is generally favoured as it avoids immediate negative impacts on existing employees, as was already discussed in Bartholomew's work [5].

Investigations into attainable configurations under different Markov system conditions have been conducted by a number of researchers, including continuous-time Markov chains [13] and non-homogeneous Markov chains [14–16].

However, variations in control methods have been explored in the literature, including the concept of pressure in states introduced by [17] and restricted recruitment as discussed in [18]. Control theory in the context of semi-Markov processes has received limited attention. The concepts of attainability and maintainability in non-homogeneous semi-Markov chains, particularly through maintaining the number of members in each seniority class within an organisational state, was first examined by [19], where Vassiliou and Papadopoulou extended the concept of maintainability by imposing that the number of members is maintained for each seniority class within an organisational state. Recently, a new concept of maintainability was developed for semi-Markov chains [20], namely state reunion maintainability (SR-maintainability), where the number of members is maintained for each organisational state. Building upon this foundation, our work introduces the parallel concept of state reunion attainability, wherein we explore the possibility of reaching a specified distribution of members across organisational states.

The definition of SR-maintainability will be our starting point to discuss attainability in the setting of time-homogeneous semi-Markov chains, as maintainability and attainability go hand in hand. In practical scenarios, the goal may involve initially achieving a specific personnel structure and subsequently ensuring its sustainability over time using consistent control mechanisms. Alternatively, starting from an already maintainable personnel structure, the objective might shift towards transforming this stable configuration to achieve a different, desired personnel structure, all while employing adaptive control strategies to navigate the complexities of such a transition. These processes necessitate a thorough understanding of how control strategies can be effectively applied to first reach the desired state distribution and then to preserve it. The dual focus on attainability and maintainability underscores the importance of strategic planning in managing population dynamics, where the initial phase of reaching an optimal structure is seamlessly followed by efforts to maintain that structure through careful control and management practices.

In Section 3 we first review the concept of attainability for Markov chains and extend this work to systems with a growth factor $1 + \alpha$, where the parameter α signifies the rate of change in the size of the system over time. When α is negative, this indicates a contraction in the system size, i.e., a decline of the number of people in the system. Conversely, when α is positive, the system expands over time. Thereafter, in Section 4, we introduce and study attainability as well as state reunion attainability for semi-Markov chains starting from the concept of SR-maintainability for semi-Markov chains. We show that a general approach to state reunion attainability, where a structure is said to be state reunion attainable if there exists an arbitrary initial structure from which it can be attained, is not appropriate and introduce the concept of (n-step) state reunion attainability starting from a subset $\mathscr{S}$ of structures. We provide a method to determine the associated region of attainable structures and illustrate these results.

2. Time-Homogeneous Markov Chain and Semi-Markov Chain Models

In this section, we provide fundamental concepts and notations that are common in previous studies on Markov and semi-Markov chain models [3,4].

For a Markov chain model with states $S_1, \ldots, S_l$:

- Let $\mathbf{P}^I \in \mathbb{R}^{l \times l}$ denote the internal transition matrix, where the ijth element $\mathbf{P}^I_{ij}$ represents the probability of transitioning from state S_i to state S_j within one time unit.
- The vector $\mathbf{w} = (w_i) \in \mathbb{R}^l$ captures the wastage probabilities for each state, where w_i is the probability of an entity leaving the system from state S_i within one time unit.
- The recruitment vector $\mathbf{r} = (r_i) \in \mathbb{R}^l$ gathers the probabilities r_i of entering the system into state S_i.

Let us further introduce Δ^{k-1} as the $(k-1)$-probability simplex, i.e., the set of all vectors $\mathbf{x} \in \mathbb{R}^k$ where $x_i \geq 0$ for all i, and $\sum_{i=1}^{k} x_i = 1$. This set represents the space of all possible population structures in a k-state system. In this paper, we will be primarily interested in Δ^{l-1}.

Population structures at times t and $t + 1$ are represented by vectors $\mathbf{s}(t)$ and $\mathbf{s}(t + 1)$, respectively, where $\mathbf{s}(t), \mathbf{s}(t+1) \in \Delta^{l-1}$. These vectors describe the distribution of entities across l states at specific time points.

Then, the evolution of the population structure in a constant-sized Markov chain from time t to $t + 1$ is described by the following equation:

$$\mathbf{s}(t + 1) = \mathbf{s}(t)(\mathbf{P}^I + \mathbf{w}'\mathbf{r})$$

where the notation $\mathbf{w}'$ refers to the transpose of the row vector $\mathbf{w}$.

A population structure $\mathbf{s} \in \Delta^{l-1}$ is said to be attainable with respect to a constant-sized Markov process defined by the internal transition matrix $\mathbf{P}^I$ if there exists a structure $\mathbf{y} \in \Delta^{l-1}$ such that $\mathbf{s}$ can be achieved from $\mathbf{y}$ in one step using control by recruitment, formally stated as follows:

$$\exists \mathbf{y}, \mathbf{r} \in \Delta^{l-1} : \mathbf{s} = \mathbf{y}(\mathbf{P}^I + \mathbf{w}'\mathbf{r})$$

Semi-Markov chain models are extensions of Markov chain models that can take into account the duration of stay in the states. Define J_n as the state following the nth transition and T_n as the time at which the nth transition occurs in a semi-Markov process. The semi-Markov kernel $\mathbf{q}$ is then given by the following [21]:

$$q_{ij}(k) = \Pr(J_{n+1} = S_j, T_{n+1} - T_n = k \mid J_n = S_i)$$

where $q_{ij}(k)$ represents the probability that the process transitions from state S_i to state S_j after exactly k time units. The semi-Markov kernel $\mathbf{q}$ can be used to obtain the sequence of transition matrices $\{\mathbf{P}(k)\}_k$ in the following way:

Theorem 1 ([22]). *For all k such that* $\sum_{h \in S} \sum_{m=0}^{k-1} q_{ih}(m) \neq 1$, *we have the following:*

$$
\mathbf{P}_{ij}(k) = \begin{cases} \dfrac{q_{ij}(k)}{1 - \sum_{h \in S} \sum_{m=0}^{k-1} q_{ih}(m)} & \text{if } i \neq j \\[2ex] 1 - \sum_{i \neq j} \dfrac{q_{ij}(k)}{1 - \sum_{h \in S} \sum_{m=0}^{k-1} q_{ih}(m)} & \text{if } i = j \end{cases}
$$

Let K denote the maximum seniority level considered within the system. The sequence of matrices $\{\mathbf{P}(k)\}_{k=0}^{K}$, with each $\mathbf{P}(k) \in \mathbb{R}^{l \times l}$, is derived from the semi-Markov kernel **q**. Here, $\mathbf{P}(k)$ specifically represents the transition probabilities for entities with state seniority k.

3. Attainability for Markov Chains

3.1. Attainability for Constant-Sized Markov Systems

When examining attainability, one needs to clarify three things: a starting structure, the means to attain a certain structure, and an optional time limit to attain the desired structure. Regarding the means to attain a certain structure, we assume that the system is under control by recruitment. The starting point and the optional time limit will be discussed in the next sections. Bartholomew [5] defined the concept of attainability as follows:

Definition 1 ([5]). *A structure* **s** *is called attainable with respect to a constant-sized Markov process defined by* $\mathbf{P}^l$ *if there exists a structure* **y** *such that* **s** *is reachable from* **y** *in one step using control by recruitment.*

The attainable region, which we will denote as $\mathscr{AR}_M$, was characterised for a constant-sized system as well [5]. We restate the theorem and formulate a slightly different proof, which will be the basis of the remainder of the results, where we will write $\mathbf{e_i}$ for the standard basis vectors in $\mathbb{R}^l$.

Theorem 2 ([5]). *The attainable region for a constant-sized Markov system,* $\mathscr{AR}_M$, *is the convex hull of the vectors* $\{\mathbf{e_i}\mathbf{P}^l + w_i\mathbf{e_j}\}_{i,j}$, *i.e., the following is true:*

$$
\mathscr{AR}_M = \text{conv}\{\mathbf{e_i}\mathbf{P}^l + w_i\mathbf{e_j}\}_{i,j}
$$

Proof. Suppose that **a** is an arbitrary attainable structure. This implies that there exist probability vectors $\mathbf{y} = \sum_{i=1}^{l} y_i \mathbf{e_i}$ and $\mathbf{r} = \sum_{j=1}^{l} r_j \mathbf{e_j}$ such that the following is true:

$$
\mathbf{a} = \mathbf{y}(\mathbf{P}^l + \mathbf{w}'\mathbf{r})
$$

Rewriting this equation, we obtain the following equalities:

$$
\begin{aligned}
\mathbf{a} &= \mathbf{y}(\mathbf{P}^l + \mathbf{w}'\mathbf{r}) \\
&= \Big(\sum_{i=1}^{l} y_i \mathbf{e_i}\Big)(\mathbf{P}^l + \mathbf{w}'\mathbf{r}) \\
&= \sum_{i=1}^{l} y_i \Big(\mathbf{e_i}\mathbf{P}^l + (\mathbf{e_i} \cdot \mathbf{w})\mathbf{r}\Big) \\
&= \sum_{i=1}^{l} y_i \Big(\mathbf{e_i}\mathbf{P}^l + w_i\Big(\sum_{j=1}^{l} r_j \mathbf{e_j}\Big)\Big) \\
&= \sum_{i=1}^{l} y_i \Big(\sum_{j=1}^{l} r_j \Big(= \mathbf{e_i}\mathbf{P}^l + w_i \mathbf{e_j}\Big)\Big)
\end{aligned} \tag{1}
$$

where we use $\mathbf{e_i} \cdot \mathbf{w}$ as the notation for the scalar product of $\mathbf{e_i}$ and $\mathbf{w}$. We conclude that $\mathbf{a} \in \text{conv}\{\mathbf{e_i}\mathbf{P}^I + w_i\mathbf{e_j}\}_{i,j}$. Note that the reverse inclusion is trivial, as every convex combination of vectors of the set $\{\mathbf{e_i}\mathbf{P}^I + w_i\mathbf{e_j}\}_{i,j}$ can be rewritten in the form $\mathbf{y}(\mathbf{P}^I + \mathbf{w}'\mathbf{r})$, where $\mathbf{y}$ and $\mathbf{r}$ are probability vectors. $\square$

This region can be useful as we know for certain that the points that belong to the complement of $\mathscr{AR}_M$ are definitely not attainable, no matter what the starting point $\mathbf{y}$ is. One can also define the concept of attainability starting from a set of structures $\mathscr{S}$.

Definition 2 (*n*-step attainability from $\mathscr{S}$). *A structure* $\mathbf{s}$ *is called n-step attainable from* $\mathscr{S}$ *with respect to a constant-sized Markov process defined by* $\mathbf{P}^I$ *if there exists a structure* $\mathbf{y} \in \mathscr{S}$ *such that* $\mathbf{s}$ *is reachable from* $\mathbf{y}$ *in n steps using control by recruitment.*

Since Equation (1) can be rewritten as $\sum_{j=1}^{l} r_j\left(\mathbf{y}\mathbf{P}^I + (\mathbf{y} \cdot \mathbf{w})\mathbf{e_j}\right)$, the following lemma holds:

Lemma 1. *If* $\mathscr{S} = \{\mathbf{v}\}$, *it follows that, for a constant-sized Markov process defined by* $\mathbf{P}^I$, *the one-step attainable region from* $\mathscr{S}$ *is given by the following:*

$$\mathscr{AR}_M^{1,\mathscr{S}} = \text{conv}\{\mathbf{v}\mathbf{P}^I + (\mathbf{v} \cdot \mathbf{w})\mathbf{e_j}\}_j$$

Lemma 1 can be used to determine, in a straightforward way, the attainable region for a finite set $\mathscr{S}$. If the set $\mathscr{S}$ is a convex set, the same technique yields the following:

Lemma 2. *If the starting region* $\mathscr{S}$ *is a convex set with vertices* $\{\mathbf{v_1}, \mathbf{v_2}, \ldots, \mathbf{v_k}\}$, *it follows that, for a constant-sized Markov process defined by* $\mathbf{P}^I$, *the one-step attainable region from* $\mathscr{S}$ *is given by the following:*

$$\mathscr{AR}_M^{1,\mathscr{S}} = \text{conv}\{\mathbf{v_i}\mathbf{P}^I + (\mathbf{v_i} \cdot \mathbf{w})\mathbf{e_j}\}_{i,j}$$

To obtain $\mathscr{AR}_M^{n,\mathscr{S}}$, one could calculate $\mathscr{AR}_M^{1,\mathscr{S}}$ and use this as the new starting region to calculate $\mathscr{AR}_M^{2,\mathscr{S}}$, and by iteratively following this procedure, one can obtain the desired $\mathscr{AR}_M^{n,\mathscr{S}}$.

3.2. Attainability for Markov Systems Subject to Growth and Contraction

In his doctoral dissertation [3], Bartholomew suggested the extension of these findings to organisations that experience growth or contraction. This research gap will be addressed in this section.

The evolution of the total size of a system that is subject to growth or contraction can be described by the following:

$$\mathbf{N}(t+1) = (1+\alpha)\mathbf{N}(t)$$

where $\mathbf{N}(t)$ corresponds to the total number of people in the organisational states at time t, and the parameter α refers to the rate of change in the size of the system over time. When α is negative, this indicates a contraction in the system size; conversely, when α is positive, this signifies growth. Note that in the case of growth or contraction, starting from a personnel structure $\mathbf{y}(t)$ at time t, $\mathbf{y}(t+1)$ is given by the following

$$\mathbf{y}(t+1) = \mathbf{y}(t)\mathbf{P}_M^I + \mathbf{r}^+(t)$$

where the additive recruitment vector $\mathbf{r}^+(t)$ is chosen such that the sum of the components of $\mathbf{y}(t+1)$ equals $1+\alpha$ instead of 1. So, when talking about the structures, we need to normalise with respect to the L^1 norm and consider $\frac{\mathbf{y}(t+1)}{||\mathbf{y}(t+1)||_1}$. Observe that the vector $\mathbf{r}^+(t)$

should not be confused with the classical recruitment vector $\mathbf{r}(t)$, which is a probability vector that corresponds to $\frac{\mathbf{r}^+(t)}{||\mathbf{r}^+(t)||_1}$.

Now, note that the maximal amount of contraction is limited by $\max_i w_i$, as being part of the wastage vector is the only way to leave the system, i.e., $\alpha \geq -\max_i w_i$. Furthermore, note that the procedure sketched in the proof of Theorem 2 is rooted in the fact that the vectors of the form $\mathbf{e_i P}^I$ have to be supplemented to achieve the desired vector, which has to sum to 1, as a constant-sized system is considered in Theorem 2. As long as $w_i \geq -\alpha$ holds for all i, the same reasoning can be repeated, i.e., we need to supplement the vectors $\mathbf{e_i P}^I$ to achieve the desired vector, of which the elements have to sum to $1 + \alpha$. This immediately yields the following:

Theorem 3. *The attainable region for a Markov system with growth factor $1 + \alpha$, where $w_i \geq -\alpha$ for all i, $\mathscr{A R}_M(1 + \alpha)$, is the convex hull of the vectors $\{\mathbf{e_i P}^I + (w_i + \alpha)\mathbf{e_j}\}_{i,j}$, i.e., the following is true:*

$$\mathscr{A R}_M(1 + \alpha) = \text{conv}\{\mathbf{e_i P}^I + (w_i + \alpha)\mathbf{e_j}\}_{i,j} \qquad (2)$$

This result covers the case of a growing system, as $\alpha > 0$ implies that $w_i \geq -\alpha$. However, this result does not indicate how to compute the attainable region for contracting systems with $w_i < -\alpha$ for some i. In the latter case, the sums of the components of some of the vectors of the form $\mathbf{e_i P}^I$ are simply too big, i.e., their L^1 norm exceeds $(1 + \alpha)$; therefore, they cannot be used as building blocks of the attainable region. Now, suppose that there exist just one i for which $w_i < -\alpha$. For all $j \neq i$, we can still supplement $\mathbf{e_j P}^I$ with the $[(w_j + \alpha)\mathbf{e_1}]_l$ to take into account all of the attainable convex combinations where $\mathbf{e_j P}^I$ contributes with a non-zero coefficient. But, for $\mathbf{e_i P}^I$, it is impossible to do this, as $\|\mathbf{e_i P}^I\|_1 > (1 + \alpha)$. Simply discarding $\mathbf{e_i P}^I$ is no option either, as there might still exist convex combinations of $\mathbf{e_i P}^I$ with the $\mathbf{e_j P}^I$ that do result in attainable structures. To resolve this problem, we should simply take into account these convex combinations. If we write

$$\{\beta_0 \mathbf{e_i P}^I + \sum_{i \neq j} \beta_j \mathbf{e_j P}^I\}_\beta :=$$

$$\{\beta_0 \mathbf{e_i P}^I + \sum_{i \neq j} \beta_j \mathbf{e_j P}^I \mid \sum_s \beta_s = 1; \forall s : 0 \leq \beta_s \leq 1, \beta_0 \neq 0, \text{with}$$

$$\|\beta_0 \mathbf{e_i P}^I + \sum_{i \neq j} \beta_j \mathbf{e_j P}^I\|_1 = (1 + \alpha)\}$$

we can use this result to state the following theorem, which includes growth as well as contraction:

Theorem 4. *The attainable region for a Markov system with growth factor $1 + \alpha$, $\mathscr{A R}_M(1 + \alpha)$, is the convex hull of the vectors $\{\mathbf{e_i P}^I_*\}_i$, where*

$$\mathbf{e_i P}^I_* = \begin{cases} \{\mathbf{e_i P}^I + (w_i + \alpha)\mathbf{e_j}\}_j, & \text{if } w_i \geq -\alpha, \\ \{\beta_0 \mathbf{e_i P}^I + \sum_{i \neq j} \beta_j \mathbf{e_j P}^I\}_\beta, & \text{if } w_i < -\alpha. \end{cases}$$

With the use of Theorem 4, one can easily generalise Lemmas 1 and 2 to systems with growth factor $1 + \alpha$.

Although this definition can be used for general starting regions $\mathscr{S}$, we argue that it can often be useful in practice to use the maintainability region $\mathscr{M R}_M$ as a starting region, as a maintainable structure might already be in place within the company, or a company could be actively working towards such a structure. Furthermore, the maintainable region is the a priori smallest known state reunion attainable set, regardless of the starting position. Note that in this case, $\mathscr{A R}_M^{n-1,\mathscr{S}} \subset \mathscr{A R}_M^{n,\mathscr{S}}$.

4. *SR*-Maintainability and *SR*-Attainability for Semi-Markov Chains

4.1. State Re-Union Maintainability

In order to study the attainability of a semi-Markov chain, we need to incorporate all of the information in the matrices $\mathbf{P}(k)$ into one matrix $\mathbf{P}_{SM}$ that characterises the semi-Markov (SM) model. This involves segregating the states $\mathbf{S}$ by their levels of organisational state seniority, with $\mathbf{P}_{SM}$ serving as the transition matrix for these seniority-based disaggregated states. This leads to Definitions 3 and 4, which were initially developed to facilitate the study of maintainability for semi-Markov chains [20]. Suppose we have l organisational states and one state that corresponds to leaving the system, which is called the wastage state. If the sequence $\{\mathbf{P}(k)\}_k$ is of length $K + 1$, we define the following:

Definition 3. *The set of seniority-based states is given by*

$$\mathbf{S_{SB}} = \{S_{a(b)} \mid 0 \leq a \leq K \text{ and } 1 \leq b \leq l\}$$

where the state $S_{a(b)}$ corresponds to the staff in organisational state b that has organisational state seniority equal to a.

Definition 4. *For $0 \leq k \leq K$, the elements of $\mathbf{P}_{SM}$ are equal to the following:*

$$(\mathbf{P}_{SM})_{ij} = 0 \quad \text{for } i - 1 \not\equiv_{K+1} k$$

and, if $i - 1 \equiv_{K+1} k$, then the following is true:

$$(\mathbf{P}_{SM})_{ij} = \begin{cases} \mathbf{P}(k)_{\lceil \frac{i}{K+1} \rceil, \lceil \frac{i}{K+1} \rceil} & \text{if } \lceil \frac{i}{K+1} \rceil = \lceil \frac{j}{K+1} \rceil \quad \text{and } (j - 1 - i) \equiv_{K+1} 0 \\ \mathbf{P}(k)_{\lceil \frac{i}{K+1} \rceil, \lceil \frac{j}{K+1} \rceil} & \text{if } \lceil \frac{i}{K+1} \rceil \neq \lceil \frac{j}{K+1} \rceil \quad \text{and } (j - 1) \equiv_{K+1} 0 \end{cases}$$

If we redefine the state set, we can view this matrix $\mathbf{P}_{SM}$ as the transition matrix with state space $\mathbf{S_{SB}}$. In this way, all of the information regarding transitions is stored in one matrix $\mathbf{P}_{SM}$, which can be used to elegantly state the definitions of state reunion maintainability and attainability. By writing the state vector at time t as $\mathbf{n_{SB}}(t)$ and the non-normalised recruitment vector, which entails the absolute recruitment counts, at time t as $\mathbf{r}_{\mathbf{SB}}^{+}(t)$, we obtain the following equations that describe the evolution of the stock vector for a system with a growth factor $1 + \alpha$:

$$\mathbf{n_{SB}}(t + 1) = \mathbf{n_{SB}}(t)\mathbf{P}_{SM} + \mathbf{r}_{\mathbf{SB}}^{+}(t)$$

$$\mathbf{N}(t + 1) = (1 + \alpha)\mathbf{N}(t)$$

The concepts of state reunion maintainability as well as state reunion attainability can be stated by the use of a reunion matrix $\mathbf{U}$, which encodes the specific seniority-based states that are to be fused.

Definition 5. *For a transition matrix $\mathbf{P}_{SM}$ with state space $\mathbf{S_{SB}}$, a $(K + 1)l \times l$ matrix $\mathbf{U} = (U_{ij})$ is called the reunion matrix if each of its l columns $\big[\mathbf{U}\big]_j$ consists of $K + 1$ ones through the following:*

$$U_{ij} = \begin{cases} 1 & \text{if } (j - 1)(K + 1) \leq i \leq j(K + 1) \\ 0 & \text{else} \end{cases}$$

We can now restate the concept of state reunion maintainability.

Definition 6 (State reunion maintainability [20]). *A structure $\mathbf{s}$ is called state reunion maintainable (SR-maintainable) for a system with growth factor $1 + \alpha$ under control by recruitment if*

there exists a path of seniority-based stock vectors $(\mathbf{n_{SB}}(t))_t$ *and if a sequence of recruitment vectors* $(\mathbf{r_{SB}^+}(t))_t$ *can be chosen such that for every* $t \in \mathbb{N}$, *the following is true:*

$$\mathbf{n_{SB}}(t+1) = \mathbf{n_{SB}}(t)\mathbf{P}_{SM} + \mathbf{r_{SB}^+}(t) \tag{3}$$

$$(1+\alpha)\mathbf{n_{SB}}(t)\mathbf{U} = \mathbf{n_{SB}}(t+1)\mathbf{U} \tag{4}$$

$$\mathbf{s} = \frac{\mathbf{n_{SB}}(t)\mathbf{U}}{||\mathbf{n_{SB}}(t)\mathbf{U}||_1} \tag{5}$$

A sequence of seniority-based stock vectors $(\mathbf{n_{SB}}(t))_t$ *that satisfies Equations (3)–(5) will be called a seniority-based path associated to the SR-maintainable personnel structure* **s**.

4.2. Attainability for Semi-Markov Chains

For semi-Markov chains, we follow a similar approach as the one in Section 3. This would yield the following definition for attainability:

Definition 7. *A structure* $\mathbf{s_{SB}}$ *is called attainable with respect to a semi-Markov process defined by* $\mathbf{P}_{SM}$ *if there exists a structure* $\mathbf{y_{SB}}$ *such that* $\mathbf{s_{SB}}$ *is reachable from* $\mathbf{y_{SB}}$ *in one step using control by recruitment.*

Remark 1. *As recruitment is only allowed in the seniority-based states with state seniority zero, most of the components of* $\mathbf{r_{SB}}$ *are zero.*

However, in the context of real-world applications, it might often be deemed less restrictive and more efficacious to focus on preserving the proportions in the organisational states instead, as is the case for state reunion maintainability.

4.3. State Re-Union Attainability

A natural way to define state reunion attainability would be the following.

Definition 8 (General state reunion attainability). *A structure* $\mathbf{s} = \mathbf{s_{SB}}\mathbf{U}$ *is called state reunion attainable with respect to a semi-Markov process defined by* $\mathbf{P}_{SM}$ *if there exists a structure* $\mathbf{y_{SB}}$ *such that* $\mathbf{s_{SB}}$ *is reachable from* $\mathbf{y_{SB}}$ *in one step using control by recruitment.*

Yet, it turns out that this approach is not informative with regard to state reunion attainability:

Lemma 3. *All structures* $\mathbf{s} = \mathbf{s_{SB}}\mathbf{U} \in \Delta^{l-1}$ *are state reunion attainable for every semi-Markov process defined by* $\mathbf{P}_{SM}$.

Proof. For the structure $\mathbf{y_{SB}}$ with all the personnel in one of the $S_{K(b)}$ states at time t, we know that none of these people will be in an internal state at time $t+1$, i.e., the stock vector at time $t+1$ will be completely determined by the recruitment vector $\mathbf{r_{SB}}$, which implies that under control by recruitment, each structure $\mathbf{s} = \mathbf{s_{SB}}\mathbf{U}$ would be attainable in this way. □

A more suitable definition of state reunion attainability would be the n-step state reunion attainability, starting from a set $\mathscr{S}$.

Definition 9 (n-step state reunion attainability from $\mathscr{S}$). *A structure* $\mathbf{s} = \mathbf{s_{SB}}\mathbf{U}$ *is called n-step state reunion attainable from $\mathscr{S}$ with respect to a semi-Markov process defined by* $\mathbf{P}_{SM}$ *if there exists a structure* $\mathbf{y_{SB}} \in \mathscr{S}$ *such that* $\mathbf{s_{SB}}$ *is reachable from* $\mathbf{y_{SB}}$ *in n steps using control by recruitment.*

We will denote, for a system subject to a growth factor of $(1 + \alpha)$, the n-step attainable set starting from $\mathscr{S}$ and the n-step state reunion attainable set starting from $\mathscr{S}$ as $\mathscr{A}\mathscr{R}_{SM}^{n,\mathscr{S}}(1 + \alpha)$ and $\mathscr{A}\mathscr{R}_{SM}^{n,\mathscr{S}}(1 + \alpha) \cdot \mathbf{U}$, respectively.

Remark 2. *Definition 9 is a generalisation of Definition 8 in the sense that they coincide for $n = 1$ with $\mathscr{S} = \Delta^{l-1}$.*

To calculate the n-step state reunion attainable structures in practice, one could use the same technique as in the proof of Theorem 2. Furthermore, this technique also yields the following results:

Lemma 4. *If $\mathscr{S} = \{\mathbf{v}\}$, it follows that the one-step state reunion attainable region from $\mathscr{S}$ for a semi-Markov process with growth factor $(1 + \alpha)$ defined by $\mathbf{P}_{SM}$ is given by the following:*

$$\mathscr{A}\mathscr{R}_{SM}^{1,\mathscr{S}}(1 + \alpha) \cdot \mathbf{U} = \text{conv}\{\mathbf{v}\mathbf{P}_{SM} + (\mathbf{v} \cdot \mathbf{w}_{SB} + \alpha)\mathbf{e}_j\}_{j|_{S_{0(b)}}} \cdot \mathbf{U}$$

Remark 3. *Note that $\mathscr{A}\mathscr{R}_{SM}^{1,\mathscr{S}}(1 + \alpha) \cdot \mathbf{U}$ is empty if $\mathbf{v} \cdot \mathbf{w}_{SB} < -\alpha$ and that only the $\mathbf{e}_j$ are considered that correspond to states with zero seniority, as these are the only states were recruitment can take place. We denote this restriction on the index j as $j|_{S_{0(b)}}$.*

Lemma 4 can be used to determine the attainable region for a finite set $\mathscr{S} = \{\mathbf{v_1}, \mathbf{v_2}, \ldots, \mathbf{v_k}\}$. We will first introduce the following notation:

$$\{\beta_0\mathbf{v_i}\mathbf{P}_{SM} + \sum_{i \neq j} \beta_j\mathbf{v_j}\mathbf{P}_{SM}\}_\beta :=$$

$$\{\beta_0\mathbf{v_i}\mathbf{P}_{SM} + \sum_{i \neq j} \beta_j\mathbf{v_j}\mathbf{P}_{SM} \mid \sum_s \beta_s = 1; \forall s : 0 \leq \beta_s \leq 1, \beta_0 \neq 0, \text{with}$$

$$||\beta_0\mathbf{v_i}\mathbf{P}_{SM} + \sum_{i \neq j} \beta_j\mathbf{v_j}\mathbf{P}_{SM}||_1 = (1 + \alpha)\}$$

If the set $\mathscr{S}$ is a convex set, we obtain the following:

Lemma 5. *If the starting region $\mathscr{S}$ is a convex set with vertices $\{\mathbf{v_1}, \mathbf{v_2}, \ldots, \mathbf{v_k}\}$, it follows that the one-step state reunion attainable region from $\mathscr{S}$ for a semi-Markov process with growth factor $(1 + \alpha)$ defined by $\mathbf{P}_{SM}$ is given by the convex hull of the vectors $\{\mathbf{v_i}\mathbf{P}_{SM}^*\}_i \cdot \mathbf{U}$, where*

$$\{\mathbf{v_i}\mathbf{P}_{SM}^*\}_i := \begin{cases} \{\mathbf{v_i}\mathbf{P}_{SM} + (\mathbf{v_i} \cdot \mathbf{w} + \alpha)\mathbf{e}_j\}_{j|_{S_{0(b)}}}, & \text{if} \quad w_i \geq -\alpha, \\ \{\beta_0\mathbf{v_i}\mathbf{P}_{SM} + \sum_{i \neq j} \beta_j\mathbf{v_j}\mathbf{P}_{SM}\}_\beta, & \text{if} \quad w_i < -\alpha. \end{cases}$$

To obtain $\mathscr{A}\mathscr{R}_{SM}^{n,\mathscr{S}}$ one could calculate $\mathscr{A}\mathscr{R}_{SM}^{1,\mathscr{S}}$ and use this as the new starting region to calculate $\mathscr{A}\mathscr{R}_{SM}^{2,\mathscr{S}}$. By iteratively following this procedure, one can obtain the desired $\mathscr{A}\mathscr{R}_{SM}^{n,\mathscr{S}}$.

4.4. Illustrations

In this section, we illustrate our findings by constructing the attainable and state reunion attainable regions for different growth factors $(1 + \alpha)$.

First, consider the Markov system defined by

$$\mathbf{P}^l = \begin{pmatrix} 0.5 & 0.4 & 0 \\ 0 & 0.6 & 0.3 \\ 0 & 0 & 0.8 \end{pmatrix}, \quad \mathbf{w} = (0.1, 0.1, 0.2)$$

for which we determine the maintainable region for the cases $\alpha \in \{0, 1, -0.15\}$.

For $\alpha = 0$, Theorem 2 yields that

$$\mathscr{A}\mathscr{R}_M(1) = \text{conv}\{\mathbf{e_i}\mathbf{P}^I + w_i\mathbf{e_j}\}_{i,j}$$

so it follows that $\mathscr{A}\mathscr{R}_M(1)$ is the convex span of the vectors $(0.6, 0.4, 0)$, $(0.5, 0.5, 0)$, $(0.5, 0.4, 0.1)$, $(0.1, 0.6, 0.3)$, $(0, 0.7, 0.3)$, $(0, 0.6, 0.4)$, $(0.2, 0, 0.8)$, $(0, 0.2, 0.8)$, and $(0, 0, 1)$.

For $\alpha = 1$, Theorem 3 implies that

$$\mathscr{A}\mathscr{R}_M(2) = \text{conv}\{\mathbf{e_i}\mathbf{P}^I + (w_i + 1)\mathbf{e_j}\}_{i,j}$$

which implies that $\mathscr{A}\mathscr{R}_M(2)$ is the convex span of the following vectors after normalisation: $(1.6, 0.4, 0)$, $(0.5, 1.5, 0)$, $(0.5, 0.4, 1.1)$, $(1.1, 0.6, 0.3)$, $(0, 1.7, 0.3)$, $(0, 0.6, 1.4)$, $(1.2, 0, 0.8)$, $(0, 1.2, 0.8)$, and $(0, 0, 2)$.

For $\alpha = -0.15$, Theorem 4 implies that

$$\mathscr{A}\mathscr{R}_M(0.85) = \text{conv}\{\mathbf{e_i}\mathbf{P}^I_*\}_i$$

which implies that $\mathscr{A}\mathscr{R}_M(0.85)$ is the convex span of the following vectors after normalisation: $(0.25, 0.2, 0.4)$, $(0, 0.3, 0.55)$, $(0.05, 0, 0.8)$, $(0, 0.05, 0.8)$, and $(0, 0, 0.85)$.

These regions are shown in Figure 1.

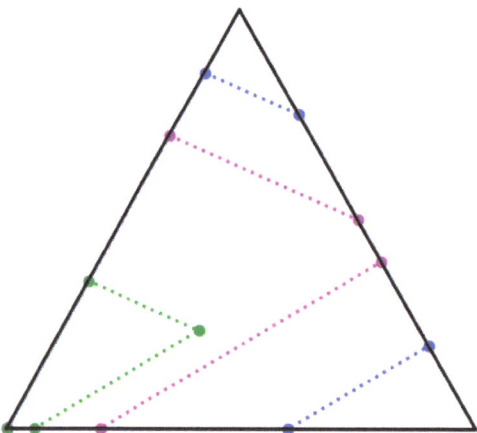

Figure 1. $\mathscr{A}\mathscr{R}_M(0)$, $\mathscr{A}\mathscr{R}_M(1)$, and $\mathscr{A}\mathscr{R}_M(0.85)$.

Furthermore, we can use the maintainable region for the constant-sized Markov system defined by $\mathbf{P}^I$ as the starting set. We know that the maintainable region is given by the following [20]:

$$\mathscr{M}\mathscr{R}_M(1) = \text{conv}\left\{\left(\frac{2}{7}, \frac{2}{7}, \frac{3}{7}\right), (0, 0.4, 0.6), (0, 0, 1)\right\}$$

If we use this region as the set $\mathscr{S}_0$, following Lemma 2, we obtain the following:

$$\mathscr{A}\mathscr{R}_M^{1,\mathscr{S}_0} = \text{conv}\{\mathbf{v_i}\mathbf{P}^I + (\mathbf{v_i} \cdot \mathbf{w})\mathbf{e_j}\}_{i,j}$$
$$= \text{conv}\{(0.2, 0, 0.8), (0, 0.2, 0.8), (0, 0, 1), (0.16, 0.24, 0.6), (0, 0.4, 0.6),$$
$$(0, 0.24, 0.76), \left(\frac{2}{7}, \frac{2}{7}, \frac{3}{7}\right), \left(\frac{1}{7}, \frac{3}{7}, \frac{3}{7}\right), \left(\frac{1}{7}, \frac{2}{7}, \frac{4}{7}\right)\}$$
$$= \text{conv}\{(0.2, 0, 0.8), (0, 0, 1), (0, 0.4, 0.6), \left(\frac{2}{7}, \frac{2}{7}, \frac{3}{7}\right), \left(\frac{1}{7}, \frac{3}{7}, \frac{3}{7}\right), \left(\frac{1}{7}, \frac{2}{7}, \frac{4}{7}\right)\}$$

So, if we define $\mathscr{S}_1 = \{(0.2, 0, 0.8), (0, 0, 1), (0, 0.4, 0.6), \left(\frac{2}{7}, \frac{2}{7}, \frac{3}{7}\right), \left(\frac{1}{7}, \frac{3}{7}, \frac{3}{7}\right)\}$, we obtain the following:

$$\mathscr{AR}_M^{2,\mathscr{S}_0} = \mathscr{AR}_M^{1,\mathscr{S}_1} = \mathrm{conv}\{(0.28, 0.08, 0.64), (0.1, 0.26, 0.64), (0.1, 0.08, 0.82),$$
$$(0.2, 0, 0.8), (0, 0.2, 0.8), (0, 0, 1), (0.16, 0.24, 0.6), (0, 0.4, 0.6), (0, 0.24, 0.76),$$
$$\left(\frac{2}{7}, \frac{2}{7}, \frac{3}{7}\right), \left(\frac{1}{7}, \frac{3}{7}, \frac{3}{7}\right), \left(\frac{1}{7}, \frac{2}{7}, \frac{4}{7}\right), \left(\frac{15}{70}, \frac{22}{70}, \frac{33}{70}\right), \left(\frac{5}{70}, \frac{32}{70}, \frac{33}{70}\right), \left(\frac{5}{70}, \frac{22}{70}, \frac{43}{70}\right)\}$$
$$= \mathrm{conv}\{(0.28, 0.08, 0.64), (0.2, 0, 0.8), (0, 0, 1), (0, 0.4, 0.6), \left(\frac{2}{7}, \frac{2}{7}, \frac{3}{7}\right),$$
$$\left(\frac{1}{7}, \frac{3}{7}, \frac{3}{7}\right), \left(\frac{5}{70}, \frac{32}{70}, \frac{33}{70}\right)\}$$

These regions are shown in Figure 2.

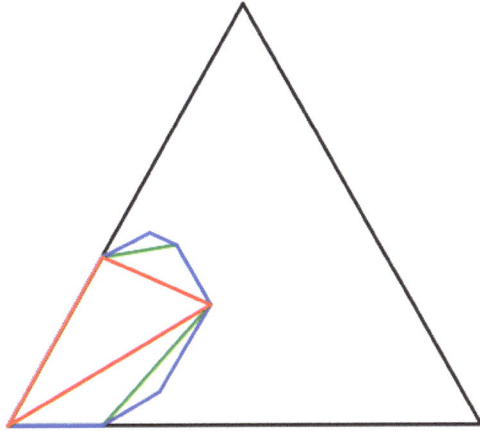

Figure 2. $\mathscr{MR}_M = \mathscr{S}_0$, $\mathscr{AR}_M^{1,\mathscr{S}_0}$ and $\mathscr{AR}_M^{2,\mathscr{S}_0}$.

Now, consider a semi-Markov system for which $\mathbf{P}(k)$ is given by the following:

$$\mathbf{P}(0) = \begin{pmatrix} 0.2 & 0.5 & 0 & 0.3 \\ 0 & 0.7 & 0.2 & 0.1 \\ 0 & 0 & 0.9 & 0.1 \\ 0 & 0 & 0 & 1 \end{pmatrix}, \mathbf{P}(1) = \begin{pmatrix} 0.6 & 0.3 & 0 & 0.1 \\ 0 & 0.5 & 0.45 & 0.05 \\ 0 & 0 & 0.9 & 0.1 \\ 0 & 0 & 0 & 1 \end{pmatrix} \text{ and } \mathbf{P}(2) = \begin{pmatrix} 0 & 0 & 0 & 1 \\ 0 & 0 & 0 & 1 \\ 0 & 0 & 0 & 1 \\ 0 & 0 & 0 & 1 \end{pmatrix}$$

We obtain, following Definition 4, the following:

$$\mathbf{P}_{SM} =$$

	$S_{0(1)}$	$S_{1(1)}$	$S_{2(1)}$	$S_{0(2)}$	$S_{1(2)}$	$S_{2(2)}$	$S_{0(3)}$	$S_{1(3)}$	$S_{2(3)}$
$S_{0(1)}$	0	0.2	0	0.5	0	0	0	0	0
$S_{1(1)}$	0	0	0.6	0.3	0	0	0	0	0
$S_{2(1)}$	0	0	0	0	0	0	0	0	0
$S_{0(2)}$	0	0	0	0	0.7	0	0.2	0	0
$S_{1(2)}$	0	0	0	0	0	0.5	0.45	0	0
$S_{2(2)}$	0	0	0	0	0	0	0	0	0
$S_{0(3)}$	0	0	0	0	0	0	0	0.9	0
$S_{1(3)}$	0	0	0	0	0	0	0	0	0.9
$S_{2(3)}$	0	0	0	0	0	0	0	0	0

and $\mathbf{w}_{SB} = (0.3, 0.1, 1, 0.1, 0.05, 1, 0.1, 0.1, 1)$.

Let $\mathscr{S} = \mathrm{conv}\{\mathbf{v_1}, \mathbf{v_2}, \mathbf{v_3}\}$ with

$$\mathbf{v_1} = \left(\frac{153{,}867}{500{,}000}, \frac{153{,}867}{2{,}500{,}000}, \frac{369{,}281}{10{,}000{,}000}, \frac{172{,}331}{1{,}000{,}000}, \frac{15{,}079}{125{,}000}, \frac{603{,}159}{10{,}000{,}000}, \frac{177{,}501}{2{,}000{,}000}, \frac{399{,}377}{5{,}000{,}000}, \frac{718{,}879}{10{,}000{,}000}\right)$$

$$\mathbf{v_2} = \left(0, 0, 0, \frac{290{,}221}{1{,}000{,}000}, \frac{2{,}031{,}547}{10{,}000{,}000}, \frac{2{,}031{,}547}{20{,}000{,}000}, \frac{7{,}473{,}191}{50{,}000{,}000}, \frac{420{,}367}{3{,}125{,}000}, \frac{12{,}106{,}569}{100{,}000{,}000}\right)$$

$$\mathbf{v_3} = \left(0, 0, 0, 0, 0, 0, \frac{36{,}900{,}369}{100{,}000{,}000}, \frac{8{,}302{,}583}{25{,}000{,}000}, \frac{29{,}889{,}299}{100{,}000{,}000}\right)$$

Using Lemma 5, we obtain that $\mathscr{AR}_{SM}^{1,\mathscr{S}} = \mathrm{conv}\{\mathbf{a_1}, \mathbf{a_2}, \mathbf{a_3}, \cdots, \mathbf{a_9}\}$ with

$$\mathbf{a_1} = (0.30773359, 0.06154672, 0.03692803, 0.17233081,$$
$$0.12063157, 0.06031578, 0.08875037, 0.07987533, 0.0718878)$$

$$\mathbf{a_2} = (0, 0.06154672, 0.03692803, 0.4800644,$$
$$0.12063157, 0.06031578, 0.08875037, 0.07987533, 0.0718878)$$

$$\mathbf{a_3} = (0, 0.06154672, 0.03692803, 0.17233081,$$
$$0.12063157, 0.06031578, 0.39648396, 0.07987533, 0.0718878)$$

$$\mathbf{a_4} = (0.290221, 0, 0, 0, 0.2031547, 0.10157735, 0.14946382, 0.13451744, 0.12106569)$$

$$\mathbf{a_5} = (0, 0, 0, 0.290221, 0.2031547, 0.10157735, 0.14946382, 0.13451744, 0.12106569)$$

$$\mathbf{a_6} = (0, 0, 0, 0, 0.2031547, 0.10157735, 0.43968482, 0.13451744, 0.12106569)$$

$$\mathbf{a_7} = (0.36900369, 0, 0, 0, 0, 0, 0, 0.33210332, 0.29889299)$$

$$\mathbf{a_8} = (0, 0, 0, 0.36900369, 0, 0, 0, 0.33210332, 0.29889299)$$

$$\mathbf{a_9} = (0, 0, 0, 0, 0, 0, 0.36900369, 0.33210332, 0.29889299)$$

A simple calculation shows that $\mathscr{AR}_{SM}^{1,\mathscr{S}} = \mathrm{conv}\{\mathbf{a_1}, \mathbf{a_3}, \mathbf{a_5}, \mathbf{a_7}\}$. Multiplying the vectors $\mathbf{a_1}, \mathbf{a_3}, \mathbf{a_5}$, and $\mathbf{a_7}$ by $\mathbf{U}$ yields $\mathscr{AR}_{SM}^{1,\mathscr{S}} \mathbf{U}$, the one-step state reunion attainable region which is the convex combination of the following vectors:

$$\left(0, \frac{58{,}494}{98{,}317}, \frac{39{,}823}{98{,}317}\right), \left(\frac{59{,}469}{603{,}901}, \frac{166{,}010}{469{,}913}, \frac{428{,}471}{781{,}529}\right), \left(\frac{60{,}941}{150{,}024}, \frac{166{,}010}{469{,}913}, \frac{126{,}519}{526{,}037}\right), \left(\frac{100}{271}, 0, \frac{171}{271}\right)$$

This region is shown in Figure 3.

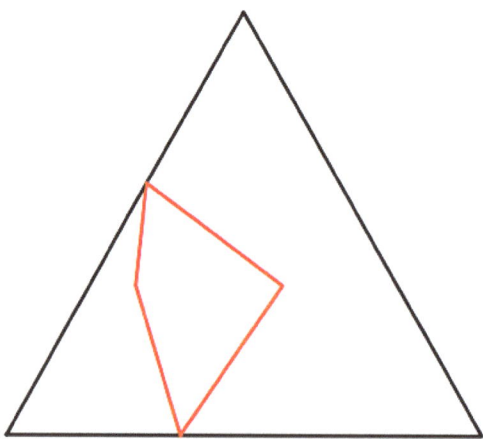

Figure 3. $\mathscr{AR}_{SM}^{1,\mathscr{S}} \cdot \mathbf{U}$.

5. Conclusions and Further Research Avenues

In this study, we explore the concept of control through recruitment, broadening the traditional concept of attainability for constant-sized Markov systems to systems subjected to growth and contraction. Furthermore, we generalise this concept to semi-Markov chains. Our exploration is characterised not only by its expansion of existing frameworks but also by the introduction of an innovative concept known as state reunion attainability (SR-attainability), based on the concept of state reunion maintainability [20]. This new concept allows us to gain important theoretical insights and identify the SR-attainable regions. Our work is distinguished by its novel method of broadening the scope of attainability and the introduction of SR-attainability, providing both theoretical understanding and practical algorithms, such as Theorem 4 and Lemma 5, for use in this field.

Future research could explore the broadening of reunion matrices, aiming to extend SR-attainability to include the attainability of various state combinations based on seniority, such as reclassification by overall seniority or pay scale. This opens the possibility of preserving selective subsets of seniority-based states, rather than encompassing all states, giving rise to a concept of partial (SR)-attainability. Consequently, this would allow for the application of other and more diverse **U**-matrices, which encode the fusion of seniority-based states (Definition 5), thereby expanding the practical use of the SR-attainability framework.

Author Contributions: Conceptualization, B.V.; validation, B.V. and M.-A.G.; writing—original draft preparation, B.V.; writing—review and editing, B.V. and M.-A.G.; visualization, B.V.; supervision, M.-A.G. All authors have read and agreed to the published version of the manuscript.

Funding: This research received no external funding.

Data Availability Statement: Data sharing is not applicable.

Conflicts of Interest: The authors declare no conflicts of interest.

References

1. Amenaghawon, V.A.; Ekhosuehi, V.U.; Osagiede, A.A. Markov manpower planning models: A review. *Int. J. Oper. Res.* **2023**, *46*, 227–250. [CrossRef]
2. Ezugwu, V.; Ologun, S. Markov chain: A predictive model for manpower planning. *J. Appl. Sci. Environ. Manag.* **2017**, *21*, 557–565. [CrossRef]
3. Bartholomew, D.J. *A Mathematical Analysis of Structural Control in a Graded Manpower System*; University of California: Berkeley, CA, USA, 1969.
4. Vassiliou, P.-C.G. *Non-Homogeneous Markov Chains and Systems: Theory and Applications*; CRC Press: Boca Raton, FL, USA , 2022.
5. Bartholomew, D.J. *Stochastic Models for Social Processes*; Wiley: Hoboken, NJ, USA, 1967.
6. Azcue, P.; Frostig, E.; Muler, N. Optimal strategies in a production inventory control model. *Methodol. Comput. Appl. Probab.* **2023**, *25*, 43. [CrossRef]
7. Fernández Cara, E.; Zuazua Iriondo, E. Control theory: History, mathematical achievements and perspectives. *Boletín Soc. Esp. Mat. Apl.* **2003**, *26*, 79–140.
8. Davies, G. Structural control in a graded manpower system. *Manag. Sci.* **1973**, *20*, 76–84. [CrossRef]
9. Davies, G. Control of grade sizes in a partially stochastic markov manpower model. *J. Appl. Probab.* **1982**, *19*, 439–443. [CrossRef]
10. Tsaklidis, G.M. The evolution of the attainable structures of a homogeneous markov system by fixed size. *J. Appl. Probab.* **1994**, *31*, 348–361. [CrossRef]
11. Vajda, S. Mathematical aspects of manpower planning. *J. Oper. Res. Soc.* **1975**, *26*, 527–542. [CrossRef]
12. Masood, H.; Podolsky, M.; Budworth, M.-H.; Karajovic, S. Uncovering the antecedents and motivational determinants of job crafting. *Career Dev. Int.* **2023**, *28*, 33–54. [CrossRef]
13. Tsaklidis, G.M. The evolution of the attainable structures of a continuous time homogeneous markov system with fixed size. *J. Appl. Probab.* **1996**, *33*, 34–47. [CrossRef]
14. Georgiou, A.; Vassiliou, P.-C. Periodicity of asymptotically attainable structures in nonhomogeneous markov systems. *Linear Algebra Appl.* **1992**, *176*, 137–174. [CrossRef]
15. Vassiliou, P.-C.; Georgiou, A. Asymptotically attainable structures in nonhomogeneous markov systems. *Oper. Res.* **1990**, *38*, 537–545. [CrossRef]
16. Vassiliou, P.-C.; Tsantas, N. Stochastic control in non-homogeneous markov systems. *Int. J. Comput. Math.* **1984**, *16*, 139–155. [CrossRef]

17. Kalamatianou, A. Attainable and maintainable structures in markov manpower systems with pressure in the grades. *J. Oper. Res. Soc.* **1987**, *38*, 183–190. [CrossRef]
18. Ossai, E. Maintainability of manpower system with restricted recruitment. *Glob. J. Math. Sci.* **2013**, *12*, 1–4. [CrossRef]
19. Vassiliou, P.-C.; Papadopoulou, A. Non-homogeneous semi-markov systems and maintainability of the state sizes. *J. Appl. Probab.* **1992**, *29*, 519–534. [CrossRef]
20. Verbeken, B.; Guerry, M.-A. State reunion maintainability for semi-markov models in manpower planning. Under review at Methodology and Computing in Applied Probability. *arXiv* **2024**, arXiv:2306.02088. [CrossRef]
21. Barbu, V.; Limnios, N. *Semi-Markov Chains and Hidden Semi-Markov Models toward Applications: Their Use in Reliability and DNA Analysis*; Springer Science & Business Media: Berlin/Heidelberg, Germany, 2009; Volume 191.
22. Verbeken, B.; Guerry, M.-A. Discrete time hybrid semi-markov models in manpower planning. *Mathematics* **2021**, *9*, 1681. [CrossRef]

Article

Cost Evaluation for Capacity Planning Based on Patients' Pathways via Semi-Markov Reward Modelling

Christina Chatzimichail, Pavlos Kolias * and Alexandra Papadopoulou

Department of Mathematics, Aristotle University of Thessaloniki, 54124 Thessaloniki, Greece; xristina.k.xatzimixail@gmail.com (C.C.); apapado@math.auth.gr (A.P.)
* Correspondence: pakolias@math.auth.gr

Abstract: In the present paper, we develop a non-homogeneous semi-Markov reward model, deriving expressions for a healthcare system's expected structure along with the expected costs generated by medical services and patients' holding times in the states. We provide a novel definition and investigation for states' availability, which is critical for capacity planning based on service demand in an environment of limited resources. The study is based on patients' mobility through hospital care, where each patient spends an amount of time in every state of the hospital (emergency room, short-term acute care, hospitalization, surgery room, and intensive care unit). Multiple outcomes, such as discharge or death, can also be taken into account. We envisage a situation where any discharges are immediately replaced by a number of new admissions that carry on the pathways of the patients who exit. By assuming an expanding system, the new idea of states' inflows is considered due to new patients who create pathways through hospital care, along with internal entrances. The theoretical results are illustrated numerically with simulated hospital data informed by aggregated public data of the Greek public health sector. The framework can be used for both strategic planning and cost evaluation purposes for hospital resources.

Keywords: healthcare; semi-Markov systems; population structure; cost evaluation

MSC: 60J10; 60J20; 60K15; 90B70; 91B70

Citation: Chatzimichail, C.; Kolias, P.; Papadopoulou, A. Cost Evaluation for Capacity Planning Based on Patients' Pathways via Semi-Markov Reward Modelling. *Mathematics* **2024**, *12*, 1430. https://doi.org/10.3390/math12101430

Academic Editor: Manuel Alberto M. Ferreira

Received: 1 April 2024
Revised: 4 May 2024
Accepted: 6 May 2024
Published: 7 May 2024

1. Introduction

Systems appear in every discipline and deterministic or stochastic mathematical modelling is applied for their study. For example, different population systems can be divided into a set of states, taking into account some of their basic characteristics, such as their socio-economic status, status or rank in a hierarchy system. Members of the system usually transition through these states in a probabilistic manner based on historical data of the visited states, as well as the duration of stay within each state. According to those parameters, a semi-Markov chain can be developed for the study of those systems [1]. One example of a mathematical model is the non-homogeneous semi-Markov model, that has been applied to numerous domains, such as manpower systems [2,3]. A broad and accessible overview of non-homogeneous Markov chains and systems can be found in [4]. Moreover, the addition of a reward process allows us to study the operational characteristics of a wide variety of other systems as well. The attachment of a reward structure in a semi-Markov model obviously increases the complexity of analysis but also provides thoroughness in modelling because in real-life, every action generates a reward, either positive or negative [5].

By using a Markov chain to study systems, we assume that the probability of transition from one category to another does not depend on the length of stay. Furthermore, the Markovian models assume that the holding times follow exponential or geometric distributions, in the continuous and discrete case, respectively. Thus, if the data do not fit

well to the aforementioned distributions, the estimations of the sojourn times will turn out to be unreliable. Hence, semi-Markov models generally provide better goodness-of-fit, as they could incorporate arbitrary distributions for the holding times, allowing flexibility. This holds true especially in cases where the holding times actually depend on the next transition. On the other hand, semi-Markov chains require higher computational workload for calculating the recursive and analytic relationships for the underlying process due to the larger number of estimated parameters. On the contrary, time dependence is a desirable characteristic to be included in the process since it provides additional useful information. In this case, the transitions of such a system are not merely described by a typical Markov chain procedure, therefore semi-Markov models are considered as more rigorous stochastic tools that provide a framework accommodating a variety of applied probability models [6–8]. Semi-Markov processes have found applications in different domains, including manpower planning, financial credit risk, word sequencing and DNA analysis [9–16].

Other stochastic models have found application in the finance and healthcare sectors. Economic assessment of medical care often compares healthcare initiatives using cost models and offers solutions that result in both cost-effective methods for the healthcare provider and advantages for the patient. Since governments all over the world are constantly faced with rising medical costs and are consequently unable to meet the demands for greater resources, such approaches are especially important when it comes to providing information that facilitates the efficient and fair allocation of limited resources [17]. In these kinds of situations, a variety of modeling approaches have been used, mostly individual-based micro-economic models like decision trees or Markov models, or population- or cohort-based macro-economic models like regression [18–20].

Previous studies developed models of patient duration of stay incorporating the use of Bayesian belief networks with Coxian phase-type distributions for modelling the length of stay of a group of elderly patients in hospital [21]. Other results and applications of the phase type distributions include modelling the cost of treating stroke patients within a healthcare facility using a mixture of Coxian phase-type models with multiple absorbing states [18,21]. Furthermore, the moments of total costs have also been obtained for an individual assuming Poisson arrivals [22]. A previous study provided important information to health service managers and policy makers to help them identify sequential patterns which require attention for efficiently managing healthcare resources and developing effective healthcare management policies via non-homogeneous Markov models [23].

Also, theoretical results for the moments and distribution of a semi-Markov cost model with discounting have been provided in analytic form for an open healthcare system [24], a Markov reward model for a healthcare system with a constant size, and in addition, with fixed growth which declines to zero as time tends to infinity [25]. The same researchers also presented a Markov reward model for a healthcare system with Poisson admissions where expressions for the distribution, the mean and variances of costs are derived [26]. A Markov model was used to describe the movements of geriatric patients within a hospital system, where the spend-down cost of running down services is estimated given that there are no more admissions and different costs assigned to states [27]. Finally, a census approach to model bed occupancy for geriatric patients by the implementation of a stochastic compartmental Markov model has been developed [28].

It has also been suggested that using Markov models for economic evaluation in healthcare sectors is an intuitive approach to handle outcomes and costs concurrently. Markov models can be easily modified in a variety of ways to expand beyond their limits, despite being criticized for their narrow assumptions. For instance, within an analytical framework like a semi-Markov model, the fundamental presumptions of the Markov model, such as the Markov property, can be modified. This method is very adaptable and can accurately capture the complexity and variety that are frequently present in diverse healthcare systems. The expected population structure of the healthcare system and the evaluation of costs generated by the hospital services of every kind (treatments, surgeries,

medical care, etc.) are parameters of great importance, and hospital managers would benefit immensely if they had advanced knowledge of patients' duration of stay and the corresponding derived costs [19,21–31].

In the present study, a non-homogeneous semi-Markov reward model is considered where rewards are random variables associated with state occupancies and transitions. The novel part of the current paper is derived from the inclusion of states' inflows and availability, which is critical for capacity planning based on services demand in an environment of fixed resources. In Section 2, the theory of the model is provided and results related to the population's structure and states' inflows are given and expressions related to state's current availability follow. Also, expressions for the expected costs generated by the system and corresponding to patients' paths are developed. Finally, in Section 3, most of the theoretical results are illustrated numerically with simulated hospital data informed from aggregated public data of the Greek public health sector. Finally, conclusions and suggestions for further research are provided in Section 4.

2. Methods

2.1. Population Structure

Let us consider a population which is stratified into a set of states $S = \{1, 2, 3, \ldots, k\}$ according to various characteristics. The states are assumed to be exclusive and exhaustive, so that each member of the system may be in one and only one state at any given time. The population structure of the system at time t is described by a vector $N(t) = [N_1(t), \ldots, N_k(t)]$, where $N_i(t)$ is the expected number of members of the system in state i at time t. Let $T(t)$ be the expected number of members of the system at time t.

In the present paper, time is considered to be a discrete parameter and we assume that the individual transitions between the states occur according to a non-homogeneous semi-Markov chain (*embedded non-homogeneous semi-Markov chain*). The embedded non-homogeneous semi-Markov chain in the system defines the stochastic process which describes the movements of every patient through the healthcare system. Thus, the patients' pathways, which are made up from transitions and successive holding times between the states, are governed by the sequence of the transition probability matrices of the Markov chain $\{P(t)\}_{t=0}^{\infty}$ and the sequence of the holding time mass function matrices $\{H(m)\}_{m=0}^{\infty}$.

Moreover, we assume that the system is open and the population is expanding, i.e., $\Delta T(t) = T(t) - T(t-1) > 0$, so at every time unit three kinds of movements can occur: *internal transitions, new entrances* and *exits*. In this respect, let us denote by $\{F(t)\}_{t=0}^{\infty}$, the sequence of substochastic matrices where $F(t) = \{f_{ij}(t)\}_{i,j \in S}$, where $f_{ij}(t)$ define the transition probabilities between the states which are controlled by the entrance time t to state i. Let also $p_{k+1}(t)$ be the row vector of wastage, whose ith element is the probability of leaving the system from i, given that the entrance in state i occurred at time t and $p_0(t)$ be the column vector of replacements, whose j-th element is the probability of entering the system in state j as a replacement of a member who entered his last state at time t. We consider that every member in the system holds a specific position (i.e., post in a company, bed in a hospital) called "membership" [32] and initially there are $T(0)$ memberships in the system. Thus, a member entering the system creates a particular membership which moves within the states with the other members. When a member leaves, the membership is taken by a new recruit and moves within the system with the replacement, and so on. Denote by $\{P(t)\}_{t=0}^{\infty}$, the sequence of stochastic matrices where $P(t) = \{p_{ij}(t)\}_{ij \in S}$, and $p_{ij}(t) = f_{ij}(t) + p_{i,k+1}(t)p_{oj}(t)$ define the transition probabilities for the memberships which equivalently define transitions between the states either with actual transitions of the members or by replacement of the leaving members by new recruits. The sequence of stochastic matrices $Q(n,t) = \{q_{ij}(n,t)\}_{i,j \in S}$, which define the interval transition probabilities for the memberships of the embedded semi-Markov chain to the system, is described by the following recursive Equation [2]:

$$Q(n,s) =^> W(n,s) + \sum_{m=1}^{n} C(s,m)Q(n-m,s+m) \tag{1}$$

where $C(s,m) = P(s) \boxtimes H(m)$ is the Hadamard product of the matrices $P(s)$ and $H(m)$, $\{H(m)\}_{m=0}^{\infty}$ is the holding time mass function matrix of the embedded semi-Markov chain, $^{>}W(n,s)$ is a diagonal matrix with elements the survival functions of the holding times in the states. It can be easily proved that $C(s,m)$ the so-called *Core matrix* of the process, is the most important parameter of the imbedded semi-Markov chain since it combines the two stochastic processes imbedded in the system, the Markov process and the one of the holding times. The analytic solution of the recursive Equation (1) is proven in [2] as follows

$$Q(n,s) =^{>}W(n,s) + C(s,\,n) + \sum_{j=2}^{n}\left[C(s,j-1) + \sum_{k=1}^{j-2} S_j(k,s,m_k)\right]\left[^{>}W(n-j+1,s+j-1) \atop + C(s+j-1,\,n-j+1)\right] \tag{2}$$

where

$$S_j(k,s,m_k) = \sum_{m_k=2}^{j-k}\sum_{m_{k-1}=1+m_k}^{j-k+1}\cdots\sum_{m_1=1+m_2}^{j-1}\prod_{r=-1}^{k-1}C(s+m_{k-r}-1,m_{k-r-1}-m_{k-r})$$

for every $j \geq k+2$ while for every $j < k+2$, $S_j(k,s,m_k) = 0$. Furthermore, the system's expected population structure can be determined by the following equation just by the basic parameters of the system as follows [2]:

$$N(t) = N(0)Q(t,0) + \sum_{m=1}^{t}\Delta T(m)r_0(m)Q(t-m,m), \tag{3}$$

where $r_0(m)$ is the recruitment vector of the system. Relation (3) completely determines the expected population structure of the system. The analytic solution for Equations (1) and (3), in relation to the basic parameters of the system, is provided in [2].

2.2. States' Inflows

In some models (e.g., healthcare modelling, manpower planning) the number of members that enter a specific state either via recruitment without replacement or internal transitions at any given time is crucial information for decision analysis and capacity planning based on service demand in an environment of limited hospital resources. The aforementioned expected number of members can be described by a vector $M(t) = [M_1(t), \ldots, M_k(t)]$, where $M_i(t)$ is the expected number of the new recruits to state i at time t creating additional memberships to the state plus the memberships which enter state i via internal transitions. Using probabilistic arguments, the above-defined expectations can be recursively defined by the following:

$$M(n) = N(0)E(n,0) + \sum_{m=1}^{n}\Delta T(m)r_0(m)E(n-m,m), \tag{4}$$

where $M(n) = [M_1(n), \ldots, M_k(n)]$ and $E(n,s)$ is the matrix where its elements equal to the entrance probabilities for the memberships for the interval $[s, s+n)$ [33].

2.3. States' Current Availability

The difference $N_i(t) - M_i(t)$ is the mean number of memberships which entered state i during the time interval $[0,t)$ and remain at that state at least until time t. Therefore, the above difference provides useful information related to the current availability of the state. Moreover, if we assume that C_i defines state's i capacity then the difference $C_i - [N_i(t) - M_i(t)]$ indicates the current availability of the state. Hence, the vector $C - [N(t) - M(t)]$, where $C = [C_1, \ldots, C_k]$, provides estimations which are critical for capacity planning based on service demand in an environment of scarce resources and investigating optimal solutions.

2.4. Attachment of Costs

Define as $y_{ij}(t)$ the cost that a membership generates at time t after entering state i during the interval $[t, t+1)$ when its successor state is j and $b_{ij}(m)$ as the cost generated by the membership's transition from state i to j, after holding time m time units in state i. Also,

define as $V(s, n, \beta) = [v_1(s, n, \beta), \ldots, v_k(s, n, \beta)]^T$, the vector whose i-th element, $v_i(s, n, \beta)$, is the expected present value of cost that is generated by a membership during the time interval $[s, s + n)$ under the condition that the membership entered state i at time s and the discount factor equals β, $0 < \beta < 1$. This coefficient is usually calculated by $\beta = \frac{1}{1-r}$, where r is the interest rate, when referring to economic rewards. It is known from [4] that:

$$V(s, n, \beta) = {}^>Y(s, n, \beta) + {}^>R(s, n, \beta) + \sum_{m=1}^n P(s) ¤ H(m) \beta^{m+s} V(s + m, n - m, \beta), \quad (5)$$

where

$$
\begin{aligned}
{}^>Y(s, n, \beta) &= \left[{}^>y_1(s, n, \beta), \ldots, {}^>y_k(s, n, \beta) \right]^T, \\
{}^>y_i(s, n, \beta) &= \sum_{x=1}^k \sum_{m=n+1}^\infty p_{ix}(s) h_{ix}(m) y_{ix}(s, n, \beta), \\
y_{ix}(s, n, \beta) &= \sum_{\mu=0}^{n-1} \beta^{\mu+s} y_{ix}(\mu + s), \\
R(s, n, \beta) &= [r_1(s, n, \beta), \ldots, r_k(s, n, \beta)]^T, \\
r_i(s, n, \beta) &= \sum_{x=1}^k \sum_{m=1}^n p_{ix}(s) h_{ix}(m) [y_{ix}(s, m, \beta) + \beta^{m+s} b_{ix}(m)].
\end{aligned}
$$

Furthermore, the analytic solution of Equation (5) can be derived if we follow the corresponding steps of a similar proof in [4]. The result is given below

$$V(s, n, \beta) = {}^>Y(s, n, \beta) + {}^>R(s, n, \beta) + \sum_{j=2}^n \left[C(s, j-1, \beta) + \sum_{k=1}^{j-2} S_j(k, s, m_k, \beta) \right] \quad (6)$$
$$[{}^>Y(s + j - 1, n - j + 1, \beta) + R(s + j - 1, \ n - j + 1, \beta)],$$

where $S_j(k, s, m_k) = \sum_{m_k=2}^{j-k} \sum_{m_{k-1}=1+m_k}^{j-k+1} \cdots \sum_{m_1=1+m_2}^{j-1} \prod_{r=-1}^{k-1} C(s + m_{k-r} - 1, m_{k-r-1} - m_{k-r})$ for every $j \geq k + 2$ while for every $j < k + 2$, $S_j(k, s, m_k) = 0$. Let us now define as $TV(s, n, \beta) = [TV_1(s, n, \beta), \ldots, TV_k(s, n, \beta)]^T$, the vector whose i-th element, $TV_i(s, n, \beta)$, is the expected present value of cost that is generated by the memberships of the system during the time interval $[s, s + n)$ under the condition that the memberships entered the system in state i at time s and the discount factor equals β [4]. Then we have

$$TV(0, t, \beta) = [N(0)]^T ¤ V(0, t, \beta) + \sum_{m=1}^t \Delta T(m) [r_0(m)]^T ¤ V(m, t - m, \beta), \quad (7)$$

where

$$
\begin{aligned}
TV(0, t, \beta) &= [TV_1(0, t, \beta), \ TV_2(0, t, \beta), \ldots, \ TV_k(0, t, \beta)]^T, \\
V(s, t, \beta) &= [v_1(s, t, \beta) \ v_2(s, t, \beta) \ldots v_k(s, t, \beta)]^T, \\
N(0) &= [N_1(0) \ N_2(0) \ldots N_k(0)] \text{and} \\
r_0(m) &\ [r_{01}(m), \ r_{02}(m), \ldots, \ r_{0k}(m)].
\end{aligned}
$$

Last, the total cost generated in the system by the memberships' pathways until time t equals to the sum of the elements of $TV(0, t, \beta)$.

3. Illustration

For the illustration, the data regarding patients' stay within each state, and the corresponding generated costs, were informed by public data of the Greek public health sector, considering a public hospital and a population of patients which are stratified into a set of hospitals' states. We denote by $S = \{$Emergency Room (ER), Short-Term Acute Care (STAC), Hospitalization (H), Surgery Room, (SR), Intensive Care Unit (ICU)$\}$ the set of states that are assumed to be exclusive and exhaustive, so that each patient of the hospital may be in one and only one state at any time given. The possible trajectories within the hospital are visualized in Figure 1. We assume that the internal transition probabilities are governed by the following substochastic matrix:

$$
F = \begin{array}{c} ER \\ STAC \\ H \\ SR \\ ICU \end{array}
\begin{bmatrix}
0.00 & 0.00 & 0.10 & 0.07 & 0.03 \\
0.00 & 0.00 & 0.15 & 0.10 & 0.05 \\
0.00 & 0.00 & 0.00 & 0.25 & 0.05 \\
0.00 & 0.00 & 0.70 & 0.00 & 0.25 \\
0.00 & 0.00 & 0.90 & 0.05 & 0.00
\end{bmatrix}.
$$

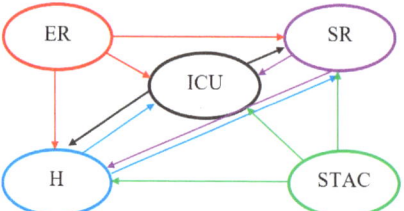

Figure 1. Visualization of the patients' pathways through the semi-Markov model.

It is assumed that a patient enters the hospital either through *ER* with probability 0.75 or through *STAC* with probability 0.25, defining p_0 = [0.75,   0.25,   0, 0,   0]. The death of the patient, the transition of the patient in other hospital or rehabilitation home for various medical reasons and the discharge to normal residence could be considered as exits from the hospital, and so the loss vector is assumed to be p_{k+1} =[0.80,   0.70,   0.70, 0.05,   0.05]. As a consequence, the matrix of the embedded Markov chain *P* is the following:

$$P = \begin{matrix} ER \\ STAC \\ H \\ OR \\ ICU \end{matrix} \begin{bmatrix} 0.6000 & 0.2000 & 0.1000 & 0.0700 & 0.0300 \\ 0.5250 & 0.1750 & 0.1500 & 0.1000 & 0.0500 \\ 0.5250 & 0.1750 & 0.0000 & 0.2500 & 0.0500 \\ 0.0375 & 0.0125 & 0.7000 & 0.0000 & 0.2500 \\ 0.0375 & 0.0125 & 0.9000 & 0.0500 & 0.0000 \end{bmatrix}.$$

One can notice that according to the matrix *P*, some patients' pathways correspond to zero probabilities. We assume that the transition probability matrix *P* is non-homogeneous, hence we add a Gaussian noise term $e_{ij}(t) \sim N\left(0, \sigma(t) :- \frac{1}{1000+t^2}\right)$, in each cell, in order to create a sequence of matrices $P(t)$, in order to impose small random deviations to the estimated transition probabilities, reflecting the irregularities that can be observed in detailed real data. The choice of a Gaussian distribution is twofold. First, the noise term has zero expectation, therefore the average point estimates of the transition probabilities are not influenced by noise. Second, the variance of the noise term converges to zero, when $t \to \infty$, hence the process evolves into a homogeneous semi-Markov chain after a long time period. The waiting time of the patients in the states *ER*, *STAC* and *SR* is one day. The stochastic matrix *P* is irreducible, therefore, the $\lim_{t\to\infty} P^t$ exists and is equal to the stable matrix *P**, which is the asymptotic matrix of the embedded Markov chain:

$$P^* = \begin{matrix} ER \\ STAC \\ H \\ OR \\ ICU \end{matrix} \begin{bmatrix} 0.4835 & 0.1611 & 0.1958 & 0.1018 & 0.0578 \\ 0.4835 & 0.1611 & 0.1958 & 0.1018 & 0.0578 \\ 0.4835 & 0.1611 & 0.1958 & 0.1018 & 0.0578 \\ 0.4835 & 0.1611 & 0.1958 & 0.1018 & 0.0578 \\ 0.4835 & 0.1611 & 0.1958 & 0.1018 & 0.0578 \end{bmatrix}.$$

Patients that exit the hospital are replaced by some of the incoming patients who occupy their corresponding memberships in the hospital. Let us also note that the rest of the incoming patients that enter the hospital through its expansion according to $\Delta T(t)$, create new memberships either through ER or STAC with probabilities 0.75 and 0.25, respectively, i.e., r_0 = [0.75,   0.25,   0, 0,   0]. In addition, based on the semi-Markov reward model, the expected healthcare cost that is generated by the patients is estimated up to a specific time point. This cost is assumed to be independent of time and includes the total daily healthcare cost that is generated by the patients, as well as the medical consumables that are necessary for their treatment.

In 2012, the Diagnosis-Related Groups (DRG) table was created, which presents the maximum budget that can be sponsored to a public hospital for all possible cases of diseases and treatments. For each disease, the DRG includes the daily healthcare cost,

the cost of health examinations, the cost of use or maintenance of medical equipment, such as respirators, stretcher chairs and any other cost associated for the treatment of the patient. According to the ministerial decree, which is published in the Government Gazette (ΦΕΚ 946Β'/27 March 2012), for any disease, the average daily healthcare cost is EUR 140. The DRG does not include the cost of medical consumables. According to a recent balance sheet of large public hospital in Greece, EUR 2,275,023.83 are spent annually for medical consumables, and on average, we assume that the cost of the medical consumables that correspond to each patient is EUR 10.62. Thus, the cost that is earned from a patient occupying either STAC or H is equal to EUR 150.62. The DRG does not include the daily healthcare cost in the ICU, as well as the cost of surgeries. According to the Government Gazette (ΦΕΚ 4898Β'/1 November 2018), the daily healthcare cost in the ICU is EUR 800 for each one of the first three days and EUR 550 for each day from the fourth day of occupying and onwards. Moreover, according to the United Mobility System, the cost of a surgery is EUR 1215.61 on average.

In this implementation, this cost is independent of patients' holding time in the states. Moreover, if the patient does not transition from the ICU to H, then the cost of transition to H as well as the cost of transition to SR is equal to the cost of use/maintenance of stretcher or chair which transfers the patient. The cost that the patient generates for making a transition from the ICU to H or SR include the cost of use/maintenance of a medical machine such as respirator that may be used due to the patient's health problem. We assume that the cost of use/maintenance of these medical machines per patient is calculated at EUR 10 on average. If the patient moves to the hospital with a private means of transportation, i.e., an ambulance is not used for the transition of the patient to hospital and also the patient does not use a stretcher or chair for the transition to ER or to STAC, then the cost of transition to ER or to STAC is zero. More generally in the current illustration, we assume that cost is generated in a hospital for the transition of the patient to the ER or to the STAC. The specific cost includes the cost of use/maintenance of the stretcher or the chair and the cost of ambulance's fuel, which according to Government Gazette is defined to be EUR 0.15/km and a patient traverses 50 km on average by ambulance. Thus, the cost of the transition of a patient to the hospital by ambulance is equal to EUR 7.5 on average and we assume that the cost of use/maintenance of the stretcher or the chair is EUR 5. As a result, the cost of the transition a patient to the ER or to the STAC is defined to be EUR 12.50. Summarizing the above information, we define the following matrix of patients' memberships, as $= \{b_{ij}\}_{i,j \in S}$:

$$
B = \begin{array}{c} ER \\ STAC \\ H \\ SR \\ ICU \end{array} \begin{bmatrix} 12.50 & 12.50 & 5.00 & 5.00 & 5.00 \\ 12.50 & 12.50 & 5.00 & 5.00 & 5.00 \\ 12.50 & 12.50 & 0.00 & 5.00 & 5.00 \\ 12.50 & 12.50 & 5.00 & 0.00 & 5.00 \\ 12.50 & 12.50 & 15.00 & 15.00 & 0.00 \end{bmatrix}.
$$

In the following, we present the estimated healthcare system's structure along with the estimated cost for three scenarios with different initial population structure, expansion rate, and holding time distributions. All the calculations have been made through R (version 4.3).

3.1. Scenario 1

In a simple scenario, we assume that the expansion of the system is equal to a constant, $\Delta T(t) = 20$, the initial system population vector is $N(0) = [231, 152, 106, 34, 77]$, and the holding time distribution of the states are described by geometric distributions, as follows:

$$
H(1) = \begin{array}{c} ER \\ STAC \\ H \\ SR \\ ICU \end{array} \begin{bmatrix} 1.00 & 1.00 & 1.00 & 1.00 & 1.00 \\ 1.00 & 1.00 & 1.00 & 1.00 & 1.00 \\ \frac{1}{8} & \frac{1}{8} & 1.00 & \frac{1}{6} & \frac{1}{10} \\ 1.00 & 1.00 & 1.00 & 1.00 & 1.00 \\ \frac{1}{5} & \frac{1}{5} & \frac{1}{3} & \frac{1}{3} & 1.00 \end{bmatrix},
$$

while for $m > 1$, we have

$$
H(m) = \begin{array}{c} ER \\ STAC \\ H \\ SR \\ ICU \end{array} \left[\begin{array}{ccccc}
0.0000 & 0.0000 & 0.0000 & 0.0000 & 0.0000 \\
0.0000 & 0.0000 & 0.0000 & 0.0000 & 0.0000 \\
\frac{1}{8}\left(\frac{7}{8}\right)^{m-1} & \frac{1}{8}\left(\frac{7}{8}\right)^{m-1} & 0.0000 & \frac{1}{6}\left(\frac{5}{6}\right)^{m-1} & \frac{1}{10}\left(\frac{9}{10}\right)^{m-1} \\
0.0000 & 0.0000 & 0.0000 & 0.0000 & 0.0000 \\
\frac{1}{5}\left(\frac{4}{5}\right)^{m-1} & \frac{1}{5}\left(\frac{4}{5}\right)^{m-1} & \frac{1}{3}\left(\frac{2}{3}\right)^{m-1} & \frac{1}{3}\left(\frac{2}{3}\right)^{m-1} & 0.0000
\end{array} \right].
$$

The estimated system structure over time $N(t)$ is presented in Figure 2 for the first 100 days by visualizing each of the components $N_i(t)$ of the five-dimensional vector. The relationship between time (measured in days) and the state size approximates a linear form. By assuming a simpler method, a linear regression model can be applied, in order to predict the number of patients within each state for a given day. For instance, based on the estimated regression coefficients (Table 1), it is expected that when $t = 10$, the estimated state size will be 62 patients within the *ICU*.

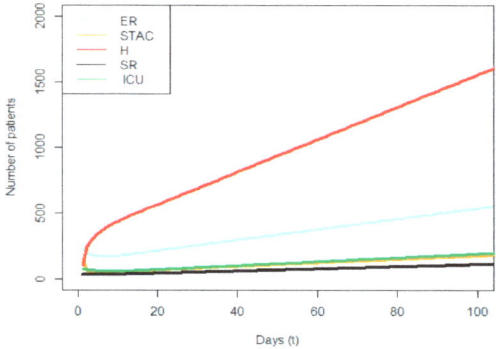

Figure 2. Evolution of $N_i(t)$, $i = 1, \ldots, 5$, $t = 1, \ldots, 100$, $\Delta T(t) = 20$, $N(0) = [231, 152, 106, 34, 77]$.

Table 1. Estimated linear regression coefficients between state size and time.

	Intercept	β (Slope)
Emergency	143.275	3.976
Short-term acute care	49.262	1.314
Hospitalization	312.6	12.4
Surgery room	27.6764	0.8401
Intensive Care Unit	47.142	1.465

Figure 3 illustrates the number of occupied beds in both hospitalization and the intensive care unit for a period of 100 days.

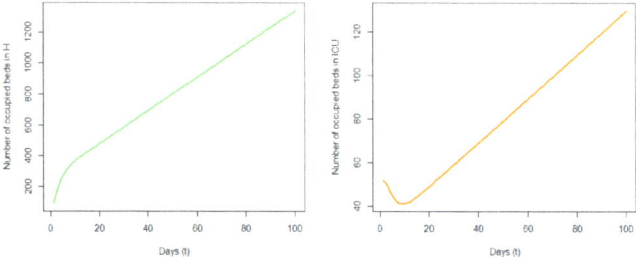

Figure 3. Expected number of occupied beds within H and the *ICU* for 100 days, with $\Delta T(t) = 20$, and $N(0) = [231, 152, 106, 34, 77]$..

Patients' memberships generate costs associated with their stay within each state, and we consider the following matrix $Y = \{y_{ij}\}_{i,j \in S}$ that summarizes these costs as:

$$Y = \begin{array}{c} ER \\ STAC \\ H \\ SR \\ ICU \end{array} \begin{bmatrix} 10.62 & 10.62 & 10.62 & 10.62 & 10.62 \\ 150.62 & 150.62 & 150.62 & 150.62 & 150.62 \\ 150.62 & 150.62 & 0.00 & 150.62 & 150.62 \\ 1215.61 & 1215.61 & 1215.61 & 0.00 & 1215.61 \\ 800.00 & 800.00 & 800.00 & 800.00 & 0.00 \end{bmatrix}.$$

During the initial time period, patients' cost within the *ICU* state is higher than the other costs, but after a week and onwards, the expected healthcare cost of all patients is higher for the state *ER* (Figure 4). In addition, the cost that is associated with medical services in the surgery rooms is the lowest for the whole time period.

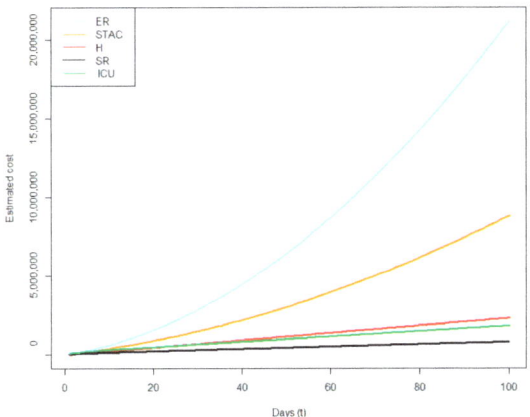

Figure 4. Expected healthcare cost for $N(0) = [231, 152, 106, 34, 77]$ and $\Delta T(t) = 20$.

The estimation of the average cost generated by a patient's treatment within a state in the hospital in the long-term is equal to EUR 218.58, and this could be calculated by the column matrix $Q^* W^{-1} R$ [4], where:

$$Q^* = \begin{array}{c} ER \\ STAC \\ H \\ SR \\ ICU \end{array} \begin{bmatrix} 0.20040 & 0.06681 & 0.61637 & 0.04220 & 0.07421 \\ 0.20040 & 0.06681 & 0.61637 & 0.04220 & 0.07421 \\ 0.20040 & 0.06681 & 0.61637 & 0.04220 & 0.07421 \\ 0.20040 & 0.06681 & 0.61637 & 0.04220 & 0.07421 \\ 0.20040 & 0.06681 & 0.61637 & 0.04220 & 0.07421 \end{bmatrix},$$

$$W^{-1} = \begin{bmatrix} 1.00 & 0.00 & 0.00 & 0.00 & 0.00 \\ 0.00 & 1.00 & 0.00 & 0.00 & 0.00 \\ 0.00 & 0.00 & 0.13 & 0.00 & 0.00 \\ 0.00 & 0.00 & 0.00 & 1.00 & 0.00 \\ 0.00 & 0.00 & 0.00 & 0.00 & 0.32 \end{bmatrix}, \text{ and } R = \begin{array}{c} ER \\ STAC \\ H \\ SR \\ ICU \end{array} \begin{bmatrix} 21 \\ 160 \\ 1151 \\ 1220 \\ 2505 \end{bmatrix}.$$

3.2. Scenario 2

Expanding the previous scenario, it is assumed that the system's expansion rate is larger for smaller values of t, and decreases later on. Hence, initially, there is an increased inflow in the hospital, however as t increases in size, we expect the number of new patients in the hospital to converge to 1, with the following rate $\Delta T(t) = \left\lfloor \frac{20}{t} + \frac{100}{t^2} \right\rfloor + 1$, while the holding time distributions are the same with the first scenario. Starting with an empty healthcare system, with $N(0) = [0, 0, 0, 0, 0]$, Figure 5 presents the evolution

of the expected structure of the system for a given period of 100 days. At 100 days, the population size reaches 327 patients, while the patients are distributed according to $N(100) = [67, 22, 200, 14, 24]$. Initially, it is observed that the populations within the emergency room and STAC unit increase, but reach a certain threshold where they drop and then remain at an approximately stable level. On the other hand, the number of patients that are hospitalized increase rapidly at the beginning, however, after two weeks the rate of increase is constant.

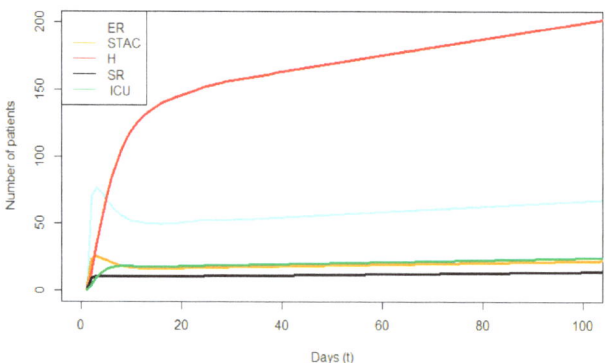

Figure 5. Evolution of $N_i(t)$, $i = 1, \ldots, 5$, $t = 1, \ldots, 100$, $\Delta T = \left\lfloor \frac{20}{t} + \frac{100}{t^2} \right\rfloor + 1$, $N(0) = [0, 0, 0, 0, 0]$.

By assuming that the hospital's resources are limited, we also consider a hospital that contains a maximum of 103 *ICU* beds, and the initial structure of the hospital is not empty, according to $N(0) = [231, 152, 106, 34, 77]$. The initial occupancy of the *ICU* is 74.76% and the total number of patients within the hospital is $T(0) = 600$. The results of the system's structure are illustrated in Figure 6, which presents that in the current hospital there is always *ICU* availability, and according to the initial population vector $N(0)$, the number of patients in the *ER* is higher than the number of the patients in any other state.

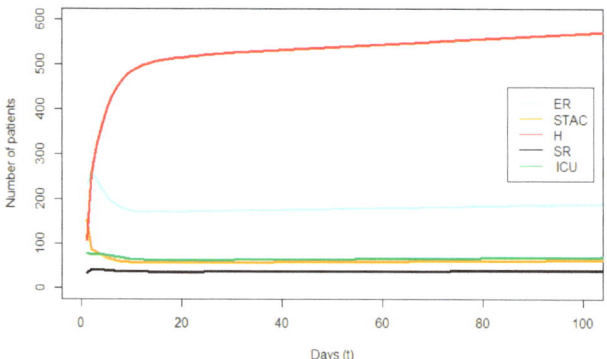

Figure 6. Evolution of $N_i(t)$, $i = 1, \ldots, 5$, $t = 1, \ldots, 100$, $\Delta T = \left\lfloor \frac{20}{t} + \frac{100}{t^2} \right\rfloor + 1$, $N(0) = [231, 152, 106, 34, 77]$.

Assuming the same population structure and expansion rate, we estimated the number of beds which are occupied in H as well as the *ICU* (Figure 7). Firstly, we observe that the estimated number of beds which are occupied in H is higher than the corresponding number of beds in the *ICU*. Initially, 106 beds are occupied in H, but for the second day, this number is estimated to be 92, and this is the only daily decrease in the number of beds occupied in H, while from the third day and onwards, we estimate that the above number is either increasing or remaining constant. The maximum daily increase in occupancies in

hospitalization beds is equal to 68 beds. Moreover, the estimated number of beds which are occupied in the *ICU* decreases for about 18 days and then increases linearly. In more detail, regarding the *ICU*, the maximum daily decrease is equal to 25 beds, since initially 77 beds are occupied, whereas for the second day, 52 beds are occupied.

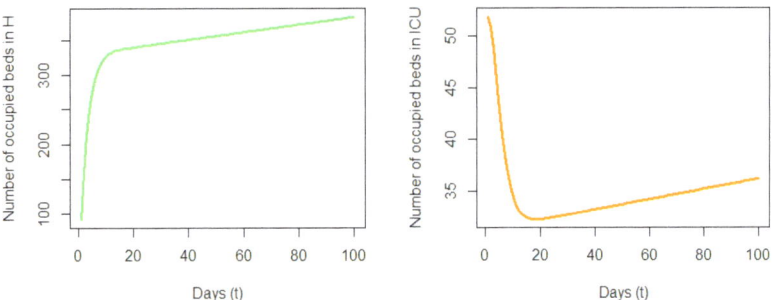

Figure 7. Expected number of occupied beds within H and the *ICU* for 100 days, $\Delta T = \left\lfloor \frac{20}{t} + \frac{100}{t^2} \right\rfloor + 1$ and $N(0) = [231, 152, 106, 34, 77]$.

According to Figure 8, the increase in the cost generated by patients' pathways through time has an approximately linear form. Initially, the cost of the *ICU* section appears to be the highest across all states, however, later on, the cost associated with *ER* surpasses all the other states, followed by *STAC*, while patients entering the surgery room generate the lowest cost.

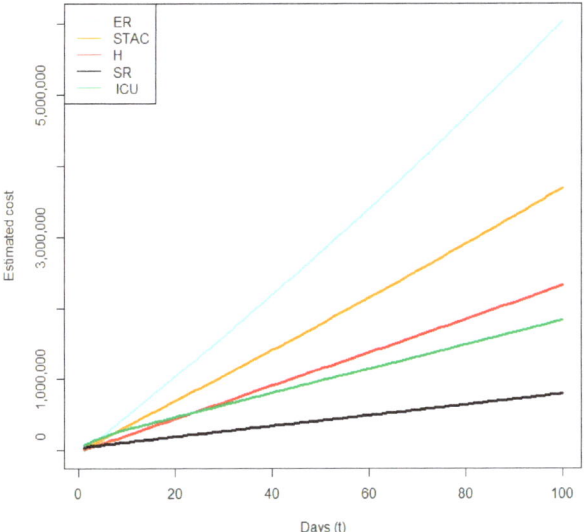

Figure 8. Expected healthcare cost for $N(0) = [231, 152, 106, 34, 77]$ and $\Delta T(t) = \left\lfloor \frac{20}{t} + \frac{100}{t^2} \right\rfloor + 1$.

3.3. Scenario 3

For the last scenario, the initial structure vector is considered to be $N(0) = [300, 152, 106, 34, 50]$, thus we assume a reduced number of patients within the *ICU*. Also, the holding time distributions were assumed to be different for the *ICU* state, e.g., the average holding time within the *ICU* before discharge is assumed to be 7 days, while the average holding time before a surgery operation or hospitalization is assumed to be 5 days. From the visualization, one can observe that the occupied *ICU* beds surpass the hospital's capacity ($N = 103$) approximately

after 5 days, then exceeds slightly after 16 days and then the number of patients within the *ICU* continues to increase (Figure 9).

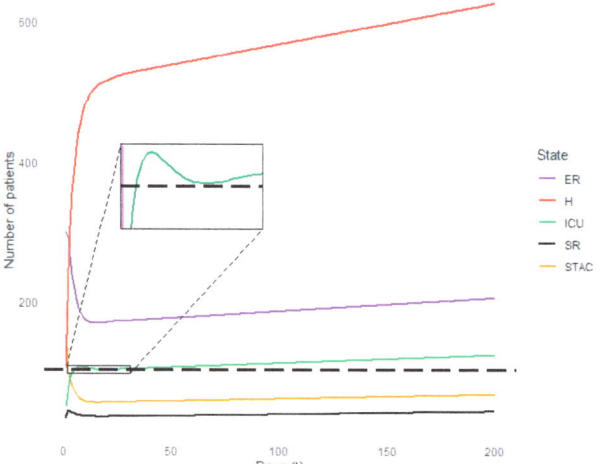

Figure 9. Evolution of $N_i(t)$, $i = 1,\ldots,5, t = 1,\ldots,100$, $\Delta T = \left\lfloor \frac{20}{t} + \frac{100}{t^2} \right\rfloor + 1$, $N(0) = [300, 152, 106, 34, 50]$, dotted line represents ICU capacity ($N = 103$ wards).

Figure 10 illustrates the number of occupied beds in both hospitalization and the intensive care unit for a period of 100 days and the visualization of the associated costs for each state are presented in Figure 11.

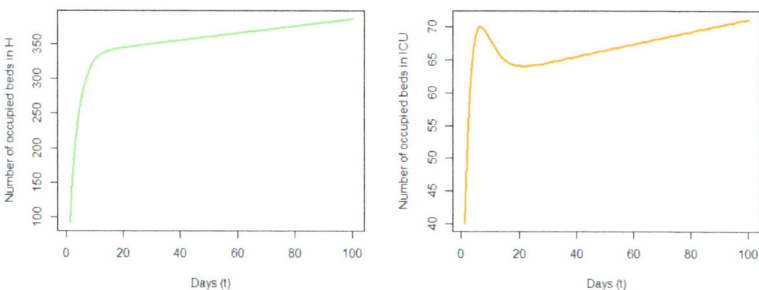

Figure 10. Expected number of beds which are occupied in H and the ICU.

It is observed that the healthcare cost that is generated initially while patients enter in any state does not exhibit strong daily changes. The expected long-term patient cost for this scenario is EUR 247.11. Therefore, a 2-day increase in the average patient's stay within the *ICU* results in a 13% larger patient cost in the long-run, compared to the first scenario, which is given by $Q^* W^{-1} R$, where:

$$Q^* = \begin{matrix} ER \\ STAC \\ H \\ SR \\ ICU \end{matrix} \begin{bmatrix} 0.19126 & 0.06376 & 0.58823 & 0.04028 & 0.11647 \\ 0.19126 & 0.06376 & 0.58823 & 0.04028 & 0.11647 \\ 0.19126 & 0.06376 & 0.58823 & 0.04028 & 0.11647 \\ 0.19126 & 0.06376 & 0.58823 & 0.04028 & 0.11647 \\ 0.19126 & 0.06376 & 0.58823 & 0.04028 & 0.11647 \end{bmatrix},$$

and

$$W^{-1} = \begin{bmatrix} 1.00 & 0.00 & 0.00 & 0.00 & 0.00 \\ 0.00 & 1.00 & 0.00 & 0.00 & 0.00 \\ 0.00 & 0.00 & 0.13 & 0.00 & 0.00 \\ 0.00 & 0.00 & 0.00 & 1.00 & 0.00 \\ 0.00 & 0.00 & 0.00 & 0.00 & 0.20 \end{bmatrix}, \text{ and } R = \begin{matrix} ER \\ STAC \\ H \\ SR \\ ICU \end{matrix} \begin{bmatrix} 21 \\ 160 \\ 1151 \\ 1220 \\ 4109 \end{bmatrix}$$

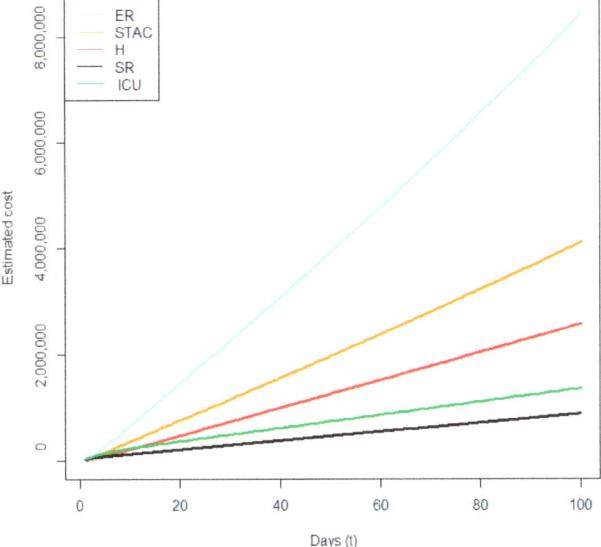

Figure 11. Expected healthcare cost for $N(0) = [300, 152, 106, 34, 50]$ and $\Delta T(t) = \left\lfloor \frac{20}{t} + \frac{100}{t^2} \right\rfloor + 1$.

4. Conclusions

The aim of the current study was to examine patients' pathways in an open healthcare system via the lens of a non-homogeneous semi-Markov reward system with discounting. The proposed model incorporated two novel components, namely states' inflows and availability. The inclusion of the inflows allows for the measurement of the expected number of new recruits of every state (i.e., new members in the system plus entrances through internal transitions), at every time point, providing an estimation of the patients' inflows to the hospital's states. This leads to the estimation of various attributes of the system, such as the capacity and the availability of the states. The model also incorporated information about costs associated with patients' transitions or stay within the states.

The theoretical results were accompanied with different case illustrations of open healthcare systems with various characteristics (initial structure, holding times distributions, and expansion rates). To our knowledge, this is the first time that the aforementioned theoretical framework is accompanied with an application to a healthcare system based on aggregated data from the Greek public health sector. Three different scenarios were developed to simulate a real healthcare system including open systems with constant or non-linear decreasing expansion rates. Through the findings, one can examine and predict the upcoming structure of the system for each state separately, aiming to assist resource allocation in healthcare units.

Through the illustration, the availability of each state is calculated providing useful information for capacity planning in a healthcare environment with limited resources. More specifically, the current availability of wards in critical units within a hospital can be estimated, such as the intensive care unit or surgery rooms. For example, in cases where the modelling procedure suggests that the number of patients exceeds the hospitals' capacity after a time period, this may serve as a warning that the current healthcare resources are

not adequate to provide medical services for all patients. Last, expressions for the expected costs generated by the system and corresponding to patients' paths are estimated as well as the average patient's long-term cost that is generated.

Our application can guide healthcare policy makers to configure different strategies in order to optimize the resources of a healthcare system, and also provide estimations of future costs under various scenarios. The results encourage the use of this model in exploring cost sensitivity arising from different treatment strategies and investigating optimal solutions.

Author Contributions: Conceptualization, A.P.; methodology, A.P.; software, P.K. and C.C.; validation, P.K., A.P. and C.C.; formal analysis, P.K. and C.C.; investigation, P.K. and C.C.; resources, P.K., A.P. and C.C.; data curation, P.K. and C.C.; writing—original draft preparation, P.K., A.P. and C.C.; writing—review and editing, P.K., A.P. and C.C.; visualization, P.K., A.P. and C.C.; supervision, A.P.; project administration, P.K. and A.P. All authors have read and agreed to the published version of the manuscript.

Funding: This research received no external funding.

Data Availability Statement: The data used in the current study were synthetic.

Conflicts of Interest: The authors declare no conflicts of interest.

References

1. Howard, R.A. *Dynamic Probabilistic Systems: Semi-Markov and Decision Processes*; Dover Publications: Mineola, NY, USA, 2007; Volume 2.
2. Vassiliou, P.-C.G.; Papadopoulou, A. Non-homogeneous Semi-Markov Systems and Maintainability of the State Sizes. *J. Appl. Probab.* **1992**, *29*, 519–534. [CrossRef]
3. Bartholomew, D.J.; Andrew, F.F.; Sally, I.M. *Statistical Techniques for Manpower Planning*; Wiley: Hoboken, NJ, USA, 1979.
4. Papadopoulou, A.A. Economic Rewards in Non-Homogeneous Semi-Markov Systems. *Commun. Stat. Theory Methods* **2004**, *33*, 681696. [CrossRef]
5. Vassiliou, P.-C.G. *Non-Homogeneous Markov Chains and Systems Theory and Applications*; Taylor and Francis Group: Milton Park, UK, 2022.
6. McClean, S.I. A Semi-Markov Model for a Multigrade Population with Poisson Recruitment. *J. Appl. Probab.* **1980**, *17*, 846–852. [CrossRef]
7. McClean, S.I. Semi-Markov Models for Manpower Planning. In *Semi-Markov Models*; Springer: Berlin/Heidelberg, Germany, 1986; pp. 283–300.
8. D'Amico, G.; Di Biase, G.; Janssen, J.; Manca, R. *Semi-Markov Migration Models for Credit Risk*; Wiley Online Library: Hoboken, NJ, USA, 2017.
9. Vassiliou, P.-C.G. Non-Homogeneous Semi-Markov and Markov Renewal Processes and Change of Measure in Credit Risk. *Mathematics* **2021**, *9*, 55. [CrossRef]
10. Janssen, J.; Manca, R. *Applied Semi-Markov Processes*; Springer Science & Business Media: Berlin/Heidelberg, Germany, 2006.
11. Janssen, J. *Semi-Markov Models: Theory and Applications*; Springer Science & Business Media: Berlin/Heidelberg, Germany, 2013.
12. Schbath, S.; Prum, B.; de Turckheim, E. Exceptional Motifs in Different Markov Chain Models for a Statistical Analysis of DNA sequences. *J. Comput. Biol.* **1995**, *2*, 417–437. [CrossRef] [PubMed]
13. De Dominicis, R.; Manca, R. Some New Results on the Transient Behaviour of Semi-Markov Reward Processes. *Methods Oper. Res.* **1986**, *53*, 387–397.
14. Vasileiou, A.; Vassiliou, P.-C.G. An Inhomogeneous Semi-Markov Model for the Term Structure of Credit Risk Spreads. *Adv. Appl. Probab.* **2006**, *38*, 171–198. [CrossRef]
15. Vassiliou, P.-C.G.; Vasileiou, A. Asymptotic Behaviour of the Survival Probabilities in an Inhomogeneous Semi-Markov Model for the Migration Process in Credit Risk. *Linear Algebra Appl.* **2013**, *438*, 2880–2903. [CrossRef]
16. Vassiliou, P.-C.G. Semi-Markov Migration Process in a Stochastic Market in Credit Risk. *Linear Algebra Appl.* **2014**, *450*, 13–43. [CrossRef]
17. Gillespie, J.; McClean, S.; Scotney, B.; Garg, L.; Barton, M.; Fullerton, K. Costing Hospital Resources for Stroke Patients Using Phase-Type Models. *Health Care Manag. Sci.* **2011**, *14*, 279–291. [CrossRef]
18. Katsaliaki, K.; Mustafee, N. Applications of Simulation within the Healthcare Context. *J. Oper. Res. Soc.* **2011**, *62*, 1431–1451. [CrossRef] [PubMed]
19. McClean, S.; Barton, M.; Garg, L.; Fullerton, K. A Modeling Framework that Combines Markov Models and Discrete-Event Simulation for Stroke Patient Care. *ACM Trans. Model. Comput. Simul.* **2011**, *21*, 1–26. [CrossRef]
20. Cooper, K.; Brailsford, S.C.; Davies, R. Choice of Modelling Technique for Evaluating Health Care Interventions. *J. Oper. Res. Soc.* **2007**, *58*, 168–176. [CrossRef]

21. Marshall, A.H.; McClean, S.I. Conditional Phase-Type Distributions for Modelling Patient Length of Stay in Hospital. *Int. Trans. Oper. Res.* **2003**, *10*, 565–576. [CrossRef]
22. McClean, S.; Garg, L.; Fullerton, K. Costing Mixed Coxian Phase-Type Systems with Poisson Arrivals. *Commun. Stat. Theory Methods* **2014**, *43*, 1437–1452. [CrossRef]
23. Garg, L.; McClean, S.; Meenan, B.; Millard, P. Non-homogeneous Markov Models for Sequential Pattern Mining of Healthcare Data. *IMA J. Manag. Math.* **2008**, *20*, 327–344. [CrossRef]
24. Papadopoulou, A.A.; Tsaklidis, G.; McClean, S.; Garg, L. On the Moments and the Distribution of the Cost of a Semi Markov Model for Healthcare Systems. *Methodol. Comput. Appl. Probab.* **2012**, *14*, 717–737. [CrossRef]
25. McClean, S.; Millard, P. Using Markov Models to Manage High Occupancy Hospital Care. In Proceedings of the 3rd International IEEE Conference Intelligent Systems, London, UK, 4–6 September 2006.
26. McClean, S.; Garg, L.; Meeman, B.; Millard, P. Using Markov Models to Find Interesting Patient Pathways. In Proceedings of the Computer Based Medical Systems Annual IEEE Symposium, Maribor, Slovenia, 20–22 June 2007; pp. 713–718.
27. McClean, S.I.; McAlea, B.; Millard, P.H. Using a Markov Reward model to Estimate Spend-Down Costs for a Geriatric Department. *J. Oper. Res. Soc.* **1998**, *49*, 1021–1025. [CrossRef]
28. Taylor, G.I.; McClean, S.I.; Millard, P.H. Stochastic Models of Geriatric Patient Bed Occupancy Behavior. *J. R Statist. Soc. A* **1999**, *163*, 39–48. [CrossRef]
29. Marshall, A.H.; McClean, S.I.; Shapcott, C.M.; Millard, P.M. Modelling Patient Duration of Stay to Facilitate Resource Management of Geriatric Hospitals. *Health Care Manag. Sci.* **2002**, *5*, 313–319. [CrossRef]
30. McClean, S.; Gillespie, T.; Scotney, B.; Fullerton, K. Using Phase Type Models to Cost a Cohort of Stroke Patients. *Eur. J. Oper. Res.* **2012**, *236*, 190–199. [CrossRef]
31. Faddy, M.J.; McClean, S.I. Analyzing Data on Lengths of Stay of Hospital Patients Using Phase-type Distributions. *Appl. Stoch. Models Bus. Ind.* **1999**, *15*, 311–317. [CrossRef]
32. Bartholomew, D.J. *Stochastic Models for Social Processes*, 3rd ed.; Wiley: Chichester, UK, 1982.
33. Papadopoulou, A.A. Counting Transitions-Entrance Probabilities in Non-Homogeneous Semi-Markov Systems. *Appl. Stochastic Models Data Anal.* **1998**, *13*, 199–206. [CrossRef]

mathematics

Article

The Arsenal of Perturbation Bounds for Finite Continuous-Time Markov Chains: A Perspective

Alexander Y. Mitrophanov

Frederick National Laboratory for Cancer Research, National Institutes of Health, Frederick, MD 21702, USA;
alex.mitrophanov@nih.gov or mitrophanov.alex@gmail.com

Abstract: Perturbation bounds are powerful tools for investigating the phenomenon of insensitivity to perturbations, also referred to as stability, for stochastic and deterministic systems. This perspective article presents a focused account of some of the main concepts and results in inequality-based perturbation theory for finite state-space, time-homogeneous, continuous-time Markov chains. The diversity of perturbation bounds and the logical relationships between them highlight the essential stability properties and factors for this class of stochastic processes. We discuss the linear time dependence of general perturbation bounds for Markov chains, as well as time-independent (i.e., time-uniform) perturbation bounds for chains whose stationary distribution is unique. Moreover, we prove some new results characterizing the absolute and relative tightness of time-uniform perturbation bounds. Specifically, we show that, in some of them, an equality is achieved. Furthermore, we analytically compare two types of time-uniform bounds known from the literature. Possibilities for generalizing Markov-chain stability results, as well as connections with stability analysis for other systems and processes, are also discussed.

Keywords: Markov stochastic process; Kolmogorov equation; differential equation; perturbation theory; sensitivity analysis; stability; robustness; ergodicity coefficient; stationary distribution

MSC: 60J27; 60J35; 34D10; 60J28; 34D20

Citation: Mitrophanov, A.Y. The Arsenal of Perturbation Bounds for Finite Continuous-Time Markov Chains: A Perspective. *Mathematics* **2024**, *12*, 1608. https://doi.org/10.3390/math12111608

Academic Editors: Panagiotis-Christos Vassiliou and Andreas C. Georgiou

Received: 4 May 2024
Revised: 18 May 2024
Accepted: 18 May 2024
Published: 21 May 2024

Correction Statement: This article has been republished with a minor change. The change does not affect the scientific content of the article and further details are available within the backmatter of the website version of this article.

1. Introduction

Perturbation bounds and related approaches for continuous-time Markov chains have been applied in research fields as diverse as reliability theory [1–3], queuing theory [4–8], quantum physics [9–12], climate science [13], biochemical kinetics [14–19], economics [20], population genetics [21], and health insurance modeling [22]. In principle, such bounds can be useful in any field where continuous-time Markov chains and their generalizations are used as mathematical models. At the same time, Markov chain perturbation bounds represent noteworthy theoretical developments that have connections with many directions of mathematical research. In this perspective article, we will summarize and highlight some distinguishing features of Markov chain perturbation bounds that illustrate both the inner logic of this research area and its usefulness for current and future applications. Specifically, we will discuss exponential vs. linear time dependence for perturbation bounds, as well as their possible time-independence (or, time-uniformity) and the connection with the rate of exponential convergence to the stationary distribution. Moreover, we will provide new results characterizing the tightness of time-uniform perturbation bounds. Additionally, we will outline the relationships between different perturbation-theory results for Markov chains and other processes and systems.

Perturbation bounds, their properties, and the connections between them constitute inequality-based perturbation theory, which can be developed for Markov chains and, generally, for stochastic and deterministic processes (i.e., mathematical objects representing systems changing over time). This complements the more traditional approach to perturbations that focuses on continuity and differentiability results, as well as asymptotic

expansions [23–28]. For quantitative studies, both perturbation bounds and perturbation expansions have their respective advantages; a comparison between them has been attempted in the case of discrete time [29]. For the purposes of this article, we emphasize that Markov chain perturbation bounds provide (1) a compact and convenient representation of the essential features defining the chain's sensitivity to perturbations and (2) a bound for the magnitude of the perturbation in the Markov chain's state probabilities given the magnitude of the perturbation in the chain's parameters and initial distribution. This magnitude is often a "summary" of the perturbation magnitudes for the chain's individual parameters, which allows the bound to hold for perturbations of different structure but the same magnitude. Note that, while the discovery of informative *lower* perturbation bounds would be very insightful, current research focuses on *upper* bounds, which is what we discuss in this article.

The primary reason for the focus on continuous time (in this perspective article, as well as in most of the author's research) is that physical time is continuous. This makes continuous-time Markov chains a natural choice for the stochastic modeling of real-world phenomena and systems. One prominent example is provided by physics and chemistry, where the (forward) Kolmogorov equations, which govern temporal changes in the Markov chain's state probabilities, have a special name: the master equation [15,30]. Yet another reason is the close connection with a powerful branch of mathematics—the theory of differential equations. Indeed, the Kolmogorov equations are a system of differential equations. One could thus anticipate that the general perturbation theory for differential equations would guide us toward the perturbation bounds we need. One of the well-known results in differential-equation theory is Gronwall's inequality and its different versions [31,32]. The application of this inequality to Markov chains (which has been attempted more than once, including an article in this Special Issue [22]) is what motivated us to write this perspective article.

Herein, we consider finite, time-homogeneous chains, because they provide excellent opportunities for illustrating the main concepts of perturbation analysis and also due to the considerable importance of such chains for applications. The possibility of generalizations to countable state spaces and time-inhomogeneous Markov chains will be indicated in the comments. Furthermore, this article focuses on *regular* perturbations, which correspond to cases where expected perturbation magnitudes can be regarded as small. This smallness is, often, not a strict mathematical requirement but a reflection of situations where such bounds can be useful. In contrast, *singular* perturbations correspond to cases where some state transitions in a Markov chain are considerably faster than others, so we could think of "large-magnitude perturbations" or multiple time scales. While the typical approach to singular perturbations centers on asymptotic expansions [25,26,28], perturbation-bound approaches to singular perturbations have also been developed [33,34]. Thus, some of the results that we discuss could, in principle, be applied to singular-perturbation problems.

This perspective article describes what can be regarded as deterministic perturbations of the Kolmogorov equations. Thus, we are in effect considering deterministic perturbations of a stochastic process (i.e., the Markov chain under study). One could possibly imagine perturbation scenarios involving various deterministic or stochastic systems under deterministic or stochastic perturbations. Clearly, each scenario would require its own theoretical developments. Yet, the types of results we discuss could be relevant in a broader context and may be applicable to other possible (and, as it might happen, far more complex) perturbation scenarios. At the very least, they can provide a relevant standard for comparison or even help generate a viable working hypothesis [35,36].

2. Continuous-Time Markov Chains and Perturbations: Notation and Some Basic Properties

Let $S = \{0, 1, \ldots, N\}$, where $N \geq 1$ is an integer, be a finite set. On this set, regarded as the state space, consider a continuous-time Markov chain $X = \{X(t), t \geq 0\}$ with constant generator (also known as the transition-rate matrix) $Q = (q_{ij})$ and vector of state

probabilities $p(t) = (p_i(t))$. Here, q_{ij} is the rate of transitions from state i to state j ($i \neq j$), and $p_i(t)$ is the probability that $X(t)$ will be in state i, given an initial distribution $p(0)$ (see, e.g., the definition of a continuous-time Markov chain in Refs. [37,38]). On the same state space, consider another Markov chain, $\widetilde{X} = \left\{ \widetilde{X}(t), \, t \geq 0 \right\}$, with generator $\widetilde{Q} = \left(\widetilde{q}_{ij} \right)$ and vector of state probabilities $\widetilde{p}(t) = \left(\widetilde{p}_i(t) \right)$. We will refer to the chains X and $\widetilde{X}$ as the unperturbed and perturbed chains, respectively, and the matrix $E := \widetilde{Q} - Q$ is the perturbation. To measure the magnitude of perturbations, we will use the l_1 norm (absolute entry sum) for vectors, which will be regarded as *row* vectors (per the tradition existing in the Markov chain literature). For matrices, we will use the corresponding subordinate norm, which is the maximum absolute row sum. We will denote l_1 vector and matrix norms by $\| \cdot \|$. Thus, for a vector $x = (x_i)$ and a matrix $A = (a_{ij})$, the norms are defined as follows:

$$\|x\| = \sum_i |x_i|, \quad \|A\| = \sup_{\|x\|=1} \|xA\| = \max_i \sum_j |a_{ij}|.$$

Importantly, for differences between probability vectors, this choice of norm corresponds to variation distance, which arguably is the most widely used distance in contemporary Markov chain theory (at least in the case of finite state spaces). For probability vectors p and $\widetilde{p}$ representing distributions on S, the variation distance, $d_{TV}(.,.)$, is commonly defined as follows:

$$d_{TV}\left(\widetilde{p}, p \right) := \sup_{A \subseteq S} \left| \widetilde{p}(A) - p(A) \right| = \frac{1}{2} \left\| \widetilde{p} - p \right\|,$$

where $\widetilde{p}(A)$ and $p(A)$ are the measures on S induced by $\widetilde{p}$ and p, respectively. Sometimes, the quantity $2d_{TV}\left(\widetilde{p}, p \right) = \left\| \widetilde{p} - p \right\|$ is used as the variation distance [18,19]. Because any two norms in a finite-dimensional space are equivalent, a bound on $\left\| \widetilde{p} - p \right\|$ will imply a bound on the vector difference in any other norm of interest, but the corresponding absolute constant may not be readily available. And even if it is, the resulting bound may not be tight (i.e., it might considerably overestimate the actual perturbation magnitude). A preferred approach would be to follow the proof of a bound in the l_1 norm and see if the same proof, perhaps with small modifications, also works for another norm of interest, such as an l_p norm (see, e.g., Ref. [39]).

Define $z(t) := \widetilde{p}(t) - p(t)$, so $\|z(t)\|$ is the magnitude of the perturbation in the state-probability vector of the chain X at time $t \geq 0$. To avoid the trivial case, we will assume throughout the article that $E \neq 0$; this assumption is necessary for some of the perturbation bounds to be strict inequalities. However, cases where $z(0) = 0$ will not be excluded. The perturbation bounds that we discuss will typically be uniform over a (finite or infinite) time interval and have the form

$$\sup_{t \in [0,T)} \|z(t)\| \leq \kappa_1(T) \|z(0)\| + \kappa_2(T) \|E\|, \quad 0 < T \leq \infty, \tag{1}$$

where $\kappa_1(T)$ and $\kappa_2(T)$ are the *condition numbers* (this term was borrowed from numerical linear algebra, where perturbation bounds are prevalent [40]). If these numbers are sufficiently small, then the chain X is well conditioned and insensitive to perturbations. While large condition numbers do not necessarily mean that the chain is sensitive, it is often implied and might as well be true. In any event, for our sensitivity assessment to be accurate, we want the bound in Equation (1) to be as tight as possible.

The use of the l_1 norm in Equation (1) offers some analytic advantages. First, because $\|p(t)\| \equiv 1$ (due to $p(t)$ being a probability vector), Equation (1) naturally provides a bound involving *relative* perturbations:

$$\sup_{t \in [0,T)} \frac{\|z(t)\|}{\|p(t)\|} \leq \kappa_1(T) \frac{\|z(0)\|}{\|p(0)\|} + \kappa_2(T) \|Q\| \frac{\|E\|}{\|Q\|}. \tag{2}$$

Equation (2) shows that the perturbation in $p(t)$ will be small if the relative perturbations in $p(0)$ and Q are both sufficiently small. In fact, using the l_1 norm, the absolute and relative perturbations of $p(t)$ are equivalent due to $\|p(t)\| \equiv 1$. At the same time, for the chain X to be well conditioned with respect to absolute perturbations in the generator, $\kappa_2(T)$ needs to be sufficiently small, whereas for it to be well conditioned with respect to relative perturbations in the generator, $\kappa_2(T)\|Q\|$ needs to be sufficiently small, as follows from Equation (2).

A second advantage of the l_1 norm is that Equation (1) can be divided by $N+1$ (i.e., the size of the state space) and thereby provide a bound on the average perturbation in a state probability of the chain X (averaged over all state-probability perturbations). For some applications, the metric $\|z(t)\|/(N+1)$ might be more informative than $\|z(t)\|$ (cf. Ref. [14]). The division by $N+1$ also allows one to control the growth of the right-hand side of Equation (1) with N, which can occur due to the nature of norm-based bounds.

Moreover, the use of the l_1 norm allows us to obtain simple perturbation bounds for the moments of the random variable $X(t)$, as demonstrated by the following statement (in which $E(\,.\,)$ and $\mathrm{var}(\,.\,)$ denote expectation and variance, respectively).

Statement 1. *The following bounds hold for all $t \geq 0$ and every positive integer m:*

$$\left| E\left(\widetilde{X}^m(t)\right) - E(X^m(t)) \right| \leq N^m \|z(t)\|,$$

$$\left| \mathrm{var}\left(\widetilde{X}(t)\right) - \mathrm{var}(X(t)) \right| \leq 3N^2 \|z(t)\|.$$

Proof. The perturbation bound for the non-central moments is a direct generalization of the corresponding result for the expectation [4]:

$$\left| E\left(\widetilde{X}^m(t)\right) - E(X^m(t)) \right| \leq \sum_{k=0}^{N} k^m \left| \widetilde{p}_k(t) - p_k(t) \right| \leq N^m \|z(t)\|.$$

Next, from the basic properties of variance, we have

$$\left| \mathrm{var}\left(\widetilde{X}(t)\right) - \mathrm{var}(X(t)) \right| \leq \left| \sum_{k=0}^{N} k^2 \left(\widetilde{p}_k(t) - p_k(t)\right) \right| + \left| \left(\sum_{k=0}^{N} k\widetilde{p}_k(t)\right)^2 - \left(\sum_{k=0}^{N} kp_k(t)\right)^2 \right|.$$

Here, the first term on the right-hand side does not exceed $N^2 \|z(t)\|$. For the second term, we have

$$\left| \left(\sum_{k=0}^{N} k\widetilde{p}_k(t)\right)^2 - \left(\sum_{k=0}^{N} kp_k(t)\right)^2 \right|$$
$$= \left| \sum_{k=0}^{N} k\widetilde{p}_k(t) - \sum_{k=0}^{N} kp_k(t) \right| \times \left(\sum_{k=0}^{N} k\widetilde{p}_k(t) + \sum_{k=0}^{N} kp_k(t) \right) \leq N\|z(t)\| \times 2N.$$

Putting everything together, we obtain

$$\left| \mathrm{var}\left(\widetilde{X}(t)\right) - \mathrm{var}(X(t)) \right| \leq N^2 \|z(t)\| + 2N^2 \|z(t)\| = 3N^2 \|z(t)\|.$$

This completes the proof. □

Notice that, in Statement 1, the mth non-central moment for both X and $\widetilde{X}$ is bounded by N^m, and this bound is attained for distributions concentrated in the state N. And if, instead of the absolute moment difference, we consider the relative difference $\left| E\left(\widetilde{X}^m(t) \right) - E(X^m(t)) \right| / N^m$, then, from Statement 1, we obtain a perturbation bound without the explicit dependence on N^m on the right-hand side. Similar relative differences can also be considered for the variances, each of which is bounded by $2N^2$.

3. Time Dependence in Perturbation Bounds: From Exponential to Linear

The forward Kolmogorov equations for chains X and $\widetilde{X}$ have the following form:

$$\frac{d\boldsymbol{p}(t)}{dt} = \boldsymbol{p}(t)\boldsymbol{Q}, \quad \frac{d\widetilde{\boldsymbol{p}}(t)}{dt} = \widetilde{\boldsymbol{p}}(t)\widetilde{\boldsymbol{Q}}, \quad t \geq 0.$$

When Gronwall's inequality is applied to these equations, Equation (1) holds on finite time intervals and takes the following explicit form [1,14,22]:

$$\sup_{t \in [0,T)} \|z(t)\| \leq e^{\|Q\|T}\|z(0)\| + \left(e^{\|Q\|T} - 1 \right) \frac{\|E\|}{\|Q\|}, \quad 0 < T < \infty. \tag{3}$$

The right-hand side of Equation (3) tends to $\|z(0)\|$ as $T \to 0$, suggesting that the bound may be informative on short- or moderate-length time intervals. However, for increasing T, the right-hand side grows exponentially, which can make the bound arbitrarily loose.

The possibility of obtaining perturbation bounds with a sub-exponential dependence on T was realized quite early [1]. This sub-exponential dependence turns out to be linear. Indeed, the following bound holds [1,14,33]:

$$\sup_{t \in [0,T)} \|z(t)\| \leq \|z(0)\| + T\|E\|, \quad 0 < T < \infty. \tag{4}$$

The derivation of Equation (4) is rather straightforward and relies on the integral representation of $z(t)$ (using the fact that the Kolmogorov equations are linear) together with some standard norm-based bounds. Using simple calculus, one can show that the right side of Equation (4) is smaller than that of Equation (3) for any $\|Q\|$ and T [14]. Overall, replacing the exponential dependence on T with a linear dependence offers tremendous improvements in bound tightness. However, there is another important conceptual difference between Equations (3) and (4). Specifically, in Equation (3), the condition numbers $\kappa_1(T)$ and $\kappa_2(T)$ depend on the parameters of X via $\|Q\|$; in other words, Equation (3) distinguishes between more well-conditioned and less well-conditioned Markov chains. However, Equation (4) does not make that distinction, and its condition numbers are the same for all Markov chains. Ideally, we would like to combine the tightness of the bound in Equation (4) with the chain-specific nature of the bound in Equation (3). How can this be achieved?

One simple and natural strategy involves reflecting chain-specific information in the choice of T, which has been suggested in the context of Markov-chain modeling of the frequently encountered biochemical reaction $A + B \rightleftharpoons AB$ (binary-complex formation and dissociation) [14]. That work investigated the nearness between the quadratic (full) and the linear (approximate) model for the reaction, and the latter was regarded as the unperturbed Markov chain. The author used the fact that the expectation of the unperturbed chain, $E(X(t))$, approached its unique stationary state $E(X(\infty))$ exponentially fast, with exponential rate μ independent of the initial conditions:

$$\Delta(t) = \Delta(0)e^{-\mu t},$$

where $\Delta(t) := E(X(t)) - E(X(\infty))$. Thus, we can define

$$T_\Delta := \frac{1}{\mu},$$

with T_Δ being the *relaxation time* for $\Delta(t)$. It is analogous to relaxation times studied in physics (cf. Ref. [41]), and such terminology has also been adopted in Markov chain convergence research.

Quite intuitively, the relaxation time T_Δ represents a relevant time scale for temporal changes in X, so we can set $T = T_\Delta$ in Equation (4) and thereby obtain a chain-specific— rather than generic—perturbation bound with increased tightness. Note, however, that in Markov chain research, relaxation time is typically defined as the inverse of the *spectral gap*, which is the spectral characteristic of the generator that defines the rate of convergence of a Markov chain to the stationary distribution [37,42]. In the case of continuous time, the spectral gap can be defined as the minimum absolute real part among all the generator's nonzero eigenvalues [18,19,37]. Notably, when the unperturbed chain is a Prendiville process, which was the case in the binary-complex formation modeling study [14], the spectral-gap definition of the relaxation time coincides with T_Δ [18]. Whereas the introduction of T_Δ assumed uniqueness of the steady state, this approach can be extended to situations where the stationary distribution of the unperturbed chain X is not necessarily unique. Indeed, Equation (4), being general, applies to such cases. All we need is a way to assess the range of relevant time scales for the unperturbed chain. This can be achieved, for example, based on subject-matter expertise in the research field where the Markov chains in question are used as mathematical models.

Setting $T = T_\Delta$ in Equation (4) provides a chain-specific value for $\kappa_2(T)$. At the same time, the value $\kappa_1(T) \equiv 1$ in Equation (4) is still generic. As we will see in the next section, in perturbation bounds suitable for very long time intervals, we also have $\kappa_1(T) \equiv 1$. This essentially is a consequence of the requirement that the bound in Equation (1) be uniform over a certain time interval. When this requirement is absent, the equivalent of $\kappa_1(T)$ can tend to 0 in the infinite-time limit. See, e.g., the bound derivation details in Refs. [18,33].

An important question in the development of Markov chain perturbation theory is the generalizability of the results to time-inhomogeneous and infinite state-space chains. The definition of time-inhomogeneity simply involves Markov chain generators that depend on the time variable: $Q(t)$ and $\widetilde{Q}(t)$, $t \geq 0$ [4,22,38]. The perturbation bound in Equation (3) was very recently extended to the case of finite, time-inhomogeneous Markov chains [22]. The bound in Equation (4) can be generalized to time-inhomogeneous chains with a countable state space [7]. While the main focus of Ref. [7] is on Markov chains demonstrating various types of infinite-time convergence (termed *ergodicity*), the finite-time bound, such as Equation (4), holds in the general case. The main necessary condition is that the theory of differential equations in the Banach (specifically, l_1) space is applicable, and a requirement for that is that the generators of the chains under consideration should be bounded. It is worth noting, however, that infinite-time convergence results can be extended to chains with unbounded generators, which serve as mathematical models, e.g., in biology [43]. Likewise, developing a perturbation theory for the case of unbounded generators could benefit some applications.

4. From Linear Time Dependence to Time Independence for Ergodic Markov Chains by Using Convergence Bounds

It turns out that bounds of the form as in Equation (4) can sometimes be considerably strengthened. For this, we need to make an additional assumption: throughout the remainder of this article, we will assume that the *stationary distribution* of X (i.e., a distribution $\pi = (\pi_i)$ satisfying $\pi Q = 0$) is *unique*. This assumption is not restrictive, because finite, time-homogeneous, continuous-time Markov chains used in applications very often possess this property. For example, in physics and chemistry, this unique stationary distribution can represent the often-studied state of thermodynamic or chemical

equilibrium. For stationary-distribution uniqueness, a frequently used sufficient condition is the irreducibility of X (or, in some applications, the positivity of all transition rates q_{ij} ($i \neq j$), which is sufficient for irreducibility), but it is not required for our purposes. What is required is a rigorous (and, preferably, tight) convergence bound for X.

If X has a unique stationary distribution, π, then there exist positive numbers C, b such that, for all initial distributions $p(0)$ and $t \geq 0$, we have

$$\|p(t) - \pi\| \leq Ce^{-bt}. \tag{5}$$

This convergence to a unique stationary distribution is the manifestation of ergodicity. Importantly, Equation (5) implies that $C \geq 1$ [19]. If Equation (5) holds, then for all initial distribution vectors $p_1(0)$ and $p_2(0)$ and all $t \geq 0$, we have

$$\|p_1(t) - p_2(t)\| \leq 2Ce^{-bt}, \tag{6}$$

where $p_1(t)$ and $p_2(t)$ are the distributions of $X(t)$ corresponding to the initial distributions $p_1(0)$ and $p_2(0)$, respectively. In the finite, time-homogeneous case, Equations (5) and (6) are equivalent convergence conditions, and they can be proven, e.g., using the properties of the l_1 *ergodicity coefficient* (also known as Dobrushin's ergodicity coefficient) for chain X [33]. However, Equation (6) is particularly convenient for generalizing perturbation and convergence results to the time-inhomogeneous case. That is why some perturbation results in the literature explicitly use a convergence bound in the form given by Equation (6). The l_1 ergodicity coefficient, $\tau_1(\, . \,)$, is defined for any real square matrix A as follows:

$$\tau_1(A) :- \sup_{\substack{\|x\| = 1 \\ xe^{\mathsf{T}} = 0}} \|xA\| = \frac{1}{2}\max_{i,j}\sum_k \left|a_{ik} - a_{jk}\right|,$$

where $e = (1 \; 1 \dots \; 1)$ and ^{T} denotes transpose. For a continuous-time chain X, ergodicity coefficients are applied to, and calculated for, the chain's transition matrices $P(t) :- \exp(Qt)$.

Since the 1990s, explicit and computable Markov chain convergence bounds have been an active research topic, and numerous such bounds have been obtained for the finite state-space case [16,18,37,44–46]. Their utility in perturbation analysis follows from Equation (5). Indeed, for any $x > 0$, define the *mixing time*, $\theta(x)$, as follows [37]:

$$\theta(x) :- \inf_{t \geq 0}\{ \, t : \; \|p(t) - \pi\| \leq x \quad \text{for all } p(0) \, \}.$$

For any extent of convergence to the stationary distribution (i.e., for any distance from the stationary distribution), the mixing time $\theta(x)$ is the time when this extent of convergence is achieved. To define a characteristic time of convergence (which is meaningful yet arbitrary), let us choose $x = 1/e$. From Equation (5), it follows that

$$\theta\left(e^{-1}\right) \leq b^{-1}(\log C + 1). \tag{7}$$

Combining this with Equation (4), we obtain

$$\sup_{t \in [0,T)} \|z(t)\| \leq \|z(0)\| + b^{-1}(\log C + 1)\|E\|, \quad T = b^{-1}(\log C + 1). \tag{8}$$

We could have obtained a simpler version of this bound if we had used the relaxation time definition $T = 1/b$ in Equation (4). However, the relaxation time is only a proxy for the mixing time [42], whereas Equation (7) provides a rigorous bound for it. The main reason to use the right-hand side of Equation (8), however, is not the rigor of the mixing-time

estimate. Rather miraculously, it turns out that the right-hand side of Equation (8) provides a perturbation bound that is uniform over $t \geq 0$:

$$\sup_{t \geq 0} \|z(t)\| \leq \|z(0)\| + b^{-1}(\log C + 1)\|E\|; \tag{9}$$

moreover, this inequality is strict for $C > 1$ [18,19]. Two sufficient conditions for $C > 1$ are that: (1) $N > 1$ and (2) $N = 1$ and the stationary distribution of the chain X is non-uniform [19]. Thus, $C > 1$ is—by far—the prevalent case.

Besides the obvious significance of the time-uniform bound, such as Equation (9), in the analysis of regular perturbations, this time-uniformity is essential in the derivation of bounds for singular perturbations [33]. Equation (9) eliminates the time-dependency on the right-hand side altogether, while preserving the chain-specific nature of the bound. This bound delivers a clear message: if, for a Markov chain, we have a convergence bound of the type shown in Equation (5) (or Equation (6)), then we "automatically" obtain a perturbation bound for that Markov chain. Moreover, (1) if a chain converges fast to its stationary distribution, then it is stable under perturbations in its generator, and (2) the main determinant of this stability is the exponential convergence rate b. Thus, obtaining perturbation bounds is another reason why mathematicians should study Markov chain convergence, which complements the list of such reasons given in the preface to the first edition of Ref. [37].

Because the derivation of Equation (9) yields a bound that holds on an infinite time interval, that approach also works for stationary distributions. Indeed, if $\tilde{\pi}$ is a (not necessarily unique) stationary distribution of $\tilde{X}$, then

$$\left\|\tilde{\pi} - \pi\right\| \leq b^{-1}(\log C + 1)\|E\|; \tag{10}$$

if $C > 1$, then this inequality is strict [18]. The perturbation bounds in Equations (9) and (10) were derived specifically for the Kolmogorov equations and use some unique features of their solutions. They rely on the notion of the ergodicity coefficient, which plays an important role in the theory of stochastic matrices [39,40,47]. (See Ref. [33] for a perturbation analysis in continuous time with more extensive use of ergodicity coefficients.) These bounds illustrate how, by exploiting the special structure of the governing equations for different classes of stochastic (and deterministic) processes, one can obtain increasingly informative and accurate perturbation and approximation results.

The strictness of the inequalities in Equations (9) and (10) for $C > 1$ helps us to avoid the futile, in this case, search for examples of equality, which the non-strict inequality in Equation (8) could encourage (and which, in general, can be very meaningful for a perturbation bound). At the same time, if the bounds in Equations (9) and (10) turned out to be strict for all possible C, including $C = 1$, then we would have been motivated to try to improve these bounds using an absolute multiplicative constant (which is another meaningful pursuit in general perturbation theory). However, this is impossible, as demonstrated by the following statement.

Statement 2. *There exist two-state Markov chains X and $\tilde{X}$ for which, in Equations (9) and (10), an equality is attained.*

Proof. First, consider Equation (10), which is non-strict for $N = 1$, suggesting that, in this case, an equality is possible. Choose $N = 1$ and choose Q so that $q_{01} = q_{10} = 1$ (the other two entries of Q are determined from the condition that row sums for any generator Q are all equal to 0). Due to this symmetry, the stationary distribution of X is uniform, i.e., $\pi = (1/2 \ 1/2)$. Now, on the same state space $S = \{0,1\}$, choose $\tilde{Q}$ so that $\tilde{q}_{01} = 1$ and $\tilde{q}_{10} = 0$. Obviously, the corresponding stationary distribution is unique and equal to $\tilde{\pi} = (0 \ 1)$. Direct calculation shows that $\|E\| = 2$ and $\left\|\tilde{\pi} - \pi\right\| = 1$. The chain X is

a special case of the Prendiville process on $S = \{0, 1\}$, and an explicit formula for its l_1 ergodicity coefficient, $\beta(t)$, is known [18]:

$$\beta(t) = e^{-(q_{01}+q_{10})t} = e^{-2t}.$$

It can be demonstrated (see Refs. [18,33]) that

$$\|\boldsymbol{p}_1(t) - \boldsymbol{p}_2(t)\| \le \beta(t)\|\boldsymbol{p}_1(0) - \boldsymbol{p}_2(0)\|,$$

where $\boldsymbol{p}_1(t)$ and $\boldsymbol{p}_2(t)$ are the distributions of $X(t)$ corresponding to arbitrary initial distributions $\boldsymbol{p}_1(0)$ and $\boldsymbol{p}_2(0)$, respectively. Using this inequality together with the general bound $\|\boldsymbol{p}_1(0) - \boldsymbol{p}_2(0)\| \le 2$, we obtain

$$\|\boldsymbol{p}_1(t) - \boldsymbol{p}_2(t)\| \le 2e^{-2t}.$$

Therefore, we can choose $C = 1$ and $b = 2$ in Equation (6). We thus have an explicit expression for every quantity on both sides of Equation (10). Substituting them all into that non-strict inequality, we obtain an equality.

Now, for the chosen chains X and $\tilde{X}$, and the chosen C and b, suppose that Equation (9) is a strict inequality. Additionally, assume that $\|z(0)\| = 0$. Then, from Equations (9) and (10), we have

$$\sup_{t\ge 0}\|z(t)\| < b^{-1}(\log C + 1)\|E\| = 1 = \left\|\tilde{\pi} - \pi\right\| = \lim_{t\to\infty}\|z(t)\|,$$

which is a contradiction. $\square$

5. Related Results and Extensions

Equation (9) is not the only time-uniform bound with a logarithmic dependence on C reported in the literature. Even though it was the first to be published [18], another bound had, in fact, been derived (and submitted for publication) earlier [19]:

$$\sup_{t\ge 0}\|z(t)\| \le \|z(0)\| + \inf_{0<y<1}\frac{b^{-1}\log(C/y)}{1-y}\|E\|. \tag{11}$$

The question then becomes, which bound is sharper—Equation (9) or Equation (11)? The following statement shows that the bound provided by Equation (9) is sharper than the one provided by Equation (11).

Statement 3. *If $C > 1$, then*

$$\log C + 1 < \inf_{0<y<1}\frac{\log(C/y)}{1-y},$$

and this expression becomes an equality for $C = 1$.

Proof. First, assume that $C > 1$. Define

$$f_C(y) := \frac{\log(C/y)}{1-y}.$$

It follows that the infimum of $f_C(y)$ over $y \in (0, 1)$ is attained at an internal point y_0 of this interval, such that

$$C = y_0 \exp\left(\frac{1-y_0}{y_0}\right) \tag{12}$$

(Proposition 1 in Ref. [19]). Taking the logarithm of Equation (12), we obtain

$$\log C + 1 = \log y_0 + \frac{1}{y_0}.$$

Therefore, because $0 < y_0 < 1$, we have that $\log y_0 < 0$ and thus

$$\log C + 1 < \frac{1}{y_0}.$$

At the same time, from the definition of $f_C(y)$ and Equation (12), it follows that

$$f_C(y_0) = \frac{1}{y_0}.$$

This equality, together with the inequality preceding it, proves Statement 3 for $C > 1$. If $C = 1$, then $f_C(y)$ monotonically decreases on $(0, 1)$ and approaches 1 as $y \uparrow 1$ (Proposition 1 in Ref. [19]), from which Statement 3 follows. $\square$

Equation (9) and the related bounds reflect the fact that fast convergence to the stationary distribution implies insensitivity to perturbations. Intuitively, the chain X will be fast converging if all the transition rates in Q are sufficiently large. This begs the question: is it possible to obtain a perturbation bound with the condition number expressed explicitly in terms of the transition rates, q_{ij}? This question has been answered in the affirmative for cases where certain additional assumptions are satisfied [19]. A particularly simple answer exists for Markov chains possessing a *strongly accessible* state, i.e., a state that can be reached from every other state in one transition. An example of such a chain is one whose transition rates q_{ij} $(i \neq j)$ are all positive. If X has a strongly accessible state, then, in Equation (1), we can set $T = \infty$, $\kappa_1(T) = 1$, and $\kappa_2(T) = 1/\delta$, where δ is the sum, over all columns, of the off-diagonal column-minimum entries of Q [19].

A related question is: if the exponential-convergence parameter, b, in Equations (9) and (10) is so influential, then could it be possible to obtain perturbation bounds where the condition number $\kappa_2(\infty)$ depends only on b or a related quantity? It turns out that the quantity N/λ, where λ is the spectral gap of Q, is a condition number for perturbations of the stationary distribution [19]. (Generally, we have that $b \leq \lambda$ [19], but this can become an equality in many practical situations). A time-uniform perturbation bound with a condition number of $66eN/((e-1)\lambda)$ has been obtained under the additional assumption that the unperturbed chain X is *reversible* (i.e., is an irreducible chain such that $\pi_i q_{ij} = \pi_j q_{ji}$ for all $i, j \in S$) [48]. Reversible chains form a special class of time-homogeneous Markov chains that is important in many applications, such as models of physical processes that possess the property of detailed balance [18,37,42,48,49]. Easily interpretable condition numbers, containing quantities such as N/λ, are very valuable for qualitative insights into determinants of Markov chain insensitivity to perturbations. At the same time, the bounds in Equations (9) and (10) are likely to be tighter due to the logarithmic dependence on C [48].

Equation (9) appears to possess all of the desired perturbation-bound attributes. However, upon a closer look, we may find that there is room for improvement. Indeed, whereas $\|z(t)\| \to \|z(0)\|$ for $t \to 0$, the right-hand side of Equation (9) does not approach $\|z(0)\|$ for small t, because it does not depend on t at all. Therefore, the bound in Equation (4), and even Equation (3), can be sharper than Equation (9) for small t. How can we handle this situation? Evidently, the only way to maximize tightness is to use Equation (9) on long time intervals and Equation (4) on short ones. For an ergodic unperturbed chain X, the inequality in Equation (4) is strict [18,33]. Thus, from Equations (4) and (9), for the prevalent case $C > 1$ we have

$$
\sup_{t \in [0,T)} \|z(t)\| < \begin{cases} \|z(0)\| + T\|E\| & \text{if} & 0 < T \le b^{-1}(\log C + 1), \\ \|z(0)\| + b^{-1}(\log C + 1)\|E\| & \text{if} & b^{-1}(\log C + 1) \le T \le \infty. \end{cases}
$$

An alternative way to improve Equation (9) via a combination of bounds allows one to handle cases differing in the balance between the magnitude of $z(0)$ and that of E. Specifically, for $C > 1$, the following bound holds [18]:

$$
\sup_{t \ge 0}\|z(t)\| < \begin{cases} b^{-1}(\log C + 1)\|E\| & \text{if} & \|E\| \ge b\|z(0)\|, \\ \|z(0)\| + b^{-1}(\log C)\|E\| & & \text{otherwise.} \end{cases}
$$

The intriguing property of the bound above is that, for $b\|z(0)\|$ small enough relative to $\|E\|$, the dependence of the right-hand side on $\|z(0)\|$ disappears altogether.

Analogs of the bound in Equation (9), including the limiting distributions (as $t \to \infty$), have been derived for time-inhomogeneous Markov chains on finite and infinite state spaces [4–6,50], and convergence bounds for such general cases are also available [16,51]. It turns out, however, that obtaining explicit convergence bounds, such as Equation (5), in the case of an infinite state space (i.e., requiring *uniform ergodicity* in continuous time; cf. Ref. [52]) can be problematic. Actually, the unperturbed Markov chain of interest may not even be uniformly ergodic. An alternative strategy is to use perturbation bounds that rely on specially selected classes of norms other than the l_1 norm (such as weighted norms), and this is an active research direction in Markov chain theory and applications [4,5,8,53–56].

6. Discussion

This perspective article is about the properties of perturbation bounds for state-probability vectors of continuous-time Markov chains. All in all, we find these properties rather remarkable. Yet, perhaps the most remarkable of them is the availability and richness of connections with perturbation theories for other classes of quantities, processes, and systems. For example, a certain choice of the pre-exponential factor in a convergence bound—i.e., the constant C in Equations (9) and (10)—can also be a condition number for the eigenvalues and, therefore, for the spectral gap of the generator Q [13,18]. One and the same quantity, expressed in terms of the ergodicity coefficients of chain X, can be used as a condition number for the chain's state-probability vectors and also for its ergodicity coefficients [33]. As yet another powerful example, the perturbation bounds discussed herein (particularly, Equation (9)) inspired the development of a perturbation theory for general state-space, discrete-time Markov chains [52]. In recent years, that theory has blossomed (see, e.g., Refs. [55–59]) and deserves a separate, detailed review (which, in fact, is about to be published in the context of Markov chain Monte Carlo methodology [60]). It should also be mentioned that perturbation bounds for the stationary distribution of finite state-space, discrete-time Markov chains form a now-classic topic in matrix analysis, which has been characterized by outstanding mutual enrichment of linear algebra and applied probability [40]. Moreover, a theory has been developed that utilizes Markov chain perturbation bounds as straightforward plug-ins to readily obtain sensitivity bounds for hidden Markov models [61]. Continuing the topic of Markov processes, we should mention finite-time perturbation bounds for diffusions [62]. Perturbation bounds for the stationary distributions of diffusions have also been obtained [63,64]; interestingly enough, they do not appear (unlike our Equation (10)) to be directly related to perturbation bounds that are uniform over $t \ge 0$. Thus, derivation and investigation of time-uniform perturbation bounds for diffusions may be a promising research topic. Finally, an intriguing interplay between established and new results can be found in the recent work on regime-switching processes, where Markov chain considerations were used to gauge approaches to perturbation analysis for processes with a more complex structure [35,36].

A different direction of perturbation research, which, conceptually, is closely related to the material of this perspective article, has recently been developed in control theory

for deterministic *contractive systems*. Such systems have convergence properties that can be defined using a generalization of Equation (6) (a generalization containing an expression of the form $C\|\boldsymbol{p}_1(0) - \boldsymbol{p}_2(0)\|$ instead of the constant C) [65,66]. Perturbation and approximation bounds for both regular [67,68] and singular [69] perturbations of contractive systems have been derived. Whereas this perturbation theory developed within the domain of differential equations independently of Markov chain theory, there appear to be possibilities for cross-fertilization. Importantly, for all of these systems, the exponential rate of infinite-time convergence plays an essential role. This is a manifestation of the pattern where the parameter governing the effects of perturbations in the initial conditions also governs the effects of perturbations in the system's parameter values, which could be suggested as a general phenomenon for dynamical systems [70]. Perhaps, in the future, such theories will converge, using the Kolmogorov equations as a shared research focus, and will continue to strengthen each other, thereby benefiting diverse applications.

These developments concern deterministic perturbations of stochastic and deterministic systems; the situation with stochastic perturbations has also been the focus of intensive research. Random perturbations of dynamical systems are a now-classic subfield of stochastic processes. Naturally for random perturbations, the rate of convergence to the unperturbed, deterministic process is typically analyzed using large-deviations theory [71,72] (as an illustration of new research, see Ref. [73]). Stochastic perturbations of stochastic systems are an area where opportunities for a relevant theory are wide open. One promising approach is to cast such a theory in the framework of stochastic processes in a random environment, where the randomness in the environment represents the perturbations, which are perhaps assumed to be small. Work in this direction has started [74,75] (including approaches based on large deviations [72]), but further progress seems to be needed before the theory is fully ready for broad applications.

7. Conclusions

The purpose of this perspective article is to illustrate the approaches and results available in the inequality-based perturbation theory for continuous-time Markov chains. Herein, our priority was to emphasize the logical interconnections between different approaches. By intention, this is not a comprehensive overview of this research field. A systematic overview should include a broader discussion of the available bounds (including the array of results centered on ergodicity coefficients for continuous-time chains [33]), a more detailed analysis of the relationships between Markov chain perturbation results in continuous and discrete time (including approaches focused on entrywise, rather than norm-based, perturbation bounds), perhaps a deeper technical dive into the proofs for the presented results, and a look into the numerical accuracy of the available perturbation bounds on practically relevant examples. It would also be informative to consider cases of unstructured perturbations of continuous-time Markov chains (i.e., cases where the perturbed system of differential equations is not a proper system of Kolmogorov equations)—a situation that can arise in numerical solution problems [1]. Each of these topics deserves a focused presentation and can motivate future studies. Contemporary perturbation theory for Markov chains is an exciting example of interdisciplinary mathematics that draws ideas and tools from probability theory, stochastic processes, differential equations, operator theory, and matrix analysis, and has the potential to impact numerous areas of applied research. We hope that this perspective article will facilitate the continued growth of this promising research direction.

Funding: This research received no external funding.

Data Availability Statement: Data are contained within the article.

Acknowledgments: The author is grateful to the Reviewers for their comments and suggestions on the manuscript.

Conflicts of Interest: The author declares no conflicts of interest.

References

1. Ramesh, A.V.; Trivedi, K. On the sensitivity of transient solutions of Markov models. In Proceedings of the 1993 ACM Sigmetrics, Santa Clara, CA, USA, 10–14 May 1993; pp. 122–134. [CrossRef]
2. Yin, L.; Smith, M.A.J.; Trivedi, K.S. Uncertainty analysis in reliability modeling. In Proceedings of the Annual Reliability and Maintainability Symposium, Philadelphia, PA, USA, 22–25 January 2001; pp. 229–234. [CrossRef]
3. Skulj, D. Application of normal cones to the computation of solutions of the nonlinear Kolmogorov backward equation. *Int. J. Approx. Reason.* **2023**, *158*, 108919. [CrossRef]
4. Zeifman, A.; Korolev, V.; Satin, Y. Two approaches to the construction of perturbation bounds for continuous-time Markov chains. *Mathematics* **2020**, *8*, 253. [CrossRef]
5. Zeifman, A.; Korolev, V.; Satin, Y.; Korotysheva, A.; Bening, V. Perturbation bounds and truncations for a class of Markovian queues. *Queueing Syst.* **2014**, *76*, 205–221. [CrossRef]
6. Zeifman, A.; Korotysheva, A. Perturbation bounds for $M_t/M_t/N$. queue with catastrophes. *Stoch. Models* **2012**, *28*, 49–62. [CrossRef]
7. Zeifman, A.I.; Isaacson, D.L. On strong ergodicity for nonhomogeneous continuous-time Markov chains. *Stoch. Proc. Appl.* **1994**, *50*, 263–273. [CrossRef]
8. Zeifman, A.I.; Korolev, V.Y.; Razumchik, R.V.; Satin, Y.A.; Kovalev, I.A. Limiting characteristics of queueing systems with vanishing perturbations. *Dokl. Math.* **2022**, *106*, 375–379. [CrossRef]
9. Erkursun-Özcan, N.; Mukhamedov, F. Stability estimates of Markov semigroups on abstract states spaces. *Mediterr. J. Math.* **2020**, *17*, 44. [CrossRef]
10. Szehr, O.; Wolf, M.M. Perturbation bounds for quantum Markov processes and their fixed points. *J. Math. Phys.* **2013**, *54*, 032203. [CrossRef]
11. Waeldchen, S.; Gertis, J.; Campbell, E.T.; Eisert, J. Renormalizing entanglement distillation. *Phys. Rev. Lett.* **2016**, *116*, 020502. [CrossRef] [PubMed]
12. Shabani, A.; Neven, H. Artificial quantum thermal bath: Engineering temperature for a many-body quantum system. *Phys. Rev. A* **2016**, *94*, 052301. [CrossRef]
13. Gutiérrez, M.S.; Lucarini, V. Response and sensitivity using Markov chains. *J. Stat. Phys.* **2020**, *179*, 1572–1593. [CrossRef]
14. Mitrophanov, A.Y. Stochastic Markov models for the process of binary complex formation and dissociation. *Mat. Model.* **2001**, *13*, 101–109.
15. Constantino, P.H.; Vlysidis, M.; Smadbeck, P.; Kaznessis, Y.N. Modeling stochasticity in biochemical reaction networks. *J. Phys. D Appl. Phys.* **2016**, *49*, 093001. [CrossRef]
16. Mitrophanov, A.Y. Note on Zeifman's bounds on the rate of convergence for birth–death processes. *J. Appl. Probab.* **2004**, *41*, 593–596. [CrossRef]
17. Thorsley, D.; Klavins, E. Approximating stochastic biochemical processes with Wasserstein pseudometrics. *IET Syst. Biol.* **2010**, *4*, 193–211. [CrossRef] [PubMed]
18. Mitrophanov, A.Y. Stability and exponential convergence of continuous-time Markov chains. *J. Appl. Probab.* **2003**, *40*, 970–979. [CrossRef]
19. Mitrophanov, A.Y. Stability estimates for finite homogeneous continuous-time Markov chains. *Theory Probab. Appl.* **2006**, *50*, 319–326. [CrossRef]
20. D'Amico, G.; De Blasis, R.; Gismondi, F. Perturbation analysis for dynamic poverty indexes. *Commun. Stat.-Theory Methods* **2023**, *52*, 6820–6839. [CrossRef]
21. Legried, B.; Terhorst, J. Rates of convergence in the two-island and isolation-with-migration models. *Theor. Popul. Biol.* **2022**, *147*, 16–27. [CrossRef] [PubMed]
22. Esquível, M.L.; Krasii, N.P.; Guerreiro, G.R. Estimation–calibration of continuous-time non-homogeneous Markov chains with finite state space. *Mathematics* **2024**, *12*, 668. [CrossRef]
23. Delebecque, F. A reduction process for perturbed Markov chains. *SIAM J. Appl. Math.* **1983**, *43*, 325–350. [CrossRef]
24. Heidergott, B.; Leahu, H.; Löpker, A.; Pflug, G. Perturbation analysis of inhomogeneous finite Markov chains. *Adv. Appl. Probab.* **2016**, *48*, 255–273. [CrossRef]
25. Khasminskii, R.Z.; Yin, G.; Zhang, Q. Asymptotic expansions of singularly perturbed systems involving rapidly fluctuating Markov chains. *SIAM J. Appl. Math.* **1996**, *56*, 277–293. [CrossRef]
26. Khasminskii, R.Z.; Yin, G.; Zhang, Q. Constructing asymptotic series for probability distributions of Markov chains with weak and strong interactions. *Quart. Appl. Math.* **1997**, *55*, 177–200. [CrossRef]
27. Zeifman, A.I. Stability for continuous-time nonhomogeneous Markov chains. *Lect. Notes Math.* **1985**, *1155*, 401–414. [CrossRef]
28. Altman, E.; Avrachenkov, K.E.; Núñez-Queija, R. Perturbation analysis for denumerable Markov chains with application to queueing models. *Adv. Appl. Probab.* **2004**, *36*, 839–853. [CrossRef]
29. Abbas, K.; Berkhout, J.; Heidergott, B. A critical account of perturbation analysis of Markov chains. *Markov Process Relat. Fields* **2016**, *22*, 227–265.
30. Briat, C.; Khammash, M. Noise in biomolecular systems: Modeling, analysis, and control implications. *Annu. Rev. Control Robot.* **2023**, *6*, 283–311. [CrossRef]
31. Barich, F. Some Gronwall-Bellman inequalities on time scales and their continuous forms: A survey. *Symmetry* **2021**, *13*, 198. [CrossRef]

32. Chandra, J.; Fleishman, B.A. On a generalization of Gronwall-Bellman lemma in partially ordered Banach spaces. *J. Math. Anal. Appl.* **1970**, *31*, 668–681. [CrossRef]
33. Mitrophanov, A.Y. Ergodicity coefficient and perturbation bounds for continuous-time Markov chains. *Math. Inequal. Appl.* **2005**, *8*, 159–168. [CrossRef]
34. Jiang, S.X.; Liu, Y.Y.; Tang, Y.C. A unified perturbation analysis framework for countable Markov chains. *Linear Algebra Appl.* **2017**, *529*, 413–440. [CrossRef]
35. Shao, J.H. Comparison theorem and stability under perturbation of transition rate matrices for regime-switching processes. *J. Appl. Probab.* **2024**, *61*, 540–557. [CrossRef]
36. Shao, J.H.; Yuan, C.G. Stability of regime-switching processes under perturbation of transition rate matrices. *Nonlinear Anal. Hybrid Syst.* **2019**, *33*, 211–226. [CrossRef]
37. Levin, D.A.; Peres, Y. *Markov Chains and Mixing Times*, 2nd ed.; American Mathematical Society: Providence, RI, USA, 2017.
38. Vassiliou, P.-C.G. *Non-Homogeneous Markov Chains and Systems: Theory and Applications*; Chapman and Hall/CRC: New York, NY, USA, 2022. [CrossRef]
39. Seneta, E. Perturbation of the stationary distribution measured by ergodicity coefficients. *Adv. Appl. Probab.* **1988**, *20*, 228–230. [CrossRef]
40. Cho, G.E.; Meyer, C.D. Comparison of perturbation bounds for the stationary distribution of a Markov chain. *Linear Algebra Appl.* **2001**, *335*, 137–150. [CrossRef]
41. Žnidarič, M. Relaxation times of dissipative many-body quantum systems. *Phys. Rev. E* **2015**, *92*, 042143. [CrossRef] [PubMed]
42. Olesker-Taylor, S.; Zanetti, L. Geometric bounds on the fastest mixing Markov chain. *Probab. Theory Relat. Fields* **2024**, *188*, 1017–1062. [CrossRef]
43. Mitrophanov, A.Y.; Borodovsky, M. Convergence rate estimation for the TKF91 model of biological sequence length evolution. *Math. Biosci.* **2007**, *209*, 470–485. [CrossRef] [PubMed]
44. Diaconis, P.; Stroock, D. Geometric bounds for eigenvalues of Markov chains. *Ann. Appl. Probab.* **1991**, *1*, 36–61. [CrossRef]
45. Fill, J.A. Eigenvalue bounds on convergence to stationarity for nonreversible Markov chains, with an application to the exclusion process. *Ann. Appl. Probab.* **1991**, *1*, 62–87. [CrossRef]
46. Szehr, O.; Reeb, D.; Wolf, M.M. Spectral convergence bounds for classical and quantum Markov processes. *Commun. Math. Phys.* **2015**, *333*, 565–595. [CrossRef]
47. Ipsen, I.C.F.; Selee, T.M. Ergodicity coefficients defined by vector norms. *SIAM J. Matrix Anal. Appl.* **2011**, *32*, 153–200. [CrossRef]
48. Mitrophanov, A.Y. The spectral gap and perturbation bounds for reversible continuous-time Markov chains. *J. Appl. Probab.* **2004**, *41*, 1219–1222. [CrossRef]
49. Mitrophanov, A.Y. Reversible Markov chains and spanning trees. *Math. Sci.* **2004**, *29*, 107–114.
50. Usov, I.; Satin, Y.; Zeifman, A.; Korolev, V. Ergodicity bounds and limiting characteristics for a modified Prendiville model. *Mathematics* **2022**, *10*, 4401. [CrossRef]
51. Zeifman, A.; Satin, Y.; Kryukova, A.; Razumchik, R.; Kiseleva, K.; Shilova, G. On three methods for bounding the rate of convergence for some continuous-time Markov chains. *Int. J. Appl. Math. Comput. Sci.* **2020**, *30*, 251–266. [CrossRef]
52. Mitrophanov, A.Y. Sensitivity and convergence of uniformly ergodic Markov chains. *J. Appl. Probab.* **2005**, *42*, 1003–1014. [CrossRef]
53. Liu, Y.Y. Perturbation analysis for continuous-time Markov chains. *Sci. China Math.* **2015**, *58*, 2633–2642. [CrossRef]
54. Liu, Y.Y.; Li, W.D. Error bounds for augmented truncation approximations of Markov chains via the perturbation method. *Adv. Appl. Probab.* **2018**, *50*, 645–669. [CrossRef]
55. Medina-Aguayo, F.; Rudolf, D.; Schweizer, N. Perturbation bounds for Monte Carlo within Metropolis via restricted approximations. *Stoch. Proc. Appl.* **2020**, *130*, 2200–2227. [CrossRef] [PubMed]
56. Negrea, J.; Rosenthal, J.S. Approximations of geometrically ergodic reversible Markov chains. *Adv. Appl. Probab.* **2021**, *53*, 981–1022. [CrossRef]
57. Levi, E.; Craiu, R.V. Finding our way in the dark: Approximate MCMC for approximate Bayesian methods. *Bayesian Anal.* **2022**, *17*, 193–221. [CrossRef]
58. Maire, F.; Friel, N.; Alquier, P. Informed sub-sampling MCMC: Approximate Bayesian inference for large datasets. *Stat. Comput.* **2019**, *29*, 449–482. [CrossRef]
59. Bouranis, L.; Friel, N.; Maire, F. Model comparison for Gibbs random fields using noisy reversible jump Markov chain Monte Carlo. *Comput. Stat. Data Anal.* **2018**, *128*, 221–241. [CrossRef]
60. Rudolf, D.; Smith, A.; Quiroz, M. Perturbations of Markov chains. *arXiv* **2024**, arXiv:2404.10251v1.
61. Mitrophanov, A.Y.; Lomsadze, A.; Borodovsky, M. Sensitivity of hidden Markov models. *J. Appl. Probab.* **2005**, *42*, 632–642. [CrossRef]
62. Bogachev, V.I.; Röckner, M.; Shaposhnikov, S.V. Distances between transition probabilities of diffusions and applications to nonlinear Fokker–Planck–Kolmogorov equations. *J. Funct. Anal.* **2016**, *271*, 1262–1300. [CrossRef]
63. Bogachev, V.I.; Kirillov, A.I.; Shaposhnikov, S.V. Distances between stationary distributions of diffusions and solvability of nonlinear Fokker–Planck–Kolmogorov equations. *Theory Probab. Appl.* **2018**, *62*, 12–34. [CrossRef]
64. Bogachev, V.I.; Miftakhov, A.F.; Shaposhnikov, S.V. Differential properties of semigroups and estimates of distances between stationary distributions of diffusions. *Dokl. Math.* **2019**, *99*, 175–180. [CrossRef]

65. Margaliot, M.; Sontag, E.D.; Tuller, T. Contraction after small transients. *Automatica* **2016**, *67*, 178–184. [CrossRef]
66. Tsukamoto, H.; Chung, S.J.; Slotine, J.J.E. Contraction theory for nonlinear stability analysis and learning-based control: A tutorial overview. *Annu. Rev. Control* **2021**, *52*, 135–169. [CrossRef]
67. Botner, M.; Zarai, Y.; Margaliot, M.; Grüne, L. On approximating contractive systems. *IEEE Trans. Autom. Control* **2017**, *62*, 6451–6457. [CrossRef]
68. Coogan, S.; Margaliot, M. Approximating the steady-state periodic solutions of contractive systems. *IEEE Trans. Autom. Control* **2019**, *64*, 847–853. [CrossRef]
69. Del Vecchio, D.; Slotine, J.J.E. A contraction theory approach to singularly perturbed systems. *IEEE Trans. Autom. Control* **2013**, *58*, 752–757. [CrossRef]
70. Kaszás, B.; Haller, G. Universal upper estimate for prediction errors under moderate model uncertainty. *Chaos* **2020**, *30*, 113144. [CrossRef] [PubMed]
71. Freidlin, M.I.; Wentzell, A.D. *Random Perturbations of Dynamical Systems*, 3rd ed.; Springer: Berlin/Heidelberg, Germany, 2012. [CrossRef]
72. Varadhan, S.R.S. Large deviations. *Ann. Probab.* **2008**, *36*, 397–419. [CrossRef]
73. Jiang, J.; Wang, J.; Zhai, J.; Zhang, T. Uniform large deviations and metastability of random dynamical systems. *arXiv* **2024**, arXiv:2402.16522v1.
74. Hoppensteadt, F.; Salehi, H.; Skorokhod, A. Markov chain with small random perturbations with applications to bacterial genetics. *Random Oper. Stoch. Equ.* **1996**, *4*, 205–227. [CrossRef]
75. Skorokhod, A.V.; Hoppensteadt, F.C.; Salehi, H.D. *Random Perturbation Methods with Applications in Science and Engineering*; Springer: New York, NY, USA, 2002. [CrossRef]

Article

On a Mixed Transient–Asymptotic Result for the Sequential Interval Reliability for Semi-Markov Chains

Guglielmo D'Amico [1,*,†] and Thomas Gkelsinis [2,†]

[1] Department of Economics, University "G. d'Annunzio" of Chieti-Pescara, 65127 Pescara, Italy
[2] Laboratory of Mathematics Raphaël Salem, University of Rouen-Normandy, UMR 6085, 76801 Saint-Étienne-du-Rouvray, France; gkelsinis@univ-rouen.fr
* Correspondence: g.damico@unich.it
† These authors contributed equally to this work.

Abstract: In this paper, we are concerned with the study of sequential interval reliability, a measure recently introduced in the literature. This measure represents the probability of the system working during a sequence of nonoverlapping time intervals. In the cited work, the authors proposed a recurrent-type formula for computing this indicator in the transient case and investigated the asymptotic behavior as all the time intervals go to infinity. The purpose of the present work is to further explore the asymptotic behavior when only some of the time intervals are allowed to go to infinity while the remaining ones are not. In this way, we provide a unique indicator that is able to describe the process evolution in the transient and asymptotic cases as well. It is important to mention that this is not a straightforward result since, in order to achieve it, we need to develop several mathematical ingredients that generalize the classical renewal and Markov renewal frameworks. A numerical example illustrates our theoretical results.

Keywords: sequential measures; convolution product; semi-Markov processes; asymptotic results

MSC: 60K15; 60K20; 90B25

Citation: D'Amico, G.; Gkelsinis, T. On a Mixed Transient–Asymptotic Result for the Sequential Interval Reliability for Semi-Markov Chains. *Mathematics* **2024**, *12*, 1842. https://doi.org/10.3390/math12121842

Academic Editors: Panagiotis-Christos Vassiliou and Andreas C. Georgiou

Received: 30 April 2024
Revised: 6 June 2024
Accepted: 12 June 2024
Published: 13 June 2024

1. Introduction

In this paper, we study a specific reliability indicator of discrete-time semi-Markov systems called sequential interval reliability (*SIR*) which has been recently introduced in [1].

The choice for semi-Markov models has a twofold meaning: on the practical side, it is important to consider flexible models able to describe real problems; on the theoretical side, it is essential to provide mathematical results for general systems that encompass interesting particular cases already studied or worthy to be investigated.

In this respect, it is well known that semi-Markov processes are among the most important modeling techniques for real-world issues in diverse applied fields, like reliability, financial mathematics, earthquake studies, bioinformatics, etc. (see, e.g., [2–5]). Furthermore, there are valuable theoretical reasons supporting the semi-Markov choice. Indeed, they generalize the Markov chain framework by taking into account the duration of stay in the states. Hence, any result established in the semi-Markov case has a corresponding particular result in the Markovian setting. The latter is recovered whenever the sojourn time in a state of the process is modeled through a memoryless distribution, the exponential one in continuous time or the geometric one in discrete time.

Several researchers have investigated the dependability metrics of semi-Markov systems.

In the literature, there is a distinction based on the choice of discrete-time or continuous-time models.

The reliability methodology for continuous-time semi-Markov processes and the corresponding statistical inference can be found in [2,6–10].

The complexities that arise from the solution of semi-Markov models in continuous time led to the development of numerical approximations based on the discrete counterpart [11–14]. Also, for this last requirement, a study has recently emerged on the theory of reliability for discrete-time semi-Markov systems and on their estimation problem (see, e.g., [15–17]).

Numerical aspects related to a corresponding R package (https://cran.r-project.org/web/packages/smmR/index.html and https://cran.r-project.org/web/packages/SMM, accessed on 11 March 2024) can be found in [18].

Employing interval-based reliability indicators is a promising approach that allows us to examine the dependency of reliability in response to a particular specification of the time interval of interest expressed in terms of a starting point and a length. This was the original idea that brought to light the notion of interval reliability for continuous-time semi-Markov models [19,20]. The analogous discrete-time models were studied in [21,22] and recently extended to include duration-dependent versions in [23]. In short, interval reliability is the probability that the system will work at any time within a fixed time interval $[t, t + p]$. This measure includes, in particular, the availability function at time t whenever $p = 0$ and the reliability function at p whenever $t = 0$.

The present work is an extension of the work developed in [1], where we proposed a new reliability measure called sequential interval reliability (*SIR*).

The *SIR* generalizes the notion of interval reliability as representing the probability that a system is in a working state during a sequence of nonoverlapping intervals that are not necessarily equi-spaced. This performance indicator is of importance in several application domains where system performance is important only for specific temporal intervals. As an example, we can think of the reliability of an air-conditioning system in an office; it is recommended that the reliability be high on working days from 8 a.m. to 5 p.m. Unreliability during the night or at the weekend is not a serious issue, and the engineer can disregard it using the SIR indicator, which has been designed according to this scope. Following the line in [24], we are also interested in taking into account the dependence on the initial and/or final backward.

In [1], we proposed a recurrent-type formula for computing this indicator in the transient case, and we investigated the asymptotic behavior as the first time point goes to infinity, and hence, all the successive time points diverge to infinity as well. The purpose of the present work is to further explore the asymptotic behavior as some other time points are allowed to go to infinity. This means that we will consider a number of time intervals over which we assess the reliability in the transient regime and the remaining ones, which diverge to infinity, over which we measure the asymptotic sequential interval reliability. This leads to a result of mixed type, simultaneously considering transient and asymptotic behaviors in a unique formula.

It is very important to stress that this is not a straightforward work; in order to achieve this, we needed to develop several mathematical ingredients, like proposing a specific operator between two sets of functions (cf. Equation (11)), introducing a new matrix convolution product (in Definition 2), investigating the relationship with the classical one (in Proposition 2), and applying renewal-type arguments (like the key renewal theorem and Markov renewal equation techniques) to the generalized framework formalized by this new matrix convolution product (cf. the proof of Theorem 2).

The rest of this article is structured as follows: in the next section, we introduce the semi-Markov framework and sequential interval reliability by recalling some previous results. The main contribution of this article, presented in Section 3, is the investigation of the asymptotic behavior of the sequential interval reliability as a time of interest goes to infinity. A numerical example is provided in Section 4, illustrating some aspects of our theoretical work.

2. Mathematical Model and System Performance Metrics

This section introduces the mathematical framework by presenting a short description of semi-Markov chains and known performability measures used in the reliability field.

2.1. Semi-Markov Chains

A semi-Markov chain is a random process that is frequently used in several applied problems. It exhibits a particular type of time dependence between events where the Markovian property holds not at every time point but only at moments when the system changes its states. Consider a generic random system taking values in the finite state space $E = \{1, \ldots, s\}$. The system evolves in time, and its behavior can be described by two sequences of random variables defined over a probability space $(\Omega, \mathcal{F}, \mathbb{P})$.

The first sequence of random variables is $J = (J_n)_{n \in \mathbb{N}}$, with $J_n : \Omega \to E$. It denotes the states successively visited by the system. The successive points when the random system changes its states are denoted by $T = (T_n)_{n \in \mathbb{N}}$, with $T_n : \Omega \to \mathbb{N}$. Let us further introduce $N(t) := \max\{n \in \mathbb{N} \mid T_n \leq t\}$ as the discrete-time counting process denoting the number of transitions within time t. Then, the process $(Z_t)_{t \in \mathbb{N}}$, defined by $Z_t = J_{N(t)}$, is called a semi-Markov chain.

If we assume that

$$\mathbb{P}(J_{n+1} = j, T_{n+1} - T_n = k | J_n, \ldots, J_0, T_n, \ldots, T_0) = \mathbb{P}(J_{n+1} = j, T_{n+1} - T_n = k | J_n), \quad (1)$$

then the process $Z = (Z_k, k \in \mathbb{N})$ is a semi-Markov chain. Property (1) allows the joint process $(J, T) = (J_n, T_n)_n$ to be a Markov renewal Chain. Whenever the probability $\mathbb{P}(J_{n+1} = j, T_{n+1} - T_n = k | J_n = i)$ is independent of the number of transitions n, the semi-Markov chain is time-homogeneous. When we relax this assumption, we deal with time-inhomogeneous semi-Markov processes; see, e.g., [25,26]. This class of stochastic processes has demonstrated high potential for describing real-life problems, among which are credit risk and financial applications; see, e.g., [27–29].

A semi-Markov chain is uniquely determined (almost surely) through an initial distribution $(\mu_i)_{i \in E}$ with $\mu_i = \mathbb{P}(Z_0 = i) = \mathbb{P}(J_0 = i)$ and a matrix of function $\mathbf{q}(t) = (q_{ij}(t))_{i,j \in E, t \in \mathbb{N}}$ called the semi-Markov kernel. The latter collects the probabilities

$$q_{ij}(t) = \mathbb{P}(J_{n+1} = j, T_{n+1} - T_n = t | J_n = i).$$

Simple probabilistic computations allow us to represent the semi-Markov kernel as

$$q_{ij}(k) = p_{ij} f_{ij}(k),$$

where $p_{ij} = \mathbb{P}(J_{n+1} = j | J_n = i)$, and $f_{ij}(k) = \mathbb{P}(T_{n+1} - T_n = k | J_n = i, J_{n+1} = j)$.

Hence, the semi-Markov kernel can be identified by providing a transition probability matrix $\mathbf{P} = (p_{ij})_{i,j \in E}$ for the embedded Markov chain J_n and a probability distribution function $f_{ij}(\cdot)$ for each couple of states i, j. The element p_{ij} represents the conditional probability of transitioning from state i to state j independently in time. The function $f_{ij}(\cdot)$ identifies the probability distribution of the sojourn time length in state i before making the next transition in state j.

The theory of semi-Markov chains is well developed, and the interested reader can find several results described in [4].

2.2. Reliability Metrics

To assess the reliability behavior of a semi-Markov system, usually the state space E is split into two subsets, U for the working states and D for the failure states; hence, $E = U \cup D$ and $E = U \cap D = \varnothing$.

The literature abounds with various measures of performance. One of the most interesting is the sequential interval reliability introduced in [1]. The main interest of this measure resides in its high generality, as it encompasses availability, reliability, and interval

reliability at the same time. Here, we report some definitions and results given in [1] for improving readability and understanding the new result that we are going to show in the next section.

Let us consider two time sequences of nonnegative times $\underline{t} := (t_i)_{i=1,\ldots,N}$ and $\underline{p} := (p_i)_{i=1,\ldots,N}$ such that the following apply:

1. $t_i < t_{i+1}$ for all $i = 1, \ldots, N-1$;
2. $t_i + p_i < t_{i+1}$ for all $i = 1, \ldots, N-1$.

Previous conditions guarantee that $\forall i, j = 1, \ldots, N$ with $i \neq j$,

$$[t_i, t_i + p_i] \bigcap [t_j, t_j + p_j] = \varnothing.$$

Hence, they form a sequence of nonoverlapping time intervals.

Sequences $\underline{t}$ and $\underline{p}$ can be considered row vectors. Hereinafter, vectors will always be intended as rows unless otherwise specified.

According to [1], for $v \in \mathbb{N}$ and $k \in E$, we can define the conditional sequential interval reliability, $SIR_k^{(N)}(v; \underline{t}, \underline{p})$, as the conditional probability that the system is in the up-states U during the time intervals $\{[t_i, t_i + p_i]\}_{i=1,\ldots,N}$, given the information set $(k, v) := \{J_{N(0)} = k, T_{N(0)} = -v\}$, i.e.,

$$
\begin{aligned}
SIR_k^{(N)}(v; \underline{t}, \underline{p}) &:= \mathbb{P}(Z_l \in U, \text{ for all } l \in [t_i, t_i + p_i], i = 1, \ldots, N \mid J_{N(0)} = k, T_{N(0)} = -v) \\
&= \mathbb{P}_{(k,v)}(Z_l \in U, \text{ for all } l \in [t_i, t_i + p_i], i = 1, \ldots, N).
\end{aligned}
\tag{2}
$$

It is important to note that the SIR function ignores the behavior of the system within two subsequent time intervals. In other words, for any discrete time point in the set $[t_i + p_i + 1, t_{i+1} - 1]$, the system is free to occupy up-states or down-states without altering the indicator's value.

A particular case of the former definition is obtained when $v = 0$; thus, we will set

$$SIR_k^{(N)}(\underline{t}, \underline{p}) := SIR_k^{(N)}(0; \underline{t}, \underline{p}) = \mathbb{P}(Z_l \in U, \text{ for all } l \in [t_i, t_i + p_i], i = 1, \ldots, N \mid J_{N(0)} = k).$$

A recursive formula for computing the sequential interval reliability of a discrete-time semi-Markov chain is known.

Proposition 1 ([1]). *Let $\underline{t} := (t_i)_{i=1,\ldots,N}$ and $\underline{p} := (p_i)_{i=1,\ldots,N}$, $N \in \mathbb{N}^*$ be two time sequences such that $\{[t_i, t_i + p_i]\}_{i=1,\ldots,N}$ is a sequence of nonoverlapping real intervals. For any $v \in \mathbb{N}$ and $k \in E$, the indicator $SIR_k^{(N)}(v; \underline{t}, \underline{p})$ is given by the following:*

$$SIR_k^{(N)}(v; \underline{t}, \underline{p}) = g_k^{(N)}(v; \underline{t}, \underline{p}) + \sum_{r \in E} \sum_{\theta=1}^{t_1} \frac{q_{kr}(v+\theta)}{\overline{H}_k(v)} SIR_r^{(N)}(0; \underline{t} - \theta \mathbf{1}_{1:N}, \underline{p}).
\tag{3}$$

Here, $\overline{H}_k(v) = \sum_{s=v+1}^{\infty} \sum_{j \in E} f_{kj}(s)$, $\mathbf{1}_{1:N}$ is a vector of 1s of length N, and $g_k^{(N)}(v; \underline{t}, \underline{p})$ is given by

$$g_k^{(N)}(v; \underline{t}, \underline{p}) := 1_{\{k \in U\}} \left[\frac{\overline{H}_k(t_N + p_N + v)}{\overline{H}_k(v)} \right.$$

$$+ \sum_{\theta = t_1 + 1}^{t_1 + p_1} \sum_{r \in E} \sum_{m \in U} \sum_{v' = 0}^{t_1 + p_1 - \theta} \frac{q_{kr}(v + \theta)}{\overline{H}_k(v)} R_{rm}^b(v'; t_1 + p_1 - \theta) SIR_m^{(N-1)}(v'; t_{2:N} - 1_{2:N}(t_1 + p_1), p_{2:N})$$

$$+ \sum_{j=2}^{N} \sum_{\theta = t_j}^{t_j + p_j} \sum_{r \in E} \frac{q_{kr}(v + \theta)}{\overline{H}_k(v)} SIR_r^{(N-j+1)}\left(0; (\theta, t_{j+1:N} - 1_{j+1:N}\theta), (t_j + p_j - \theta, p_{j+1:N})\right)$$

$$+ \sum_{j=1}^{N-1} \sum_{\theta = t_j + p_j + 1}^{t_{j+1} - 1} \sum_{r \in E} \frac{q_{kr}(v + \theta)}{\overline{H}_k(v)} SIR_r^{(N-j)}\left(0; t_{j+1:N} - 1_{j+1:N}\theta, p_{j+1:N}\right) \right], \tag{4}$$

where $1_{\{k \in U\}}$ is the indicator function of the event $\{k \in U\}$, and $R_{ij}^b(v; t)$ is the reliability with the final backward defined by

$$R_{ij}^b(v; t) := \mathbb{P}(Z_s \in U, \text{ for all } s \in \{0, \ldots, t - v\}, Z_t = j, B_t = v \mid Z_0 = i, T_{N(0)} = 0). \tag{5}$$

Remark 1. *Equation (3) is a recurrent-type formula. The unknown function $SIR_k^{(N)}(v; \underline{t}, \underline{p})$ depends on itself but is evaluated at different values of the variables. First, we observe that the value of the backward recurrence time process is v on the left-hand side of the formula and is reset to zero on the right-hand side. This is due to the Markovian property of the semi-Markov process at transition times. The vector $\underline{t}$ of the initial points of the N intervals is shifted according to the time θ of the first transition when occurring before the initial time t_1 of the first interval. This transition occurs with probability $\frac{q_{kr}(v + \theta)}{\overline{H}_k(v)}$ in the state r. The summations over all possible states $r \in E$ and times $\theta \in \{1, 2, \ldots, t_1\}$ consider all the possible cases.*

The function $g_k^{(N)}(v; \underline{t}, \underline{p})$ considers the remaining possibilities, which consist of transitions inside one of the intervals $[t_j, t_j + p_j]$ or between two intervals, i.e., $[t_j + p_j + 1, t_{j+1} - 1]$ or exceeding the considered time horizon $t_N + p_N$. Then, a further recursion shows the dependence of $SIR_k^{(N)}$ on $SIR_k^{(M)}$ for every positive integer $M < N$.

If $v = 0$, Equation (3) collapses into

$$SIR_k^{(N)}(\underline{t}, \underline{p}) = g_k^{(N)}(\underline{t}, \underline{p}) + \sum_{r \in E} \sum_{\theta = 1}^{t_1} q_{kr}(\theta) SIR_r^{(N)}(\underline{t} - \theta 1_{1:N}, \underline{p}), \tag{6}$$

where we have set $g_k^{(N)}(\underline{t}, \underline{p}) := g_k^{(N)}(0; \underline{t}, \underline{p})$.

In [1], the asymptotic analysis of the sequential interval reliability $SIR_k^{(N)}(v; t_{1:N}, b_{1:N})$ was also studied, allowing the time point t_1 to go to infinity. As a result of the sequence t_i rising, we see that all these time points also diverge to infinity. The next result given in Theorem 1 answers this question.

Theorem 1 ([1]). *For an ergodic semi-Markov chain, under the previous notations,*

$$\lim_{t_1 \to \infty} SIR_k^{(N)}(v; \underline{t}, \underline{p}) = \lim_{t_1 \to \infty} SIR_k^{(N)}(\underline{t}, \underline{p}) = \frac{1}{\sum_{i \in E} \nu(i) m_i} \sum_{j \in U} \nu(j) \sum_{t_1 \geq 0} g_j^{(N)}(\underline{t}, \underline{p}), \tag{7}$$

where $(\nu(i))_{i \in E}$ represents the stationary distribution of the embedded Markov chain $(J_n)_{n \in \mathbb{N}}$, and m_i is the mean sojourn time in state $i \in E$, so it is the mean time of the distribution $(h_i(k))_{k \in \mathbb{N}}, i \in E$. The form of the function $g_j^{(N)}(\underline{t}, \underline{p})$ is given in Equation (4).

3. A Mixed Transient–Asymptotic Result for the Sequential Interval Reliability

It is possible to generalize and combine Proposition 1 with Theorem 1, allowing t_h, $h \geq 2$ to go to infinity at any time. Hence, the main question we want to answer is about the value of

$$\lim_{t_h \to \infty} SIR_k^{(N)}(\underline{t}, \underline{p}).$$

We observe that a positive answer to this problem will provide a mixed result because the part of the probability $SIR^{(N)}(\underline{t}, \underline{p})$ corresponding to the time intervals $\{[t_i, t_i + p_i]\}_{i=1,\ldots,h-1}$ is devoted to the description of the behavior of the system in the transient case, while the part containing the remaining intervals $\{[t_i, t_i + p_i]\}_{i=h,\ldots,N}$, having considered $t_h \to \infty$, is responsible for the description of the asymptotic behavior of the system.

First, we present some definitions related to matrix convolution products and some new operations necessary for the proof of our main result. Let $\mathcal{M}_E$ be the set of real matrices of dimension E, and let $\mathcal{M}_E(\mathbb{N})$ be the set of matrix-valued functions defined on $\mathbb{N}$, with values in $\mathcal{M}_E$. A matrix of functions $\mathbf{A} \in \mathcal{M}_E(\mathbb{N})$ can be interpreted in two different ways. First, if we fix any time $t \in \mathbb{N}$, we obtain $\mathbf{A}(t) \in \mathcal{M}_E$, which is a real-valued matrix. The second possibility consists of fixing a couple of states $i, j \in E$, and then, the element $A_{ij}(\cdot)$ is a function of the time. A special element of $\mathcal{M}_E(\mathbb{N})$ is the null matrix $\mathbf{0} := (\mathbf{0}(t); t \in \mathbb{N})$, with $\mathbf{0}(t) := \mathbf{0}$ for any $t \in \mathbb{N}$.

Definition 1. *Let $\mathbf{A}, \mathbf{B} \in \mathcal{M}_E(\mathbb{N})$, where their matrix convolution product $\mathbf{A} * \mathbf{B}$ is defined as the matrix-valued function $\mathbf{C} \in \mathcal{M}_E(\mathbb{N})$ such that*

$$C_{ij}(t) := \sum_{r \in E} \sum_{s=0}^{t} A_{ir}(t-s) B_{rj}(s), \quad i, j \in E, \quad t \in \mathbb{N}. \tag{8}$$

In matrix form,

$$\mathbf{C}(t) := \sum_{s=0}^{t} \mathbf{A}(t-s) \mathbf{B}(s), \quad k \in \mathbb{N}.$$

Define a matrix-valued function $\boldsymbol{\delta I} = (d_{ij}(t); i, j \in E) \in \mathcal{M}_E(\mathbb{N})$ such that $d_{ii}(0) = 1$, $\forall i \in E$, and $d_{ij}(t) = 0$ otherwise. It is simple to realize that $\boldsymbol{\delta I}$ is the identity element for the matrix convolution product. Hence, iterating the convolution operation, we can easily obtain the n-fold convolution for any element $\mathbf{A} \in \mathcal{M}_E(\mathbb{N})$. Indeed, $\mathbf{A}^{(n)}$ can be obtained recursively as follows:

$$\mathbf{A}^{(0)} := \boldsymbol{\delta I}, \quad \mathbf{A}^{(1)} := \mathbf{A} \quad \text{and} \quad \mathbf{A}^{(n)} := \mathbf{A} * \mathbf{A}^{(n-1)}, \quad n \geq 2.$$

Second, let us introduce two sets of functions that will be useful in our proof. So, for $h, N \in \mathbb{N}$, first, let us define

$$\mathcal{A}(h; N) := \left\{ f : D_{\mathcal{A}(h;N)} \to \mathbb{R} \right\}, \tag{9}$$

where the domain $D_{\mathcal{A}}(h; N)$ is defined by

$$
\begin{aligned}
D_{\mathcal{A}}(h; N) \quad := \quad & \big\{ (\underline{x}, \underline{z}, \underline{w}) \in \mathbb{N}^{h-1} \times \mathbb{N}^{N-h} \times \mathbb{N}^{N} \mid \underline{x} = (x_1, \ldots, x_{h-1}), x_i \leq x_{i+1}, \\
& \forall i = 1, \ldots, h-2; \underline{z} = (z_{h+1}, \ldots, z_N), z_i \geq 0, \forall i = h+1, \ldots, N-1; \\
& \underline{w} = (w_1, \ldots, w_N), 0 \leq w_i \leq x_{i+1} - x_i, \forall i = 1, \ldots, h-1, \\
& 0 \leq w_i \leq z_{i+1}, \forall i = h, \ldots, N, \\
& \text{having set } z_{N+1} := \infty \big\}.
\end{aligned}
$$

Similarly, for $h, N \in \mathbb{N}$, let us define a set of one-variable functions indexed by three vectors of parameters

$$\mathcal{B}_{\underline{s},\underline{l},\underline{p}}(h;N) := \left\{ \widetilde{f} : \mathbb{N} \to \mathbb{R} \mid y = \widetilde{f}(t_1; \underline{s}, \underline{l}, \underline{p}) \right\}, \text{ such that}$$

$$t_1 \in \mathbb{N},$$

$$\underline{s} \in \mathbb{N}^{h-1}, \underline{s} = (s_1, \ldots, s_{h-1}), 0 \le s_i \, \forall i = 1, \ldots, h-1,$$

$$\underline{l} \in \mathbb{N}^{N-h}, \underline{l} = (l_{h+1}, \ldots, l_N), 0 \le l_i, \, \forall i = h+1, \ldots, N,$$ (10)

$$\underline{p} \in \mathbb{N}^N, 0 \le p_i \le s_i, \, \forall i = 1, \ldots, h-1$$

$$0 \le p_i \le l_{i+1}, \, \forall i = h, \ldots, N, \text{ having set } l_{N+1} := \infty.$$

Let us consider an operator acting on these two sets, $\Phi : \mathcal{A}(h;N) \to \mathcal{B}_{\underline{s},\underline{l},\underline{p}}(h;N)$ such that $\forall y = f(\underline{x}, \underline{z}, \underline{w}) \in \mathcal{A}(h;N)$, we have that

$$\Phi(f(\underline{x}, \underline{z}, \underline{w})) := \widetilde{f}(t_1; \underline{s}, \underline{l}, \underline{p}),$$ (11)

where

$$t_1 = x_1; \; s_i = x_{i+1} - x_i =: \Delta x_i \, \forall i = 1, \ldots, h-1,$$

$$l_i = z_i \, \forall i = h+1, \ldots, N,$$

$$p_i = w_i \, \forall i = h+1, \ldots, N,$$

and

$$\widetilde{f}(x_1; \Delta \underline{x}, \underline{z}, \underline{w}) = f(\underline{x}, \underline{z}, \underline{w}).$$

The operator Φ maps any function $f(\underline{x}, \underline{z}, \underline{w}) \in \mathcal{A}(h;N)$ to an element of the set of functions $\mathcal{B}_{\underline{s},\underline{l},\underline{p}}(h;N)$ in such a way as to preserve the values of the images. Hence, to a vectorial function, we associate a scalar function, namely of the variable t_1, with the parameter set $\Theta = \{s_{1:h-1}, l_{h+1:N}, w_{1:N}\}$.

It is simple to realize that operator (11) is bijective and satisfies the following two properties:

- the image of a product is equal to the product of the images:
  $\forall f(\underline{x}^1, \underline{z}^1, \underline{w}^1), h(\underline{x}^2, \underline{z}^2, \underline{w}^2) \in \mathcal{A}(h;N)$, it results that

$$\Phi(f(\underline{x}^1, \underline{z}^1, \underline{w}^1) \cdot h(\underline{x}^2, \underline{z}^2, \underline{w}^2)) = \Phi(f(\underline{x}^1, \underline{z}^1, \underline{w}^1)) \cdot \Phi(h(\underline{x}^2, \underline{z}^2, \underline{w}^2)),$$

This property is sometimes referred to as Cauchy's multiplicative functional equation.
- The image of a sum is equal to the sum of the images:
  $\forall f(\underline{x}^1, \underline{z}^1, \underline{w}^1), h(\underline{x}^2, \underline{z}^2, \underline{w}^2) \in \mathcal{A}(h;N)$, it results that

$$\Phi(f(\underline{x}^1, \underline{z}^1, \underline{w}^1) + h(\underline{x}^2, \underline{z}^2, \underline{w}^2)) = \Phi(f(\underline{x}^1, \underline{z}^1, \underline{w}^1)) + \Phi(h(\underline{x}^2, \underline{z}^2, \underline{w}^2))$$

This property is sometimes referred to as Cauchy's additive functional equation.

The last point before presenting our main result about the mixed transient–asymptotic behavior of the SIR function is to introduce a new matrix convolution product, which is important for our framework, and to see the relationship between the classical matrix convolution product and the one defined in [1].

Definition 2. *Let* $\mathbf{A} \in \mathcal{M}_E(\mathbb{N})$ *be a matrix-valued function, and let* $\mathbf{b} = (b_1, \ldots, b_s)^T$ *be a vector-valued function such that every component* $b_r \in \mathcal{A}(h;N), r \in E$. *Let* $\underline{t} := (t_i)_{i=1,\ldots,N}$ *and* $\underline{p} := (p_i)_{i=1,\ldots,N}, N \in \mathbb{N}^*$ *be two time sequences such that* $\{[t_i, t_i + p_i]\}_{i=1,\ldots,N}$ *is a sequence of nonoverlapping real intervals, and set* $l_{h+1:N} = (l_{h+1}, \ldots, l_N)$ *with* $l_i := t_i - t_{i-1}$, $\forall i = h+1, \ldots, N$ *and* $x_{1:h-1} = (x_1, \ldots, x_{h-1})$ *with* $x_i := t_i, \, \forall i = 1, \ldots, h-1$. *The matrix convolution product* $*_h$ *is defined by*

$$(\mathbf{A} *_h \mathbf{b})_k(x_{1:h-1}, l_{h+1:N}, p_{1:N}) := \sum_{r \in E} \sum_{\theta=1}^{t_1} A_{kr}(\theta) b_r(x_{1:h-1} - \theta \mathbf{1}_{1:h-1}, l_{h+1:N}, p_{1:N}),$$

or, in matrix form,

$$(\mathbf{A} *_h \mathbf{b})(x_{1:h-1}, l_{h+1:N}, p_{1:N}) := \sum_{\theta=1}^{t_1} \mathbf{A}(\theta) \mathbf{b}(x_{1:h-1} - \theta \mathbf{1}_{1:h-1}, l_{h+1:N}, p_{1:N}).$$

The next result presents a relationship between the new matrix convolution product introduced above and the classical one defined in (8).

Proposition 2. *Let* $\mathbf{q} \in \mathcal{M}_E(\mathbb{N})$ *be a semi-Markov kernel, and let* $\mathbf{f} = (f_1, \ldots, f_s)^T$ *be a vector-valued function such that every component* $f_r \in \mathcal{A}(h; N), r \in E$. *Then,* $\forall (\underline{x}, \underline{z}, \underline{w}) \in \mathbb{N}^{h-1} \times \mathbb{N}^{N-h} \times \mathbb{N}^N$, *it results that*

$$\Phi\big((\mathbf{q} *_h \mathbf{f})_k(\underline{x}, \underline{z}, \underline{w})\big) = \big(\mathbf{q} * \tilde{\mathbf{f}}\big)_k(x_1; s_{1:h-1}, l_{h+1:N}, \underline{w}),$$

where $s_i = x_{i+1} - x_i, \forall i = 1, \ldots, h-1$, *and* $l_{i+1} = x_{i+1} - x_i, \forall i = h, \ldots, N-1$.

Proof. By the definitions of the operator Φ and of the $*_h$ convolution product, we have

$$\Phi\big((\mathbf{q} *_h \mathbf{f})_k(\underline{x}, \underline{z}, \underline{w})\big) = \Phi\Big(\sum_{r \in E} \sum_{\theta=1}^{x_1} q_{kr}(\theta) \cdot f_r(x_{1:h-1} - \theta \mathbf{1}_{1:h-1}, l_{h+1:N}, w_{1:N})\Big)$$

$$= \sum_{r \in E} \sum_{\theta=1}^{t_1} \Phi\big(q_{kr}(\theta) \cdot f_r(x_{1:h-1} - \theta \mathbf{1}_{1:h-1}, l_{h+1:N}, w_{1:N})\big), \tag{12}$$

where the last equality is due to the additivity property of the Φ-operator. Next, we observe that any function $i : \{1, 2, \ldots, x_1\} \to \mathbb{R}$ can be seen as an element of the set of function $\mathcal{A}(h; N)$ by simply observing that $\forall \theta \in \{1, 2, \ldots, x_1\}$, we can write $i(\theta) = i(\theta, \underline{0}, \tilde{\underline{0}})$, where $\underline{\theta} = (\theta, \ldots, \theta) \in \mathbb{N}^{h-1}, \underline{0} = (0, \ldots, 0) \in \mathbb{N}^{N-h}$, and $\tilde{\underline{0}} = (0, \ldots, 0) \in \mathbb{N}^N$. Thus, in also using the second property of the Φ-operator (multiplicative property), Equation (12) becomes

$$= \sum_{r \in E} \sum_{\theta=1}^{t_1} \Phi\big(q_{kr}(\underline{\theta}, \underline{0}, \tilde{\underline{0}}) \cdot f_r(x_{1:h-1} - \theta \mathbf{1}_{1:h-1}, l_{h+1:N}, w_{1:N})\big)$$

$$= \sum_{r \in E} \sum_{\theta=1}^{t_1} \Phi\big(q_{kr}(\underline{\theta}, \underline{0}, \tilde{\underline{0}})\big) \cdot \Phi\big(f_r(x_{1:h-1} - \theta \mathbf{1}_{1:h-1}, l_{h+1:N}, w_{1:N})\big)$$

$$= \sum_{r \in E} \sum_{\theta=1}^{t_1} q_{kr}(\theta) \cdot \tilde{f}_r(x_1 - \theta; s_{1:h-1}, l_{h+1:N}, w_{1:N})), \tag{13}$$

where $s_i = x_{i+1} - \theta - (x_i - \theta) = x_{i+1} - x_i$.

The proof is complete once we observe that Equation (13) coincides with the ordinary convolution product $\big(q * \tilde{f}\big)_k(x_1; s_{1:h-1}, l_{h+1:N}, w_{1:N})$. $\square$

Now, we are in the position of formulating the main result of this study, but first, we introduce a notation that we will also use in the proof of our main result.

Assume for the moment that the $\lim_{t_h \to \infty} SIR_k^{(N)}(\underline{t}, \underline{p})$ exists, and denote it by the following notation:

$$\lim_{t_h \to \infty} SIR_k^{(N)}(\underline{t}, \underline{p}) = \begin{cases} \mathcal{L}_k^{(N)}(t_{1:h-1}, l_{h+1:N}, p_{1:N}) & \text{if } 2 \leq h \leq N, \\ \mathcal{L}^{(N)}(l_{2:N}, p_{1:N}) & \text{if } h = 1 \wedge N > 1 \\ \mathcal{L}^{(1)}(p) & \text{if } h = 1 \wedge N = 1. \end{cases}$$

Theorem 2. *Assume that the semi-Markov chain is ergodic. Let $\underline{t} := (t_i)_{i=1,\ldots,N}$ and $\underline{p} := (p_i)_{i=1,\ldots,N}$, $N \in \mathbb{N}^*$ be two time sequences such that $\{[t_i, t_i + p_i]\}_{i=1,\ldots,N}$ is a sequence of nonoverlapping real intervals. Then, $\forall 1 \leq h \leq N$, it results that*

$$\mathcal{L}_k^{(N)}(t_{1:h-1}, l_{h+1:N}, p_{1:N}) := \lim_{t_h \to \infty} SIR_k^{(N)}(\underline{t}, \underline{p})$$

$$= \sum_{r \in E} \sum_{\theta=1}^{t_1} \psi_{kr}(\theta) \mathcal{G}_r^{(N)}(t_{1:h-1} - \theta \mathbf{1}_{1:h-1}, l_{h+1:N}, p_{1:N}), \tag{14}$$

where the function $\mathcal{G}_r^{(N)}(t_{1:h-1} - \theta \mathbf{1}_{1:h-1}, l_{h+1:N}, p_{1:N})$ is fully determined in Equation (31), and the convention $x_{1:0} = \varnothing$ is used.

Proof of Theorem 2. First, we observe that the theorem is true for $h = 1$, which was proved in Theorem 1 in [1]. Indeed, the authors proved that

$$\lim_{t_1 \to \infty} SIR^{(N)}(\underline{t}, \underline{p}) = \lim_{t_1 \to \infty} \mu\psi * \widetilde{g}(t_1; l_{2:N}, p_{1:N}) =: \mathcal{L}^{(N)}(l_{2:N}, p_{1:N})$$

$$= \sum_{i \in E} \mu_i \sum_{j \in U} \frac{1}{\mu_{jj}} \sum_{t_1 \geq 0} g_j^{(N)}(\underline{t}, \underline{p}) = \frac{1}{\sum_{i \in E} \nu(i) m_i} \sum_{j \in U} \nu(j) \sum_{t_1 \geq 0} g_j^{(N)}(\underline{t}, \underline{p}),$$

where μ_{jj} is the mean recurrence time to state j for the semi-Markov chain.

Now, we assume that the statement in the theorem is true $\forall n \leq N - 1$, and we proceed to verify its overall validity using the mathematical induction principle.

Based on Equation (3), and taking the limit for t_h going to infinity, we have

$$\lim_{t_h \to +\infty} SIR_k^{(N)}(\underline{t}, \underline{p}) = \lim_{t_h \to +\infty} g_k^{(N)}(\underline{t}, \underline{p}) + \sum_{r \in E} \sum_{\theta=1}^{t_1} q_{kr}(\theta) \lim_{t_h \to +\infty} SIR_r^{(N)}(\underline{t} - \theta \mathbf{1}_{1:N}, \underline{p}). \tag{15}$$

Now, we begin to evaluate $\lim_{t_h \to +\infty} g_k^{(N)}(\underline{t}, \underline{p})$.

According to Equation (4), we have

$$\lim_{t_h \to +\infty} g_k^{(N)}(\underline{t}, \underline{p}) := \lim_{t_h \to +\infty} \left\{ \mathbf{1}_{\{k \in U\}} \left[\overline{H}_k(t_N + p_N) \right. \right.$$

$$+ \sum_{\theta=t_1+1}^{t_1+p_1} \sum_{r \in E} \sum_{m \in U} \sum_{v'=0}^{t_1+p_1-\theta} q_{kr}(\theta) R_{rm}^b(v'; t_1 + p_1 - \theta) SIR_m^{(N-1)}(v'; t_{2:N} - \mathbf{1}_{2:N} \cdot (t_1 + p_1), p_{2:N})$$

$$+ \sum_{j=2}^{h-1} \sum_{\theta=t_j}^{t_j+p_j} \sum_{r \in E} q_{kr}(\theta) SIR_r^{(N-j+1)}\left(0; ((\theta, t_{j+1:N}) - \mathbf{1}_{j:N} \cdot \theta), (t_j + p_j - \theta, p_{j+1:N})\right)$$

$$+ \sum_{j=h}^{N} \sum_{\theta=t_j}^{t_j+p_j} \sum_{r \in E} q_{kr}(\theta) SIR_r^{(N-j+1)}\left(0; ((\theta, t_{j+1:N}) - \mathbf{1}_{j:N} \cdot \theta), (t_j + p_j - \theta, p_{j+1:N})\right) \Big]$$

$$+ \sum_{j=1}^{h} \sum_{\theta=t_j+p_j+1}^{t_{j+1}-1} \sum_{r \in E} q_{kr}(\theta) SIR_r^{(N-j)}(0, t_{j+1:N} - \mathbf{1}_{j+1:N} \cdot \theta, p_{j+1:N})$$

$$+ \sum_{j=h}^{N-1} \sum_{\theta=t_j+p_j+1}^{t_{j+1}-1} \sum_{r \in E} q_{kr}(\theta) SIR_r^{(N-j)}(0, t_{j+1:N} - \mathbf{1}_{j+1:N} \cdot \theta, p_{j+1:N}) \Bigg\}, \tag{16}$$

The next step is the computation of the previous limits for each of its components that we are going to enumerate for the sake of clarity:

$$(1) \quad \lim_{t_h \to +\infty} \overline{H}_k(t_N + p_N) = \lim_{t_h \to +\infty} \overline{H}_k\left(t_h + \sum_{s=h+1}^{N} l_s + p_N\right) = \overline{H}_k(\infty) = 0. \tag{17}$$

$$(2) \quad \lim_{t_h \to +\infty} \sum_{\theta=t_1+1}^{t_1+p_1} \sum_{r \in E} \sum_{m \in U} \sum_{v'=0}^{t_1+p_1-\theta} q_{kr}(\theta) R_{rm}^b(v'; t_1 + p_1 - \theta)$$

$$\cdot SIR_m^{(N-1)}(v'; t_{2:N} - \mathbf{1}_{2:N} \cdot (t_1 + p_1), p_{2:N}) \tag{18}$$

$$= \sum_{\theta=t_1+1}^{t_1+p_1} \sum_{r \in E} \sum_{m \in U} \sum_{v'=0}^{t_1+p_1-\theta} q_{kr}(\theta) R_{rm}^b(v'; t_1 + p_1 - \theta)$$

$$\cdot \lim_{t_h \to +\infty} SIR_m^{(N-1)}(t_{2:N} - \mathbf{1}_{2:N} \cdot (t_1 + p_1), p_{2:N}), \tag{19}$$

Here, in the last equality, we used the fact that $\forall v' \in \mathbb{N}$ for an ergodic semi-Markov process,

$$\lim_{t_h \to +\infty} SIR_m^{(N-1)}(v'; t_{2:N} - \mathbf{1}_{2:N} \cdot (t_1 + p_1), p_{2:N}) = \lim_{t_h \to +\infty} SIR_m^{(N-1)}(t_{2:N} - \mathbf{1}_{2:N} \cdot (t_1 + p_1), p_{2:N}).$$

Moreover, using the inductive hypothesis, we obtain

$$\lim_{t_h \to +\infty} SIR_m^{(N-1)}(t_{2:N} - \mathbf{1}_{2:N} \cdot (t_1 + p_1), p_{2:N})$$

$$= \lim_{t_{h-1}^* \to +\infty} SIR_m^{(N-1)}(t_{1:N-1}^*, p_{1:N-1}^*) = \mathcal{L}_m^{(N-1)}(t_{1:h-2}^*, l_{h:N-1}^*, p_{1:N-1}^*), \tag{20}$$

where

$$t_j^* = t_{j+1} - (t_1 + p_1) \quad \forall j = 1, \dots, N-1,$$

$$l_j^* = t_j^* - t_{j-1}^* \quad \forall j = 2, \dots, N-1,$$

$$p_j^* = p_{j+1} \quad \forall j = 1, \dots, N-1.$$

A substitution of (20) in (18) produces

$$= \sum_{\theta=t_1+1}^{t_1+p_1} \sum_{r \in E} \sum_{m \in U} \sum_{v'=0}^{t_1+p_1-\theta} q_{kr}(\theta) R_{rm}^b(v'; t_1 + p_1 - \theta) \mathcal{L}_m^{(N-1)}(t_{1:h-2}^*, l_{h:N-1}^*, p_{1:N-1}^*)$$

$$= \sum_{\theta=t_1+1}^{t_1+p_1} \sum_{r \in E} \sum_{m \in U} q_{kr}(\theta) R_{rm}^b(t_1 + p_1 - \theta) \mathcal{L}_m^{(N-1)}(t_{1:h-2}^*, l_{h:N-1}^*, p_{1:N-1}^*),$$

having observed that $\sum_{v'=0}^{t_1+p_1-\theta} R_{rm}^b(v'; t_1 + p_1 - \theta) = R_{rm}^b(t_1 + p_1 - \theta)$.

$$(3) \quad \lim_{t_h \to +\infty} \sum_{j=2}^{h-1} \sum_{\theta=t_j}^{t_j+p_j} \sum_{r \in E} q_{kr}(\theta) SIR_r^{(N-j+1)}((\theta, t_{j+1:N}) - \mathbf{1}_{j:N} \cdot \theta), (t_j + p_j - \theta, p_{j+1:N}))$$

$$= \sum_{j=2}^{h-1} \sum_{\theta=t_j}^{t_j+p_j} \sum_{r \in E} q_{kr}(\theta) \lim_{t_h \to +\infty} SIR_r^{(N-j+1)}((\theta, t_{j+1:N}) - \mathbf{1}_{j:N} \cdot \theta), (t_j + p_j - \theta, p_{j+1:N})). \tag{21}$$

Now, through a change in variables

$$\dot{t}_s = \begin{cases} 0 & \text{if } s = 1, \\ t_{j+s-1} - \theta & \text{for } s = 2, \dots, N-j+1, \end{cases}$$

$$\dot{p}_s = \begin{cases} t_j + p_j - \theta & \text{if } s = 1, \\ p_{j+s-1} & \text{for } s = 2, \dots, N-j+1, \end{cases}$$

we obtain that

$$\lim_{t_h \to +\infty} SIR_r^{(N-j+1)}\left((\theta, t_{j+1:N}) - \mathbf{1}_{j:N} \cdot \theta\right), (t_j + p_j - \theta, p_{j+1:N})$$

$$= \lim_{t_{h-j+1} \to +\infty} SIR_r^{(N-j+1)}(\dot{t}_{1:N-j+1}, \dot{p}_{1:N-j+1}) = \mathcal{L}_r^{(N-j+1)}(\dot{t}_{1:h-j}, \dot{t}_{h-j+2:N-j+1}, \dot{p}_{1:N-j+1}), \tag{22}$$

where the last equality is due to the inductive hypothesis. A substitution of (22) in (21) produces

$$\sum_{j=2}^{h-1} \sum_{\theta=t_j}^{t_j+p_j} \sum_{r \in E} q_{kr}(\theta) \mathcal{L}_r^{(N-j+1)}(\dot{t}_{1:h-j}, \dot{t}_{h-j+2:N-j+1}, \dot{p}_{1:N-j+1}). \tag{23}$$

$$(4) \quad \sum_{j=h}^{N} \sum_{\theta=t_j}^{t_j+p_j} \sum_{r \in E} q_{kr}(\theta) SIR_r^{(N-j)}(0, t_{j+1:N} - \mathbf{1}_{j+1:N} \cdot \theta, p_{j+1:N})$$

$$\le \sum_{j=h}^{N} \sum_{\theta=t_j}^{t_j+p_j} \sum_{r \in E} q_{kr}(\theta) = \sum_{j=h}^{N} (H_k(t_j + p_j) - H_k(t_j)). \tag{24}$$

Now, observe that if $t_h \to +\infty$, all times t_s with $s \ge h$ go to infinity as well; hence, we have

$$\lim_{t_h \to +\infty} \sum_{j=h}^{N} \sum_{\theta=t_j}^{t_j+p_j} \sum_{r \in E} q_{kr}(\theta) SIR_r^{(N-j)}(0, t_{j+1:N} - \mathbf{1}_{j+1:N} \cdot \theta, p_{j+1:N})$$

$$\le \lim_{t_h \to +\infty} \sum_{j=h}^{N} (H_k(t_j + p_j) - H_k(t_j)) = \sum_{j=h}^{N} \lim_{t_j \to +\infty} (H_k(t_j + p_j) - H_k(t_j)) = 0. \tag{25}$$

$$(5) \quad \lim_{t_h \to +\infty} \sum_{j=1}^{h-1} \sum_{\theta=t_j+p_j+1}^{t_{j+1}-1} \sum_{r \in E} q_{kr}(\theta) SIR_r^{(N-j)}(t_{j+1:N} - \mathbf{1}_{j+1:N} \cdot \theta, p_{j+1:N})$$

$$\lim_{t_h \to +\infty} \left(\sum_{j=1}^{h-2} \sum_{\theta=t_j+p_j+1}^{t_{j+1}-1} \sum_{r \in E} q_{kr}(\theta) SIR_r^{(N-j)}(t_{j+1:N} - \mathbf{1}_{j+1:N} \cdot \theta, p_{j+1:N}) \right.$$

$$\left. + \sum_{\theta=t_{h-1}+p_{h-1}+1}^{t_h-1} \sum_{r \in E} q_{kr}(\theta) SIR_r^{(N-h+1)}(t_{h:N} - \mathbf{1}_{h:N} \cdot \theta, p_{h:N}) \right). \tag{26}$$

Let us consider the above:

$$\lim_{t_h \to +\infty} \sum_{\theta=t_{h-1}+p_{h-1}+1}^{t_h-1} \sum_{r \in E} q_{kr}(\theta) SIR_r^{(N-h+1)}(t_{h:N} - \mathbf{1}_{h:N} \cdot \theta, p_{h:N}).$$

To this end, we observe that

$$\lim_{t_h \to +\infty} SIR_r^{(N-h+1)}(t_{h:N} - \mathbf{1}_{h:N} \cdot \theta, p_{h:N})$$

$$= \lim_{\tilde{t}_1 \to +\infty} SIR_r^{(N-h+1)}(\tilde{t}_{1:N-h+1}, \tilde{p}_{1:N-h+1}) = \mathcal{L}^{(N-h+1)}(\tilde{t}_{2:N-h+1}, \tilde{p}_{1:N-h+1}), \tag{27}$$

where the last equality is a consequence of the inductive hypothesis and

$$\tilde{t}_j = t_{h-1+j} - \theta \ \forall j = 1, \ldots, N-h+1,$$

$$\tilde{p}_j = p_{h-1+j} \ \forall j = 1, \ldots, N-h+1,$$

$$\tilde{l}_s = \begin{cases} \tilde{t}_s - \tilde{t}_{s-1} & \text{for } s = 2, \ldots, N-h+1, \\ 0 & \text{for } s = 1, \end{cases}$$

Moreover, we observe that

$$\sum_{\theta=t_{h-1}+p_{h-1}+1}^{t_h-1} \sum_{r \in E} q_{kr}(\theta) = \sum_{\theta=t_{h-1}+p_{h-1}+1}^{t_h-1} h_k(\theta) = \overline{H}_k(t_{h-1} + p_{h-1}),$$

Then, from the key renewal theorem (see, e.g., [4]), we obtain that

$$\lim_{t_h \to +\infty} \sum_{\theta=t_{h-1}+p_{h-1}+1}^{t_h-1} \sum_{r \in E} q_{kr}(\theta) SIR_r^{(N-h+1)}(t_{h:N} - \mathbf{1}_{h:N} \cdot \theta, p_{h:N})$$

$$= \overline{H}_k(t_{h-1} + p_{h-1}) \mathcal{L}^{(N-h+1)}(\tilde{l}_{2:N-h+1}, \tilde{p}_{1:N-h+1}).$$

It remains to compute

$$\lim_{t_h \to +\infty} \sum_{j=1}^{h-2} \sum_{\theta=t_j+p_j+1}^{t_{j+1}-1} \sum_{r \in E} q_{kr}(\theta) SIR_r^{(N-j)}(t_{j+1:N} - \mathbf{1}_{j+1:N} \cdot \theta, p_{j+1:N})$$

$$= \sum_{j=1}^{h-2} \sum_{\theta=t_j+p_j+1}^{t_{j+1}-1} \sum_{r \in E} q_{kr}(\theta) \lim_{t_h \to +\infty} SIR_r^{(N-j)}(t_{j+1:N} - \mathbf{1}_{j+1:N} \cdot \theta, p_{j+1:N}).$$

Now, set

$$\hat{t}_s = t_{j+s} - \theta \ \forall s = 1, \ldots, N-j,$$

$$\hat{p}_s = p_{j+s} - \theta \ \forall s = 1, \ldots, N-j,$$

and observe that

$$\lim_{t_h \to +\infty} SIR_r^{(N-j)}(t_{j+1:N} - \mathbf{1}_{j+1:N} \cdot \theta, p_{j+1:N})$$

$$= \lim_{\hat{t}_{h-j} \to +\infty} SIR_r^{(N-j)}(\hat{t}_{1:N-j}, \hat{p}_{1:N-j}) = \mathcal{L}_r^{(N-j)}(\hat{t}_{1:h-j-1}, \hat{l}_{h-j+1:N-j}, \hat{p}_{1:N-j}),$$

where in the last equality, we used the inductive hypothesis. Therefore, we may conclude that limit (26) is equal to

$$\overline{H}_k(t_{h-1} + p_{h-1}) \mathcal{L}^{(N-h+1)}(\tilde{l}_{2:N-h+1}, \tilde{p}_{1:N-h+1})$$

$$+ \sum_{j=1}^{h-2} \sum_{\theta=t_j+p_j+1}^{t_{j+1}-1} \sum_{r \in E} q_{kr}(\theta) \mathcal{L}_r^{(N-j)}(\hat{t}_{1:h-j-1}, \hat{l}_{h-j+1:N-j}, \hat{p}_{1:N-j}). \tag{28}$$

It remains to compute

$$(6) \quad \lim_{t_h \to +\infty} \sum_{j=h}^{N-1} \sum_{\theta=t_j+p_j+1}^{t_{j+1}-1} \sum_{r \in E} q_{kr}(\theta) SIR_r^{(N-j)}(t_{j+1:N} - \mathbf{1}_{j+1:N} \cdot \theta, p_{j+1:N}).$$

Clearly, this limit is upper bounded by

$$\lim_{t_h \to +\infty} \sum_{j=h}^{N-1} \sum_{\theta=t_j+p_j+1}^{t_{j+1}-1} \sum_{r \in E} q_{kr}(\theta). \tag{29}$$

Now, set $a = \theta - (t_j + p_j + 1)$ to obtain the equality of (29) with

$$\lim_{t_h \to +\infty} \sum_{j=h}^{N-1} \sum_{a=0}^{(t_{j+1}-1)-(t_j+p_j+1)} \sum_{r \in E} q_{kr}(a + t_j + p_j + 1) = \sum_{j=h}^{N-1} \sum_{a=0}^{t_{j+1}-t_j-p_j-2} \sum_{r \in E} q_{kr}(\infty) = 0 \quad (30)$$

The limits from (1) to (6) computed before provide the following result:

$$\lim_{t_h \to +\infty} g_k^{(N)}(\underline{t}, \underline{p}) = 1_{k \in U} \Bigg\{ \sum_{\theta=t_1+1}^{t_1+p_1} \sum_{r \in E} \sum_{m \in U} q_{kr}(\theta) R_{rm}^b(t_1 + p_1 - \theta) \mathcal{L}_m^{(N-1)}(t_{1:h-2}^*, l_{h:N-1}^*, p_{1:N-1}^*)$$

$$+ \sum_{j=2}^{h-1} \sum_{\theta=t_j}^{t_j+p_j} \sum_{r \in E} q_{kr}(\theta) \mathcal{L}_r^{(N-j+1)}(\dot{t}_{1:h-j}, \dot{l}_{h-j+2:N-j+1}, \dot{p}_{1:N-j+1}) \Bigg\}$$

$$+ \overline{H}_k(t_{h-1} + p_{h-1}) \mathcal{L}^{(N-h+1)}(\tilde{l}_{2:N-h+1}, \tilde{p}_{1:N-h+1})$$

$$+ \sum_{j=1}^{h-2} \sum_{\theta=t_j+p_j+1}^{t_{j+1}-1} \sum_{r \in E} q_{kr}(\theta) \mathcal{L}_r^{(N-j)}(\hat{t}_{1:h-j-1}, \hat{l}_{h-j+1:N-j}, \hat{p}_{1:N-j}) =: \mathcal{G}_k^{(N)}(t_{1:h-1}, l_{h+1:N}, p_{1:N}). \quad (31)$$

According to previous computations, Equation (15) can be expressed as

$$\mathcal{L}_k^{(N)}(t_{1:h-1}, l_{h+1:N}, p_{1:N}) = \mathcal{G}_k^{(N)}(t_{1:h-1}, l_{h+1:N}, p_{1:N})$$

$$\sum_{r \in E} \sum_{\theta=1}^{t_1} q_{kr}(\theta) \mathcal{L}_r^{(N)}(t_{1:h-1} - \mathbf{1}_{1:h-1} \cdot \theta, l_{h+1:N}, p_{1:N}). \quad (32)$$

By applying the Φ-operator, we transform Equation (32) into an ordinary Markov renewal equation:

$$\tilde{\mathcal{L}}_k^{(N)}(t_1; s_{1:h-1}, l_{h+1:N}, p_{1:N}) = \tilde{\mathcal{G}}_k^{(N)}(t_1; s_{1:h-1}, l_{h+1:N}, p_{1:N})$$

$$\sum_{r \in E} \sum_{\theta=1}^{t_1} q_{kr}(\theta) \tilde{\mathcal{L}}_r^{(N)}(t_1 - \theta; s_{1:h-1}, l_{h+1:N}, p_{1:N}). \quad (33)$$

Equation (33) can be expressed in a more compact form denoted by $\Theta = \{s_{1:h-1}, l_{h+1:N}, p_{1:N}\}$, the set of parameters of the transformed function, and using a matrix-form representation:

$$\tilde{\mathcal{L}}_k^{(N)}(t_1; \Theta) = \tilde{\mathcal{G}}_k^{(N)}(t_1; \Theta) + (\mathbf{q} * \tilde{\mathcal{L}}^{(N)})_k(t_1; \Theta).$$

The solution of this Markov renewal equation is well known (cf. [4]), and it is given by

$$\tilde{\mathcal{L}}^{(N)}(t_1; \Theta) = (\boldsymbol{\psi} * \tilde{\mathcal{G}}^{(N)})(t_1; \Theta),$$

or element-wise,

$$\tilde{\mathcal{L}}_k^{(N)}(t_1; \Theta) = \sum_{r \in E} \sum_{\theta=1}^{t_1} \psi_{kr}(\theta) \tilde{\mathcal{G}}_r^{(N)}(t_1 - \theta; \Theta)$$

$$= \sum_{r \in E} \sum_{\theta=1}^{t_1} \psi_{kr}(\theta) \mathcal{G}_r^{(N)}(t_{1:h-1} - \mathbf{1}_{1:h-1} \cdot \theta, l_{h+1:N}, p_{1:N})$$

$$= \mathcal{L}_k^{(N)}(t_{1:h-1}, l_{h+1:N}, p_{1:N}) = \lim_{t_h \to +\infty} SIR_k^{(N)}(\underline{t}, \underline{p}),$$

which concludes the proof. $\square$

Remark 2. *Observe that the function $\mathcal{G}^{(N)}$ depends on the $\mathcal{L}^{(\diamond)}$ at the number of intervals $\diamond < N$; hence, it should be evaluated recursively in the number of intervals.*

Example 1. *As an application of Theorem 2, we can obtain an explicit representation of the mixed transient–asymptotic result of the sequential interval reliability for $N = 2$:*

$$\lim_{t_2 \to \infty} SIR_k^{(2)}(t_{1:2}, p_{1:2})$$

$$= \sum_{r \in E} \sum_{\theta=1}^{t_1} \psi_{kr}(\theta) \cdot \left[1_{\{r \in U\}} \sum_{x=t_1-\theta+1}^{t_1-\theta+p_1} \sum_{v \in E} q_{rv}(x) R_v(t_1 - \theta + p_1 - x) + \overline{H}_r(t_1 + p_1) \right] \cdot IR(\infty, p_2),$$

where $IR(\infty, p_2)$ is the asymptotic value of the interval reliability function, which can be recovered from Theorem 1 once we observe that if $t_i + p_i = t_{i+1} - 1$ for all $i = 1, \ldots, N - 1$ and $v = 0$, then

$$SIR_k^{(N)}(0; \underline{t}, \underline{p}) = IR(t_1, t_N + p_N - t_1).$$

4. A Numerical Example

In this section, we will present a numerical example considering three semi-Markov models that govern three different repairable systems. The difference among these systems is located in the difficulty of repairing them through a repairability index (transition probability). In order to make it clear, we fully present the setting of the experiment. The state space of the systems consists of three possible states, $E = \{1, 2, 3\}$, where the operational states are the first two, $U = \{1, 2\}$, and the non-working state is the last one, $D = \{3\}$. The first state is considered to be a fully operational state, while the second one is thought to be barely operational.

The transitions of the repairable semi-Markov models are shown in the following flowgraph, Figure 1.

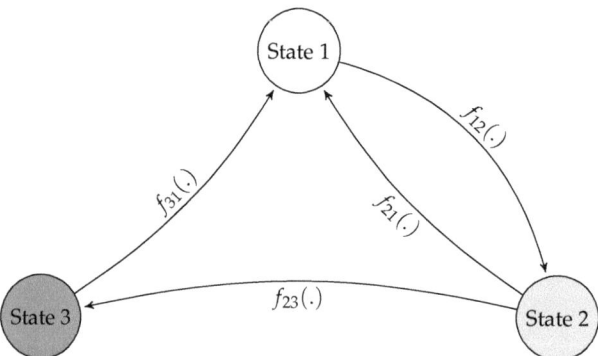

Figure 1. Semi-Markov model.

The transition matrix P of the embedded Markov chain J_n along with the initial distribution μ are given by

$$P = \begin{pmatrix} 0 & 1 & 0 \\ p_{21} & 0 & 1 - p_{21} \\ 1 & 0 & 0 \end{pmatrix}, \ \mu = (1, 0, 0).$$

Now, let X_{ij} be the conditional sojourn time of the SMCs, and Z is state i, given that the next state is j ($j \neq i$). The conditional sojourn times are given as follows:

$$X_{12} \sim \text{Geometric}(0.3)\,,$$
$$X_{21} \sim \text{discrete Weibull}(0.9, 1.1)\,,$$
$$X_{23} \sim \text{discrete Weibull}(0.4, 1.3)\,,$$
$$X_{31} \sim \text{discrete Weibull}(0.6, 1.8)\,.$$

The difficulty of repairing the system is located in the transition probability p_{21} of going from the barely operated state, 2, back to the fully operational state, 1. The three models are classified according to the probability p_{21} (repairability index) as easily repairable for $p_{21} = 0.9$ (Model 1), repairable for $p_{21} = 0.5$ (Model 2), and difficult to repair for $p_{21} = 0.1$ (Model 3).

Figures 2–4 illustrate each model's conditional sequential interval reliability for two time-varying intervals as the time t_2 is moving forward through time. This is the probability that the system will be operational in the time intervals $[1, 2]$ and $[k + 2, k + 3]$ for $k \in \{15, \ldots, 30\}$. It can be easily identified that, as time t_2 becomes large enough, each system's sequential interval reliability tends to converge to the asymptotic analogous $\lim_{t_2 \to \infty} SIR_k^{(N)}(v; \underline{t}, \underline{p})$. On the other hand, Figures 5–7 depict each model's conditional sequential interval reliability for two nonoverlapping, contiguous time intervals as the time t_1 is moving forward through time. Also, in this case, the sequential interval reliability function exhibits a tendency to converge asymptotically, as expected from our theoretical result.

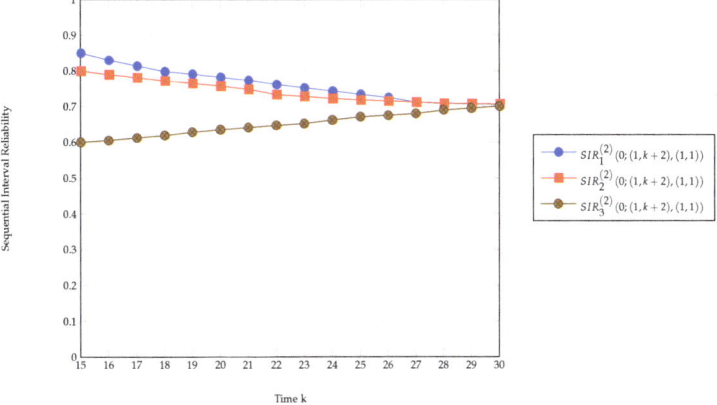

Figure 2. Model 1. Sequential interval reliability plot with two separate time-varying intervals.

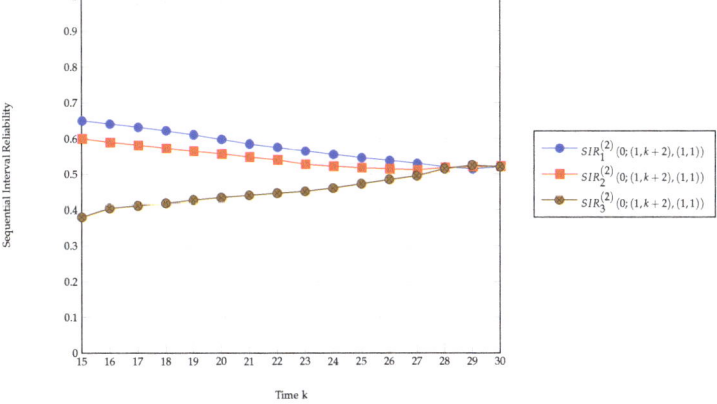

Figure 3. Model 2. Sequential interval reliability plot with two separate time-varying intervals.

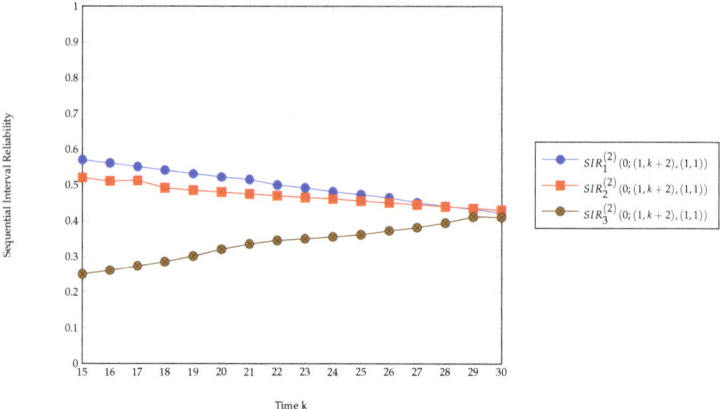

Figure 4. Model 3. Sequential interval reliability plot with two separate time-varying intervals.

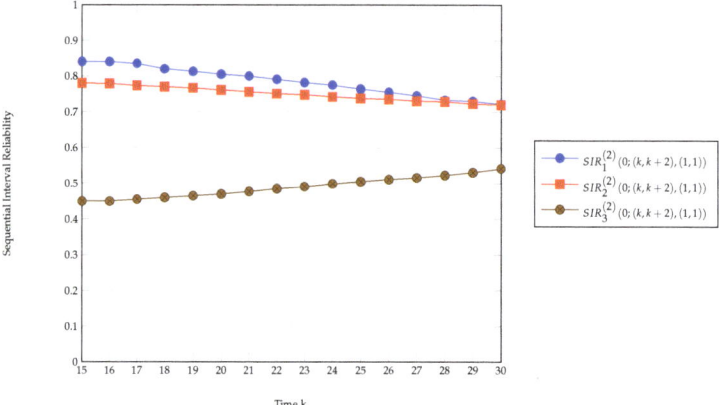

Figure 5. Model 1. Sequential interval reliability plot with two nonoverlapping, contiguous time intervals.

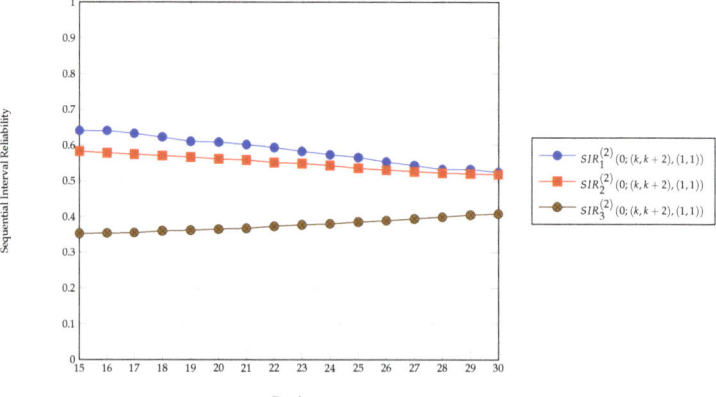

Figure 6. Model 2. Sequential interval reliability plot with two nonoverlapping, contiguous time intervals.

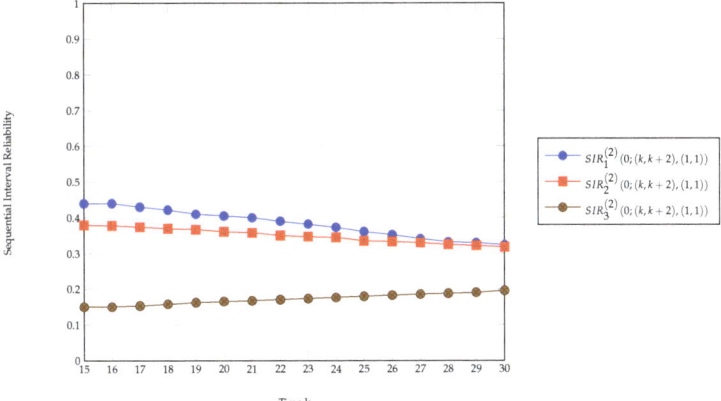

Figure 7. Model 3. Sequential interval reliability plot with two nonoverlapping, contiguous time intervals.

5. Conclusions

This paper presents a new result for the sequential interval reliability (SIR), an indicator recently introduced in the literature. The new result provides a mixed transient and asymptotic description for the system, merging these two aspects into a unique measure. The achievement of this result needs dedicated mathematical development, which includes several innovative aspects. Indeed, this paper introduces a specific operator acting between two sets of functions, a new matrix convolution product, and the use of classical results in probability theory such as the key renewal theorem and Markov renewal equation techniques in the generalized framework. Future work may include an evaluation of this indicator and related transient–asymptotic results in different applied problems involving the use of real data.

Author Contributions: Conceptualization, G.D.; methodology, G.D.; software, T.G.; validation, G.D. and T.G.; formal analysis, G.D.; investigation, G.D. and T.G.; resources, G.D. and T.G.; data curation, T.G.; writing—original draft preparation, G.D. and T.G.; writing—review and editing, G.D. and T.G.; visualization, T.G.; supervision, G.D.; project administration, G.D.; funding acquisition, G.D. All authors have read and agreed to the published version of the manuscript.

Funding: Guglielmo D'Amico acknowledges the financial support from the program MUR PRIN 2022 n. 2022ETEHRM "Stochastic models and techniques for the management of wind farms and power systems". Guglielmo D'Amico is a member of the Gruppo Nazionale Calcolo Scientifico-Istituto Nazionale di Alta Matematica (GNCS-INdAM).

Data Availability Statement: Data are contained within the article.

Acknowledgments: The authors would like to express their gratitude to Panagiotis- Christos Vassiliou and Andreas C. Georgiou for the opportunity to submit the present manuscript to the Special Issue *Stochastic Processes and Their Applications: In Honor of Prof. Sally McClean* for possible publication.

Conflicts of Interest: The authors declare no conflicts of interest.

References

1. Barbu, V.S.; D'Amico, G.; Gkelsinis, T. Sequential interval reliability for discrete-time homogeneous semi-Markov repairable systems. *Mathematics* **2021**, *9*, 1997. [CrossRef]
2. Limnios, N.; Oprisan, G. *Semi-Markov Processes and Reliability*; Springer Science & Business Media: Berlin/Heidelberg, Germany, 2001.
3. Janssen, J.; Manca, R. *Applied Semi-Markov Processes*; Springer Science & Business Media: Berlin/Heidelberg, Germany, 2006.
4. Barbu, V.S.; Limnios, N. *Semi-Markov Chains and Hidden Semi-Markov Models toward Applications: Their Use in Reliability and DNA Analysis*; Springer Science & Business Media: Berlin/Heidelberg, Germany, 2009; Volume 191.
5. Vassiliou, P.C.; Georgiou, A.C. Markov and Semi-Markov Chains, processes, systems, and emerging related fields, 2021.
6. Limnios, N. Dependability analysis of semi-Markov systems. *Reliab. Eng. Syst. Saf.* **1997**, *55*, 203–207. [CrossRef]

7. Ouhbi, B.; Limnios, N. Nonparametric reliability estimation of semi-Markov processes. *J. Stat. Plan. Inference* **2003**, *109*, 155–165. [CrossRef]
8. D'Amico, G. Age-usage semi-Markov models. *Appl. Math. Model.* **2011**, *35*, 4354–4366. [CrossRef]
9. Votsi, I.; Gayraud, G.; Barbu, V.; Limnios, N. Hypotheses testing and posterior concentration rates for semi-Markov processes. *Stat. Inference Stoch. Process.* **2021**, *24*, 707–732. [CrossRef]
10. D'Amico, G.; Petroni, F. ROCOF of higher order for semi-Markov processes. *Appl. Math. Comput.* **2023**, *441*, 127719. [CrossRef]
11. das Chagas Moura, M.; Droguett, E.L. Mathematical formulation and numerical treatment based on transition frequency densities and quadrature methods for non-homogeneous semi-Markov processes. *Reliab. Eng. Syst. Saf.* **2009**, *94*, 342–349. [CrossRef]
12. Blasi, A.; Janssen, J.; Manca, R. Numerical treatment of homogeneous and non-homogeneous semi-Markov reliability models. *Commun. Stat. Theory Methods* **2004**, *33*, 697–714. [CrossRef]
13. Corradi, G.; Janssen, J.; Manca, R. Numerical treatment of homogeneous semi-Markov processes in transient case—A straightforward approach. *Methodol. Comput. Appl. Probab.* **2004**, *6*, 233–246. [CrossRef]
14. Wu, B.; Maya, B.I.G.; Limnios, N. Using semi-Markov chains to solve semi-Markov processes. *Methodol. Comput. Appl. Probab.* **2021**, *23*, 1419–1431. [CrossRef]
15. Barbu, V.; Boussemart, M.; Limnios, N. Discrete-time semi-Markov model for reliability and survival analysis. *Commun. Stat.-Theory Methods* **2004**, *33*, 2833–2868. [CrossRef]
16. Trevezas, S.; Limnios, N. Exact MLE and asymptotic properties for nonparametric semi-Markov models. *J. Nonparametric Stat.* **2011**, *23*, 719–739. [CrossRef]
17. D'Amico, G. Single-use reliability computation of a semi-Markovian system. *Appl. Math.* **2014**, *59*, 571–588. [CrossRef]
18. Barbu, V.S.; Berard, C.; Cellier, D.; Sautreuil, M.; Vergne, N. Sequential interval reliability for discrete-time homogeneous semi-Markov repairable systems. *R J.* **2018**, *10*, 226–247. [CrossRef]
19. Csenki, A. On the interval reliability of systems modelled by finite semi-Markov processes. *Microelectron. Reliab.* **1994**, *34*, 1319–1335. [CrossRef]
20. Csenki, A. An integral equation approach to the interval reliability of systems modelled by finite semi-Markov processes. *Reliab. Eng. Syst. Saf.* **1995**, *47*, 37–45. [CrossRef]
21. Georgiadis, S.; Limnios, N. Interval reliability for semi-Markov systems in discrete time. *J. Soc. Fr. Stat.* **2014**, *155*, 152–166.
22. Georgiadis, S.; Limnios, N. Nonparametric estimation of interval reliability for discrete-time semi-Markov systems. *J. Stat. Theory Pract.* **2016**, *10*, 20–39. [CrossRef]
23. D'Amico, G.; Manca, R.; Petroni, F.; Selvamuthu, D. On the computation of some interval reliability indicators for semi-Markov systems. *Mathematics* **2021**, *9*, 575. [CrossRef]
24. D'Amico, G.; Janssen, J.; Manca, R. Initial and final backward and forward discrete time non-homogeneous semi-Markov credit risk models. *Methodol. Comput. Appl. Probab.* **2010**, *12*, 215–225. [CrossRef]
25. De Dominicis, R.; Manca, R. An algorithmic approach to non-homogeneous semi-Markov processes. *Commun. Stat.-Simul. Comput.* **1984**, *13*, 823–838. [CrossRef]
26. Vassiliou, P.C.; Papadopoulou, A. Non-homogeneous semi-Markov systems and maintainability of the state sizes. *J. Appl. Probab.* **1992**, *29*, 519–534. [CrossRef]
27. Vasileiou, A.; Vassiliou, P.C. An inhomogeneous semi-Markov model for the term structure of credit risk spreads. *Adv. Appl. Probab.* **2006**, *38*, 171–198. [CrossRef]
28. D'Amico, G.; Janssen, J.; Manca, R. Downward migration credit risk problem: A non-homogeneous backward semi-Markov reliability approach. *J. Oper. Res. Soc.* **2016**, *67*, 393–401. [CrossRef]
29. Vassiliou, P.C. Non-homogeneous semi-Markov and Markov renewal processes and change of measure in credit risk. *Mathematics* **2020**, *9*, 55. [CrossRef]

Article

A Throughput Analysis Using a Non-Saturated Markov Chain Model for LTE-LAA and WLAN Coexistence

Mun-Suk Kim

Department of Computer Science and Engineering, Sejong University, Seoul 05006, Republic of Korea; msk@sejong.ac.kr

Abstract: To address the severe spectrum shortage in mobile networks, the 3rd Generation Partnership Project (3GPP) standardized Long Term Evolution (LTE)-License Assisted Access (LAA) technology. The LTE-LAA system ensures efficient coexistence with other existing unlicensed systems by incorporating listen-before-talk functionality and conducting random backoff operations similar to those in the IEEE 802.11 distributed coordination function. In this paper, we propose an analytical model to calculate the throughput of each system in a scenario where a single LTE-LAA system shares an unlicensed channel with multiple wireless local area network (WLAN) systems. The LTE-LAA system is utilized for supplementary downlink transmission from the LTE-LAA eNodeB (eNB) to LTE-LAA devices. Our proposed analytical model uses a Markov chain to represent the random backoff operations of the LTE-LAA eNB and WLAN nodes under non-saturated traffic conditions and to calculate the impact of the clear channel assessment (CCA) performed by the LTE-LAA eNB. Through numerical results, we demonstrate how the throughput of both the LTE-LAA and WLAN systems is determined by the contention window size and CCA threshold of the LTE-LAA eNB.

Keywords: license assisted access; coexistence; clear channel assessment; Markov chain

MSC: 60J10

Academic Editors: Panagiotis-Christos Vassiliou and Andreas C. Georgiou

Received: 6 November 2024
Revised: 19 December 2024
Accepted: 26 December 2024
Published: 27 December 2024

Citation: Kim, M.-S. A Throughput Analysis Using a Non-Saturated Markov Chain Model for LTE-LAA and WLAN Coexistence. *Mathematics* 2025, 13, 59. https://doi.org/10.3390/math13010059

1. Introduction

The rapid growth of mobile devices and the rise of diverse mobile applications have led to a severe spectrum shortage in mobile networks. To tackle this issue, the 3rd Generation Partnership Project (3GPP) has standardized Long Term Evolution (LTE)-License Assisted Access (LAA) technology, enabling the use of unlicensed spectrum bands to support downlink transmission in mobile networks [1,2]. LTE-LAA incorporates listen-before-talk functionality to ensure efficient coexistence with other existing unlicensed systems, especially widely deployed wireless local area networks (WLANs). LTE-LAA with the listen-before-talk feature was established as a global standard in 3GPP Release 13 to facilitate coexistence in the unlicensed band [3].

Recently, numerous studies have been conducted to ensure reasonable coexistence between LTE and WLAN systems in unlicensed bands [4–14]. Specifically, several studies have evaluated the performance of LTE-LAA systems employing listen-before-talk and random backoff mechanisms, similar to the IEEE 802.11 distributed coordination function, for accessing unlicensed channels [11–14]. The studies [11,12] presented simulation results on the throughput of LTE-LAA and WLAN systems under varying congestion conditions, while the study [13] provided experimental results on interference between LTE-LAA and

WLAN systems. The study [14] proposed an analytical model to evaluate the throughput of each system under saturated conditions, where both LTE-LAA and WLAN systems consistently have data to transmit.

In this paper, we propose an analytical model to calculate the throughput for each system in a scenario where a single LTE-LAA system, dedicated to downlink transmission, shares an unlicensed channel with multiple WLAN systems. Unlike prior studies on the performance analysis of LTE-LAA and WLAN systems, our study employs a Markov chain approach to model the random backoff operations of LTE-LAA eNodeB (eNB) and WLAN nodes under non-saturated traffic conditions. The Markov chain approach is limited by the need to define LTE-LAA eNB and WLAN node transmissions in discrete timeslots. Nevertheless, it enables a clear and detailed analysis of all sequential random backoff operations in the distributed coordination function of LTE-LAA and WLAN. In addition, we analyze the throughput of LTE-LAA and WLAN systems by integrating the impact of the clear channel assessment (CCA) threshold, which represents the sensitivity level required to detect ongoing transmissions, with Markov chain modeling of random backoff operations. Through numerical results, we demonstrate that the CCA threshold and contention window size of the LTE-LAA eNB play a crucial role in balancing the performance between LTE-LAA and WLAN systems. With a larger contention window size set at the LTE-LAA eNB, the LTE-LAA eNB experienced a longer backoff period, allowing WLAN nodes greater opportunities for channel access. As the CCA threshold set at the LTE-LAA eNB decreased, the LTE-LAA eNB became more sensitive to concurrent WLAN transmissions, which reduced its opportunities for channel access.

The remainder of this paper is organized as follows. Our proposed analytical model is detailed in Section 2. Section 3 discusses the numerical results. Finally, Section 4 concludes this paper.

2. Analysis of LTE-LAA and WLAN System Throughputs

We used a Markov chain model to analyze the throughput of LTE-LAA and WLAN systems in a scenario where a single LTE-LAA system shares the unlicensed spectrum with multiple WLAN basic service sets. Figure 1 shows an LTE-LAA eNB located at the center, with multiple LTE-LAA devices distributed within the coverage area of the LTE-LAA cell, which supports only downlink transmissions from the LTE-LAA eNB to LTE-LAA devices. We define the CCA region as the area where WLAN transmissions are detectable by the LTE-LAA eNB, with R_{cca} representing its radius. Additionally, we define an interfering region, where WLAN transmissions can interfere with LTE-LAA devices but remain undetectable by the LTE-LAA eNB; R_I denotes the distance from the LTE-LAA eNB to the outer boundary of this interfering region.

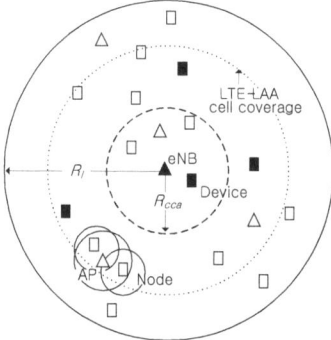

Figure 1. An example scenario where LTE-LAA and WLAN systems coexist.

2.1. Random Backoff Operations in LTE-LAA eNB

LTE-LAA eNB competes with multiple WLAN nodes for channel access by utilizing channel sensing and backoff mechanisms similar to those employed in WLAN systems, as shown in Figure 2.

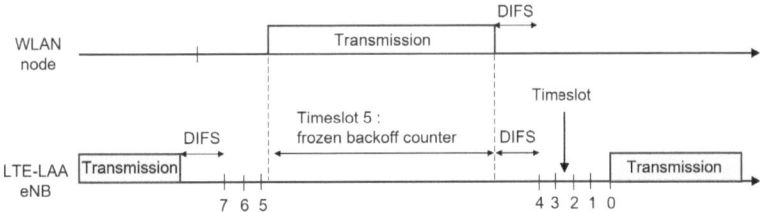

Figure 2. Example of the random backoff operations of LTE-LAA eNB.

The LTE-LAA eNB, when handling a new packet, first listens to the target channel to measure the energy level over a duration equal to the distributed inter-frame space (DIFS). If the measured energy level is below the predefined CCA threshold, the LTE-LAA eNB initiates transmission. Otherwise, if the channel is detected as busy, the LTE-LAA eNB continues monitoring until the channel is idle for a DIFS duration. Once the channel is deemed idle, the LTE-LAA eNB generates a random backoff time before transmitting to reduce the probability of collisions with packets transmitted by WLAN nodes. Furthermore, to prevent channel capture, the LTE-LAA eNB must wait for a random backoff interval between two consecutive new packet transmissions, even if the channel is sensed as idle during a DIFS duration. The LTE-LAA eNB operates on a discrete-time backoff scale, where the time following an idle DIFS is divided into fixed-length timeslots. The LTE-LAA eNB is allowed to transmit only at the beginning of each timeslot. For each packet transmission, the LTE-LAA eNB randomly selects a number from the range $[0, W - 1]$, where W is referred to as the contention window. The LTE-LAA eNB then counts down the corresponding number of idle timeslots before initiating transmission. The backoff counter decreases as long as the channel is sensed as idle. If a transmission is detected on the channel, the counter is "frozen" and resumes only after the channel has been idle for a DIFS duration. The LTE-LAA eNB initiates transmission when the backoff counter reaches zero.

Figure 2 illustrates an example scenario of the random backoff operations of an LTE-LAA eNB. The LTE-LAA eNB and a WLAN node share the same unlicensed channel. After completing a packet transmission, the LTE-LAA eNB waits for a DIFS duration and selects a backoff counter value of 7 before transmitting the next packet. In this scenario, we assume that the WLAN node transmits a packet in the middle of the timeslot corresponding to a backoff counter value of 5 for the LTE-LAA eNB. As a result of the channel being sensed as busy, the backoff timer is frozen at 5 and resumes decrementing only when the channel is sensed as idle for a DIFS duration. As illustrated in Figure 2, the backoff counter of the LTE-LAA eNB remains frozen during the transmission of a WLAN node, which can cause the time interval between two consecutive timeslot beginnings to be significantly longer than the timeslot size, σ. Specifically, this interval equals the timeslot size, σ, when no other WLAN nodes are transmitting, but it corresponds to the time between two consecutive backoff counter decrements when transmissions from other WLAN nodes are present.

2.2. Markov Chain Model for Random Backoff Operations in LTE-LAA eNB

In this section, referring to [15], we use a Markov chain model to study the random backoff operations of the LTE-LAA eNB, as described in Section 2.1, under non-saturated conditions where packets are not always present in the queue of the LTE-LAA eNB. We

then derive the stationary probability τ, representing the probability of the LTE-LAA eNB transmitting a packet during a randomly selected timeslot.

The LTE-LAA eNB shares an unlicensed channel with multiple WLAN nodes. To avoid collisions with packets transmitted by other WLAN nodes, the LTE-LAA eNB generates a random backoff counter before transmitting. Let $c(t)$ denote the stochastic process representing the backoff counter for the LTE-LAA eNB. A discrete, integer-based time scale is adopted, where t and $t+1$ represent the beginning of two consecutive timeslots. The backoff counter of the LTE-LAA eNB decreases at the beginning of each timeslot.

Assuming non-saturated conditions where the LTE-LAA eNB does not always have packets waiting in its queue for transmission, our Markov chain model, referring to [15], includes two types of states: the post-backoff stage and the backoff stage. The post-backoff stage represents the state where the LTE-LAA eNB has no packets in its queue awaiting transmission, while the backoff stage corresponds to the state where a packet is waiting to be transmitted. Let $s(t)$ be the stochastic process indicating whether the LTE-LAA eNB is in the post-backoff stage or the backoff stage at time t. Specifically, if $s(t) = -1$, it indicates that the LTE-LAA eNB is in the post-backoff stage at time t, and if $s(t) = 0$, it indicates that the LTE-LAA eNB is in the backoff stage at time t.

The bidimensional process $\{s(t), c(t)\}$ can be represented using a discrete-time Markov chain, as illustrated in Figure 3. The stochastic process $s(t)$, representing the post-backoff stage or the backoff stage, takes values of -1 or 0, while the stochastic process $c(t)$, representing the backoff counter, ranges from 0 to $W-1$. Thus, the state space, consisting of a finite set of states, can be expressed as follows:

$$\mathcal{S} = \{(-1,0), \cdots, (-1,k_2), \cdots, (-1,W-1), (0,0), \cdots, (0,k_2), \cdots, (0,W-1)\} \quad (1)$$

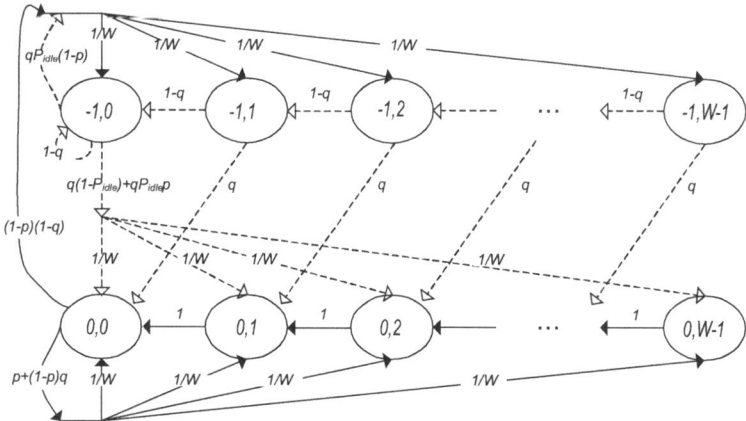

Figure 3. Markov chain model for random backoff operations in LTE-LAA eNB.

Let $P[k_1', k_2'|k_1, k_2]$ denote the probability of transitioning from state (k_1, k_2) to state (k_1', k_2'). In our Markov chain model, since the transition probabilities are independent of the time at which the transition occurs, the transition probability $P[k_1', k_2'|k_1, k_2]$ can be expressed as follows:

$$P[k_1', k_2'|k_1, k_2] = P[s(t+1) = k_1', c(t+1) = k_2'|s(t) = k_1, c(t) = k_2], \quad \text{for any } t = 0, 1, \cdots \quad (2)$$

In the backoff states, while the medium is sensed as idle, the state $(0, k_2)$ is decremented by 1 to $(0, k_2 - 1)$ in each timeslot. However, in the post-backoff states, if there is at least one packet awaiting transmission at the start of a timeslot, the state $(-1, k_2)$ transitions to

the backoff state $(0, k_2 - 1)$. Otherwise, similar to the backoff states, the state $(-1, k_2)$ is decremented by 1 to $(-1, k_2 - 1)$. Thus, we have for $1 \leq k_2 \leq W - 1$

$$
\begin{aligned}
P[0, k_2 - 1 \mid 0, k_2] &= p_1 = 1 \\
P[-1, k_2 - 1 \mid -1, k_2] &= p_2 = 1 - q \\
P[0, k_2 - 1 \mid -1, k_2] &= p_3 = q
\end{aligned}
\tag{3}
$$

where q is the probability that there is at least one packet awaiting transmission at the start of each backoff counter decrement.

In the backoff state $(0, 0)$, the LTE-LAA eNB transmits; following the transmission, it returns to the post-backoff state with a new k_2, i.e., state $(-1, k_2)$, selected from $[0, W - 1]$, provided no collision occurs and there are no packets awaiting transmission in the queue. Thus, this transition probability is

$$
P[-1, k_2 \mid 0, 0] = p_4 = \frac{(1 - p)(1 - q)}{W}
\tag{4}
$$

where p is the probability of a collision occurring between transmissions from the LTE-LAA eNB and WLAN nodes within the CCA range. However, if a collision occurs, or if the transmission is successful and there is at least one packet remaining in the buffer, the LTE-LAA eNB reenters the backoff state with a new k_2 chosen within the range $[0, W - 1]$.

$$
P[0, k_2 \mid 0, 0] = p_5 = \frac{p}{W} + \frac{(1 - p)q}{W}
\tag{5}
$$

In addition, we consider the state $(-1, 0)$, where post-backoff is complete but there are no packets awaiting transmission in the buffer. Suppose a packet arrives in the buffer while in state $(-1, 0)$. If the medium is sensed as busy during an additional timeslot, the LTE-LAA eNB enters a new backoff state $(0, k_2)$; otherwise, it transmits immediately. If a collision occurs following the transmission, the LTE-LAA eNB again enters a backoff state $(0, k_2)$. Therefore, the probability of this transition is

$$
P[0, k_2 \mid -1, 0] = p_6 = \frac{q(1 - P_{idle})}{W} + \frac{q P_{idle} p}{W}
\tag{6}
$$

where P_{idle} represents the probability that the medium is sensed as idle during a timeslot. If the transmission succeeds without a collision, the LTE-LAA eNB returns to the state $(-1, k_2)$, where k_2 is selected from $[0, W - 1]$. Thus, we have

$$
\begin{aligned}
P[-1, 0 \mid -1, 0] &= p_7 = 1 - q + \frac{q P_{idle}(1 - p)}{W} \\
P[-1, k_2 \mid -1, 0] &= p_8 = \frac{q P_{idle}(1 - p)}{W}, \quad \text{for } 1 \leq k_2 \leq W - 1
\end{aligned}
\tag{7}
$$

Let P denote the transition probability matrix of the Markov chain model illustrated in Figure 3. Then, using Equations (3)–(7), we can express the transition probability matrix P as shown in Figure 4.

Let $b(0, k_2)$ and $b(-1, k_2)$ denote the stationary probabilities of being in the states $(0, k_2)$ and $(-1, k_2)$, representing the backoff and post-backoff states, respectively. Then, these stationary probabilities can be expressed as follows:

$$
\begin{aligned}
b(0, k_2) &= \lim_{t \to \infty} P[s(t) = 0, c(t) = k_2], \\
b(-1, k_2) &= \lim_{t \to \infty} P[s(t) = -1, c(t) = k_2], \quad \text{for } 0 \leq k_2 \leq W - 1
\end{aligned}
\tag{8}
$$

Taking into account all stationary state probabilities, we derive the following normalization condition:

$$\sum_{k_2=0}^{W-1} b(-1,k_2) + \sum_{k_2=0}^{W-1} b(0,k_2) = 1 \tag{9}$$

Using Equations (3)–(7), we express all stationary state probabilities in terms of $b(-1,k_2)$. Then, by applying the normalization equation in Equation (9), we can further express $b(-1,k_2)$ in terms of p, P_{idle}, q, and W.

$$
\begin{array}{c|cccccccccc}
 & (-1,0) & & (-1,k_2) & & (-1,W-1) & (0,0) & & (0,k_2) & & (0,W-1) \\
\hline
(-1,0) & p_7 & \cdots & p_8 & \cdots & p_8 & p_6 & \cdots & p_6 & \cdots & p_6 \\
\vdots & \vdots & & \vdots & & \vdots & \vdots & & \vdots & & \vdots \\
(-1,k_2) & 0 & \cdots & p_2\ 0 & \cdots & 0 & 0 & \cdots & p_3\ 0 & \cdots & 0 \\
\vdots & \vdots & & \vdots & & \vdots & \vdots & & \vdots & & \vdots \\
(-1,W-1) & 0 & \cdots & 0 & \cdots & p_2\ 0 & 0 & \cdots & 0 & \cdots & p_3\ 0 \\
(0,0) & p_4 & \cdots & p_4 & \cdots & p_4 & p_5 & \cdots & p_5 & \cdots & p_5 \\
\vdots & \vdots & & \vdots & & \vdots & \vdots & & \vdots & & \vdots \\
(0,k_2) & 0 & \cdots & 0 & \cdots & 0 & 0 & \cdots & 1\ 0 & \cdots & 0 \\
\vdots & \vdots & & \vdots & & \vdots & \vdots & & \vdots & & \vdots \\
(0,W-1) & 0 & \cdots & 0 & \cdots & 0 & 0 & \cdots & 0 & \cdots & 1\ 0
\end{array}
$$

Figure 4. Transition probability matrix, P, of the Markov chain model for random backoff operations in LTE-LAA eNB.

A transition into the state $(-1, W-1)$ from the state $(-1,0)$ occurs as described in Equation (7). In addition, a transition into the state $(-1, W-1)$ from the state $(0,0)$ occurs as described in Equation (4). Thus, the stationary probability of the state $(-1, W-1)$ is given by

$$b(-1,W-1) = b(-1,0)\frac{q(1-p)P_{idle}}{W} + b(0,0)\frac{(1-p)(1-q)}{W} \tag{10}$$

Referring to Equation (3), for $1 \le k_2 \le W-2$, we can express $b(-1,k_2)$ as $b(-1,k_2) = (1-q)b(0,k_2+1)_e + b(-1,W-1)$, while for $k_2 = 0$, the relation $qb(-1,0) = (1-q)b(-1,1) + b(-1,W-1)$ holds. By straightforward recursion, this leads to $qb(-1,0) = b(-1,W-1)\cdot(1-(1-q)^W)/q$. Thus, using Equation (10), we have

$$\frac{b(-1,0)}{b(0,0)} = \frac{1-q}{q}\left(\frac{(1-p)(1-(1-q)^W)}{qW - P_{idle}(1-p)(1-(1-q)^W)}\right) \tag{11}$$

Using these equations, we determine the first sum in Equation (9),

$$\sum_{k_2=0}^{W-1} b(-1,k_2) = b(-1,0)\cdot\frac{qW}{1-(1-q)^W} \tag{12}$$

Referring to Equations (5) and (6), in the same manner as Equation (10), the stationary probability of the state $(W-1)$ is given by

$$b(0,W-1) = b(-1,0)\cdot\left(\frac{q(1-P_{idle})}{W} + \frac{qP_{idle}p}{W}\right) + b(0,0)\cdot\left(\frac{p}{W} + \frac{(1-p)q}{W}\right) \tag{13}$$

We can express $b(0,k_2)$ in terms of $b(0,W-1)$ and $b(-1,W-1)$ because $b(0,k_2) = b(0,k_2+1) + b(0,W-1) + qb(-1,k_2+1)$ for $0 \le k_2 \le W-2$. Thus, using Equations (10), (11), and (13), the second sum in Equation (9) is

$$\sum_{k_2=0}^{W-1} b(0, k_2) = b(-1, 0) \cdot \left[\frac{q^2 w - q + q(1-q)^W}{1 - (1-q)^W} + \frac{(1-q)^2\{1 - (1-q)^{W-2}\} - q(1-q)(W-2)}{1 - (1-q)^W} \right.$$

$$\left. + \frac{q^2(W-1)(W-2)}{2\{1 - (1-q)^W\}} + \frac{q(W+1)\{1 - P_{idle}(1-p)\}}{2} + \right. \tag{14}$$

$$\left. \frac{q(W+1)[qW - P_{idle}(1-p)\{1 - (1-q)^W\}]\{(1-p)q + p\}}{2(1-q)(1-p)\{1 - (1-q)^W\}} \right]$$

The LTE-LAA eNB attempts transmission in the following two cases: (i) when a packet arrives in the buffer and the medium is sensed as idle in the state $(-1, 0)$, and (ii) when the LTE-LAA eNB is in the state $(0, 0)$. Thus, the transmission probability is $\tau = q P_{idle} b(-1, 0) + b(0, 0)$. Using Equation (11), it can be expressed as follows:

$$\tau = b(-1, 0) \left(\frac{q^2 W - q^2 P_{idle}(1-p)(1 - (1-q)^W)}{(1-p)(1-q)(1 - (1-q)^W)} \right) \tag{15}$$

where τ can be expressed in terms of p, P_{idle}, q, and W from Equations (9), (12), and (14). Thus, given p, P_{idle}, q, and W, we can calculate the transmission probability of the LTE-LAA eNB using Equation (15). In Section 2.4, the transmission probability τ is used to calculate the throughputs of both LTE-LAA and WLAN systems.

2.3. Interference Measured at an LTE-LAA Device

It is assumed that the LTE-LAA eNB uses an omnidirectional antenna, as illustrated in Figure 5; its transmission power, denoted by P_e, is fixed in accordance with regulations for unlicensed band usage. Let $P_{rx,u}$ represent the received signal power at an LTE-LAA device u from the LTE-LAA eNB, and let P_I denote the cumulative interference from concurrent transmissions by multiple WLAN nodes. Then, $P_{rx,u} = K r_u^{-\eta} P_e$, where K is a constant and η is the propagation loss exponent [16]. The signal to interference plus noise ratio (SINR) at the LTE-LAA device u can then be obtained as follows:

$$\gamma = \frac{P_{rx,u}}{P_I + P_N} \tag{16}$$

where P_N is the noise.

To calculate P_I, we approximate the interference from discrete WLAN nodes as a continuous field with an equivalent node density [16,17]. In this model, the continuous field is defined by the density of interfering WLAN nodes, denoted as λ_n. Let I_b represent the set of WLAN basic service sets in the interfering region, and σ_i represent the channel utilization of each WLAN basic service set i. Then, the density is given by $\lambda_n = \sum_{i \in I_b} \sigma_i / A_I$, where A_I is the area of the interfering region, calculated as $A_I = \pi(R_I^2 - R_{cca}^2)$ [16].

We consider a scenario where an LTE-LAA device experiences interference from transmissions by WLAN nodes located in the interfering region, as shown in Figure 5a. Let ν represent the distance between the LTE-LAA device and an interfering WLAN node. Figure 5b depicts a polar coordinate system centered at the LTE-LAA eNB. Let y be the distance between the LTE-LAA eNB and an infinitesimal element of the interfering region, which is given by

$$y = \alpha(R_I - R_{cca}) + R_{cca} \tag{17}$$

where $\alpha \in [0,1]$ is a scaling factor. When $\alpha = 0$ and $\alpha = 1$, the infinitesimal element is located at the boundary of the CCA range and the outer boundary of the interfering region, respectively.

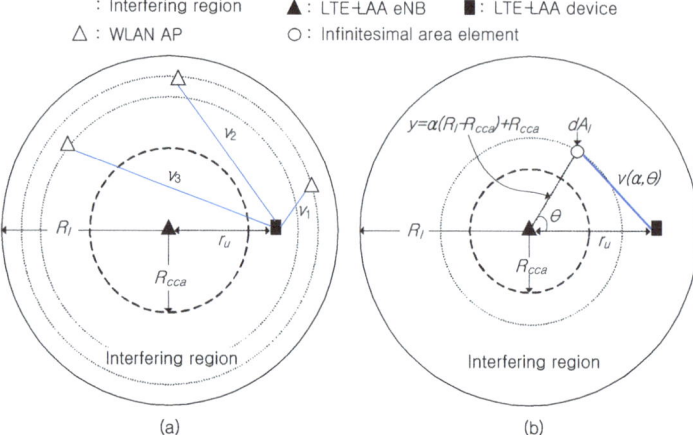

: Interfering region   ▲ : LTE-LAA eNB   ■ : LTE-LAA device
△ : WLAN AP   ○ : Infinitesimal area element

(a)   (b)

Figure 5. (a) A scenario where an LTE-LAA device is interfered by three WLAN APs and (b) estimation of distance between the LTE-LAA device and an infinitesimal element in a polar coordinate system (the shaded area is the interfering region).

Let θ denote a polar angle in the polar coordinate system; then, given a scaling factor α and a polar angle θ, the distance v can be obtained as follows:

$$v(\alpha, \theta) = \begin{cases} |y - r_u|, & \text{for } \theta = 0 \\ \sqrt{y^2 + r_u^2 - 2 \cdot y \cdot r_u \cdot \cos\theta}, & \text{for } 0 < \theta < \pi \\ y + r_u, & \text{for } \theta = \pi, \end{cases} \tag{18}$$

As shown in Figure 5b, an infinitesimal element of the interfering region can be given by

$$dA_I = y \cdot dy d\theta \tag{19}$$

From the equation above, the total number of interfering WLAN nodes contained in the infinitesimal element is given by $\lambda_n \cdot dA_I = \lambda_n \cdot y \cdot dy d\theta$; then, using Equation (18), their interference power is $P_n K v(\alpha, \theta)^{-\eta} \cdot \lambda_n \cdot dA_I$ where P_n is the transmit power of a WLAN node. Thus, in the interfering region, the average interference power measured at the LTE-LAA device is

$$P_I \simeq 2\lambda_n P_n K \cdot \int_0^\pi \int_0^1 v(\alpha, \theta)^{-\eta} \cdot (R_I - R_{cca}) d\alpha d\theta \tag{20}$$

Here, referring to Equation (17), we use the relation $dy = (R_I - R_{cca}) \cdot d\alpha$.

Thus, using Equations (16) and (20), we can calculate the average SINR for each LTE-LAA device, which will then be used to estimate the data rate of the LTE-LAA system in Section 2.4. We adopt the Shannon capacity as the LTE-LAA rate function, allowing us to estimate the LTE-LAA rate as follows [18,19]:

$$R_{laa}(\gamma) \approx \kappa_{bw} \cdot \kappa_c \cdot B \log_2(1 + \gamma/\kappa_{sinr}) \tag{21}$$

where B represents the bandwidth of a subchannel, and κ_{bw} is the system efficiency factor accounting for various system-level overheads. The parameters κ_c and κ_{sinr} together adjust for the SINR implementation efficiency of the modulation and coding schemes [19].

2.4. Throughput of LTE-LAA and WLAN Systems

In this subsection, we analyze the throughput of LTE-LAA and WLAN systems based on the random backoff operations of WLAN nodes and the random backoff operations of the LTE-LAA eNB, as explained in Section 2.2.

The WLAN nodes employ random backoff operations, similar to those of LTE-LAA eNB described in Section 2.1, to control access to the shared wireless channel. The study in [15] analyzed the random backoff operations of WLAN nodes using a non-saturated Markov chain, with post-backoff and backoff stages denoted as $(0, k_2)_e$ and (k_1, k_2), respectively. Figure 6 illustrates the first two stages of the Markov chain model proposed in [15]. The following notations are used in this subsection:

- k_1: Backoff stage number.
- k_2: Value of the backoff counter.
- W_0: Minimum contention window size.
- $b(0, 0)_e$: Stationary probabilities of being in the post-backoff states $(0, 0)_e$.
- p_l: Collision probability of WLAN node l.
- q_l: Probability of at least one packet awaiting transmission in the buffer of WLAN node l in a timeslot.
- P_{idle}^l: Probability that WLAN node l senses the medium as idle in a timeslot.
- τ_l: Probability that WLAN node l is attempting transmission in a timeslot.
- $L(T)$: Set of WLAN nodes located within the CCA ranges of the nodes in the set T, which does not include the nodes in the set T.
- L': Set of WLAN nodes located in the CCA range of the LTE-LAA eNB.

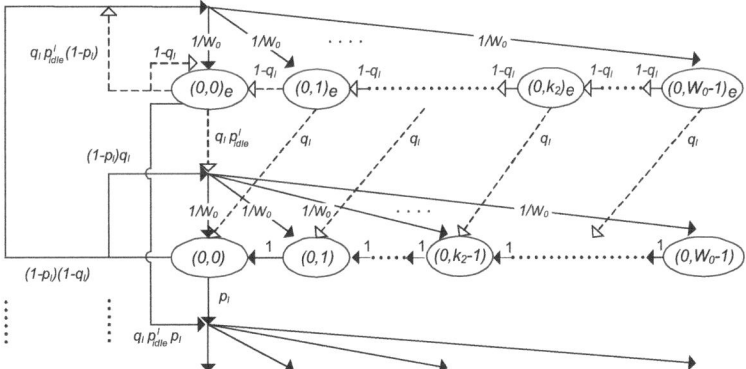

Figure 6. Markov chain model for the random backoff operations of a WLAN node.

Then, referring to [15], the transmission probability τ_l can be obtained as follows:

$$\tau_l = b(0, 0)_e \cdot \left(\frac{q_l^2 W_0}{(1 - p_l)(1 - q_l)(1 - (1 - q_l)^{W_0})} - \frac{q_l^2 P_{idle}^l}{1 - q_l} \right) \tag{22}$$

To simplify the analysis, we disregard the hidden-node problem; specifically, we assume that, for any transmitting and receiving pair of WLAN nodes, the receiver can only sense transmissions from WLAN nodes located within the CCA range of the transmitter. Thus,

considering the transmissions of both the LTE-LAA eNB and WLAN nodes within the CCA range of transmitter l, the collision probability p_l in Equation (22) is given by

$$1 - p_l = (1 - \tau) \cdot \prod_{l' \in L(\{l\})} (1 - \tau_{l'}) \tag{23}$$

where the transmission probability of the LTE-LAA eNB, τ, can be obtained from Equation (15). Using Equation (23), $P_{idle}^l = 1 - p_l$.

The probability that at least one WLAN node within the CCA range of the LTE-LAA eNB attempts transmission is given by

$$\tau_w = 1 - \prod_{l' \in L'} (1 - \tau_{l'}) \tag{24}$$

The channel usage state may be occupied due to either a successful transmission or a collision among transmissions; otherwise, the medium may be idle. Using Equations (15) and (24), the probability that the LTE-LAA eNB or at least one of WLAN nodes will attempt transmission is

$$P_{tr} = 1 - (1 - \tau)(1 - \tau_w) \tag{25}$$

The probabilities that the LTE-LAA eNB and the WLAN nodes within the CCA range transmit without collision are, respectively,

$$P_{u,s} = \tau(1 - \tau_w)$$
$$P_{w,s} = \tau_w(1 - p_w)(1 - \tau) \tag{26}$$

The probability that the transmission from the LTE-LAA eNB is interfered with by transmissions from WLAN nodes within the CCA range is given by

$$P_{u,c} = \tau_w \cdot \tau \tag{27}$$

The probability of a collision occurring among transmissions of WLAN nodes within the CCA range is

$$P_{w,c} = \tau_w \cdot p_w \cdot (1 - \tau) \tag{28}$$

Suppose that n_l WLAN nodes, labeled $l_1, l_2, \ldots, l_{n_l}$, are attempting transmission in a timeslot. For all these transmissions to succeed, the LTE-LAA eNB must remain idle, each WLAN node must be outside the CCA range of the others, and none of the WLAN nodes in the set $L(l_1, l_2, \ldots, l_{n_l})$ should transmit. Thus, the probability of all these transmissions succeeding is

$$P_{succ}(T) = (1 - \tau) \cdot \mathcal{A}(T) \cdot \prod_{l' \in L(T)} (1 - \tau_{l'}) \tag{29}$$

where $T = \{l_1, l_2, \cdots, l_{n_l}\}$ and $\mathcal{A}(T)$ is an indicator function. If each node in T is outside the CCA range of every other node in T, then $\mathcal{A}(T) = 1$; otherwise, $\mathcal{A}(T) = 0$.

Using Equation (29), the probability that all transmissions succeed when some WLAN nodes located within the CCA range of the LTE-LAA eNB transmit in a timeslot is

$$P_{w,s} = \prod_{T \subset L'} \left(P_{succ}(T) \cdot \prod_{l'' \in T} \tau_{l''} \right) \tag{30}$$

Using the equation above, the probability of a collision occurring among transmissions from WLAN nodes located within the CCA range of the LTE-LAA eNB is

$$P_{w,c} = (1 - \tau) \cdot (\tau_w - P_{w,s}) \tag{31}$$

Let T_{laa} denote the expected time for a transmission by the LTE-LAA eNB, and let $T_{w,s}$ and $T_{w,c}$ denote the expected times for a successful transmission by a WLAN node and a collision experienced by the WLAN node, respectively. Using P_{tr}, $P_{u,s}$, $P_{u,c}$, $P_{w,s}$, and $P_{w,c}$ in Equations (25)–(28), (30), and (31), respectively, the expected time spent per channel state is

$$E_s = (1 - P_{tr})\sigma + P_{u,s}T_{laa} + P_{w,s}T_{w,s} + P_{u,c} \cdot \max\{T_{laa}, T_{w,c}\} + P_{w,c}T_{w,c} \tag{32}$$

where σ is the timeslot size.

Let R_W denote the data rate of the WLAN system, as defined in the 802.11 standard [20]. The throughput of the WLAN system can then be obtained as follows:

$$S_w = \frac{P_{w,s}T_{w,s}^{data}R_W}{E_s} \tag{33}$$

Here, $T_{w,s}^{data}$ represents the portion of $T_{w,s}$ during which data is transmitted.

Unlike for the WLAN system, we account for throughput degradation due to collisions to estimate the throughput of the LTE-LAA system. Let $P_{I,in}$ represent the average interference power caused by WLAN nodes within the CCA range. Then, similarly to Equation (20), we can calculate $P_{I,in}$; however, in this case, $y = \alpha \cdot R_{cca}$ and $dy = R_{cca} \cdot d\alpha$. Thus, $P_{I,in}$ is given by

$$P_{I,in} \simeq 2\lambda_{n,in}P_nK \cdot \int_0^\pi \int_0^1 v(\alpha,\theta)^{-\eta} \cdot R_{cca}d\alpha d\theta \tag{34}$$

where $\lambda_{n,in}$ represents the average number of WLAN nodes transmitting simultaneously within the CCA range. Let γ_{in} denote the SINR measured during a collision. Then, referring to Equation (16), it is given by $\gamma_{in} = \frac{P_{rx,u}}{P_I + P_{I,in} + P_N}$. Thus, using Equation (21), the throughput of the LTE-LAA system is

$$S_{laa} = \frac{T_{laa}^{data} \cdot \{P_{u,s}R_{laa}(\gamma) + P_{u,c}R_{laa}(\gamma_{in})\}}{E_s} \tag{35}$$

Here, T_{laa}^{data} represents the portion of T_{laa} during which data is transmitted, and γ denotes the SINR measured when there is no interference from WLAN nodes within the CCA range, which can be calculated using Equation (16). If multiple LTE-LAA devices are present, γ and γ_{in} are computed as the average SINRs across all LTE-LAA devices.

3. Performance Evaluation

We obtained numerical results for the throughput of each system in a coexistence scenario involving LTE-LAA and WLAN systems. As illustrated in Figure 1, we assumed a scenario for performance evaluation where a single LTE-LAA small cell coexists with multiple WLAN access points (APs) operating at a carrier frequency of 5.8 GHz over a 20 MHz bandwidth. Within the LTE-LAA cell, 10 LTE-LAA devices were uniformly distributed, and within a cell of radius R_I, five or fifteen APs were also uniformly located. Each AP was connected to five WLAN nodes. The urban micro non-line-of-sight model for a hexagonal cell layout was used to estimate the path loss [12]. Here, with r representing the distance in meters and f_c the carrier frequency in GHz, the path loss was given by

$PL = 36.7 \log_{10}(r) + 22.7 + 26 \log_{10}(f_c)$ (dB). This yields the corresponding values of $K = 10^{-7.254}$ and $\eta = 3.67$ [18]. The other parameters required for our performance evaluation were as follows: $P_a = 20$ dBm, $P_s = 17$ dBm, $P_e = 30$ dBm, $P_N = -90$ dBm, $W_0 = 16$, $R_I = 40$ m, $\kappa_{bw} = 0.6726$, $\kappa_c = 0.75$, $\kappa_{sinr} = 1$, $B = 20$ MHz, $DIFS = 34$ µs, $SIFS = 16$ µs, $\sigma = 9$ µs.

The WLAN transmission rate, R_W, was set to 72 Mbps, while the rate for LTE-LAA can be calculated using Equation (21). The medium access control and physical layer header sizes were set to 272 bits and 128 bits, respectively. The acknowledgment packet was configured with 336 bits, and the payload size was 12,000 bits. The durations $T_{u,s}$, $T_{u,c}$, $T_{w,s}$, and $T_{w,c}$ were influenced by R_W, R_U, the sizes of headers, acknowledgments, and payload, as well as DIFS, SIFS, and the propagation delay [21]. The propagation delay was set to 2 µs.

To examine how the contention window size W at the LTE-LAA eNB affects throughput, Figures 7 and 8 present the average throughput versus W for LTE-LAA, WLAN, and the total system (i.e., LTE-LAA+WLAN). It can be observed that, as W increases, the average WLAN throughput increases while the throughput of the LTE-LAA system decreases. This is due to the LTE-LAA eNB experiencing longer backoff durations as W increases, allowing WLAN nodes more frequent access to the channel. Moreover, Figures 7 and 8 illustrate that the average throughput of the LTE-LAA system is lower when fifteen APs are positioned within a cell radius R_I, compared to when only five APs are positioned. This is due to the fact that having fifteen APs increases the number of WLAN basic service sets within the CCA range compared to having only five APs.

Figures 9 and 10 demonstrate that the average throughput of both LTE-LAA and WLAN systems is highly influenced by the CCA threshold, P_{cca}, at the LTE-LAA eNB. These figures also reveal distinct operational behaviors between the two systems. For WLAN, the average throughput continuously decreases as P_{cca} increases. In contrast, the LTE-LAA throughput, shown in Figure 10, increases as P_{cca} approaches -79 dBm and then gradually declines as P_{cca} continues to increase. Note that a higher CCA threshold reduces the number of WLAN basic service sets within the CCA range, while the interference experienced by the LTE-LAA device, caused by concurrent transmissions of WLAN nodes in the interfering area, intensifies with an increase in P_{cca}.

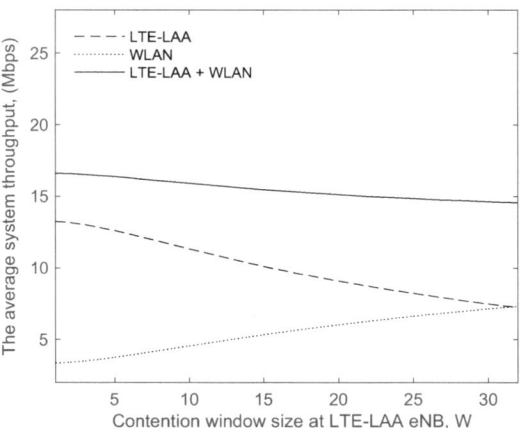

Figure 7. Average throughputs of LTE-LAA and WLAN systems versus W when five APs are positioned within a cell radius R_I.

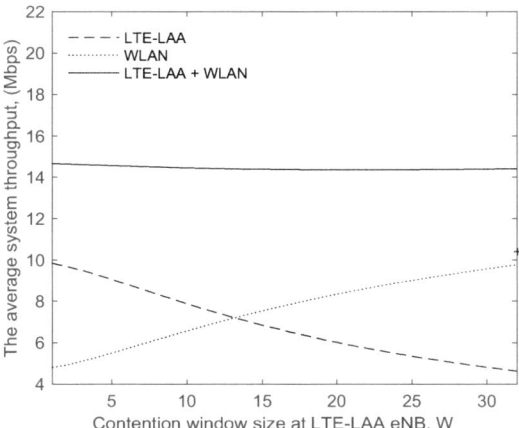

Figure 8. Average throughputs of LTE-LAA and WLAN systems versus W when 15 APs are positioned within a cell radius R_l.

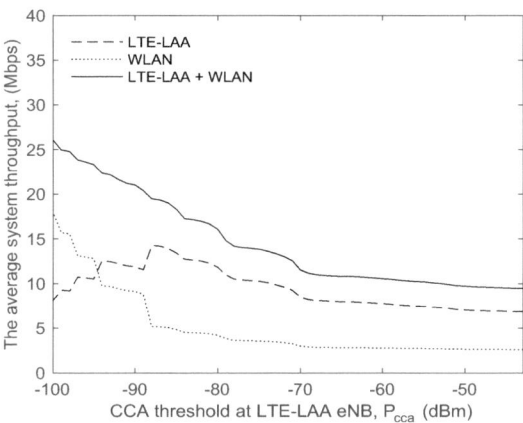

Figure 9. Average throughputs of LTE-LAA and WLAN systems versus P_{cca} when 5 APs are positioned within a cell radius R_l.

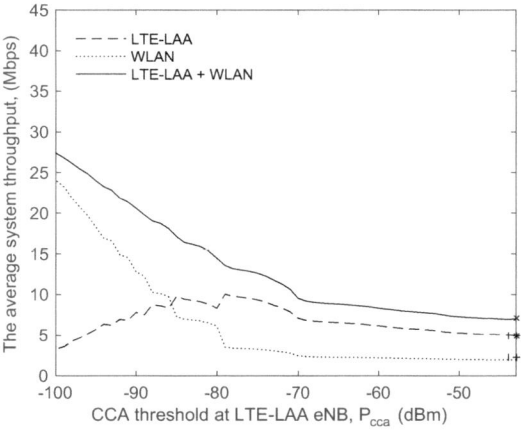

Figure 10. Average throughputs of LTE-LAA and WLAN systems versus P_{cca} when 15 APs are positioned within a cell radius R_l.

4. Conclusions

We proposed an analytical model using a Markov chain approach to represent the random backoff and CCA operations of LTE-LAA and WLAN systems in a coexistence scenario, thereby enabling throughput calculations for both systems. Numerical results demonstrated that the CCA threshold and contention window size configured at the LTE-LAA eNB were critical in balancing the throughput between LTE-LAA and WLAN systems. A larger contention window size set at the LTE-LAA eNB led to longer backoff periods, thereby increasing channel access opportunities for WLAN nodes. Similarly, a lower CCA threshold at the LTE-LAA eNB heightened its sensitivity to concurrent WLAN transmissions, resulting in fewer channel access opportunities for the LTE-LAA eNB.

Funding: This work was supported by Institute of Information & communications Technology Planning & Evaluation (IITP) under the metaverse support program to nurture the best talents (IITP-2024-RS-2023-00254529) grant funded by the Korea government (MSIT), and this research was supported by the MSIT (Ministry of Science and ICT), Korea, under the ITRC (Information Technology Research Center) support program (IITP-2024-2021-0-01816) supervised by the IITP (Institute for Information & Communications Technology Planning & Evaluation), and this work was supported by the National Research Foundation of Korea (NRF) grant funded by the Korea government (MSIT) (No. NRF-2022R1G1A1012117).

Data Availability Statement: Data are contained within the article.

Conflicts of Interest: The author declares no conflicts of interest.

Abbreviations

Notations for our proposed throughput study.

Notation	Description
$P[k_1', k_2'|k_1, k_2]$	Transition probability from state (k_1', k_2') to state (k_1, k_2)
$b(0, k_2)$	Stationary probability of being in backoff state $(0, k_2)$
$b(-1, k_2)$	Stationary probability of being in post-backoff state $(-1, k_2)$
W	Contention window size of LTE-LAA eNB
P_{cca}	CCA threshold of LTE-LAA eNB
q	Probability of at least one packet awaiting transmission at the start of a timeslot
τ	Probability that the LTE-LAA eNB is attempting transmission in a timeslot
τ_w	Probability that WLAN nodes located in the CCA range are attempting transmission in a timeslot
P_{idle}	Probability that the medium will be sensed as idle in a timeslot
p	Collision probability of LTE-LAA eNB
p_w	Probability of a collision among WLAN nodes located in the CCA range
R_I	Distance between LTE-LAA eNB and the outer boundary of the interfering region
R_{cca}	Radius of the CCA range of LTE-LAA eNB
$R_{laa}(\cdot)$	Data rate of LTE-LAA eNB
R_W	Data rate of a WLAN transmission

References

1. Feasibility Study on Licensed-Assisted Access to Unlicensed Spectrum. Available online: https://portal.3gpp.org/desktopmodules/Specifications/SpecificationDetails.aspx?specificationId=2579 (accessed on 6 December 2024).
2. Review of Regulatory Requirements for Unlicensed Spectrum. Available online: https://www.3gpp.org/ftp/workshop/2014-06-13_LTE-U/Docs/RWS-140015.zip (accessed on 6 December 2024).
3. Progress on LAA and Its Relationship to LTE-U and MulteFire. Available online: https://www.qualcomm.com/media/documents/files/laa-webinar-feb-2016.pdf (accessed on 6 December 2024).

4. Guo, Z.; Li, M.; Krunz, M. Exploiting Successive Interference Cancellation for Spectrum Sharing Over Unlicensed Bands. *IEEE Trans. Mobile Comput.* **2024**, *23*, 2348–2455. [CrossRef]

5. Yairnezhad, R.; Ekici, E. A novel scheduling algorithm for LTE on unlicensed bands to ensure fair coexistence with Wi-Fi. *Comput. Netw.* **2024**, *241*, 110232. [CrossRef]

6. Zhang, R.; Wang, M.; Cai, L.X.; Zheng, Z.; Shen, X.; Xie, L.L. LTE-unlicensed: The future of spectrum aggregation for cellular networks. *IEEE Wirel. Commun.* **2015**, *22*, 150–159. [CrossRef]

7. Ratasuk, R.; Mangalvedhe, N.; Ghosh, A. LTE in unlicensed spectrum using licensed-assisted access. In Proceedings of the 2014 IEEE Globecom Workshops (GC Wkshps), Austin, TX, USA, 8–12 December 2014; pp. 746–751.

8. Jeon, J.; Niu, H.; Li, Q.; Papathanassiou, A.; Wu, G. LTE with listen-before-talk in unlicensed spectrum. In Proceedings of the 2015 IEEE International Conference on Comunication Workshop (ICCW), London, UK, 8–12 June 2015; pp. 2320–2324.

9. Song, Y.; Sung, K.W.; Han, Y. Coexistence of Wi-Fi and Cellular With Listen-Before-Talk in Unlicensed Spectrum. *IEEE Commun. Lett.* **2016**, *20*, 161–164. [CrossRef]

10. Ko, H.; Lee, J.; Pack, S. A Fair Listen-Before-Talk Algorithm for Coexistence of LTE-U and WLAN. *IEEE Trans. Veh. Technol.* **2016**, *65*, 10116–10120. [CrossRef]

11. Bojovic, B.; Giupponi, L.; Ali, Z.; Miozzo, M. Evaluating Unlicensed LTE Technologies: LAA vs LTE-U. *IEEE Access* **2019**, *7*, 89714–89751. [CrossRef]

12. Jeon, J.; Li, Q.C.; Niu, H.; Papathanassiou, A.; Wu, G. LTE in the unlicensed spectrum: A novel coexistence analysis with WLAN systems. In Proceedings of the 2014 IEEE Global Communications Conference, Austin, TX, USA, 8–12 December 2014; pp. 3459–3464.

13. Bhausaheb, E.S.; Vijayabaskar, V. An Opportunistic Coexistence Analysis of LTE and Wi-Fi in Unlicensed 5 GHz Frequency Band. *Wirel. Pers. Commun.* **2023**, *130*, 269–280. [CrossRef]

14. Ren, Q.; Zheng, J.; Xiao, J.; Zhang, Y. Performance Analysis of an LAA and WiFi Coexistence System Using the LAA Category-4 LBT Procedure With GAP. *IEEE Trans. Veh. Technol.* **2021**, *70*, 8007–8018. [CrossRef]

15. Malone, D.; Duffy, K.; Leith, D. Modeling the 802.11 Distributed Coordination Function in Nonsaturated Heterogeneous Conditions. *IEEE/ACM Trans. Netw.* **2007**, *15*, 159–172. [CrossRef]

16. Jeon, J.; Niu, H.; Li, Q.C.; Papathanassiou, A.; Wu, G. LTE in the unlicensed spectrum: Evaluating coexistence mechanisms. In Proceedings of the 2014 IEEE Globecom Workshops (GC Wkshps), Austin, TX, USA, 8–12 December 2014; pp. 740–745.

17. Kelif, J.M.; Coupechoux, M.; Godlewski, P. A Fluid Model for Performance Analysis in Cellular Networks. *EURASIP J. Wirel. Commun. Netw.* **2010**, *2010*, 435189. [CrossRef]

18. Liu, F.; Bala, E.; Erkip, E.; Beluri, M.C.; Yang, R. Small Cell Traffic Balancing Over Licensed and Unlicensed Bands. *IEEE Trans. Veh. Technol.* **2015**, *12*, 5850–5865. [CrossRef]

19. Mogensen, P.; Na, W.; Kovacs, I.Z.; Frederiksen, F.; Pokhariyal, A.; Pedersen, K.I.; Kolding, T.; Hugl, K.; Kuusela, M. LTE Capacity Compared to the Shannon Bound. In Proceedings of the 2007 IEEE 65th Vehicular Technology Conference—VTC2007-Spring, Dublin, Ireland, 22–25 April 2007; pp. 1234–1238.

20. *IEEE Std 802.11-2007*; IEEE Standard for Information Technology—Telecommunications and Information Exchange Between Systems—Local and Metropolitan Area Networks—Specific Requirements—Part 11: Wireless LAN Medium Access Control (MAC) and Physical Layer (PHY) Specifications. IEEE Standards: Piscataway, NJ, USA, 2007. Available online: https://standards.ieee.org/ieee/802.11/3605/ (accessed on 6 December 2024).

21. Martorell, G.; Femenias, G.; Riera-Palou, P. Non-saturated IEEE 802.11 networks. A hierarchical 3D Markov model. *Comput. Netw.* **2015**, *80*, 27–50. [CrossRef]

MDPI AG
Grosspeteranlage 5
4052 Basel
Switzerland
Tel.: +41 61 683 77 34

Mathematics Editorial Office
E-mail: mathematics@mdpi.com
www.mdpi.com/journal/mathematics